Where to Wear 2006

FASHION SHOPPING FROM A-Z

Fairchild & Gallagher

NEW YORK • LONDON

PUBLISHERS
Jill Fairchild, Gerri Gallagher & Julie Craik

SERIES COPY EDITOR
John Graham

SERIES DESIGN/PRODUCTION ARTIST
Jeff Baker & Cynthia Roberts
at BookMechanics

2006 EDITOR
Emmah Duffus

2006 WRITERS
Emmah Duffus
Charlotte Purssord

PREVIOUS WRITERS
Ateh Damachi
Daisy Finer
Alice Rose
Erica Youngren

COVER DESIGN
Richard Chapman

CARTOGRAPHER
Candida Kennedy

DISTRIBUTION, SALES AND MARKETING
The Julie Craik Consultancy

Where to Wear, London, 2006 Edition

ISBN 0-9766877-4-7

Table of Contents

Introduction

Dear London Shopper,

Welcome to *Where to Wear*, the world's most detailed and authoritative directory of London's clothing and accessory stores.

Written by a team of international fashion journalists, *Where to Wear* tells you what ordinary guidebooks don't: where to find out-of-the-way boutiques and designer discount outlets; the best places for vintage, for wedding dresses, for childrenswear; where to go for budget-busting extravagance or bargain-basement trophies. From the globally famous names of Bond Street and Sloane Street to hidden treasure-houses, *Where to Wear* shows visitors where to begin and Londoners where to go next. Each of our guides is updated annually, to give you the latest lowdown on shopping hotspots.

If we wouldn't go there, we don't recommend it. If the merchandise is hot but the staff are frosty, we let you know. If the changing-room mirrors make you look more like a supertanker than a supermodel, we're not afraid to say so.

The directory is organized alphabetically, with two indexes at the back (by category and by neighbourhood). Our favourite stores are marked with a star (☆)—see page 2 for more details. To make life even easier for you, we've included ten pages of user-friendly maps. And because we know that a shopping trip involves more than just shops, we list the chicest lunch spots, the best day spas, where to have your Jimmy Choos repaired, and much else besides.

Shopping has never been easier! So rev up your credit card and get going, and make sure to keep *Where to Wear* in your handbag, briefcase or backpack.

—Jill Fairchild, Gerri Gallagher & Julie Craik

p.s. We love feedback! Please e-mail us on

uk@wheretowear.com or usa@wheretowear.com

Jill Fairchild, daughter of fashion world legend and *W* magazine founder John Fairchild, worked as an intern at *Glamour* magazine, *GQ* and *Vogue*. Ms Fairchild has also worked for Ailes Communications, a television production company, and in the late Eighties she founded and ran her own accessories company.

Gerri Gallagher is a Condé Nast editor who has lived in Europe for 20 years. She was the managing editor of Fairchild Publication's *W Europe* from 1990 to 1993 and is currently associate editor of *Tatler* magazine in London.

Julie Craik, *Where to Wear* partner and director of sales, marketing and distribution has worked in publishing for 20 years. Before joining *Where to Wear* she was associate publisher of *Tatler* magazine and had previously worked for the National Magazine Company.

Where to Wear 2006

Best Picks

Size Conversion Chart

Best Picks

Here are our particular favourites (marked ☆ in the Directory)

**Because we're worth it—
for instant cheer on a rainy day…**

Agent Provocateur
Anya Hindmarch
Boyd

Brora
Butler & Wilson
Cozmo Jenks

Heidi Klein
Paul Smith
Space.NK

**Show-stoppers—
these stores have to be seen to be believed…**

Courtezan
Harrods
Harvey Nichols

Matthew Williamson
Selfridges
Steinberg & Tolkien

Great style, fantastic prices…

Accessorize
Gap
Kew
Miss Selfridge

Monsoon
Oasis
Top Shop
Zara

If money were no object…

Bottega Veneta
Brioni
Chloé

The Cross
Dover Street Market
Ermenegildo Zegna

Henry Poole
Jimmy Choo
Matches

Pitter-patter of tiny feet...

9 London
Blossom
Push

...and for the kids themselves

Daisy & Tom
Lucky Me (mail order)
Marie-Chantal
Semmalina

Ever-reliable...

Browns
Emma Hope
Fenwick
Hilditch & Key

Joseph
Liberty
Turnbull & Asser
Whistles

If we could take the whole shop home...

Anna
Coco Ribbon
Collette Dinnigan

Diane von Furstenberg
Egg
Microzine

Selina Blow
Souvenir
Start

Clothing & Shoe Size Equivalents

Children's Clothing

American	3	4	5	6	6X
Continental	98	104	110	116	122
British	18	20	22	24	26

Children's Shoes

American	8	9	10	11	12	12	1	2	3
Continental	24	25	27	28	29	30	32	33	34
British	7	8	9	10	11	12	13	1	2

Ladies' Coats, Dresses, Skirts

American	3	5	7	9	11	12	13	14	15
Continental	36	38	38	40	40	42	42	44	44
British	8	10	11	12	13	14	15	16	17

Ladies' Blouses and Sweaters

American	10	12	14	16	18	20
Continental	38	40	42	44	46	48
British	32	34	36	38	40	42

Ladies' Hosiery

American	8	8.5	9	9.5	10	10.5
Continental	1	2	3	4	5	6
British	8	8.5	9	9.5	10	10.5

Ladies' Shoes

American	5	6	7	8	9	10
Continental	36	37	38	39	40	41
British	3.5	4.5	5.5	6.5	7.5	8.5

Men's Suits

American	34	36	38	40	42	44	46	48
Continental	44	46	48	50	52	54	56	58
British	34	36	38	40	42	44	46	48

Men's Shirts

American	14	15	15.5	16	16.5	17	17.5	18
Continental	37	38	39	41	42	43	44	45
British	14	15	15.5	16	16	17	17.5	18

Men's Shoes

American	7	8	9	10	11	12	13
Continental	39.5	41	42	43	44.5	46	47
British	6	7	8	9	10	11	12

Alphabetical Store Directory

The 1920s–1970s Crazy Clothes Connection

Lose yourself in this oasis of vintage clothing which specialises in designer labels and sells everything from Twenties flapper dresses to Seventies flares, as well as some Eighties gear that would give Tina Turner a run for her money. You might bump into Kate Moss or Naomi Campbell looking at prom dresses and platform shoes, or Robbie Williams trying on crocodile boots, leather jackets or morning suits. If you're a stickler for authenticity at fancy dress parties, a hire option is also available. *crazyclothes.co.uk*

Affordable to expensive   *Amex/MC/V*

020 7221 3989   **tube: Ladbroke Grove**
134 Lancaster Road   Tues-Sat 11-7
London W11

☆ 9 London

This ultra-stylish maternity shop has been so successful that it has moved from its Knightsbridge basement to a prime location on Hollywood Road. Adela King and Emily Evans have filled their girly haven with the sort of fashionable gems expectant mums are desperate to find: Diane von Furstenberg wrap dresses, Juicy Couture maternity jeans, Maternelle bras by Elle Macpherson and swimwear by Melissa Odabash. They also stock jeans by Earl and Rock & Republic as well as a range of pregnancy pieces by Liz Lange and Malene Birger. To top it off, a brilliant customising service means if you still want to wear your favourite pair of pre-pregnancy trousers, the girls will make it possible; just cut off the waistband, take out the zip, put in an elastic panel and hey presto! There is no excuse for looking frumpy any more. *9london.co.uk*

Expensive   *MC/V*

020 7352 7600   **tube: Earls Court**
8 Hollywood Road   Mon-Sat 10-6
London SW10

40 Savile Row

Established in 1938, this bespoke tailor is a whippersnapper amongst the elder statesmen of Savile Row, with a striking window display and a trendy, youthful feel. The confident no-frills service offers handmade suits for men and women from £2,400 and laser-cut made-to-measure suits for men from a very-good-value £650. Attention to detail is key here: custom-made shirts come with a choice of 14 different collars and 5 cuff finishes. The cut is traditional English, the fabrics wide-ranging and up-to-the-minute and the details engaging and quirky. *40savilerow.co.uk*

Very expensive   *Amex/MC/V*

020 7287 6740   **tube: Piccadilly Circus/Oxford Circus**
40 Savile Row   Mon-Fri 10-6:30, Sat 10-6
London W1

Absolute Vintage

A well-known stop on the Brick Lane vintage trail, but not one that particularly inspired us. Absolute Vintage offers racks upon racks of jeans, leather jackets, raincoats, shirts and dresses from the last few decades, and over a thousand pairs of shoes and boots. We weren't convinced by the quality or content—head round the corner to Rokit for a classier selection.

Affordable   *Amex/MC/V*

020 7247 3883   **tube: Liverpool Street**
15 Hanbury Street   Tues-Sat 12-7, Sun 11-7
London E1   (Monday by appointment)

Abu Jani Sandeep Khosla

Abu Jani and Sandeep Khosla are known affectionately in their native India as "the boys". They are India's foremost design duo and Bollywood's favourite costume creators, and they claim to make heirlooms not garments—Princess Michael of Kent is a fan. Beautifully crafted, their clothes are the height of Indian style, replete with classic chikan work, fine embroidery and mini mirrors. Luxurious fabrics and contemporary spins on traditional styles ensure this clothing would not look out of place at the Oscars, where it is indeed frequently seen (on Dames Judi Dench, for example, and Maggie Smith). The atmospheric shop is a testament to the boys' talents, with Indian woodwork screens, beautiful rugs and the smoky smell of incense in the air.   *ajsk.com*

Very expensive   *Amex/MC/V*

020 7584 7713   **tube: Knightsbridge**
55 Beauchamp Place   Mon-Sat 10-6
London SW3

à la mode

They're known for discovering hot new design talent but à la mode still pays homage to the big names, from Marc Jacobs to Marni. The gentle staff encourage a mix-and-match method, blending simple, feminine styles from a multitude of designers. Given their serious approach to fashion, the relaxed environment, bright spacious store and pretty pieces are a pleasant surprise.

Expensive   *Amex/MC/V*

020 7730 7180   **tube: Sloane Square**
10 Symons Street   Mon-Sat 10-7
London SW3

☆ Accessorize

It's like stepping into a sweet shop full of jewellery, bags, scarves, belts, sarongs, flip-flops, hats... We guarantee you won't leave Accessorize empty-handed. And, like Starbucks, if you miss one store, don't worry—there will be another round the next corner. Pop in to spruce up an outfit or just to buy an inexpensive girly treat. There is something for everyone from tweenies to seniors. Best of all, you'll probably get away with telling your friends your new earrings came from a chic boutique in Chelsea and cost a fortune (unless they've got an identical pair, obviously.) *accessorize.co.uk*

Affordable   *Amex/MC/V*

020 7629 0038   **tube: Oxford Circus**
293 Oxford Street   Mon-Sat 9:30-7:30 (Thurs 9:30-8)
London W1   Sun 11-6:30

020 7734 4750   **tube: Oxford Circus**
35-36 Great Marlborough Street   Mon-Sat 10-7
London W1   (Thurs 10-7:30) Sun 12-6

020 7491 9424   **tube: Oxford Circus/Bond Street**
386 Oxford Street   Mon-Sat 9:30-8
London W1   (Thurs 9:30-9), Sun 11-6

020 7494 0566   **tube: Piccadilly Circus**
1 Piccadilly Circus   Mon-Sat 10-9, Sun 12-8
London W1

020 7287 8673 (Sale Shop)   **tube: Piccadilly Circus**
Trocadero Centre, Coventry Street   Daily 10-9:45
London W1   (Thurs-Sat 10-11)

020 7580 7187   **tube: Oxford Circus**
The Plaza, 120 Oxford Street   Mon-Sat 10-7
London W1   (Thurs 10-8), Sun 12-6

020 7240 2107   **tube: Covent Garden**
25 The Market   Mon-Fri 9-8
London WC2   Sat-Sun 11-7

020 7240 6102   **tube: Covent Garden**
35 Neal Street   Mon-Fri 11-7, Sat 10-7
London WC2   Sun 12-6

020 7379 3623   **tube: Covent Garden**
5-6 James Street   Mon-Sat 10-8, Sun 11-6
London WC2

020 7591 0049   **tube: Sloane Square**
102 King's Road   Mon-Sat 9:30-7
London SW3   Sun 12-6

020 7581 3972   **tube: Knightsbridge**
53 Brompton Road   Mon-Sat 9:30-7:30, Sun 12-6
London SW3

020 7792 9508   **tube: Queensway/Bayswater**
Whiteley's, Queensway   Mon-Wed 10-8, Thurs-Sat 10-9
London W2   Sun 11-7:15

020 7937 1433   **tube: High Street Kensington**
123a Kensington High Street   Mon-Sat 9-7 (Thurs 9-8)
London W8   Sun 11-7:30

020 7727 3406   **tube: Ladbroke Grove**
237 Portobello Road   Mon-Sat 10-6, Sun 11-5
London W11

020 7726 8305   **tube: Bank**
84 Cheapside   Mon-Fri 8-7
London EC2

Ad Hoc

Trendy teenage girls flock to this den of eccentric accessories for racy fripperies guaranteed to upset old-fashioned fathers. The King's Road has lost much of its colour since its Sixties heyday, but thankfully punk, glam and rock'n'roll live on in the colourful collection of wigs, feather boas, string vests (yes, apparently they're fashionable), fishnet stockings, glitter make-up, and diamanté belts. Pink knickers are decorated with images of Elvis Presley and wellington boots are scattered with flowery patterns. Loud pop music pumps out all day, the doorway is scattered with coloured sequins and the changing-room only just accommodates the waif-like figures who frequent it. Full of character, this is the place to take your rebellious goddaughter for some birthday trinkets.

Affordable   *Amex/MC/V*

020 7376 8829   **tube: Sloane Square**
153 King's Road   Mon-Sat 10-6:30 (Wed 10-7)
London SW3   Sun 12-6

Adolfo Dominguez

The style of this Spanish label and the snoozy store ambience certainly won't quicken your pulse, but the two floors of merchandise will cover you top to toe, from outerwear to shoes. For shoppers who seek solace in the classics (cotton T-shirts, pinstriped suits, beaded eveningwear and simple knits) the well-tailored women's and menswear might just suffice. A new sportswear range and a selection of homewares continue the blah theme. Fashion followers could skip this stop.   *adolfodominguez.com*

Moderate   *Amex/MC/V*

020 7494 3395   **tube: Piccadilly Circus**
129 Regent Street   Mon-Sat 10-7 (Thurs 10-8)
London W1   Sun 12-6

020 7836 5013   **tube: Covent Garden**
15 Endell Street   Mon-Sat 10:30-7, Sun 12-6
London WC2

Aftershock

If Cher is your soulmate when it comes to sequins and beads, this shop is for you. Everything, from cropped trousers and loose linen shirts to halterneck tops and long evening gowns, comes adorned with shimmering decorations. The prettiest of the lot are the chiffon sleeveless tops in muted greens, pinks and blues, dazzling with clusters of matching sequins, with sizes going up to a generous extra large. Accessories come in the shape of bags—straw, beach, glitzy evening—with matching shoes and flip-flops, and the diamanté and crystal jewellery has an appropriate bling-quotient. If the total ensemble is a bit too much, choose carefully and you could go home with your next party outfit.   *aftershockplc.com*

Moderate   *Amex/MC/V*

020 7499 2858
12 South Molton Street
London W1

tube: Bond Street
Mon-Sat 10:30-7, Sun 12-6

020 7352 7353
194 King's Road
London SW3

tube: Sloane Square
Mon-Sat 10-6:30, Sun 12-6

☆ Agent Provocateur   ♀

Men driving past the suitably provocative window displays need to concentrate to keep their eyes on the road. This lingerie lair is saucy and sexy, with staff wearing nurses' outfits, fishnet stockings and fluffy pink mules. Vampish satin, silk and lace creations—plus everything from jewelled manacles to their own heady fragrance—are presented with sex-kitten kitsch. Strait-laced people, be prepared—some of the treats in store may make you blush.   *agentprovocateur.com*

Expensive   *Amex/MC/V*

020 7235 0229
16 Pont Street
London SW1

tube: Knightsbridge/Sloane Square
Mon-Sat 10-6

020 7439 0229
6 Broadwick Street
London W1

tube: Oxford Circus
Mon-Sat 11-7

020 7243 1292
305 Westbourne Grove
London W11

tube: Notting Hill Gate
Mon-Fri 10:30-6:30
Sat 10:30-7

020 7623 0229
5 Royal Exchange
London EC3

tube: Bank
Mon-Fri 10:30-6:30 (Thurs 10:30-7)

agnès b.   ♂♀

How do the French do that chic thing so effortlessly? Luckily for those of us not blessed with Gallic flair, the short cut is a trip to agnès b. The collection is sheer heaven for women who favour understated femininity infused with youth, including fine cotton tops, tailored skirts, trousers and knits. Men will appreciate the sleek tailoring of the sports jackets, trousers and button-down shirts. Some accessories are also available, and even the carrier bags have a certain je ne sais quoi. (The make-up line is being discontinued, but fans will still be able to buy the apricot cream tinted moisturiser.)   *agnesb.com*

Moderate   *Amex/MC/V*

020 7379 1992
35-36 Floral Street
London WC2

tube: Covent Garden
Mon-Fri 10:30-6:30 (Thurs 10:30-7)
Sat 10:30-7, Sun 12-5

020 7225 3477
111 Fulham Road
London SW3

tube: South Kensington
Mon 11-6, Tues-Sat 10-6 (Wed 10-7)
Sun 12-5

020 7431 1995
58-62 Heath Street
London NW3

tube: Hampstead
Mon-Sat 10-6
Sun 12-6

020 7935 5556   **tube: Baker Street/Bond Street**
40-41 Marylebone High Street   Mon 11-6, Tues, Fri-Sat 10-6
London W1   Wed-Thurs 10-7, Sun 12-5

020 7792 1947   **tube: Notting Hill Gate**
233-235 Westbourne Grove   Mon 10:30-6:30
London W11   Tues-Sat 10-6:30, Sun 12-5

020 7730 2255 (M)   **tube: Sloane Square**
31-32 Duke of York Square   Mon, Tues, Fri 10-6
London SW3   Wed, Thurs, Sat 10-7, Sun 12-5

Aimé

There's a "The Cross" feel to this Ledbury Road boutique. It all began when two sisters, Val and Venda Heng Vong, grew nostalgic for their native France. Rather than go home, they brought home to Notting Hill with French fashion's best and brightest labels: Madame à Paris, APC, Les Prairies de Paris, Claudie Pierlot and Isabel Marant. In addition to clothing, their sleek boutique houses handbags and shoes, Asian-style crockery, candles, glassware and an assortment of CDs that changes every two weeks.   *aimelondon.com*

Affordable to moderate   *Amex/MC/V*

020 7221 7070   **tube: Notting Hill Gate**
32 Ledbury Road   Mon-Sat 10:30-7
London W11

Alberta Ferretti

Ultra-feminine and super-sophisticated, Ferretti is the princess of pretty party dresses. Her fabrics (lots of chiffon) are soft and sheer, while the cuts are body-conscious but not clinging. Dresses, skirts, sleek suits and blouses are the staples, in colours that range from brooding blue to baby pink, some with girlish patterns. Philosophy, her lovely diffusion line, is housed upstairs.   *aeffe.com*

Very expensive   *Amex/MC/V*

020 7235 2349   **tube: Knightsbridge**
205-206 Sloane Street   Mon-Sat 10-6 (Wed 10-7)
London SW1

Aldo

This French-Canadian shoe store chain has taken the high street by storm. The collections are style-savvy yet wearable, offering shoes, boots, and sneakers principally crafted from black or tan leather. For women there is something for every occasion: cowboy boots decorated with embroidered patterns, wedges enhanced with blossoming flowers, pointy patchwork slip-ons and simple black ankle boots. For men there are loafers, square-toed lace-ups and trendy trainers. A collection of suede and leather jackets, handbags and sunglasses tops off this desirable selection.   *aldoshoes.com*

Affordable   *Amex/MC/V*

020 7499 4348   **tube: Oxford Circus/Bond Street**
309 Oxford Street   Mon-Sat 10-8 (Thurs 10-9)
London W1   Sun 12-6

020 7836 7692
3-7 Neal Street
London WC2

tube: Covent Garden
Mon-Wed 10-7, Thurs-Sat 10-8
Sun 12-6

020 7937 7996
141 Kensington High Street
London W8

tube: High Street Kensington
(opening hours as above)

Alexander McQueen ♀

Don't be put off by the doorman, or the sculptural, gallery-white space designed by William Russell. Step bravely into the outlandish world of fashion's favourite bad boy. McQueen's spectacular fashion shows are legendary; so too is his brutally sharp and accurate tailoring. His signature silhouette comprises sharp shoulders, stiff collars and reed-slim trousers, but when he gets romantic he is equally effective. Floaty Thirties-style evening wear sits beside precision-cut black corsets, which would look perfect on Alicia Keys at the Grammys. Cheeky cherry-patterned footwear and jewellery are also available. *alexandermcqueen.com*

Expensive   *Amex/MC/V*

020 7355 0080
4-5 Old Bond Street
London W1

tube: Green Park
Mon-Sat 10-6 (Thurs 10-7)

All Saints ♂♀

This cool store is full of daylight, making a pleasant change from the dingy atmosphere of some of its nearby competitors. You'll find girly skirts with a gothic twist, punk-inspired ribbed tops, corsets and Fifties-style Sandra Dee pastels. Blazers, distressed jeans and crucifix-adorned tops will satisfy the wannabe rock star in any man. Accessories include rosary beads (very David Beckham) and cravats for faux fops. *allsaintslondon.co.uk*

Affordable to moderate   *Amex/MC/V*

020 7494 3909
6 Foubert's Place
London W1

tube: Oxford Circus
Mon-Sat 10-7 (Thurs 10-8)
Sun 12-6

020 7730 0404
Unit 3, Duke of York Square
London SW3

tube: Sloane Square
Mon-Sat 10-6:30
(Wed 10-7), Sun 12-6

020 7379 3749
5 Earlham Street
London WC2

tube: Covent Garden
Mon-Sat 10:30-7
(Thurs 10:30-8), Sun 12-6

Allegra Hicks ♀

The ultimate chill-out attire, the kaftan, is still summer's must-have item and Allegra Hicks is where to head for the best. Her new shop is a calm oasis of casual comfortable clothing. Loose and floaty, her kaftans come in an array of summer colours from pale lilac to flaming orange. Her eye for detail is ever present in the delicately embroidered patterns of simple shapes and flowers. You'll also find a selection of bohemian handbags and semi-precious jewellery by

Celia Forner and Osanna Visconti. Underwear by Elle Macpherson rounds out the collection and makes this store a perfect stop-off before your departure... for home or that beach-side villa. *allegrahicks.com*

Directory

Expensive *Amex/MC/V*
020 7235 8989 **tube: Sloane Square**
28 Cadogan Place Mon-Sat 10-6
London SW1

Amanda Wakeley

You won't be disappointed: whether it's a sophisticated cocktail dress, a modern ballgown or a Twenties-style beaded chiffon dresses, Amanda Wakeley is the place to go if you are after beautiful sexy eveningwear. Light loose materials ensure the styles are as comfortable as everyday wear, while modern cuts (and slits up the thigh) add a naughty edge. The Sposa ready-to-wear bridal collection is elegant and simple, and the classic suits, in neutral beige and black, are also worth a look. If you are planning a night at the opera, a glamorous party or a wedding, save yourself time and make Wakeley your first stop-off. Audrey Hepburn would definitely approve. *amandawakeley.com*

Expensive *Amex/MC/V*
020 7590 9105 **tube: South Kensington**
80 Fulham Road Mon-Sat 10-6 (Wed 10-7)
London SW3

American Classics

As the name suggests the clothing here is peppered with style icons from the USA: loads of Levi's, Hawaiian shirts, boots by Redwing and baseball caps emblazoned with motorcycle motifs. It's the sort of kit worn by wannabe kids in American high school dramas—less clean-cut than the boy-next-door in Ralph Lauren look, not as daring as the leather-clad rebels with serious attitude. Skater-style Stüssy is a taste of California and Vans sneakers still rate highly on the Richter scale of cool.

Moderate *Amex/MC/V*
020 7352 2853 **tube: Sloane Square**
398 King's Road Mon-Sat 10-6:30, Sun 12-5
London SW10

020 7831 1210 **tube: Covent Garden**
20 Endell Street Mon-Sat 10-6:30, Sun 12:30-5:30
London WC2

Ananya

Indian clothing is renowned for its colour and finery. For a taste, hotfoot it to this Aladdin's cave in Notting Hill. Designer Anu Mirchandin's boutique is crammed with eye-catching, boldly shimmering pieces, all in beautiful textiles from her native country. You'll find hand-beaded trousers and appliqué jewelled skirts, funky little embroidered tops and comfortable cotton kaftans with matching trousers. Far from looking like fancy dress, the delicately detailed clothing is Bollywood cool and has been spotted on the likes of Claudia Schiffer, Rachel Hunter and Jemma Kidd. Other bits on offer include raffia bags depicting Indian gods, paste jewellery and antique mirrored photo frames.

Moderate   *Amex/MC/V*

020 7792 3339   **tube: Notting Hill Gate**
196 Kensington Park Road   Mon-Sat 10-6
London W11

Anderson & Sheppard

Here is a Savile Row institution that has resisted any modernization. The relatively spacious interior is dominated by vast rolls of cloth and has a distinctly late-Fifties feel. Renowned for their tact, A&S politely discourage contact with the press, although it is common knowledge that Prince Charles and Calvin Klein are fans of their signature cut, which is softer and less sculpted than elsewhere on the Row. They also sell a limited range of covetable cashmere sweaters, ties, umbrellas, suspenders, sheepskin slippers and flat caps to complete the look, as well as lambswool picnic rugs in shades from bright yellow to sombre brown.

Expensive to very expensive   *Amex/MC/V*

020 7734 1420   **tube: Piccadilly Circus/Green Park**
32 Old Burlington Street   Mon-Fri 8:30-5
London W1

Anello and Davide

What began in 1922 as a theatre and dance footwear specialist has pirouetted into a modern-day temple of traditional handmade designs. The shop has recently had a refit and, bizarrely, a huge fish tank doubles as the cash desk; but then it's worth remembering that this was the company that made Dorothy's magic ruby slippers in the Wizard of Oz, a world in which anything is possible. Made in Italy, new styles appear every month from killer and kitten heels to glamorous Roman sandals and colourful wedges. There is also a stunning bridal collection crafted from the finest fabrics, silk, satin and embroidered dupion. In London magical transportation would be a godsend so, once you've purchased, "close your eyes and click your heels together three times…" You never know…   *handmadeshoes.co.uk*

Expensive   *MC/V*

020 7938 2255   **tube: High Street Kensington**
15 St Alban's Grove   Tues-Fri 10-5, Sat 10-4
London W8

020 7935 7793   **tube: Bond Street**
20-21 St Christopher's Place   Mon-Sat 10-6 (Thurs 11-7)
London W1   Sun 12-4

Angela Stone

Angela Stone has been designing evening and bridal wear for 13 years and the understated style of her creations has attracted a loyal clientele. Light and fluid, dresses come in beautiful fabrics—satin, silk and crepe—with something to suit every occasion. Brides will find a host of classic cuts in the made-to-measure range, starting at a reasonable £850, but the styles really are simple so don't expect flamboyance. Off the peg, the leading look at the moment is modern Audrey Hepburn, with Fifties-style skirts in bright brash colours, flighty feather hats and pretty pearl jewellery. The sexy beaded corsets (from £250) pick up the pace and look great teamed with a pair of slim-fitting jeans and high heels. *angelastone.com*

Expensive *Amex/MC/V*

020 7371 5199 **tube: Parsons Green**
257 New King's Road Mon-Sat 9-6
London SW6

Angels

Dress doesn't come any fancier—this is the Rolls-Royce of costume-hire shops. From medieval damsels to can-can dancers to comic book heros, if you've been invited to a fancy dress party there's no better place to kit yourself out. Jerry Hall, Elton John, and Mick Jagger have all picked from Angels' time-travelling racks. The selection dates from 1066 to the 1970s and comes with all the trimmings—gold masks, powdered wigs, feather boas and make-up. Quality is top-notch so expect to pay accordingly. *fancydress.com*

Moderate to expensive *Amex/MC/V*

020 7836 5678 **tube: Leicester Square**
119 Shaftesbury Avenue Mon-Fri 9-5:30
London WC2 (last fitting at 4:30)

Ann Harvey

Desperate Housewives glamour this ain't, but Ann Harvey offers a great staple range in plus sizes from 16 to 28. The selection might whisper "middle age, middle management", but its diversity—evening wear, suits, jeans, accessories, swimwear—plus the friendly atmosphere and reasonable prices give this modest shop a firm following.

Affordable *Amex/MC/V*

020 7408 1131 **tube: Oxford Circus**
266 Oxford Street Mon-Sat 10-7 (Thurs 10-8)
London W1 Sun 12-6

Ann Wiberg

The warm, friendly manager will help with the array of off-beat customised Scandinavian designs. You'll find funky deconstructed T-shirts, ruffles and lovingly made turquoise strapless couture dresses perfect for any red carpet event. Check out the delicate jewellery by up-and-coming Danish designer Jane Konig. *annwiberg.com*

Moderate to expensive *Amex/MC/V*

020 7229 8160 **tube: Notting Hill Gate**
170 Westbourne Grove Mon-Fri 10:30-6, Sat 10-7
London W11

☆ Anna

Claudia Schiffer, Gwyneth Paltrow, Gwen Stefani, Sadie Frost and a host of trendy London ladies flock to these small, cosy boutiques which offer the best in grown-up girly clothing. A smattering of hot designer labels—Fake London, Gharani Strok, Boyd, Velvet and Saltwater—sit alongside some trusty old favourites—Whistles, Nicole Farhi, Cashmere Studio, Margaret Howell and 120% Linen. It's worth checking out their shoe collection too – we loved the Spanish riding boots by Penelope Chilvers, the jewelled sandals by Maliparmi as well as the heels and slingbacks by L'Autre Chose. The young, refreshingly friendly staff will happily help you pick just one incredible piece to blend with rest of your wardrobe. *shopatanna.co.uk*

Expensive   *Amex/MC/V*

020 7483 0411   **tube: Chalk Farm**
126 Regent's Park Road   Mon-Sat 10-6, Sun 12-6
London NW1

020 7731 7300   **tube: Fulham Broadway**
590 King's Road   Mon-Sat 10-6
London SW6

Anne Fontaine

The shops smell delicious with scented candles flickering, and the crisp white shirts in all manner of styles are accompanied by little packages of dried rosebuds. Based in France, Anne Fontaine is taking the classic white shirt to fashionable frontiers. Select a simple button-down for winter or one embellished with lighthearted ruffles for spring. Superior quality, creative cuts and seasonal details keep the selection fresh. Every collection comes with the occasional touch of colour and a bit of basic black.   *annefontaine.com*

Moderate   *Amex/MC/V*

020 7584 7703   **tube: South Kensington**
151 Fulham Road   Mon-Sat 10-6:30, Sun 12-5
London SW3

020 7408 2280   **tube: Bond Street**
30 New Bond Street   Mon-Sat 10-6:30
London W1

020 7838 9210   **tube: Sloane Square**
14 Sloane Street   Mon-Sat 10-6:30
London SW1   Sun 12-5

Anthony J. Hewitt/Airey & Wheeler

Established Savile Row tailors Anthony J. Hewitt took over Airey & Wheeler a few years ago, revamping the famous tropical clothing range and putting the accent on high-quality linen suits, pinfeather cotton suits and super-100 (the finest worsted) wool suits. The Anthony J. Hewitt side of the business continues to concentrate on handmade bespoke suits but has also introduced an innovative made-to-measure service in Dormeuil fabrics. With prices starting around

£600, this offers outstanding value to first-time Savile Row customers.

Expensive Amex/MC/V

020 7734 1505 **tube: Piccadilly Circus/Oxford Circus**
9 Savile Row Mon-Fri 9-5:30, Sat 9-12
London W1 (by appointment only)

Antique Boutique ♂

Don't let the name mislead you. Nothing here is actually antique, but you will find one-off pieces in styles that ooze modern street cred. There are beautiful handmade leather cowboy boots, cool jeans customised with studs, King T-shirts and heaps of groovy baseball caps. The staff are nowhere near as intimidating as they first appear and the rap music is user-friendly, although it might scare your granny. With few shops dedicated to the cool male shopper who would not be seen anywhere in a suit, this is a real find.

Expensive Amex/MC/V

020 7352 0901 **tube: Sloane Square**
155 King's Road Mon-Sat 10-7, Sun 12-6
London SW3

☆ Anya Hindmarch ♀

This iconic British handbag and accessories designer is a favourite with the likes of Jemima Khan, Jennifer Aniston and Claudia Schiffer. Her "Be a Bag" range, where a photo of your nearest and dearest is digitally printed onto the style of your choice, has become a London institution. A trademark tiny bow is the stamp of her classic design sense, but Hindmarch's great talent is her ability to inject as much whimsy into a basic black leather wallet as into her sequined evening bags, Fifties print beach satchels and more recently her shoes, T-shirts, bikins, kaftans and scarves. *anyahindmarch.com*

Expensive Amex/MC/V

020 7838 9177 **tube: Knightsbridge/Sloane Square**
15-17 Pont Street Mon-Sat 10-6 (Wed 10-7)
London SW1

020 792 4427 **tube: Notting Hill Gate**
63 Ledbury Road Mon-Sat10:30-6 (Thurs 10:30-7)
London W11

Aquaint ♀

Soothing orchid plants and a friendly staff will make you want to linger in this small new boutique which offers a fresh, feminine selection of womenswear from promising young designers and more established names like Ashley Isham, Lanvin, Hussein Chalayan and Roland Mouret. Everything here has been carefully crafted, right down to the details like silk-covered buttons and striking stitching. There's an array of accessories to play with too: shoes by Betty Jackson and art deco jewellery from Lara Bohinc.

Moderate to expensive Amex/MC/V

020 7240 9677
38 Monmouth Street
London WC2

tube: **Leicester Square**
Mon-Sat 10-6

Aquascutum

Quintessentially English, this luxury brand is proud of its heritage and renowned for its gentleman's tailoring, weatherproof trench coats and macs for town and country wear. Not quite as fashion-forward as its rival Burberry, but there is however an ever-expanding collection for younger customers. Fruity coloured striped shirts and cashmere scoop neck jumpers with sewn-in white shirt collars are perfect for a working wardrobe.   aquascutum.co.uk

Expensive   *Amex/MC/V*

020 7675 8200
100 Regent Street
London W1

tube: **Piccadilly Circus**
Mon-Sat 10-6:30 (Thurs 10-7)
Sun 12-5

Armand Basi

Born half a century ago in Barcelona as a small knitwear shop, Basi has moved from its staid Mayfair premises to a cooler Notting Hill location. The selection includes women's trousers, skirts, dresses and tops, and a smattering of younger, hipper streetwear. For men, there are casual shirts and trousers. Colours tend towards muted earth tones, but—like London skies—there are occasional bursts of brightness.   armandbasi.com

Moderate   *Amex/MC/V*

020 7727 7789
189 Westbourne Grove
London W11

tube: **Notting Hill Gate**
Mon-Fri 10:30-6
Sat 10-6, Sun 12-5

Armani Collezioni

Resting somewhere between Giorgio Armani's signature label and his street-style Emporio line, Collezioni features all the sleek minimalism we've come to associate with the name—at less damaging prices. Simple monotones resonate throughout this beautifully tailored collection, with suits, shirts and ties for men, lovely knits and silky skirts for women.   armani.com

Expensive   *Amex/MC/V*

020 7491 9888
43 New Bond Street
London W1

tube: **Bond Street**
Mon-Fri 10-6 (Thurs 10-7)
Sat 10-6:30

Arrogant Cat

Cool cats will welcome this sharp new shop for urban wear. The interior is immediately striking, with walls and floors painted pitch black, gilded baroque mirrors and changing-rooms dramatically draped in curtains decorated with huge red amaryllises. Funky vibes beat throughout the two floors and downstairs the purple day-bed and boudoir-style mirrored furniture are also for sale. The clothing is more Notting Hill than Chelsea chic—long skirts printed with images of the Mona Lisa smoking a joint, delicate tops dripping with beading and a fantastic selection of vintage pieces chosen to blend in with the ultra-modern collection. The Great Portland Street store has similarly OTT decor, but doesn't carry vintage.   arrogantcat.co.uk

Expensive   *Amex/MC/V*

020 7349 9070   **tube: Sloane Square**
311 King's Road   Mon-Sat 10-7 (Thurs 11-8)
London SW3   Sun 11-6

020 7836 6970   **tube: Covent Garden**
42 Shorts Gardens   (opening hours as above)
London WC2

020 7323 0886   **tube: Oxford Circus**
18 Great Portland Street   (opening hours as above)
London W1

Atticus
When you feel like putting a fashionable foot forward, hot-foot it to Atticus where prices are only mildly damaging and the staff are, refreshingly, more than happy to help. Brown suede cowboy boots, leather slip-ons with white stitching and pink kitten heels with flowers at the toes are all perfect for play-time or those moments when style speaks louder than sense.

Moderate   *Amex/MC/V*

020 7376 0059   **tube: High Street Kensington**
14 Kensington Church Street   Mon-Sat 10-7 (Thurs 10-8)
London W8   Sun 12-6

Audley
Crafted from the finest leather, Audley shoes are hard to find fault with and they're dangerously affordable too. The designs are fresh and original, with plenty of nods to the catwalk in the form of conical heels, peep toes and Prada-esque patent lace-ups. The colour palette is broad and so is the selection, from casual loafers to wedding slippers. They also offer a bespoke service, for those desperate to design their own, and don't miss their small accessories range, especially the leather-lined bags in eye-catching designs.   audley.com

Moderate   *Amex/MC/V*

020 7730 2903   **tube: Sloane Square**
72 Duke of York Square   Mon-Sat 10-6 (Wed 10-7)
London SW3   Sun 12-5

Austin Reed
A £12.3 million redevelopment of the Regent Street flagship store has bounced this brand into the 21st century, providing a bar and stress-relieving treatment rooms to entertain

the shopping-fatigued husband. Still more basic than bold, and not quite setting Regent Street alight, the selection at Austin Reed covers all the bases. However, all that is set to change with the introduction of Guest Brands which include labels like Hugo Boss, Hilfiger and Patrick Cox footwear. The smaller womenswear collection fits the same sensibility. It's a look better for blending in than for getting noticed, but what's wrong with that?   austinreed.co.uk

Moderate to expensive   *Amex/MC/V*

020 7734 6789   **tube: Piccadilly Circus**
103-113 Regent Street   Mon-Sat 10-7 (Thurs 10-8)
London W1   Sun 12-6

020 7213 9998   **tube: Bank (exit 8 or 9)**
1 Poultry   Mon-Fri 9-6:30
London EC2

020 7283 3347   **tube: Monument**
13-23 Fenchurch Street   Mon-Fri 9-5:30
London EC3

020 7588 7674   **tube: Liverpool Street**
1-14 Liverpool Street   Mon-Fri 8:30-6
London EC2

Austique   ♀

A shop full of all the things girls love. Think of all the gorgeous new labels you see in the glossies that you never know where to buy—Esther Franklin dresses, Trelise Cooper skirts, colourful Woo underwear from New York, Zimmermann bikinis sold all year round and silk beaded dresses by Jessica Starr (daughter of Mr and Mrs Monsoon and Accessorise). Prices reflect exclusivity but there is a treat for everyone from Mor body butter—a favourite moisturiser in Australia—to Zoe and Zen jewellery.   austique.co.uk

Affordable to expensive   *Amex/MC/V*

0870 345 0800   **tube: Sloane Square**
330 King's Road   Mon-Sat 10:30-6:30
London SW3   Sun 12-5

Avi Rossini   ♂

Looking for super-luxe tailoring with an English bent? Maybe you know the Rodeo Drive store and think Rossini is LA native? Nope, he's based right here on London's answer to Fashion Avenue. Although the service can be rude and abrupt, it is still worth ducking into his Bond Street store for sumptuous suits and sportswear, including leather-trimmed jeans. Focusing on feel, fit, finish and finesse, the designer turns out haute-ticketed custom ensembles and off-the-rack items. With Avi's guidance, many fans weave their crest or logo into his top-notch fabrics.

Expensive   *Amex/MC/V*

020 7409 0879   **tube: Bond Street/Green Park**
46 New Bond Street   Mon-Sat 9:30-6:30 (Thurs 9:30-7)
London W1

Aware

You have to be a bit suspicious of a man who takes pride in his underwear—strip off the average British male and you're more than likely to find a pair of M&S boxer shorts. But for an upgrade, point him in the direction of Old Compton Street in Soho: this shop features designer underwear and beach accessories, from boxer-briefs by Boss to D&G flip-flops, with the emphasis on international labels such as Armani and Ralph Lauren. It might remind you of those bare-chested Italians at the beach, posing in their Speedos but hey, it's got to be an improvement on those ancient boxer shorts.   *awareunderwear.com*

Moderate   *Amex/MC/V*

020 7287 3789   **tube: Leicester Square**
25a Old Compton Street   Mon-Sat 11-8
London W1   Sun 1-7

Ballantyne Cashmere

Wear sunglasses: the interior of Ballantyne's Westbourne Grove flagship is a kaleidoscope of colour and in-your-face prints in orange and green, all influenced by Forties fabric designer Joseph Frank. The men's and women's clothes are equally colourful, with hot pink polo shirts, striped green and white jackets, and the signature deep V- and scoop-neck cashmere jumpers. In a city brimming with cashmere shops, Ballantyne knows how to give it a bit of fashion edge.   *ballantyne-cashmere.co.uk*

Expensive   *Amex/MC/V*

020 7792 2563   **tube: Notting Hill Gate**
303 Westbourne Grove   Mon-Fri 10:30-6:30
London W11   Sat 10-6

Bally

Another brand trying to make the leap into the luxury world of Gucci and Louis Vuitton, this Swiss company has a history of producing fine shoes. The sophisticated selection of handbags and shoes, muted in tone but with an occasional splash of primary colour, is chic enough to pass muster without screaming "designer", while the "B" logo'd bags and shoes have been hot commodities among the world's fashion editors. It's harder to get excited about the clothing range, which continues the classic theme.   *bally.com*

Expensive   *Amex/MC/V*

020 7491 7062   **tube: Bond Street**
116 New Bond Street   Mon-Sat 10-6 (Thurs 10-7)
London W1   Sun 12-6

020 7493 2250   **tube: Green Park**
30 Old Bond Street   (opening hours as above
London W1   but closed Sun)

020 7589 9084   **tube: Sloane Square**
92 King's Road   Mon-Sat 10-6:30 (Wed 10-7)
London SW3   Sun 12-5

Bang Bang

This clothing exchange is the perfect antidote to cookie-cutter shopping, with secondhand designer pieces that will even thrill vintage diehards. With two floors of delicious designerwear and funky dressing-rooms with denim curtains, Bang Bang's exceptional selection of labels spans the fashion timeline from Yves Saint Laurent and Pucci to Betsey Johnson and Nicole Farhi. There's also stock from Zara, Top Shop, Gap and a fair bit of vintage. A plethora of little bits—costume jewellery, beaded handbags, leather gloves—means that those in the market for something small won't be left out. Choose wisely, and you'll get some bang bang for your buck.

Affordable to expensive   *Amex/MC/V*

020 7631 4191   **tube: Goodge Street**
21 Goodge Street   Mon-Fri 10-6:30, Sat 11-6
London W1

Barker Shoes

Established in a Northamptonshire village in 1880, Barker remains a traditional provider of men's footwear with a small-town devotion to the virtues of craftsmanship and comfort. The selection is basic, led by brown and black leather and suede lace-ups, slip-ons and ankle boots. The store brings a pleasant, unpretentious air to big-city shopping. A small women's range is also available.   *barker-shoes.co.uk*

Expensive   *Amex/MC/V*

020 7494 3069   **tube: Oxford Circus**
215 Regent Street   Mon-Sat 10-6:30 (Thurs 10-7:30)
London W1   Sun 11-5

Barkers of Kensington   (see House of Fraser)

Base

Specializing in sizes 16-28, Base provides modern staples for the plus-size set. Looks remain simple and flattering, if not terribly exciting: colourful coats, linen dresses, trouser-suits and silk tops. There is also a wide assortment of wraps and chunky jewellery. The staff are helpful and understanding—this is a good starting point for rebuilding a seasonal wardrobe.   *base-fashions.co.uk*

Moderate   *Amex/MC/V*

020 7240 8914   tube: Covent Garden/Leicester Square
55 Monmouth Street   Mon-Sat 10-6
London WC2

Base London

This funky men's clothing and footwear shop is aimed at creative twentysomethings—fans include TV presenters, soap stars and media types. The selection of classic casual T-shirts, regular shirts, knitwear and loafers comes in a generous colour palette, and the staff are young, approachable and keen to help. *baselondon.com*

Affordable to moderate — *Amex/MC/V*

020 7287 2865
30 Carnaby Street
London W1

tube: Oxford Circus
Mon-Sat 10:30-7, Sun 12-6

Basia Zarzycka

Like the twinkling display bursting around the entrance, Basia's personality fills her shop. It's a bride's grotto of jewels and accessories. Draped over antique mannequins and dangling from silk flowers is an eclectic mix of jewellery, antique beaded bags, feathered headbands and crystal tiaras. Inspired by nature you will find marcasite bumble-bees, crystal butterflies and silk flower corsages in every colour in the rainbow. Her magical elves create couture wedding gowns downstairs (from £5,500), or you can simply choose a sparkly pair of earrings or a hair slide to glamorise jeans. *basias.com*

Moderate to very expensive — *MC/V*

020 7730 1660
52 Sloane Square
London SW1

tube: Sloane Square
Mon-Sat 10-6

Bates Gentleman's Hatter

For over 90 years this tiny family-run store has supplied discerning gentlemen with the finest headwear. Their speciality is flat wool tweed caps, Gatsby style, but you'll also find top hats, bowlers, fedoras, trilbies and panamas. Styles named The Deerstalker, The Weekender or The Racing Hat are most likely to be found on the heads of the English sporting gentry, but the shop also draws stylists and big names from entertainment such as David Bowie, Diana Ross and Tom Jones. Service is proper, clipped English style, friendly and knowledgeable. *bates-hats.co.uk*

Expensive — *Amex/MC/V*

020 7734 2722
21a Jermyn Street
London SW1

tube: Piccadilly Circus
Mon-Fri 9-5:15, Sat 9:30-4

Beatrice von Tresckow

Older women with a penchant for bright colours and exotic looks flock to this Sloaney Fulham Road store. Taffeta gowns, long velvet jackets and curve-enhancing corsets are shamelessly intermingled in the selection of old-fashioned, made-to-order eveningwear. Fuchsia, purple, turquoise and green are the colours in charge, embroidery and beading are intricate, and decorative details prevail. And we thought no one went to hunt balls anymore. *beatricevontresckow.com*

Expensive — *Amex/MC/V*

020 7351 5354
273 Fulham Road
London SW10

tube: South Kensington
Mon-Sat 10-6 (Wed 10-7)

020 7243 8747
9 Portobello Road
London W11

tube: **Notting Hill Gate**
Mon-Sat 10-6

Beau Monde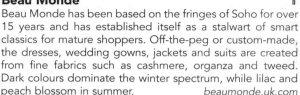

Beau Monde has been based on the fringes of Soho for over 15 years and has established itself as a stalwart of smart classics for mature shoppers. Off-the-peg or custom-made, the dresses, wedding gowns, jackets and suits are created from fine fabrics such as cashmere, organza and tweed. Dark colours dominate the winter spectrum, while lilac and peach blossom in summer. *beaumonde.uk.com*

Moderate to expensive   *Amex/MC/V*

020 7734 6563
20 Kingly Street
London W1

tube: **Oxford Circus**
Mon-Sat 10:30-6:30 (Thurs 10:30-7)
(by appointment)

Belinda Robertson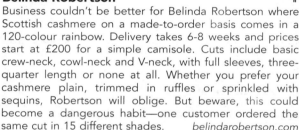

Business couldn't be better for Belinda Robertson where Scottish cashmere on a made-to-order basis comes in a 120-colour rainbow. Delivery takes 6-8 weeks and prices start at £200 for a simple camisole. Cuts include basic crew-neck, cowl-neck and V-neck, with full sleeves, three-quarter length or none at all. Whether you prefer your cashmere plain, trimmed in ruffles or sprinkled with sequins, Robertson will oblige. But beware, this could become a dangerous habit—one customer ordered the same cut in 15 different shades. *belindarobertson.com*

Expensive   *Amex/MC/V*

020 7235 0519
4 West Halkin Street
London SW1

tube: **Knightsbridge**
Mon-Fri 10-6:30, Sat 10-6:30
Sun 12-5 (seasonal)

Ben de Lisi

After a lingering lunch at Olivo, young ladies with hours to kill and cash to burn sneak across the street for a peek through Ben de Lisi's racks. This chic and dressy shop, on one of London's poshest blocks, offers a hip-meets-refined com-bination of cashmere sweater sets, tank tops, tweed trousers and some of the sexiest eveningwear in town. Modern cuts and a playful approach to fabrics might remind you of Joseph. De Lisi's future looks similarly bright, though for their menswear you still have to go to Harrods because they don't yet have the space in Elizabeth Street. *bendelisi.com*

Very expensive   *Amex/MC/V*

020 7730 2994
40 Elizabeth Street
London SW1

tube: **Sloane Square/Victoria**
Mon-Fri 10-6, Sat 12-5

Berk

Housed in Mayfair's prestigious Burlington Arcade, these two small English shops are heaped with cashmere cardi-gans, pullovers and scarves. If you only have time for one cashmere stop, Berk might be the place as it offers a wide selection for both women and men. Also in stock: John Smedley fine-gauge wool and cotton knitwear and Ballantyne cashmere, again for both sexes.

Expensive   *Amex/MC/V*

020 7493 0028   **tube: Green Park/Piccadilly Circus**
46-49 Burlington Arcade   Mon-Fri 9-5:30, Sat 9:30-5:30
London W1

020 7493 1430   **tube: Green Park/Piccadilly Circus**
6 Burlington Arcade   (opening hours as above)
London W1

Berluti

Italian in name but of French provenance, Berluti is best known for its innovative, design-led ready-to-wear shoes, though it does also offer a bespoke service. For the man with no need for specially tailored shoes this means getting bespoke looks and quality for about half the price and in a fraction of the time. The staff have been known to take a selection of shoes out to hotels for clients in a hurry, and will even open the store by appointment if need be. Ready-to-wear starts at £440, and the bespoke service at £2,000.   *berluti.com*

Expensive   *Amex/MC/V*

020 7437 1740   **tube: Oxford Circus**
43 Conduit Street   Mon-Sat 10-6:30
London W1

Bernini

The traditional haunts of the well-dressed gentleman are Savile Row and Jermyn Street but Bond Street has more and more offerings every year. At the elegantly reserved Bernini, gents will find tuxedos, three-piece suits, blazers and sports jackets with typical Italian flair. A shop for the international playboy, or indeed the aspiring playboy.   *bernini.com*

Expensive   *Amex/MC/V*

020 7491 7865   **tube: Bond Street**
95-96 New Bond Street   Mon-Sat 10-7
London W1   (Thurs 10-8), Sun 12-6

Bertie

Trendy shoe fanatics flock here for designer spin-offs at prices so modest you can afford to indulge. Styles range from bold-coloured slingbacks, flesh-toned open-toed high heels, leather loafers and terry-towelling wedges, and the stock seems to vary slightly according to location: the South Molton branch attracts a more mature twentysomething fashion flock, while the Covent Garden crowd is young and club-cool. Always worth a look.   *theshoestudio.com*

Affordable   *Amex/MC/V*

020 7493 5033   **tube: Bond Street**
36 South Molton Street   Mon-Sat 10-7
London W1   (Thurs 10-8), Sun 12-6

020 7836 7223
25 Long Acre
London WC2

tube: Covent Garden
(opening hours as above)

Bertie Golightly

In a neighbourhood where women would sooner go naked than admit they are wearing used goods, Roberta Gibbs's immaculate secondhand store, known simply as Bertie's, is a storming success. Gibbs is vigilant about banishing that straight-from-the-attic musty state of disrepair, and condition is superlative. Christian Dior, Valentino, Prada, Chanel—they've all been here, sometimes with the tags still on. The space is packed with handbags, beaded gowns, suits and shoes, which doesn't make for the most dignified shopping experience. But for a pair of last season's Ferragamos even the most proper of ladies will drop to her knees and dig.   *bertiego.co.uk*

Moderate   *Amex/MC/V*

020 7584 7270
48 Beauchamp Place
London SW3

tube: Knightsbridge
Mon-Sat 10-6 (Wed 10-7)
Sun 12-5

Bertie Wooster

Quintessentially English, stepping into Bertie Wooster will take you back to a time when gentlemen dressed proper. No trainers, no T-shirts. We're talking dapper dandies, billiards, cigars and shooting trips at the country estate. The old hunting prints on the walls, the foxes comically dressed in riding kit in the window, and the racks of thick tweeds lend this secondhand gentlemen's store a distinguished Horse and Hound feel. The selection, a combination of vintage and contemporary suits, shirts, jackets and hats, offers London's Everyman the chance to dress like an English country gent—at a fraction of Savile Row prices. You'll also find antique leather cigar cases, silver cufflink boxes and gold tiepins, as well as shoes and a selection of boxer shorts.   *bertie-wooster.co.uk*

Moderate   *Amex/MC/V*

020 7352 5662
284 Fulham Road
London SW10

tube: Fulham Broadway
Mon-Fri 10-6 (Thurs 10-7)
Sat 10-4:30

Betsey Johnson

Known for her celebration of the exuberant, the embellished and the over-the-top, Betsey Johnson is an American designer with a flamboyant flair for fashion. Her London shop is suitably wild, with bright yellow wallpaper splashed with a chintz floral pattern. This playful ethos reverberates throughout the collection, in whimsical separates and sexy eveningwear—diamanté bikinis, white tank tops decorated with feathers and red tube dresses embellished with pistols. Johnson's quirky-meets-sex-bomb effect means you'll never be able to guess what's coming next.   *betseyjohnson.com*

Expensive   *Amex/MC/V*

020 7591 0005   **tube: South Kensington**
106 Draycott Avenue   Mon-Sat 10:30-6 (Wed 10:30-7)
London SW3   Sun 12-5

Betty Jackson

A directional classicist, British designer Betty Jackson offers modern women an easy, contemporary approach to dressing smartly. From the selection of simple basics you can create a chic, fundamental wardrobe that won't need to be scrapped after a single season. For fall, expect the usual suspects—soft knitwear and sheepskin coats, as well as a smattering of decorative surprises, like pretty Chinese tops.

bettyjackson.com

Expensive   *Amex/MC/V*

020 7589 7884   **tube: South Kensington**
311 Brompton Road   Mon-Fri 10:30-6:30
London SW3   Sat 10:30-6, Sun 12-5

Bill Amberg

Bill Amberg has moved to fabulous new premises and is definitely worth a visit. Imagine anything for the home—table tops, doors, couches, bags, wallets, even wine racks—and Amberg has probably rendered it in hide. At the more mainstream end of the spectrum, handbags and briefcases come in a wide variety of colours and styles from woven to wood-finish. His fur-lined papoose and leather bouncing chair have been a hit with cool mummies like Kate Winslet and Cindy Crawford. Amberg has been appointed head designer of leather goods at Dunhill and is collaborating on a luggage range with Aston Martin—busy times for the king of leather. *billamberg.com*

Expensive   *Amex/MC/V*

020 7727 3560   **tube: Notting Hill Gate/Bayswater**
21-22 Chepstow Corner   Mon-Sat 10-6 (Thurs 10-7)
London W2

Birkenstock

This shop is a refreshingly open space with a wholesome outdoor feel. If you've never gone through a hippy phase you might not have come across these exceptionally comfortable sandals, which feature a footbed specially designed to conform to your feet. The brand has attracted a celeb following (Gwyneth adores hers), and supermodel Heidi Klum has designed a more expensive, limited-edition collection. But there is something for everyone in the large selection of leather and suede sandals, clogs and slip-ons which come in a variety of colours, patterns and styles. There is also a great selection of colourful sandals for kids. *birkenstock.co.uk*

Affordable to expensive   *Amex/MC/V*

020 7240 2783   **tube: Covent Garden**
70 Neal Street   Mon-Sat 10:30-7 (Thurs 10-8:30)
London WC2   Sun 12-6

Blackout II

This is a vintage shop on the outskirts of Covent Garden where you can both buy and sell. It has a large supply of handbags from the Thirties to the Eighties and a great selection of "dead stock" shoes—not as creepy as it sounds, this means shoes which were never sold and therefore have never been worn. Find everything from beaded evening gowns to Seventies plaid trousersuits to denim, as well as a greatest-hits assortment of accessories. Bring your stylistic vision and your sense of adventure—you may have to dig around for the perfect find. *blackout2.com*

Affordable   *Amex/MC/V*

020 7240 5006   **tube: Covent Garden**
51 Endell Street   Mon-Fri 11-7, Sat 11:30-6:30
London WC2

Blooming Marvellous

OK, so it's not the most glamorous or stylish maternity shop, but mums-to-be will find all the essentials they need here, from massive knickers (scary) to comfy trousers to packs of T-shirts which expand to fit ballooning bellies. Organised types can stock up on baby bits too. There are jumpers, blankets, bottles and bibs as well as larger necessities like baby seats and prams. Nothing will make you shout for joy but no matter, the new arrival most definitely will.

Affordable   *Amex/MC/V*

020 7371 0500   **tube: Parsons Green**
725 Fulham Road   Mon-Fri 10-6 (Thurs 10-7)
London SW6   Sat 9:30-5:30, Sun 11-5

☆ Blossom

Pregnant women rejoice. This is a peaceful oasis on Walton Street where tunes by Norah Jones will calm your frayed nerves, young smiling staff will cheer you, and the chicest maternity wear in town will restore your sense of style. The founders of Blossom are on a mission to provide everything a pregnant woman or new mother might need, from baby massage vouchers and lavender bath salts to designer wear suitable for pregnancy. Hip names to hand include Antik Batik, Megan Park and Myla. There is also a jeans bar with a host of the hottest denim labels such as Citizens of Humanity, with waistbands replaced by bump-hugging jersey panels. Best of all, Matthew Williamson, Alice Temperley and Gharani Strok have all made special pregnancy pieces exclusively for Blossom. If you are saving your pennies for the new arrival, the boxed "Pregnancy Survival Kit" by Belly Basics is a bestseller and contains a tunic top, straight-legged trousers, a flattering skirt and a three-quarter length sleeved dress, all in basic black. *blossommotherandchild.com*

Expensive   *Amex/MC/V*

020 7589 7500   **tube: South Kensington**
164 Walton Street   Mon-Sat 10-6, Sun 12-5
London SW3

Blue Velvet

At last Blue Velvet has had a major makeover and the shop is looking fresher and younger for it. Still more of a wander-in shop than a destination in its own right, this is a solid place to start your search for smart work shoes and every-day classics. Nothing quite reaches the height of fashion but the range is varied and the styles contemporary, from ever-popular black loafers to knee-high brown suede boots. If comfort is more of a priority for you than the latest trend, this could be the perfect fit. *bluevelvetshoes.com*

Moderate   *MC/V*

020 7376 7442   **tube: Sloane Square**
174 King's Road   Mon-Sat 10-7, Sun 11-6
London SW3

Blunauta

Cashmere sweater sets, linen tops, simple cotton shift dress-es and embroidered silk bags rest comfortably in this bright, breezy shop. Organized by colour, the racks are easy to nav-igate for complementary separates—a concept that seems to drive this collection, which is apparently geared more towards comfort than trend. *blunauta.it*

Moderate to expensive   *Amex/MC/V*

020 7240 1018   **tube: Covent Garden**
69-76 Long Acre   Mon-Sat 10-7
London WC2   Sun 12-6

Bodas

Lingerie is too flowery a word for this refreshingly basic bra and underwear shop with only a handful of styles to choose from, all in soft supportive cotton or a slightly sexier stretch mesh. For bras there are padded, seamless and strapless variations; and below the belt, everything from low-riding hipster thongs to old-fashioned French knickers. They also have comfortable pyjamas and kimonos for lounging around the house. It's Calvin Klein simplicity, without the hype. *bodas.co.uk*

Affordable to moderate   *MC/V*

020 7229 4464   **tube: Notting Hill Gate**
38b Ledbury Road   Mon-Sat 10-6
London W11   Sun 12-4

020 7626 3210   **tube: Bank**
29 Lime Street   Mon-Fri 10-6:30
London EC3

Bonpoint

There's something about the French—they dress kids like kids, with just the right dose of cute and not a hint of sickly sweetness: floral dresses and headbands with bows, striped T-shirts and dungarees, baby jumpsuits declaring "jolie comme maman" ("pretty like Mummy"). There is also a gor-geous range of silver rattles and an ingenious collapsible crib. Most children's stores make us go melty, but this one really sent us into gooey fits (but that may just be because of the upmarket prices). Notice that the Victoria Grove shop, as in France, likes to close for lunch. *bonpoint.com*

Moderate to expensive *Amex/MC/V*

020 7792 2515
197 Westbourne Grove
London W11

tube: Notting Hill Gate
Mon-Sat 10-6

020 7584 5131
17 Victoria Grove
London W8

tube: Gloucester Road
Mon-Fri 9-1, 2-5, Sat 10-1

020 7235 1441
15 Sloane Street
London SW1

tube: Knightsbridge
Mon-Sat 10-6

020 7495 1680
38 Old Bond Street
London W1

tube: Green Park/Bond Street
Mon-Sat 10-6

☆ Bottega Veneta

Synonymous with low-key sophisticated glamour, this luxurious Italian label combines impeccable craftsmanship with super-soft leather. At the huge Sloane Street flagship store you'll find sumptuous silk scarves, square-toed shoes and the ever popular signature woven bags, which have been going strong since the Seventies. You'll also find a smattering of ready-to-wear for both men and women, mostly simple separates such as cashmere pullovers and leather jackets. The pieces are displayed in glass cases like works of art and command fierce prices. *bottegaveneta.co.uk*

Very expensive *Amex/MC/V*

020 7838 9394
33 Sloane Street
London SW1

tube: Knightsbridge
Mon-Sat 10-6 (Wed 10-7)

020 7629 5598
15 Old Bond Street
London W1

tube: Green Park/Bond Street
Mon-Sat 10-6 (Thurs 10-7)

Boxfresh

A purveyor of hip urban clothes, Boxfresh emphasizes comfort and style in a young, contemporary look tinged with retro. Spread over three floors, you'll find print T-shirts, tracksuit jackets, patch-pocket shirts, baggy jeans and chinos, appealing to the preppy club kid. In summer, you'll find fun flip-flops, beach balls, lilos and tennis sets. Cool, simple and not overly style-conscious. *boxfresh.co.uk*

Affordable *Amex/MC/V*

020 7240 4742
13 Shorts Gardens
London WC2

tube: Covent Garden
Mon-Sat 10:30-7
Sun 12:30-5:30

☆ Boyd

Tracey Boyd's roughed-up style adds a daring edge to the posh gentility of Elizabeth Street where you'll also find Philip

Treacy and Ben de Lisi. Lace blouses and pleated skirts have a sexy, naughty edge and the rock/glam spirit of the collection brings to mind Stella McCartney or Luella Bartley. Party dresses and girlish separates are her forte, and the new luxury raincoats made of waterproof lace are a winner. New to the store is Tracey Boyd's House: an ever-changing collection of vases, stationery, cushions, linen and vintage furniture. *traceyboyd.com*

Expensive   *Amex/MC/V*

020 7730 3939   **tube: Sloane Square/Victoria**
42 Elizabeth Street   Mon-Fri 10-6, Sat 12-5
London SW1

☆ Brioni

At last, one of the greatest names in tailoring has come to London. Brioni opened their first shop here in a four-storey, 18th-century house in the heart of Mayfair. What can one say of this most stellar of all stellar fashion houses? They dressed Gregory Peck in Roman Holiday and Pierce Brosnan's James Bond. They employ 800 tailors, maybe more, in Abruzzi where every single garment is hand-stitched. They run their own tailoring school (four-year courses) so the unequalled skills and traditions do not disappear. They use 2,000 fabrics, including naturally the very best: Sea Island cotton, brushed Egyptian cotton, 190s, vicuña, the finest cashmere. Words cannot describe the quality—you have to go there and feel the stuff. It isn't cheap, of course. Mens' shirts start at £180 and off-the-peg suits at £1,940. The made-to-measure range is £2,700-£10,000, but if you take the full body-shape bespoke service (for which you have to go to the master-tailor in the Milan atelier), you get a wonderfully figure-flattering result with bill to match—there probably isn't any limit. Two other things about Brioni are not generally known. One, they also make shoes and coloured briefcases of remarkable elegance. Two, this quintessentially menswear name (they were the first to stage a menswear catwalk show, back in 1952) started doing womenswear two years ago. The top end of women's fashion is a crowded room, of course, and they haven't fully defined the Brioni woman yet, but watch this space. *brioni.it*

Very expensive   *Amex/MC/V*

020 7491 7700   **tube: Green Park/Bond Street**
32 Bruton Street   Mon-Sat 10-6 (Thurs 10-7)
London W1

Broadway

This is not necessarily the type of shop you come to north London for—the clothing is as basic and inoffensive as you will find on any shopping street. Shoes by Unisa, Great Plains turtlenecks and cotton separates from Jackpot make for some snoozy countrywear, but there are some highlights such as embroidered tops by Uttam London and bags by

B.Young. A bit bland for a neighbourhood moving steadily upmarket, but a reliable source for the locals. (There are also more restaurants per yard on Upper Street, from pricey posh to cheap eaterie, than on any other street in London.)

Moderate *Amex/MC/V*

020 7359 5655 **tube: Highbury & Islington**
152 Upper Street Mon-Sat 9:30-6 (Thurs-Fri 10-7)
London N1 Sun 11-5

☆ Brora

The days are growing colder, it's raining, and it will soon be dark by teatime. All you want to do is forget about work, curl up on the sofa with a good video and indulge in a cup of steaming hot chocolate. In an ideal world you would be stylishly dressed, head to toe, in cosy cashmere from one of our favourite shops, beloved Brora. Their soft roomy trousers, simply styled jumpers and striped socks are the chicest around; indispensable for slobbing around or long-haul flights, but also fashionable enough to wear every day. Team a Brora cardigan in crisp white with a pair of fresh blue jeans and you are ready for (almost) anything. The collection—more modern than classic—comes in a mouth-watering colour palette, from basic black to lime to strawberry. Equally fine accessories are on offer, such as picnic baskets, scarves, blankets and socks. Don't miss it. *brora.co.uk*

Expensive *Amex/MC/V*

020 7352 3697 **tube: Sloane Square**
344 King's Road Mon-Sat 10-6, Sun 12-5
London SW3

020 7224 5040 **tube: Baker Street**
81 Marylebone High Street (opening hours as above)
London W1

020 7229 1515 **tube: Notting Hill Gate**
66-68 Ledbury Road (opening hours as above)
London W11

020 7354 4246 **tube: Highbury & Islington**
186 Upper Street Mon-Sat 10:30-6:30
London N1 Sun 12-5

020 8971 9146 **tube: Wimbledon**
17 High Street Mon-Sat 10-6, Sun 12-5
London SW19

☆ Browns

Like many venerable Mayfair ladies, this elite emporium has had a face-lift, giving her a more contemporary, open plan feel. A favourite of fashion editors and stylists, Browns has nurtured design talent, from Dolce & Gabbana to Stella McCartney, for more than 25 years, maintaining South Molton Street's reputation as a fashion-lover's destination. Check out the dazzling array of talent on offer such as new-comer Jenny Dyer's coveted crepe dresses or Sissi Rossi's soft kangaroo-skin handbags, amongst other impressive labels like Jil Sander, Marni, Alexander McQueen and

Helmut Lang. The below-ground floor offers an assortment of housewares, including cushions, candles and throws. Impeccably dressed staff can be snooty and the selection is glamorously grown-up—in styles and prices. Still, it's a perennial favourite with those in the know, and a good place for picking up fashion industry gossip. *brownsfashion.com*

Expensive to very expensive *Amex/MC/V*

020 7514 0000 **tube: Bond Street**
23-27 South Molton Street Mon-Sat 10-6:30
London W1 (Thurs 10-7)

020 7514 0040 **tube: Knightsbridge**
6c Sloane Street Mon-Sat 10-6 (Wed 10-7)
London SW1

Browns Focus
This offshoot of the renowned boutique targets a younger, edgier shopper. The black tiled walls and ceiling call to mind a rather daunting, chichi nightclub, and the young girls at the counter by the door are reminiscent of clipboard chicks—if your name's not down, you're way too uncool to shop here. Lurking amidst the selection: Marc Jacobs jeans, Martin Margiela DIY decal T-shirts (decals are sold separately so you can iron them on wherever you wish), and hip creations by Australian designer Willow. Always a step ahead of the mainstream. *brownsfashion.com*

Expensive to very expensive *Amex/MC/V*

020 7514 0063/4 **tube: Bond Street**
38-39 South Molton Street Mon-Sat 10-6:30
London W1 (Thurs 10-7)

Browns Labels For Less
Across the street, this small shop makes up the final part of the magic triangle of the Browns group. It's packed with a mixed bag of the season's leftovers at marked down prices. Some of the same names offered at its full-price counterpart are available here at up to 80% off (Chloé, Marc Jacobs, Sonia Rykiel and Matthew Williamson), though you may have to dig deep to find them—it can feel like a posh jumble sale. Compared with the mother shop, the atmosphere here is low on sophistication, but you'll be too dazzled by the prices to notice. *brownsfashion.com*

Affordable to moderate *Amex/MC/V*

020 7514 0052 **tube: Bond Street**
50 South Molton Street (opening hours as above)
London W1

Bruce Oldfield
Renowned for sophisticated couture, Oldfield has found his niche in Knightsbridge. The sales staff can be à bit reticent but the dresses, in such fabrics as silk, crepe and chiffon, are classically glamorous with low backs and dramatic necklines. Antique lace and hand-printed patterns give some gowns a precious quality—suitable for fancy cocktail par-

ties but hardly serious fashion. Other styles, including the wedding dresses, are attracting a younger, fashion-conscious following. *bruceoldfield.com*

Expensive *Amex/MC/V*

020 7584 1363 tube: **Knightsbridge**
27 Beauchamp Place Mon-Fri 9:30-6, Sat 11-5
London SW3

B-Store

Seconds from the mainstream buzz of Regent Street, on the increasingly trendy Conduit Street, this store has the potential to be too-cool-for-skool. But the assistants are welcoming and whether you are Gwen Stefani's stylist or just looking for some groovy wedges to spice up a tired wardrobe, the staff will cheerfully help you. There are Richard Michon dresses, men's white leather lace-ups from Buddahood or B-Store's own spotty heels. Step into fashion land and be inspired. *buddahood.co.uk*

Moderate to expensive *Amex/MC/V*

020 7499 6828 tube: **Oxford Circus**
6 Conduit Street Mon-Fri 10:30-6:30
London W1 Sat 10-6

Budd

Squeeze into this tiny shop and find every accoutrement a gentleman could ever need: traditional shirts in a selection of colours and styles, including the house striped design, dressing-gowns, silk waistcoats, cufflinks, elegant pyjamas. As one client (and *Where to Wear* reader) told us: "Budd offers more accessories for black and white tie than any other place I know. It's a feast for sartorial eyes."

Expensive *Amex/MC/V*

020 7493 0139 tube: **Piccadilly Circus/Green Park**
1a & 3 Piccadilly Arcade Mon-Thurs 9-5:30
London W1 Fri 9-5, Sat 10-5

Buffalo Boots

Their funky platform trainers come in a kaleidoscope of colours and were made famous by the Spice Girls. If Nineties Girl Power isn't to your taste, you will also find traditional strappy sparkly heels in bronze, pink and white. There's a good selection of skater shoes, and who doesn't need an Elvis print handbag? It's also a great place to drag a moody teenager. High or low, these sneakers make a statement. *buffalo-boots.com*

Affordable to moderate *Amex/MC/V*

020 7379 1051 tube: **Covent Garden**
65-67 Neal Street Mon-Sat 10:30-7, Sun 12-5
London WC2

020 7424 9014 tube: **Camden Town**
190 Camden High Street Wed-Sun 11-6:30
London NW1

Bumpsville

You won't find any black in here. From the multicoloured flower rug and the pink and yellow painted rails, to the colourful maternity dresses and the kids' spotty socks that come in an egg box, the founders of the West Village boutique next door designed this store to uplift mothers-to-be and children alike. A wall-sized photo of the owner as a baby looks down approvingly on her own designs, as well as Antik Batik kaftans and Ollie and Nic bags which sit alongside baby Ugg boots and teeny rainbow sweaters. *bumpsville.com*

Moderate   *MC/V*

020 7727 1213   **tube: Notting Hill Gate**
33 Kensington Park Road   Mon-Fri 10:30-6:30
London W11   Sat 10-6

Burberry

It's still going strong following its groundbreaking metamorphosis from stodgy institution to chic global power-brand. The signature black, red and camel Burberry plaid is now found on only 15% of worldwide sales. It's still evident, of course, on everything from umbrellas and boxer shorts to skirts, shirts, trousers, berets and knitwear, but it's best used as subtle detailing on bikinis, cashmere sweaters and baby clothes unless you want to be branded a Chav. The ready-to-wear collections feature plenty of plaid-free choice, from sleekly tailored jackets and trousers to sparkly eveningwear and the macs are, of course, one of life's most worthwhile investments. *burberry.com*

Expensive   *Amex/MC/V*

020 7839 5222   **tube: Bond Street**
21-23 New Bond Street   Mon-Sat 10-7, Sun 12-6
London W1

020 7581 3585   **tube: Knightsbridge**
2 Brompton Road   (opening hours as above)
London SW1

020 7806 1316   **tube: Piccadilly Circus**
165 Regent Street   (opening hours as above)
London W1

Burro

A subdued atmosphere complements Burro's collection of colourful men's and women's streetwear. Designs are individual and off the high street track. Patterns can veer to the abstract, and excessively brightly coloured stripes and polka dots prevail. There is a cool, vintage flavour to the collection that keeps it from being as cheesy as it may sound, and there's also an eclectic music selection on sale. *burro.co.uk*

Affordable to moderate   *Amex/MC/V*

020 7240 5120   **tube: Covent Garden**
44 Monmouth Street   Mon-Sat 10:30-7
London WC2   Sun 12-6

☆ Butler & Wilson

Step into this Aladdin's cave of sparkly trinkets, beaded slippers, purses and serious costume jewellery bling which would not look out of place at a film premiere. The ground floor of the Fulham Road location features a large, lovely selection of vintage and costume accessories, from delicate drop earrings, "lazy lizard" hairpins and silver art deco pieces, to diamanté necklaces and beaded slippers. Upstairs, the glamorous pearl evening bags and original flapper dresses make us want to raise our flutes of champagne (vintage, of course) to the past, while modern gypsy shirts and crocheted belts are straight off the fashion pages. The South Molton Street branch has more quirky miscellanea and a dose of oriental kitsch, from pretty photo albums and kittycat puzzles to sparkling tiaras and bucket bags printed with geishas. Both stores demonstrate the playful and distinctly English approach to fashion, making Butler & Wilson a big hit with American shoppers. *butlerandwilson.co.uk*

Affordable to expensive   *Amex/MC/V*

020 7409 2955   **tube: Bond Street**
20 South Molton Street   Mon-Sat 10-6 (Thurs 10-7)
London W1   Sun 12-6

020 7352 3045   **tube: South Kensington**
189 Fulham Road   Mon-Sat 10-6 (Wed 10-7)
London SW3   Sun 12-6

Calvin Klein Lingerie

Remember the time when a Calvin Klein waistband peeking above jeans was the sign of a desirable male? Those days are long gone, but still, where would we be without our Calvins? Now that his New Bond Street clothing store has closed, you'll have to head to a department store to find his sleek-chic suits, clingy knits, shirts, dresses, skirts, relaxed sweaters and beautifully basic eveningwear.

Moderate to expensive   *Amex/MC/V*

020 7495 2916   **tube: Bond Street**
65 New Bond Street   Mon-Sat 10-6:30 (Thurs 10-7)
London W1

020 7495 2916   **tube: Bond Street**
65 South Molton Street   (opening hours as above)
London W1

020 7838 0647   **tube: Sloane Square**
68 King's Road   Mon-Sat 10-6:30
London SW3   Sun 12-6

Camden Market

The appeal of Camden Market is that it never pretends to be anything other than what it is—rough, ready and packed with retro-chic. If you're serious about shopping, get there early. Or simply drift along with the tide of spectators, absorbing the busy vibe. The southern end of the market on Camden High Street is dominated by club-style sneaker and sportswear stalls, more mainstream than underground, with all the vendors selling much the same stuff. You're better off crossing the canal, where Camden Lock offers the first signs of promise. Several levels packed to the rafters with eclectic furniture, bohemian jewellery, ethnic homeware and used books make this a hippy's paradise. *camdenlock.net*

Affordable to moderate	*Cash/cheque preferred*
(no phone)	**tube: Camden Town/Chalk Farm**
Camden High Street	Thurs-Sun 9-5:30
London NW1	
(no phone)	**tube: Chalk Farm/Camden Town**
Camden Lock	Many stalls open Mon-Sun 10-6
London NW1	(outdoor stalls Sat-Sun 10-6)

Camper

Round toes and comfy rubber soles ensure that while Campers may not be seen on the party circuit they do attract a loyal following. The layout of the Covent Garden store is ingenious, with the entire collection displayed on a giant rectangular table which customers circle in search of their perfect choice. Though the shop can be packed on a Saturday afternoon, this is an efficient way to see the whole lot in one heap. The shoes are hip without being flashy, and hot with the boho Notting Hill set. *camper.com*

Moderate	*Amex/MC/V*
020 7584 5439	**tube: Knightsbridge**
35 Brompton Road	Mon-Sat 10:30-7, Sun 12-6
London SW3	
020 7379 8678	**tube: Covent Garden**
39 Floral Street	(opening hours as above)
London WC2	
020 7629 2722	**tube: Green Park**
8-11 Royal Arcade	Mon-Sat 10-6 (Thurs 10-6:30)
28 Old Bond Street	
London W1	
020 7792 4004	**tube: Notting Hill Gate**
214 Westbourne Grove	Mon-Sat 10:30-7
London W11	Sun 12-6
020 7287 5988	**tube: Oxford Circus**
57 Foubert's Place	Mon-Sat 10-7
London W1	Sun 12-6

Canali

The menswear in this bright airy shop rests somewhere between fashion-conscious and beyond caring, with each floor devoted to a different department: shoes, coats and suits and sportswear. Canali targets the natty dresser with an eye for patterns and tailoring—in their words, "Think Cary Grant in *To Catch a Thief*." *canali.it*

Expensive	*Amex/MC/V*
020 7499 5605	**tube: Bond Street**
122 New Bond Street	Mon-Sat 9:30-6:30
London W1	(Thurs 9:30-7)

Caramel Baby & Child

Forget primary colours and logos. Caramel offers some of the chicest baby clothing around in soft beige, creams and pastels. Their small sweaters, tiny trousers and darling dresses will make your heart melt like hot butter and brown sugar. Featuring embroidered patterns and pastels, Caramel's adorable designs are only enhanced by the intimate space, where scented candles keep everything smelling sweet. Up to age eight.

Expensive   *Amex/MC/V*

020 7589 7001   **tube: South Kensington/Knightsbridge**
291 Brompton Road   Mon-Sat 10-6:30, Sun 12-5
London SW3

Carhartt

Like an underground nightclub that the right people just know about, this American streetwear shop has a boxy minimal feel to it, with a cool bass line thumping in the background. Their durable collection features bright, stripy T-shirts, nylon baseball jackets, bags, hooded sweatshirts and, of course, their trademark carpenter trousers. For womenswear in a similar spirit, head to their new Earlham Street shop. If you can bear the schlepp to East London, check out their clearance warehouse at 18 Ellingfort Road but call ahead to see if they're open (020 8986 8875).   *carhartt.com*

Affordable to moderate   *Amex/MC/V*

020 7836 5659   **tube: Covent Garden**
56 Neal Street   Mon-Sat 11-6:30 (Thurs 11-7)
London WC2   Sat 11-6:30, Sun 12-5:30
020 7287 6411   **tube: Oxford Circus**
13 Newburgh Street   Mon-Sat 11-6:30, Sun 1-5
London W1

Caroline Charles

Quintessentially elegant clothing featuring classic, couture-quality pieces—this is Ann Taylor for the designer dresser. Those who opt for timeless over trendy will find comfort in the solid-coloured selection of linen dresses, full-length skirts, crisp shirts and suits. There is also an assortment of dressy, beaded eveningwear and matching accessories.   *carolinecharles.co.uk*

Expensive   *Amex/MC/V*

020 7225 3197   **tube: Knightsbridge**
56-57 Beauchamp Place   Mon-Sat 10-6
London SW3

Caroline Holmes

Femme fatale, pretty princess or modern minimalist...whatever style a bride wants to embody, Caroline Holmes can bring it to life. With three separate couture collections (Glamour, Classic and Contemporary) there's something for everyone, be it strapless bodice and evening gloves or short sleeves and a bias cut. Visits are by appointment only, and service comes with all the bridal salon trimmings—tons of attention and that made-just-for-you feel. As the weather warms, business booms, so you're liable to face a battle of the brides if you don't call well in advance. *carolineholmes.com*

Very expensive   *Amex/MC/V*

020 7823 7678   **tube: South Kensington**
176 Walton Street   Mon-Sat 10-5:30 (by appointment)
London SW3

Cashmere London

There are those who merely love cashmere and then there are those who are obsessed with it. This shop is definitely for the latter, with a stunning selection of the highest quality Scottish cashmere in a glorious 10-colour rainbow. If you're not satisfied with the season's palette special orders can be placed, with 150 shades and multiple styles to choose from. You will also find layered chiffon skirts, pretty kaftans and handbags, all in the same pleasing palette as the cashmere.

Expensive   *Amex/MC/V*

020 7838 1133   **tube: South Kensington/Knightsbridge**
180 Walton Street   Mon-Sat 10-6:30
London SW3

Cath Kidston

Cath Kidston is the queen of domestic retro. Her petal-patterned ironing-board covers have graced the pages of Vogue, catapulting household chores to the forefront of fashion. Whether that's a good thing or not, we can't help but love her. It's all so idyllic, so English, so cosy. From summer strawberries to red roses, her pretty patterns are addictive and if vintage linens, distressed wardrobes and china teacups get you excited then you'll soon become a fan. Clothing-wise, there are soft cotton jumpers with patches of floral fabric on the elbows, warm winter dressing-gowns and confectionery-sweet children's wear.   *cathkidston.co.uk*

Moderate   *Amex/MC/V*

020 7584 3232   **tube: South Kensington/Sloane Square**
12 Cale Street   Mon-Sat 10-6
London SW3   Sun 12-5

020 7221 4000   **tube: Holland Park**
8 Clarendon Cross   (opening hours as above)
London W11

020 7731 6531   **tube: Parsons Green**
668 Fulham Road   (opening hours as above)
London SW6

020 7935 6555   **tube: Baker Street**
51 Marylebone High Street   Mon-Sat 10-7, Sun 11–5
London W1

020 7836 4803   **tube: Covent Garden**
28-32 Shelton Street   Mon-Sat 10-7 (Thurs 10-8)
London WC2   Sun 12-5

020 8944 1001
3 High Street
London SW19

Catherine Buckley ♀

Catherine Buckley is famous for her handmade vintage-style wedding dresses. Worn by Elizabeth Taylor, Patsy Kensit and Joanna Lumley, her designs are for the bride who wants to wear something unusual and flamboyant, rather than simple and classic. With names like Titania, Gainsborough and Out of Africa, you can imagine how some of these dresses look—romantic, stylized and from another era. Antique lace veils are also available, and there's also a dyeing service for shoes. *catherinebuckley.com*

Expensive   *Amex/MC/V*

020 7229 8786
116 Kensington Park Road
London W11

tube: Notting Hill Gate
(by appointment)

Catherine Walker ♀

Lady Helen Taylor, Lady Gabriella Windsor and the late Diana, Princess of Wales, are just a few of the stylish society ladies to have worn one of Walker's wonderful dresses. Sophisticated and graceful, her clothing is famous for its ability to flatter the female form with elongated lines and bias cuts, exquisite embroideries, provocative sheer panels and appliquéd lace. With such superb craftsmanship and quality, it is no surprise that prices are way out of most people's league. *catherinewalker.com*

Very expensive   *Amex/MC/V*

020 7581 8811
46 Fulham Road
London SW3

tube: South Kensington
Mon-Sat 10-6 (by appointment)

Cathryn Grosvenor ♀

It would be easy to miss this discreet store tucked away in a charming but lesser-known part of Chelsea, but it is well worth a visit. The best luxury knits are on hand here, from Egyptian cotton to cashmere and if, after scanning the racks, you're still not satisfied, their made-to-order service lets you pick the precise style and colour (from 100 shades) that please. Co-stars include a range of lovely scarves and jewellery.

Expensive   *Amex/MC/V*

020 7584 2112
3 Elystan Street
London SW3

tube: South Kensington/Sloane Square
Mon-Fri 10-5:30, Sat 10-5:30

Catimini ♀

Dressing the little ones with flair is a simple task at Catimini. Soft and cosy, the enchanting collection comes in shades of navy, olive, ruby and tangerine, embellished with ethnic patterns and embroidered animals. There's also a small selection of shoes and a colourful assortment of hats, gloves and scarves. For children up to 14. A recent refurb means that there is now a larger play area for children, with a table and crayons to amuse them while you flex Daddy's Amex. *catimini.com*

Expensive   *Amex/MC/V*

020 7629 8099   **tube: Bond Street**
52a South Molton Street   Mon-Sat 10-6:30 (Thurs 10-7)
London W1   Sun 11:30-5:30

020 7824 8897   **tube: Sloane Square**
33c King's Road   (opening hours as above)
London SW3

Caz

Be warned. Once you've worn a pair of Caz wide-legged trousers or cuddled up in one of the soft, pretty cardigans, there will be no going back to scratchy old wool. It is an expensive predicament, but Londoners can't live without their cashmere and it's an addiction Caz feeds happily with bright solid, striped and two-toned cardigan sets, short-sleeved sweaters, tank tops and shawls. Juicy Couture T-shirts and a lightweight Scottish cashmere blend mean that even in the summer months nobody has to abstain.

Expensive   *Amex/MC/V*

020 7589 1920   **tube: South Kensington**
177 Draycott Avenue   Mon-Fri 10-6 (Wed 10-6:30)
London SW3   Sat 10:30-6, Sun 1-5:30

Cecil Gee

Low-key seems to be the sales mantra at this refreshingly relaxed emporium where customers are left to sift in peace through Versace, Burberry, Dolce & Gabbana, Hugo Boss and other high-end designers. The selection is as understat-ed as the ambience and includes suits, shirts, sweaters, trousers and accessories. There is also a fast-growing wom-enswear selection in some shops. *cecilgee.co.uk*

Affordable to moderate   *Amex/MC/V*

020 7629 4441   **tube: Bond Street**
92 New Bond Street   Mon-Sat 10-7
London W1   Sun 12-6

020 7491 2292   **tube: Oxford Circus**
287 Oxford Street   Mon-Sat 10-7 (Thurs 10-8)
London W1   Sun 12-6

020 7436 8752   **tube: Oxford Circus**
170 Oxford Street   (opening hours as above)
London W1

020 7376 1268   **tube: High Street Kensington**
172 Kensington High Street   Mon-Sat 10-6:30
London W8   Sun 11-5

020 7626 5011   **tube: Bank**
153 Fenchurch Street   Mon-Fri 8:30-6
London EC3

020 7513 1824
27 Canada Square
London E14

tube: Canary Wharf
Mon-Fri 9-7, Sat 10-6
Sun 12-6

Celine

Keeping the classic shapes and luxurious double facing synonymous with the Celine label, Roberto Menichetti's second collection is more loyal to Celine's faithful following than was his debut. He has now moved on, and as we went to press Celine were about to announce a new designer, but the colourful Scholl sandals continue to be a summer bestseller, proving as much of a hit as the matching shoes and bag combinations. *celine.com*

Expensive to very expensive Amex/MC/V

020 7297 4999
160 New Bond Street
London W1

tube: Bond Street/Green Park
Mon-Sat 10-6 (Thurs 10-6:30)

Chanel

On the street that dreams are made of, Coco Chanel's spirit lives on in the wonderful designs of fashion maestro Karl Lagerfeld. Accessories, shoes and cosmetics can be found on the ground floor while the ready-to-wear collection hangs upstairs on trademark black shiny rails. Bows on cropped trousers and pretty cocktail dresses strike the perfect balance between catwalk and classic Chanel, and beautiful jewellery to complement new outfits can be found at the fine jewellery store just a few doors away at 173 New Bond Street. *chanel.com*

Expensive to very expensive Amex/MC/V

020 7493 5040
26 Old Bond Street
London W1

tube: Green Park
Mon-Sat 10-6

020 7235 6631
167-169 Sloane Street
London SW1

tube: Knightsbridge
Mon-Sat 10-6

020 7581 8620
278-280 Brompton Road
London SW3

tube: South Kensington
Mon-Sat 10-6
Sun 1-5

The Changing Room

If you're suffocating on bustling Oxford Street, take a breather at this out-of-the-way boutique. Designs range from soft feminine slip dresses to smart business suits, featuring Renato Nucci, Pleats Please, Yoshiki Hishinuna and Adolfo Dominguez. Long scarves, bags and jewellery (check out K.Mo's pearl and silver pieces) are worth a look. Styles rate high on character and low on fuss, creating an effect that is funky and fun. *the-changingroom.com*

Moderate to expensive Amex/MC/V

020 7408 1596
10a Gees Court
London W1

tube: Bond Street
Mon-Sat 10:30-6:30
(Thurs 10:30-7:30)

Charles Tyrwhitt

Clean-cut, simple and timeless, this is one of the more affordable shirt shops on Jermyn Street. Sure, if you have the money and the inclination you can find even better quality elsewhere, but for young professionals who need a stack of shirts in their wardrobe, Charles Tyrwhitt is an excellent option. The CT Woman line is as stylish, sexy and smart as the men's range, great for the woman who means business. Good mail order service too. *ctshirts.co.uk*

Moderate   *Amex/MC/V*

020 7839 6060   **tube: Piccadilly Circus/Green Park**
92 Jermyn Street   Mon-Sat 9:30-6 (Thurs 9:30-7)
London SW1   Sun 11-5

020 7329 1779   **tube: St Paul's/Mansion House**
43 Bow Lane   Mon-Fri 9:30-6 (Thurs 9:30-7)
London EC4

The Chelsea Collections

This is a very Chelsea store, selling posh, conservative clothing to posh, conservative people. Daddies bring their precious daughters here for sweet-sixteen silk gowns or a hat for their first Ascot. True trendsetters would blanch at the hot-pink, chiffon ballet skirts and peacock-blue feathered hats but in posh social terms this place sits safely within proper bounds. Garden party guests and mothers of the bride could don a smart ensemble here, topped by a Catherine Goodison hat, with elegant wraps and handbags to complete the effect. If all you're lacking is a suitable hat, there's also a made-to-measure milliner service. *chelseacollections.co.uk*

Expensive   *Amex/MC/V*

020 7581 5792   **tube: South Kensington**
90 Fulham Road   Mon-Sat 10-6
London SW3

☆ Chloé

Phoebe Philo continues to inject a winning dose of street cred into this luxurious, romantic and quintessentially French label. Her sexy daywear is ever popular and low-slung jeans, delicate feminine blouses and sharply tailored trousers are perfect wardrobe staples for sassy modern women. Stars like Kate Hudson, Cameron Diaz and Kate Moss are all fans and the London flagship store, with black satin-lined changing-rooms, is suitably glamorous. The ground floor is dedicated to shoes and you'll also find a smattering of sexy swimwear, leather goods and accessories. *chloe.com*

Very expensive   *Amex/MC/V*

020 7823 5348   **tube: Sloane Street**
152-153 Sloane Street   Mon-Sat 10-6 (Wed 10-7)
London SW1

Christian Dior

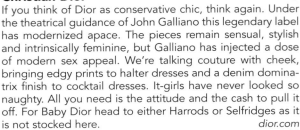

If you think of Dior as conservative chic, think again. Under the theatrical guidance of John Galliano this legendary label has modernized apace. The pieces remain sensual, stylish and intrinsically feminine, but Galliano has injected a dose of modern sex appeal. We're talking couture with cheek, bringing edgy prints to halter dresses and a denim dominatrix finish to cocktail dresses. It-girls have never looked so naughty. All you need is the attitude and the cash to pull it off. For Baby Dior head to either Harrods or Selfridges as it is not stocked here. *dior.com*

Very expensive *Amex/MC/V*

020 7235 1357 **tube: Knightsbridge**
31 Sloane Street Mon-Sat 10-6:30 (Wed 10-7)
London SW1 Sun 12-5

Christian Louboutin

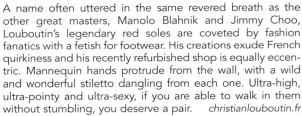

A name often uttered in the same revered breath as the other great masters, Manolo Blahnik and Jimmy Choo, Louboutin's legendary red soles are coveted by fashion fanatics with a fetish for footwear. His creations exude French quirkiness and his recently refurbished shop is equally eccentric. Mannequin hands protrude from the wall, with a wild and wonderful stiletto dangling from each one. Ultra-high, ultra-pointy and ultra-sexy, if you are able to walk in them without stumbling, you deserve a pair. *christianlouboutin.fr*

Expensive *Amex/MC/V*

020 7245 0386 **tube: Knightsbridge**
23 Motcomb Street Mon-Fri 10-6, Sat 11-6
London SW1

Christiana Couture

A wedding is the perfect excuse to indulgent your romantic side and Christiana Couture is a winner of the "Full Romantic British Bridal Award". Her silk bias-cut dress, with a cowl neck and low V back trimmed with pearls and crystals and finished off with a detachable silk chiffon train, is delicate and feminine. Most of her designs incorporate details such as cascading silk flowers, silk-covered buttons or fluted chiffon sleeves. The made-to-measure service starts at £2,900. *christianacouture.com*

Very expensive *MC/V*

020 7976 5252 **tube: Pimlico**
53 Moreton Street (by appointment)
London SW1

Church's

A well-known name for top quality, classic men's brogues, Church's is part-owned by Prada, which can only mean good things for the venerable English brand. At the very least they'll maintain their hard-earned reputation for fine leather shoes sold in a sophisticated setting where the women's line echoes the men's, but in softer forms. *churchsshoes.com*

Moderate to expensive   *Amex/MC/V*

020 7493 1474   **tube: Bond Street**
133 New Bond Street   Mon-Sat 9:30-6 (Thurs 9:30-7)
London W1

020 7493 8307   **tube: Green Park/Piccadilly Circus**
58-59 Burlington Arcade   Mon-Sat 9:30-6
London W1

020 7734 2438   **tube: Oxford Circus**
201 Regent Street   Mon-Sat 10-6:30 (Thurs 10-7:30)
London W1   Sun 12-6

020 7930 8210   **tube: Piccadilly Circus/Green Park**
108-110 Jermyn Street   Mon-Sat 9:30-6
London SW1

020 7589 9136   **tube: Knightsbridge**
143 Brompton Road   Mon-Tues 10-6
London SW3   Wed-Sat 10-6:30, Sun 11-5

020 7929 7015   **tube: Bank**
28 Royal Exchange   Mon-Fri 9-5:30
London EC3

020 7831 1846   **tube: Chancery Lane**
89 Chancery Lane   Mon-Fri 9-5:30
London WC2

020 7606 1587   **tube: Bank**
90 Cheapside   Mon-Fri 9-5:30
London EC2

020 7538 9730   **tube: Canary Wharf**
Cabot Place East   Mon-Fri 9-7
London E14   Sat 10-6:30, Sun 12-6

Claire's Accessories   👨👩

When Britney starts a necklace trend, it's bound to turn up
at Claire's. Their target is teens, but don't be surprised to
find twenty- and thirtysomethings stocking up on hoop earrings, hair toggles and sparkly belts (trend-setting TV pre-
senter Cat Deeley and actress Denise van Outen have been
spotted shopping there.) The cheap prices justify a brilliant
bulk-buy, though it's not nearly as nice as Accessorize and
the quality is just this side of junk. Still, it's all glittery and
girly, and sometimes that's just what we want. And you can
get your pre-teen ears pierced, if you have to. *claires.co.uk*

Affordable   *MC/V*

020 7734 4748   **tube: Piccadilly Circus**
Trocadero Centre   Mon-Thurs 10-9
13 Coventry Street   Fri-Sun 10-11:30
London W1

020 7376 9205   **tube: High Street Kensington**
169 Kensington High Street   Mon-Sat 9-7:30
London W8   Sun 11-6

020 7580 5504   **tube: Oxford Circus**
108 Oxford Street   Mon-Sat 9-7, Sun 12-6:30
London W1

020 7408 0342
West One Shopping Centre
Oxford Street
London W1

tube: Bond Street
(opening hours as above)

020 7637 5211
18-20 Oxford Street
London W1

tube: Tottenham Court Road
(opening hours as above)

Clarks

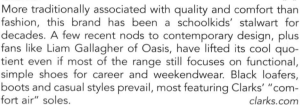

More traditionally associated with quality and comfort than fashion, this brand has been a schoolkids' stalwart for decades. A few recent nods to contemporary design, plus fans like Liam Gallagher of Oasis, have lifted its cool quotient even if most of the range still focuses on functional, simple shoes for career and weekendwear. Black loafers, boots and casual styles prevail, most featuring Clarks' "comfort air" soles.   *clarks.com*

Moderate   *Amex/MC/V*

020 7734 1339
203 Regent Street
London W1

tube: Oxford Circus
Mon-Fri 11-7 (Thurs 11-8)
Sat 10-6:30, Sun 12-6

020 7734 5294
101 Regent Street
London W1

tube: Piccadilly Circus
Mon-Fri 11-7 (Thurs 10-8)
Sat 10-6:30, Sun 12-6

020 7437 2593
15 Oxford Street
London W1

tube: Tottenham Court Road
Mon-Fri 10-7 (Thurs 10-8)
Sat 10-6:30, Sun 12-7

020 7499 0305
260 Oxford Street
London W1

tube: Oxford Circus
Mon-Sat 10-8
Sun 12-6

020 7629 9609
476 Oxford Street
London W1

tube: Marble Arch
Mon-Fri 10-8, Sat 10-7
Sun 12-7

020 7405 3500
121 High Holborn
London WC1

tube: Holborn
Mon-Fri 10-6
Sat 10-5

020 7937 4135
98 Kensington High Street
London W8

tube: High Street Kensington
Mon-Sat 10-6:30
Sun 12-6

Claudia Sebire

Chelsea ladies have long frequented this smart boutique. The selection is tailored and refined, from tweed suits to cashmere cardigans. Gilets by Karma and Strenesse bags are similarly luxe—no matter if you've never heard of them. Other labels like Marc Cain and Trixi Schober add an extra layer of polish.

Moderate   *Amex/MC/V*

020 7835 1327   **tube: South Kensington/Gloucester Road**
136 Fulham Road   Mon-Sat 10-6
London SW10

Clio

More suited to a rich international clientele than to the young and fashion-conscious, this store features bright and jewelled evening shoes in every colour of the rainbow. Shapes are dowdy, styles are brazen and prices exceed reason—perfect for the flashy Bond Street brigade.

Expensive   *Amex/MC/V*

020 7493 2018   **tube: Bond Street**
75 New Bond Street   Mon-Sat 10-6:30 (Thurs 10-8)
London W1

Club (formerly Designer Club)

Even on the dreariest London day these whitewashed walls create a sunny setting for the fine selection of chic, feminine tops, skirts and eveningwear. Sassy designs from Missoni, Ungaro and Valentino as well as shoes by top Italian designers such as Dolce & Gabbana and Sergio Rossi corner the market in sexy international style.

Expensive   *Amex/MC/V*

020 7235 2242   **tube: Knightsbridge**
9 West Halkin Street   Mon-Fri 10-6, Sat 11-6
London SW1

Clusaz

Quietly nestling on a side street with a devoted local clientele, this small shop savours its distance from Islington's main drag. Seek respite in bias-cut silk dresses by Poleci, Chine suede jackets, Nicole Farhi knits and the best from Tara Jarmon.

Moderate   *Amex/MC/V*

020 7359 5596   **tube: Angel**
56 Cross Street   Mon-Sat 10:30-6:30, Sun 1-5:30
London N1

cm store

This store brings hip-hop style to the King's Road and—be warned—you will need the wallet of P Diddy to afford a shopping spree here. As Dolly Parton says, "You've no idea how expensive it is to look this cheap." The shelves are piled high with every imaginable style of jean, many of them customised with embroidery or gold chain belts. There are canvas skirts decorated with images of reefer-smoking rastas, and the velour sweatsuits in baby pink, with "Juicy" emblazoned across the rear are just so J-Lo. Combat trousers, dozens of T-shirts with naughty slogans and plenty of jumpers for the lads ensure this store won't disappoint those wanting to buy into the pop culture lifestyle.

Expensive   *Amex/MC/V*

020 7351 9361   **tube: Sloane Square**
121 King's Road   Mon-Sat 10-7, Sun 12-6
London SW3

Coccinelle

The clean and simple way in which these chic bags and wallets are displayed reflects the refined designs and high-quality manufacturing. The selection is high end style for the younger set. Colours include rich reds, greens and golds and the Parma leather is especially supple. Bags come with matching wallets and there is a small collection of shoes, sunglasses, key chains, scarves and jewellery. Definitely a name to look out for.

Moderate *Amex/MC/V*

020 7730 7657 **tube: Sloane Square**
13 Duke of York Square Mon-Sat 10-7, Sun 11-6
London SW3

Cochinechine

It had only been open for a month when we visited, but Cochinechine has all the makings of a superstar. Exceptionally friendly staff, an exciting range of designers from Ann-Louise Roswald to Eley Kishimoto and, downstairs, spacious changing-rooms with beautiful shell-shaped sofas covered in a pink V.V. Rouleaux print. A favourite hangout for chic Hampstead mummies who drop in on the way back from the school run. Lucky them.   *cochinechine.com*

Expensive *Amex/MC/V*

020 7435 9377 **tube: Hampstead**
74 Heath Street Mon-Sat 10-6
London NW3 Sun 12-6

☆ Coco Ribbon

You might want to move in to either of these boutiques. They are pure girly pads where everything you see is for sale: from the embroidered silk knickers by Kolita to the Empire-style bedside tables and the rose hair-bands strewn on top of the romantic dressing-table. There are Moroccan sequined slippers, lavender heart bags, flower fairy lights and chic scatter cushions. You'll find itsy-bitsy bikinis by Zimmermann, stylish cashmere knitwear by Cameron Taylor, Matthew Williamson accessories, as well as Coco Ribbon's own label A Beautiful Life: an ever-growing range of lingerie, cashmere, CDs and candles. The new store in Sloane Street has a slightly more grown-up feel to it with a greater emphasis on fashion and homewear, reflected in the designers they carry, Temperley, Sass & Bide and Willow, and the interior design service they offer.   *cocoribbon.com*

Affordable to moderate *Amex/MC/V*

020 7229 4904 **tube: Ladbroke Grove**
21 Kensington Park Road Daily 10-6
London W11

020 7730 8555 **tube: Sloane Square**
133 Sloane Street Mon-Sat 10:30-6:30
London SW1 Sun 12:30-5:30

☆ Collette Dinnigan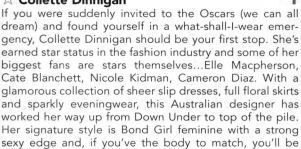

If you were suddenly invited to the Oscars (we can all dream) and found yourself in a what-shall-I-wear emergency, Collette Dinnigan should be your first stop. She's earned star status in the fashion industry and some of her biggest fans are stars themselves...Elle Macpherson, Cate Blanchett, Nicole Kidman, Cameron Diaz. With a glamorous collection of sheer slip dresses, full floral skirts and sparkly eveningwear, this Australian designer has worked her way up from Down Under to top of the pile. Her signature style is Bond Girl feminine with a strong sexy edge and, if you've the body to match, you'll be dressed to kill.   *collettedinnigan.com*

Expensive   *Amex/MC/V*
020 7589 8897   **tube: South Kensington**
26 Cale Street   Mon-Sat 10-6
London SW3

Comme des Garçons

Just off the heavily beaten Bond Street trail, this store's minimalist decor provides the perfect background to the overwhelming designs, whose strong colours and avant-garde cuts make for some high-concept fashion. From bitter chocolate deconstructed jackets and oversized palazzo pants to double-breasted satin coats and jackets with huge ruffled shoulders, this collection expresses its individuality through the unlikely combination of details. It's a look best suited to the bold and seriously style-savvy.

Affordable to very expensive   *Amex/MC/V*
020 7518 0680   **tube: Green Park**
17-18 Dover Street   Mon-Sat 11-6 (Thurs 11-7)
London W1

Connolly

If you like your leather, come here...it won't disappoint. Originally famous for providing leather for the interiors of Rolls-Royce, Jaguar and Aston Martin, Connolly was bought in 1999 by Joseph (of Joseph fame) and Isabel Ettedgui. They have extended its appeal as a logo-free luxury brand for those who prefer to enjoy their wealth with a bit of stealth. The stores sell an eclectic mix of chicly understated leather accessories, cashmere knitwear, shoes and other outlandish treats from cocktail sets to tool kits, and we are over the moon that the Grosvenor Crescent store has re-opened.

Affordable to very expensive   *Amex/MC/V*
020 7439 2510   **tube: Oxford Circus**
41 Conduit Street   Mon-Sat 10-6 (Thurs 10-7)
London W1

020 7235 3883   **tube: Hyde Park Corner**
32 Grosvenor Crescent Mews   Mon-Thurs 10-6
London SW1

Cornucopia

In a city where vintage comes at a premium, it is refreshing to find somewhere affordable. There are gems to be found here even if, compared with others on the secondhand circuit, this shop seems a little shabby. Racks are filled to the rafters and everything has a straight-from-the-attic smell (and the antique shoes are a little sad, with worn-down heels and crushed toes). There are mid-century dresses and tops in abundance, and some truly old goodies hanging up high. Like most vintage stores, you never quite know what you're going to get but if you're in the neighbourhood, have a look.

Affordable   *MC/V*

020 7828 5752   **tube: Victoria**
12 Upper Tachbrook Street   Mon-Sat 11-6
London SW1

☆ Courtezan

Sometimes a new shop comes along which is so original and imaginative that you can be sure it is soon going to become an institution, and Courtezan is one such shop. For a start it is styled like an 18th-century French interior with a trompe l'oeil ceiling, beautifully hand-painted wallpaper and baroque mirrors. In the window, stone cherubs are strewn with silk roses and mannequin legs are set up as if ready to cancan, wearing pink fishnet stockings with velvet ties. Designer Gail Berry's clothing is theatrical and dramatic, with bustles, ruffles and petticoats that evoke Victorian romanticism. Exquisite coats embellished with dragonflies hang beside tailored bodices and antique silk pyjamas. Heavy satins and rich silks create an old-world feel, while shocking pink underdresses add rock-style humour. Only the supremely confident will get away with wearing it; the meek will look like they've landed a part in Les Misérables. *courtezan.com*

Expensive   *MC/V*

020 7584 0044   **tube: South Kensington**
84 Fulham Road   Mon-Sat 10-6
London SW3

Couverture

Silk nightgowns, cotton kimonos, hand-stitched duvet covers and Indian cotton sheets—the soporific supplies at Couverture will make you want to head straight back to bed. Other covetables include vintage ceramics, cushions printed with little dolls and sequined goatskin slippers. It doesn't get much cosier than this. Zzz… *couverture.co.uk*

Moderate   *Amex/MC/V*

020 7795 1200   **tube: Sloane Square**
310 King's Road   Mon-Sat 10-6
London SW3

☆ Cozmo Jenks

Nobody knows better than society girl Cozmo Jenks that a hat can make or break an outfit. Crystal mesh headpieces and wide-brimmed Ascot hats have propelled her collections on to the fashion and society pages of every glossy magazine and have added cool to the catwalks of London Fashion Week. Prices reflect her It-girl status but her hats will be sure to add some of her eclectic style to everything from party dresses to jeans. Alternatively, check out her ready-to-wear collection in Harrods, Harvey Nichols and Selfridges. *cozmojenks.co.uk*

Expensive | *Cash/cheque*

020 7823 9758 | **tube: Sloane Square**
London SW3 | (by appointment)

Crew Clothing

Anyone prone to seasickness might not want to climb aboard...the clothing here is for the sailors among us, and there's no excuse for wearing it on terra firma. Fleece jackets, sweatshirts, turtlenecks and polos are perfect for parading the decks, but it's practicality that's important here, not fashion, and practical is such a boring word.

crewclothing.co.uk

Affordable | *MC/V*

020 7371 0483 | **tube: Parsons Green**
203 New King's Road | Mon-Sat 10-6:30, Sun 11-5
London SW6

020 7730 7820 | **tube: Sloane Square**
Unit 6, B Block | Mon-Sat 10-6 (Wed 10-7) Sun 12-6
Duke of York Square
London SW3

Crockett & Jones

Handcrafted in the finest leathers, Crockett & Jones shoes take up to eight weeks to manufacture and offer an exceptional combination of comfort, elegance and durability. Service is top-notch, and styles are the best English classics: brogues, derbys and oxfords. C&J prove that contrary to popular opinion, when it comes to town and country shoes for gentlemen, they really do make 'em like they used to. *crockettandjones.co.uk*

Expensive | *Amex/MC/V*

020 7976 2684 | **tube: Piccadilly Circus/Green Park**
69 Jermyn Street | Mon-Sat 9-6
London SW1

020 7499 6676 | **tube: Green Park/Piccadilly Circus**
20-21 Burlington Arcade | (opening hours as above)
London W1

020 7929 2111 | **tube: Bank**
25 Royal Exchange | Mon-Fri 9-6
London EC3

Crombie

Since the beginning of the 19th century, this authentic British brand has produced coats and suits in a stunning selection of fabrics. The eponymous Crombie coat, with its distinctive velvet collar, is sold in several variations, along with a classic selection of suits for both men and women. Traditional navys and greys sit beside heathery tweeds and herringbones, and the refined elegant styles look perfectly at home in this modern, airy store. A travelling tailor service means if you are chained to an office desk you can still be measured up for a new suit. *crombie.co.uk*

Expensive   *Amex/MC/V*

020 7839 1375   **tube: Piccadilly Circus/Green Park**
99 Jermyn Street   Mon-Sat 10-7, Sun 10:30-4:30
London SW1

020 7408 1583   **tube: Bond Street**
105 New Bond Street   Mon-Sat 10-7, Sun 12-6
London W1

☆ The Cross

On a tiny residential block in Holland Park, Sam Robinson and Sarah Kean have created a shopper's paradise of dreamy bright colours and girly knick-knacks. Their white-washed space offers a feast of original fashion from designers such as Jenny Dyer, Missoni, Goat and Issa as well as playful, lighthearted gifts, though we think the kids' section is in danger of overtaking the shop. You'll find tub toys and alphabet soaps, glitter candles, beauty products, handmade greeting cards and flower-shaped fairy lights. Downstairs is a den of desirables—check out the stunning jewellery by Pippa Small and Claire van Holthe, whose pearl and semi-precious earrings and bracelets have attracted fans such as Paris Hilton, Liv Tyler and Elle Macpherson. You'll want to take the whole shop home…until you've seen the price tag.

Expensive to very expensive   *Amex/MC/V*

020 7727 6760   **tube: Holland Park**
139-141 Portland Road   Mon-Sat 11-5:30
London W11

Cyberdog

Sounding like the title of a Sigourney Weaver movie, Cyberdog offers futuristic fashion: black walls covered in glowing neon clothing accompanied by a banging techno beat. T-shirts are splashed with video game graphics or feature an electroluminescent plastic panel that flashes a pattern of light to the beat of music—perfect for clubbing. Find customised camouflage-print microminis, cargo pants with padded knees and tank tops with thick black rubber shoulder straps. Perfect clothing for the trilennium. *cyberdog.net*

Affordable   *Amex/MC/V*

020 7482 2842   **tube: Camden Town**
Stables Market, Chalk Farm Road   Mon-Sat 11-6, Sun 12-7
London NW1

D&G

There was a time, not long ago, when it didn't come younger or funkier than Dolce & Gabbana. Now D&G is exactly that: a younger, funkier version of the main Dolce & Gabbana line, for men, women and children. The grey, white and orange decor gives this shop a pulsating club-like feel, and the clothing is similarly upbeat. Sunglasses, wallets, chunky silver and gold bracelets and watches complete the look. Watch out for Posh and Becks with their boys shopping for the entire family. *dolcegabbana.it*

Expensive to very expensive   *Amex/MC/V*

020 7495 9250   **tube: Bond Street**
53-55 New Bond Street   Mon-Sat 10-6
London W1   (Thurs 10-6:30)

☆ Daisy & Tom 👤

Chelsea's yummy mummy brigade can't resist this never-never land of children's clothing, furniture and toys. Puppet shows, a train set and a working merry-go-round create a fantastically kid-friendly environment. Clothing includes overalls and colourful jumpers, fairy costumes for girls and Noddy outfits for boys. Classic board games, Barbie dolls and Lego sets are also available, as well as a huge selection of huggable fluffy toys. There's even a hair salon where super-friendly staff will discipline unruly mops. *daisyandtom.com*

Affordable to expensive   *Amex/MC/V*

020 7352 5000   **tube: Sloane Square**
181-183 King's Road   Mon-Wed, Fri 9:30-6
London SW3   Thurs, Sat 10-7, Sun 11-5

Daks

As London's fashion pack bemoans the overexposure in recent years of Burberry's plaid, Daks is attempting to fill the coolness gap with its own subtler signature check. Designers Bruce Montgomery and Anthony Cuthberstow continue to create a classically British look in beige check, favouring romantic floral prints and bright stripes. For women there are elegant narrow trousers, fitted jackets and wrap dresses; for men, cord suits, cotton shirts and preppy knits. None of it is exciting enough to reach the cult status of Burberry, but this label does attract international fans from the Far East to Canada. *daks.com*

Expensive   *Amex/MC/V*

020 7409 4040   **tube: Green Park**
10 Old Bond Street   Mon-Sat 10-6 (Thurs 10-7)
London W1

020 7839 9980 (M)   **tube: Piccadilly Circus**
101 Jermyn Street   Mon-Sat 9-6
London SW1

Davies & Son

Sitting oddly, but not uncomfortably, among the newer shops on the west side of Savile Row, Davies & Son is a thoroughly traditional, all-bespoke tailors which moved into the Row from Old Burlington Street at the end of the Nineties. An informal, friendly air is combined with traditionally high standards of service for a largely overseas clientele, which includes European royalty (and we don't mean the Beckhams). Suits, still made round the corner in Old Burlington Street, start from a relatively modest, for Savile Row, £2,300. *daviesandsonsavilerow.com*

Very expensive *Amex/MC/V*

020 7434 3016 **tube: Piccadilly Circus/Oxford Circus**
38 Savile Row Mon-Fri 9-5:30, Sat 9:30-1
London W1

Debenhams

Don't be put off by the fact that Debenhams is the archetypal Oxford Street department store: there is real value for money here if you know what to look for. Reasonable prices are the primary pull in the clothing lines, which include exclusive collections by designers Jasper Conran, FrostFrench, Elspeth Gibson, Myla, Gharani Strok, Theo Fennell and Ben de Lisi. With a full selection of clothing, accessories, cosmetics, housewares and furniture, the airy store is a comfortable if not wildly inspiring place to shop. *debenhams.com*

Affordable to moderate *Amex/MC/V*

0844 561 6161 **tube: Bond Street/Oxford Circus**
334-348 Oxford Street Mon-Tues 9:30-8, Wed 10-8
London W1 Thurs 9:30-9, Fri-Sat 9:30-8, Sun 12-6

Dege & Skinner

The large, well-lit and very welcoming premises of Dege & Skinner play host to a firm with a long tradition of military tailoring (the company still makes uniforms for the Queen's cavalry regiments and the Beefeaters at the Tower of London) which has influenced the extremely elegant, high-waisted house style. The suits, coats and (uniquely) shirts are all handmade on the premises, for every occasion from Ascot to a day's shooting. A bespoke service is available, and there is also a wide range of well-chosen gentleman's accessories. Come here to play Lord of the Manor—you may even bump into Lady Madonna. *dege-skinner.co.uk*

Expensive to very expensive *Amex/MC/V*

020 7287 2941 **tube: Piccadilly Circus/Oxford Circus**
10 Savile Row Mon-Fri 9:15-5:15, Sat 9:30-12:30
London W1

Designer Bargains

If you've got the patience, they've got the labels: Prada, Versace, Gucci, DKNY and Chanel are all likely to be lurking in the tightly packed racks at this musty secondhand shop.

Handbags by Celine, Voyage cardigans and denim by Anne Klein make up a mix that is mature but occasionally a little stuffy. The shoe selection is the standout, featuring Manolo Blahnik and Jimmy Choo stilettos in exceptionally good shape. And if you're in the market for an Ascot hat, this could be just the place. Don't get carried away though: this shop still requires a healthy wallet, because prices are only bargains in comparison with the original price tags (Jimmy Choos, for example, come in at around £175.)

Moderate   *Amex/MC/V*

020 7795 6777   **tube: High Street Kensington**
29 Kensington Church Street   Mon-Sat 10-6
London W8

Design Works

This West End shop offers a fresh, younger take on the suits/shirts/shoes/accessories theme. You'll find well-cut suits in khaki, stone, beige and black with shirts in a wide palette of pastels. The finger is firmly on the fashion pulse, with the exclusive clothing lines updated four times a year. A shoe collection ranges from classic lace-up boots to funky wool and brogue styles. Large chunky vintage-feel watches are also on sale to complete the look.   *abahouse.co.jp*

Moderate to expensive   *Amex/MC/V*

020 7434 1968   **tube: Oxford Circus**
42-44 Broadwick Street   Mon-Fri 10:30-7
London W1   Sat 11-6 winter, 12-7 summer

☆ Diane von Furstenberg

With the opening of her first London store, von Furstenberg is injecting some New York glamour into the already painfully hip Ledbury Road. There is a whiff of Studio 54 about the interior, which is a shrine to all things glam. You'll find wedges, flip-flops, sunglasses and make-up by DvF along with her signature wrap-around dresses. If you happen to be Madonna or a fellow A-lister, you can slip through the corridor in the basement and end up in Matches across the road to avoid being papped.   *dvflondon.com*

Expensive   *Amex/MC/V*

020 7221 1120   **tube: Notting Hill Gate**
83 Ledbury Road   Daily 10-6 (Sun 12-6)
London W11

Diesel

Welcome to the Diesel lifestyle. This urban-minded, tongue-in-cheek Italian label doesn't pull any punches with its own brand of young, hip street style. One of the first retailers to feature live DJs, Diesel is best known for its wide selection of jeans which come in a variety of colours and cuts. Amongst the T-shirts, baggy pants, button-down shirts and jackets, you will also find wallets, underwear, luggage, shoes and fragrances.   *diesel.com*

Moderate   *Amex/MC/V*

020 7497 5543
43 Earlham Street
London WC2

tube: **Covent Garden**
Mon-Sat 10-7 (Thurs 10-8)
Sun 12-6

020 7434 3113
24 Carnaby Street
London W1

tube: **Oxford Circus**
Mon-Sat 10-7, Sun 12-6

020 7376 1785
38a Kensington High Street
London W8

tube: **High Street Kensington**
Mon-Sat 10-7 (Thurs 10-8)
Sun 12-6

020 7225 3225
72 King's Road
London SW3

tube: **Sloane Square**
Mon-Sat 10-7 (Wed 10-8)
Sun 12-6

The Dispensary 👤👩👤

The only thing you'll dispense with is your hard-earned cash. It's all too tempting—cool old school parkas, ruched jersey dresses, Mavi dark or distressed denim and T-shirts from Antoni & Alison could entice even the most ardent avoiders of trend. Harrison, Duffer, Only Hearts, Fiorucci and Dispensary's own label are also included. Label-conscious 0-12 year olds are also catered for with trendy party wear and fun shoes. Great for logo lovers.

Moderate to expensive   *Amex/MC/V*

020 7727 8797
200 Kensington Park Road
London W11

tube: **Notting Hill Gate**
Mon-Sat 10:30-6:30
Sun 12-5

020 7287 8145 (W)
9 Newburgh Street
London W1

tube: **Oxford Circus**
(opening hours as above)

020 7287 2262 (M)
8 Newburgh Street
London W1

tube: **Oxford Circus**
Mon-Sat 10:30-6:30

Diverse 👤👩

Not for the faint-hearted: this is one of those boutiques where the staff look you up and down as you enter. It's Islington's equivalent to Matches in Notting Hill, and no wonder: the selection is Grade A, including Chloé, Clements Ribeiro, Diane von Furstenburg, Missoni, Paper Denim and Fake London. Don't neglect the equally cool home collection upstairs: Chinese lanterns, leather coasters and Japanese soup bowls. The menswear selection up the block has a bit more street flavour, with brands like Diesel Style Lab, Maharishi, DSquared2 and Marc Jacobs. (The huge multicoloured light installation on the wall is also for sale, if you've got a spare £3,000.)

Expensive   *Amex/MC/V*

020 7359 8877
294 Upper Street
London N1

tube: **Angel**
Mon-Sat 10:30-6:30 (Thurs 10:30-7:30)
Sun 12:30-5:30

020 7359 0081 (M)
286 Upper Street
London N1

tube: **Angel**
(opening hours as above)

Diverse Kids

An eye-catching wave-shaped rail displays a gorgeous range of childrens' (0-12) designer clothing and shoes at the junior branch of Islington's smartest clothing shop (see above). We loved the dresses by Antik Batik, jeans by Paper Denim and fab clothing by Lolita and Quincy.

Expensive   *Amex/MC/V*

020 7226 6863   **tube: Angel**
46 Cross Street   Daily 10:30-6 (Sun 12-5:30)
London N1

DKNY

Welcome to Donna Karan's industrial emporium, where a large collection of clothing, from denim to eveningwear to accessories, is more casual and street-styled than her signature line. A sea of neutral jersey tops and covetable Prada/Mulberry-esque bags (but for about half the price) are highly desirable. At DKNY, Karan's catwalk chic also goes up to a merciful size 18 on selected items. Men will find plenty of choices, too, though styles tend to be simpler. Featuring an in-store café and a pumped-up sound system, the atmosphere recreates the energy of New York City streets—fashionable, loud, and splashed with colour.   *dkny.com*

Moderate to expensive   *Amex/MC/V*

020 7499 6238   **tube: Green Park**
27 Old Bond Street   Mon-Sat 10:30-6:30 (Thurs 10:30-7)
London W1   Sun 12-6

Dockers

Dockers made khakis what they are today, so it's no surprise this store is a temple to dress-down-Friday style. Stock up on weekend staples like V-neck T-shirts and classic, regular or slim-fit trousers. The label has injected a bit more hip into its image with techno-fabrics, snowboard styles and cargo pants aimed at a younger crowd. There's also a selection of outerwear, shirts and underwear.   *dockers-uk.co.uk*

Affordable to moderate   *Amex/MC/V*

020 7240 7908   **tube: Covent Garden**
Unit 8, North Piazza   Mon-Wed 10-7, Thurs-Fri 10-8
London WC2   Sat 10-7:30, Sun 11-6

Dolce & Gabbana

Enter the hallowed halls of this fashion dynamo and be transported to a world of fabulousness. (Watch out for Victoria Beckham—this is one of her favourites.) The theatrical gilded mirrors and velvet thrones add to the rock and roll feel of the shop. Whether you're after the must-have handbag of the season, sunglasses or just a corseted black dress to show off every curve, you'll find it here.   *dolcegabbana.it*

Expensive to very expensive   *Amex/MC/V*

020 7659 9000   **tube: Green Park**
6-8 Old Bond Street   Mon-Sat 10-6 (Thurs 10-7)
London W1

020 7201 0980 (W)   **tube: Knightsbridge**
175 Sloane Street   Mon-Sat 10-6 (Wed 10-7)
London SW1

Dollargrand

Colourful, unusual handbags are hard to come by but Dollargrand offers a cheering alternative to ubiquitous brown and black leather. The label has been stocked in Selfridges for years but now has its first stand-alone store—bright, young and fun. The daring designs come in unique shapes and boldly rendered patterns. A polka-dot print is very French Riviera, perfect for St Tropez, and the flamboyant flower pattern screams Caribbean. Evening bags are more glamorous, with a strong Fifties vibe. Live out your Sandra Dee fantasies and invest in a sorbet-shaded clutch made from soft satin with a tiny clasp.   *dollargrand.co.uk*

Moderate   *Amex/MC/V*
0845 108 4454   tube: Sloane Square
124a King's Road   Mon-Sat 10-6 (Wed 10-7), Sun 12-5
London SW3

Dolly Diamond

Vintage here dates from the Victorian period, though Diamond (real name, Pauline) has a particular weakness for the Fifties. Evening dresses are her passion, including Pucci, Chanel and the ever-elusive Dior. There are also plenty of leather jackets and everyday accessories in stock. Stroll to the back for a shoe selection, rare not just in its variety but for its exceptional condition.   *dollydiamond.com*

Affordable to expensive   *Amex/MC/V*
020 7792 2479   **tube: Notting Hill Gate**
51 Pembridge Road   Mon-Fri 10:30-6:30
London W11   Sat 9:30-6:30, Sun 12-6

Donna Karan

Bless Donna Karan for her love of the female form. In sharp contrast to the boisterous DKNY down the street, the Donna Karan store is a modern museum of sophisticated designs. Her celebrated structured approach has softened a bit, rendering loose tops (off-the-shoulder, in drapey shapes) and suits that are not quite so power-packed. Black is, as always, this New Yorker's colour of choice. Skirts with girlish details, like asymmetric hemlines and layers of ruffles, add a bit of bohemian flavour. The store also stocks her plush bedding and sleepwear ranges, along with sunglasses, belts and practical yet highly desirable bags.   *donnakaran.com*

Expensive   *Amex/MC/V*
020 7495 3100   **tube: Bond Street/Green Park**
19 New Bond Street   Mon-Sat 10-6 (Thurs 10-7)
London W1

Dormeuil

One of the most famous suiting fabric manufacturers in the world has its London headquarters and showroom here, selling mainly to tailors but also to customers whose tailor might not have the exact fabric they require. There is a vast selection of cloths in luxury yarns. *dormeuil.com*

Moderate to expensive Amex/MC/V

020 7437 1144 **tube: Piccadilly Circus**
35 Sackville Street Mon-Fri 9-5
London W1

Dorothy Perkins

Beloved of teenagers on pocket money budgets, this massive, multi-level store is a sometime source for affordable basics. The clothes are not as directional as Topshop, but a large assortment of casual, business and eveningwear is on offer. As you enter, you are assaulted with the season's latest styles and colours, whether it's a sea of sunshine yellow or a mountain of Fifties-inspired cardigans. Underwear, jewellery, shoes, maternity, petites and plus-sizes are all located upstairs. *dorothyperkins.co.uk*

Affordable Amex/MC/V

020 7494 3769 **tube: Oxford Circus**
189 Oxford Street Mon-Sat 9-8 (Thurs 9-9)
London W1 Sun 10-6

020 7255 2116 **tube: Tottenham Court Road**
118-132 New Oxford Street Mon-Fri 9-8, Sat 9-7
London WC1 Sun 12-6

020 7495 0578 **tube: Bond Street**
West One Shopping Centre Mon-Sat 10-7 (Thurs 10-8)
379 Oxford Street Sun 10-6
London W1

020 7931 7605 **tube: Victoria**
Victoria Station Mon-Fri 8-8, Sat 10-7, Sun 11-6
London SW1

020 7405 8309 **tube: Holborn**
8-13 High Holborn Mon-Fri 8-6:30
London WC1

020 7512 9707 **tube: Canary Wharf**
24 Canada Place Mon-Fri 9-7, Sat 10-6, Sun 12-6
London E14

Douglas Hayward

A quirky, verging on eccentric, bespoke tailor who's a favourite with everyone from actor Sir Michael Caine to photographer Terry O'Neill. The interior looks like a slightly dishevelled drawing-room in an English country house and you may be surprised by the teddy bears in the window until you realise just who these teddy bears are. They are made by Steiff, the famous German company which has been the Rolls-Royce of teddy bears (Teddybären!) for 102 years, and they are dressed by Ralph Lauren (retail price close to $1,000) so they are the best-dressed and most collectable teddies in the world. Inside, the store provides its renowned bespoke service, and also offers a broad selection of colourful shirts, sweaters, ties, beachwear, towels and hats. Shirts have soft collars and sweaters are whimsically coloured, so this store is aimed at artists as well as, perhaps more than, tycoons.

Expensive to very expensive   *Amex/MC/V*

020 7499 5574   **tube: Bond Street/Green Park**
95 Mount Street   Mon-Fri 9-5:30
London W1

☆ **Dover Street Market**

This is Rei Kawakubo's (of Comme des Garçons) notion of a street market in a Mayfair townhouse. She wants to combine an "atmosphere of beautiful chaos" with the energy of a local market, and all of it preferably avant garde. What you get is six floors of extremely minimalist decor (shiny steel, a generally unfinished look) containing a lot of Comme des Garçons but also a concession system by which other designers create their own displays and control their own space. There are fashionable names here (Martin Margiela, Alaïa, Hedi Slimane, Alber Elbaz, Junya Watanabe) and some beautiful stuff in heart-stopping fabrics. But you will also find newer names—Boudicca from East London, Raf Simons from Belgium, Peachboo and Krejberg (she's Indian, he's Danish ex-Kenzo) and many more. The concession system means that the displays change all the time, but what you can be sure of is that everything will always be equally heart-stoppingly expensive: simple chinos, tops or short-sleeved shirts at £300, men's jackets £750, a silk top from Lanvin £1,050, an evening dress from Alaïa £1,520. The jury is still out on Dover Street Market—the Japanese are mad for it but it has attracted criticism as well as praise—but if it works it will be a lovely place.

Very expensive   *Amex/MC/V*

020 7518 0680   **tube: Green Park**
17 Dover Street   Mon-Sat 11-6 (Thurs 11-7)
London W1

Dressage

This is one of those secret gems that those-in-the-know like to keep to themselves. What's the attraction? The store will sell your old clothes (freshly washed and ironed, please) on your behalf, so not only do you clear some space in your wardrobe you may even make some money too. They are quite fussy about what they'll take—only top quality, nearly new goods—but this too has its advantages. The shelves are piled high with exciting relics, from a pair of unworn Chanel shoes for just £130 to a vintage Yves Saint Laurent dress. You'll need a few hours to sift through it all, but we promise it will be well worth the effort.

Moderate to expensive   *Amex/MC/V*

020 7736 3696   **tube: Parsons Green**
299 New King's Road   Mon-Sat 10-6
London SW6   Sun 11-5

Directory

Duchamp

This husband and wife team (they design everything between them) sell colourful men's accessories to groomed gentlemen who are happy to pay for handcrafted cufflinks and unique silk ties. Shirts, finely knit polo tops and socks come in bright and pastel stripes, spots, checks and florals and the silver cufflinks are finished in colourful enamel and Swarovski crystal. Jonathan Ross is a big fan.

Moderate to expensive   *MC/V*

020 7243 3970   **tube: Notting Hill Gate**
75 Ledbury Road   Mon-Sat 10-6
London W11

Due Passi

Due Passi offers a signature shoe collection that doesn't exactly stand out. Designs tend to be more classic and Italian-influenced, which translates into basic black boots and loafers as well as strappy sandals. A clothing line has been introduced, which doesn't scream glamour but has a practical, worky feel. Overall, reliable and well-priced, but we were a bit underwhelmed.

Moderate   *Amex/MC/V*

020 7224 1921   **tube: Bond Street**
27 James Street   Mon-Sat 10-7 (Thurs 10-8), Sun 12-6
London W1

020 7795 0300   **tube: Sloane Square**
192 King's Road   Mon-Fri 9:30-6:30, Sat 10-7
London SW3   Sun 11-6

Duffer of St George

Duffer is most famous for its in-your-face casual clothing. The super-stylish shop offers own-label and designer off-the-peg suits, coats, casual clothes and accessories, ranging from trendy raincoats (Mackintoshes, of course) and sweats by Spruce to battered denim from PRPS as well as a few pieces for women.

Moderate to expensive   *Amex/MC/V*

020 7379 4660   **tube: Covent Garden**
29 & 34 Shorts Gardens   Mon-Fri 10:30-7
London WC2   Sat 10:30-6:30, Sun 1-5

Dune

For 10 years Dune has offered affordable, stylish, simple leather designs—if you're overwhelmed by London's sea of shoe stores, you could do worse than start here. Whether you're working overtime or carousing in clubs, Dune is likely to have something suitable. Selection ranges from sensible loafers to glittering gold boots.   *dune.co.uk*

Affordable   *Amex/MC/V*

020 7491 3626   **tube: Bond Street**
18 South Molton Street   Mon-Sat 10:30-7 (Thurs 10-8)
London W1   Sun 12-6

020 7795 6336
66 Kensington High Street
London W8

tube: **High Street Kensington**
(opening hours as above)

020 7636 8307
The Plaza, 120 Oxford Street
London W1

tube: **Oxford Circus**
(opening hours as above)

020 7824 8440
33b King's Road
London SW3

tube: **Sloane Square**
Mon-Sat 10-6:30 (Wed 10-7)
Sun 12-6

020 7792 4105
Whiteley's, Queensway
London W2

tube: **Queensway/Bayswater**
Mon-Wed 10-8
Thurs-Sat 10:30-8:30, Sun 12-6

Dunhill

Dunhill has stepped into the 21st century with its refurbished store at 48 Jermyn Street. While the in-store barber makes busy with his cut-throat razor, you can check the cricket scores on your personal TV. In the bespoke room, an innovative light system recreates the light conditions at any time of the day anywhere in the world to enable you to see the fabrics at their best. Back in the land of here and now, Dunhill's luxurious menswear is sold alongside accessories and cigars. There's casualwear too, as well as the pricey suits and formal shirts. This is a one-stop shop for the jet set. Almost as an afterthought, they have a sideline in games—backgammon, chess, Monopoly, bridge etc—many of them handmade by master-craftsman Max Parker and as fine as anything in Europe.   *dunhill.com*

Expensive   *Amex/MC/V*

020 7290 8622
48 Jermyn Street
London SW1

tube: **Piccadilly Circus/Green Park**
Mon-Fri 9:30-6:30 (Thurs 9:30-7)
Sat 10-6:30

Earl Jean

The Notting Hill store reflects this brand's sky-high cool rating. You'll find Eighties rock-chick skinny jeans, denim skirts, low-rise jeans, cords in a host of colours, and gorgeous maternity wear. Jewellery is heart-shaped, star-shaped and chunky. The host of celebrity fans can't be wrong: we want it all, and we want it now.   *earljean.com*

Moderate to expensive   *Amex/MC/V*

020 7792 5211
40 Ledbury Road
W11

tube: **Notting Hill Gate**
Mon-Sat 10-6 (Thurs-Fri 10-7)
Sun 11-6

East

As the name suggests, this shop is inspired by all things oriental. A gentle Asian influence infuses the designs, and dresses, loose blouses and comfortable trousers are simply cut so the patterns can shine through, with roomy styles to suit more mature shoppers. Elegant, feminine prints come in pastels from soft pink to bright turquoise, and don't miss the cruise range, which comes in louder, brighter greens, yellows and burnt oranges. Accessories are also available. *east.co.uk*

Affordable to moderate *Amex/MC/V*

020 7836 6685 **tube: Covent Garden**
16 The Piazza Mon-Sat 10-7 (Thurs 10-8), Sun 11-5
London WC2

020 7351 5070 **tube: South Kensington**
192 Fulham Road Mon-Sat 10-6, Sun 11-6
London SW10

020 7361 1645 **tube: High Street Kensington**
143 Kensington High Street Mon-Sat 10-7
London W8 (Thurs 10-8), Sun 11-5

020 7376 3161 **tube: Sloane Square**
105 King's Road Mon-Sat 10-6:30 (Wed 10-7)
London SW3 Sun 12-6

Eda Lingerie 👤

Ultra-feminine and intricately decorated, the matching bras and knickers at Eda are perfect if you can't quite afford La Perla but want something more distinctive than M&S. Stretch net is embroidered with elaborate designs, most of them floral and all intricately detailed. Though not prohibitively priced, the selection seems too special for everyday; there's a separate collection for brides. *eda-lingerie.com*

Moderate to expensive *Amex/MC/V*

020 7584 0435 **tube: Sloane Square**
132 King's Road Mon-Sat 10-6:30 (Wed 10-7)
London SW3 Sun 12-5

Ede & Ravenscroft 👤

It's like stepping into an episode of Brideshead Revisited. London's oldest gentleman's outfitters have been in business since 1689 and have made the coronation robes for the last 11 British monarchs. This store is worth a visit just for its exquisite English country house interior, complete with chandeliers. E&R sell the complete gentleman's wardrobe, off-the-peg and made-to-measure, down to shoes, hats, cufflinks and evening dress. *edeandravenscroft.co.uk*

Expensive *Amex/MC/V*

020 7734 5450 **tube: Piccadilly Circus**
8 Burlington Gardens Mon-Fri 9-6, Sat 10-6
London W1

020 7405 3906 **tube: Chancery Lane**
93 Chancery Lane Mon-Fri 8:45-6, Sat 10-3
London WC2

020 7929 1848 **tube: Bank/Monument**
2 Gracechurch Street Mon-Fri 9-5:30
London EC3

Edward Green 👤

Don't be put off by the slightly stiff-upper-lip service. There are plenty of shoe stores in the Burlington Arcade, but those who appreciate real quality and English style head straight for Edward Green. The styles are traditional, and the quality and finish are a byword for excellence amongst the global brotherhood of shoe fanatics. Ready-to-wear gentleman's shoes start at £445 (but they'll still be 60-70% handmade). There is also a fantastic repair service and they will make to order in a style and leather of your choice. *edwardgreen.com*

Expensive   *Amex/MC/V*

020 7499 6377   **tube: Green Park/Piccadilly Circus**
12-13 Burlington Arcade   Mon-Sat 9-5:30
London W1

☆ Egg

One of London's secret gems, tucked away in a white-washed residential mews in Knightsbridge, Egg orbits in its own soothing universe. Maureen Doherty's fans, who include Donna Karan and Issey Miyake, scour the store for raw, handwoven cotton and silk separates, knitwear by Eskandar, indigo-blue Chinese working clothes, simple plimsolls and panama hats. There are also regular exhibitions of ceramics and exhibited across the street.

Moderate   *MC/V*

020 7235 9315   **tube: Hyde Park Corner/Knightsbridge**
36 & 69 Kinnerton Street   Tues-Sat 10-6
London SW1

Egoshego

From trainers by Gola to Timberlands to Puma sneakers to Penelope sandals, this clinically white shop with clubby sound track offers an eclectic blend of shoes. The large variety also includes rounded flat slip-ons for good girls and biker boots with kitten heels for their naughtier sisters. Other brands include Custom, Art, New Rock, Converse and Diesel. *egoshegoshoes.com*

Affordable   *Amex/MC/V*

020 7836 9260   **tube: Covent Garden**
76 Neal Street   Mon-Sat 10:30-7 (Thurs 10:30-8)
London WC2   Sun 12-6

020 7229 9519   **tube: Notting Hill Gate**
158 Portobello Road   Mon-Fri 10-6, Sat 9:30-6:30
London W11   Sun 11-5

Elégance

Youngsters may scoff at the naff name, but this store is a real asset to shoppers of a certain age who appreciate styles like the double-breasted, piqué coat-dress, durable sweet-pastel suits or blouses and trousers in shades of purple, yellow and blue.

Affordable to expensive   *Amex/MC/V*

020 7409 7210   **tube: Green Park**
14a Grafton Street   Mon-Fri 9:30-6 (Thurs 10-7)
London W1   Sat 10-6

Directory

Eliot Zed

There are so many sexy shoe shops that tired old Eliot Zed looks in need of a makeover, but the shoes here do serve a function. Like it or not, fashion is still seduced by the stiletto, which means chic, flat-heeled shoes are not that easy to come by. Enter Eliot Zed, where the soft leather footwear collection proves that comfort and style don't always contradict each other. If you're after something a bit naughtier, there are strappy sandals with a cork wedge and black kitten heels with white stitching and a bow at the toe. Men have their own signature collection, as well as leather loafers and sandals from Hardridge.

Moderate   *Amex/MC/V*

020 7589 2155   **tube: South Kensington**
117-119 Walton Street (women)   Mon-Sat 10:30-6
London SW3   (Wed 10-7)
                                        some Sundays 2-5 (call to check)

020 7355 1504   **tube: Bond Street**
4 Avery Row (men)   Mon-Fri 10-6 (Thurs 10-7)
London W1   Sat 1-6

Ellis Brigham

Whether you're headed to the peaks of Snowdonia or the valleys of the Alps, this is the place to rent or buy equipment for every type of outdoor pursuit. Flex more than your credit card by hopping on the indoor ice-climbing wall, which is a permanent feature. There's also a superior selection of outerwear and footwear brands, including Columbia, Bombfire and Volcom.   *ellis-brigham.com*

Moderate to expensive   *Amex/MC/V*

020 7395 1010   **tube: Covent Garden**
3-11 Southampton Street   Mon-Fri 10-7 (Thurs 10-7:30)
London WC2   Sat 9:30-6:30, Sun 11:30-5;30

020 7937 6889   **tube: High Street Kensington**
178 Kensington High Street   Mon-Fri 10-7 (Thurs 10-7:30)
London W8   Sat 9:30-6:30, Sun 11-5

Elspeth Gibson

British designer Elspeth Gibson is a favourite with It-girls and Voguettes. You need an appointment to visit her small and exclusive shop, but once you have entered her regal realm you'll understand the appeal. Frilly and free-spirited, with a touch of 19th-century grandeur thrown in, Gibson's party dresses embody the ethereal, wispy qualities of fairytale romance. Ruffled sleeves, scalloped edges and intricate layers are all eye-catching details and fabrics are suitably fine. What a shame us mere mortals can't just stroll in off the street.   *elspethgibson.com*

Expensive   *Amex/MC/V*

020 7235 0601   **tube: Knightsbridge**
7 Pont Street   (by appointment)
London SW1

Emanuel Ungaro

This French designer known for colourful prints is making a comeback with his fanciful tailored basics for the jet set. Couture eveningwear (only available in Paris) is the speciality of the house but there's plenty of everyday fare, from faultless black and brown wool suits to cropped trousers and ruffled blouses. Summer brings an extra dose of feminine flourish, with must-have Lolita minidresses and long halterneck evening dresses. *emanuelungaro.com*

Expensive to very expensive   Amex/MC/V

020 7629 0550   **tube: Bond Street**
150-151 New Bond Street   Mon-Sat 10-6 (Thurs 10-7)
London W1

Ember

More vintage-in-training than the real thing, this is a good spot for students going through their grungy retro phase. The ample selection of Sandra Dee-style Fifties dresses is priced from £10, while the so-lame-they're-cool Hawaiian shirts start even lower. Certainly fun, but not for the experienced aficionado—although we can't fault the warm service.

Affordable to moderate   *Cash/cheque preferred*

(no phone)   **tube: Ladbroke Grove**
206 Portobello Road   Daily 12-6
London W11

☆ Emma Hope

A clever mix of sophistication and wearability, Emma Hope's shoes are revered for their beautiful shape and decorative detail. Flats, mules, boots, plimsolls and slingbacks are all faultless in design with plenty of cheerful colour adding quintessential English flair. Regal deep purples and dark reds are mixed with limey greens and bright yellows. Stylewise, there are extremes—pastel patent slides or gold kitten heels—but most rest pleasingly in the quirky middle. Well-heeled brides know that Emma Hope wedding shoes will give them blister-free nuptials. *emmahope.co.uk*

Expensive   Amex/MC/V

020 7259 9566   **tube: Sloane Square**
53 Sloane Square   Mon-Sat 10-6 (Wed 10-7)
London SW1   Sun 12-5

020 7313 7493   **tube: Notting Hill Gate**
207 Westbourne Grove   Mon-Sat 10-6 (Thurs 10-7)
London W11   Sun 12-5

020 7833 2367   **tube: Angel**
33 Amwell Street (opening hours as above but closed Sun)
London EC1

Emma Somerset

Classic French luxury clothing has been Emma Somerset's speciality for years. Don't be shy about having to ring the bell to gain entrance. Once inside, you'll find a selection

with maximum appeal and the bare minimum of embellish-
ment (a subtle stripe or frilled skirt hem). It's a sophisticated
look that never risks much and, consequently, rarely looks
out of place. *emmasomerset.co.uk*

Expensive *Amex/MC/V*

020 7235 6977 **tube: Knightsbridge/Hyde Park Corner**
69 Knightsbridge Mon-Fri 9:30-6 (Wed 9:30-7)
London SW1 Sat 10-6

Emma Willis

One of the few women on a very male thoroughfare, Emma
Willis offers bespoke and off-the-peg clothing, from traditional shirts for men to ruffled chiffon blouses for women.
Garments can be personalised with a choice of buttons, collars, linings and cuffs, and styles can be adjusted to suit
tastes and flatter shapes. Renowned for her luxurious fabrics
and the quality and craftsmanship of her designs, Emma
Willis sets a high standard to rival even the grandest of her
Jermyn Street competitors. *emmawillis.com*

Expensive *Amex/MC/V*

020 7930 9980 **tube: Piccadilly Circus/Green Park**
66 Jermyn Street Mon-Sat 10-6
London SW1

Emmett Shirts

Emmett shirt designs are the epitome of traditional-with-a-
twist, merging Jermyn Street tailoring with the contemporary edge of British fashion. Bright colour combinations,
such as purple and yellow stripes or an orange and blue
check, will scare off conservative gentlemen but more
adventurous types will revel in the fresh spin. Fine fabrics
range from poplin to royal twill and some styles feature contrasting patterns beneath the cuffs and collars. The store
only ever makes 25 of any particular shirt and the stock
changes every few weeks, so City slickers can be sure they
are investing in a modern classic. *emmettshirts.com*

Moderate *Amex/MC/V*

020 7351 7529 **tube: Sloane Square**
380 King's Road Mon-Sat 10-6:30, Sun 12-5:30
London SW3

020 7247 1563 **tube: Liverpool Street/Moorgate**
4 Eldon Street Mon-Fri 10-6:30
London EC2

Emporio Armani

Saving the trends for his mainline collection, Giorgio Armani
designs wearable clothes for Emporio and lots of them. At
the store's entrance, a line-up of well-dressed mannequins
invites you inside where you can stock up on a whole
wardrobe of men's and womenswear. From stylish sportswear to business suits plus brilliantly fitting jeans and a host
of accessories in between, you never leave empty-handed.
Dance music and a hip crew of assistants create a funky
buzz. *emporioarmani.com*

Moderate to expensive   *Amex/MC/V*

020 7491 8080   **tube: Bond Street**
51 New Bond Street   Mon-Fri 10-6 (Thurs 10-7)
London W1   Sat 10-6:30, Sun 12-6

020 7823 8818   **tube: Knightsbridge**
191 Brompton Road   Mon-Fri 10-6 (Wed 10-7)
London SW3   Sat 10-6:30, Sun 12-6

Episode

Nothing really caught our attention among the racks of colourful suits and separates here—which is not to say that Episode doesn't serve a useful purpose. There are plenty of variations on the office two-piece, from blue pinstripe to silver, while black ruffled bias-cuts skirts and red leather jackets are a bit more unbuttoned. Easy accessories (with multiple takes on the basic black pump) mix seamlessly with the straight-shooting collection.   *episodegb.com*

Moderate   *Amex/MC/V*

020 7628 8691   **tube: Liverpool Street**
135 Bishopsgate   Mon-Fri 10-6:30
London EC2

020 7355 1410   **tube: Bond Street/Green Park**
69 New Bond Street   Mon-Sat 10-6:30 (Thurs 10-7:30)
London W1   Sun 12-5

Episode

Not to be confused with the high street store of the same name (see above), this well-organised vintage shop originated in Amsterdam. As you browse the racks, humming along to Serge Gainsbourg, you will find plenty of goodies, but not the usual embarras de choix (merci, Serge) of your average, overwhelming vintage emporium. Check out the neatly arranged hats downstairs, particularly for men. Prices are moderate and staff helpful.

Moderate   *MC/V*

020 7485 9927   **tube: Chalk Farm/Camden Town**
26 Chalk Farm Road   Mon-Fri 11-7, Sat-Sun 10-7
London NW1

☆ Ermenegildo Zegna

Arguably the finest Italian cloth and suit manufacturer takes on traditional English outfitters on their own patch. With over 900 different blends, Zegna's cloth is much finer and softer than English suits generally are. Lightweight wool, linen, mohair, cashmere and silk are used to great effect, and Zegna also has a sports line using the latest fabric technology for weekending thirtysomethings. Luxury menswear doesn't get better than this.   *zegna.com*

Very expensive   *Amex/MC/V*

020 7518 2700   **tube: Bond Street/Oxford Circus**
37-38 New Bond Street   Mon-Sat 10-6 (Thurs 10-7)
London W1

Escada

Escada has global glitz appeal. Every Oscar night brings this label back to the fashion headlines when hoards of Escada-clad starlets glide along the red carpet to the flash of a billion bulbs. If you fancy your own paparazzi moment, this is the place to stop for luxurious eveningwear that's a touch naughtier than the basic ballgown. A less formal selection offers suits, dresses, shirts, skirts and trousers, as well as denim and soft knitwear from Escada Sport. *escada.com*

Very expensive *Amex/MC/V*
020 7245 9800 **tube: Knightsbridge**
194-195 Sloane Street Mon-Sat 10-6 (Wed 10-7)
London SW1

Escapade

Given the French predilection for sophisticated style, you might expect this dressy daywear to sparkle a bit more brightly than it does. For the prices, the fabrics (from wrinkled silk blouses to tight shiny trousers) don't quite make the mark, and the less-than-friendly staff don't add to the experience. The prime location amidst some of London's best boutiques makes it even more of a letdown.

Expensive *MC/V*
020 7376 5767 **tube: Sloane Square**
141 King's Road Mon-Sat 10-7, Sun 12-6
London SW3

Eskandar

With influences drawn from France, India and Eskandar's homeland, Iran, the clothing here is decidedly different from the mainstream. Lovely soft fabrics, mostly linen and cotton, combine with gentle colours like beige, cream and dove-blue in a collection that is comfortable, bohemian and refreshingly non-designer: no logos, no metal fixings, no trendy spins. The overall look harks back to simple peasant dress, with boxy baggy sweaters, round-neck linen tops and gathered floor-length skirts. A gorgeous selection of home-wares includes antique monogrammed sheets, red striped linen tea towels, old wine goblets and lots of heavy white china, and the latest range for the bath and body is to die for. *eskandar.com*

Expensive *Amex/MC/V*
020 7351 7333 **tube: Fulham Broadway**
134 Lots Road Mon-Fri 10-6, Sat 10:30-5:30
London SW10

Esprit

The name might take you back to the candy-coloured Eighties, but new owners have resuscitated this ailing label. The Regent Street flagship houses everything imaginable—trendy street clothes for boys and girls, smart suits for women, activewear for men, loads of accessories and even a toy collection and a body line. Well worth a look if you've been wondering where this label has been since Ronnie Reagan was President. *esprit.com*

Affordable *Amex/MC/V*

020 7025 7745 **tube: Oxford Circus**
178-182 Regent Street Mon-Sat 10-7 (Thurs 10-8)
London W1 Sun 12-6

020 7493 5453 **tube: Oxford Circus**
283 Oxford Street Mon-Sat 10-8 (Thurs 10-9)
London W1 (men & women only) Sun 12-6

Ethos 👨👩

Don't be fooled by the straightforward, old-fashioned interior of this cosy little shoe store hidden away at the back of Bishopsgate Arcade. Lo and behold, here is a great selection from Marc Jacobs and Jaime Mascaro, sexy pumps by Dolce & Gabbana, plus Kenzo, Sonia Rykiel and Patrick Cox—all at marginally discounted prices. Ethos also sells Mulberry wallets and handbags. Two steps away from Liverpool Street Station—who would have known?

Moderate to expensive *MC/V*

020 7638 6565 **tube: Liverpool Street**
1 Bishopsgate Arcade Mon-Fri 10:30-7
London EC2

Etro 👨👩

A label with a dedicated following for its strong colours, striking patterns and innovative fabrics, Etro is bursting with Italian flair. Women will find bold blouses, wide-legged trousers and flouncy dresses; for men there are loud suits with zingy linings and a bright assortment of ties and shirts. With its combination of eccentric design and beautiful craftsmanship, Etro is a perfect choice for the confident dresser who craves a designer dash of flash. If the vibrant colours and stripes are not for you, have a look at the homeware selection which ranges from pillows to ashtrays.

Expensive *Amex/MC/V*

020 7495 5767 **tube: Green Park**
14 Old Bond Street Mon-Sat 10-6
London W1

Euforia 👩

After eight successful years in one Notting Hill location, Annette Olivieri has opened her equally quirky second shop. Her creative collection incorporates kitsch and retro influences and includes good quality bags, casual shoes, jewellery and a limited selection of bikinis. You'll also find the latest international fashion magazines, as well as a selection of art books and postcards. *euforia-world.com*

Moderate *Amex/MC/V*

020 8968 1903 **tube: Ladbroke Grove**
7 Portobello Green Arcade Thurs-Sat 10:30-6
London W10

020 7243 1808
61b Lancaster Road
London W11

tube: Ladbroke Grove
Mon-Sat 10:30-6:30

Exclusivo

The cluttered window tells you everything about this tiny Hampstead designer secondhand store. We're sure there are gems to be found here, but after ten minutes of fossicking amongst crowded rails, dodging other customers and breathing in that fusty, dusty vintage air, we'd had enough. Come and have a go if you think you're brave enough.

Moderate   *Amex/MC/V*

020 7431 8618
24 Hampstead High Street
London NW3

tube: Hampstead
Daily 11:30-6

F.Pinet

This old-fashioned shoe store, with its gilded mirrors and velvet chairs, offers genteel service of a sort associated with Bond Street's early days. But the selection itself is surprisingly modern, with Stuart Weitzman slingbacks and a chic children's section with Italian fashion brands such as D&G. The generous men's selection includes such labels as Mauri and Moreschi, with some exotic styles in crocodile, ostrich and snake skins. Pinet's own brand is also here, of course.

Moderate to expensive   *Amex/MC/V*

020 7629 2174
47-48 New Bond Street
London W1

tube: Bond Street
Mon-Fri 10-6:30 (Thurs 10-7)
Sat 10-6:30

Fabri

Another Italian invader, Fabri sells Italian suits and sportswear amidst the more traditional British names dominating Jermyn Street and its tributary arcades. Smart casual trousers and jackets and patterned knitwear are aimed at a 35-plus business clientele looking for a more relaxed option than the stiff collars on the rest of the street. Marble floors and mirrors lend an early Eighties vibe.

Expensive   *Amex/MC/V*

020 7839 1155
75 Jermyn Street
London SW1

tube: Piccadilly Circus/Green Park
Mon-Sat 10-6

Faith

Maintaining its emphasis on affordability and style, Faith recreates the latest trends in footwear from the chunkiest soles to the highest heels. An offbeat selection, displayed on two separate floors, is a breeze to browse—so long as you don't mind the masses of purposeful teens and twentysomethings. (Kelly from Destiny's Child is said to have been ushered in through the back door.) Check out the lower floor for vintage shoes and funky trainers. Faith offers a student discount to all with applicable ID.   *faith.co.uk*

Affordable MC/V

020 7580 9561 **tube: Oxford Circus**
192-194 Oxford Street Mon-Sat 10-8
London W1 Sun 12-6

020 7495 7263 **tube: Marble Arch**
488 Oxford Street Mon-Sat 10-6, Sun 11-5
London W1

Fallan & Harvey 🛉

Is your life missing something? How about a pair of made-to-measure pyjamas? A classic bespoke tailor of good reputation, Fallan & Harvey will make anything you like from a vast selection of colourful fabrics. (Bespoke shirtmakers Crichton used to share the building—sadly, no longer.)

Expensive Amex/MC/V

020 7437 8573 **tube: Piccadilly Circus**
7 Sackville Street Mon-Fri 9-5
London W1

Farrutx 🛉

This sassy shoe brand comes from the Spanish island of Majorca. The imaginative styles create a perfect balance between sophistication and playfulness with beaded flowers, lemon-coloured ankle straps, wedge heels and pointy toes. Some designs feature a bit too much plastic for comfort, but summer styles are wearable and versatile with splashes of colour and flattering heels. Worth a look if you are in the area. *farrutx.com*

Moderate Amex/MC/V

020 7838 0100 **tube: South Kensington**
151 Fulham Road Mon-Sat 10-6, Sun 1-6
London SW3

Fat Face 🛉🛉🛉

Inspired by the surf, ski and snowboarding aesthetic (the shop's motto is "Life is Out There"), the casual sportswear at Fat Face is young, fun and ready to go. Summer and winter alike, the colourful kit is made to take a knock or two, so if you're into high-octane sports or enjoy the outdoor life, look no further. This sort of look is also trendy amongst try-hard teenagers who hang out in the baggy trousers and logo-splashed T-shirts. *fatface.com*

Moderate Amex/MC/V

020 7497 6464 **tube: Covent Garden**
13 Thomas Neals Centre Mon-Sat 10-7, Sun 12-6
London WC2

020 7384 3115 **tube: Parsons Green**
827 Fulham Road Mon-Sat 9:30-6:30, Sun 11-5
London SW6

020 7581 9380 **tube: Sloane Square**
126 King's Road Mon-Fri 10-7
London SW3 Sat 9-7, Sun 10-6

020 8947 4350
18 The Broadway
London SW19

tube: Wimbledon
Mon-Wed, Fri 9-6:30, Thurs 9-8
Sat 9-6:30, Sun 10-6

Favourbrook

Think Hugh Grant, *Four Weddings and a Funeral* and sprawling country pads...Favourbrook is as British as Twining's Breakfast Tea. Velvet dinner jackets and and brocade waistcoats are such specialities that the waistcoats have their own dedicated shop at 19 Piccadilly Arcade, opposite the women's store. There are smoking jackets and cavalry twill trousers for men, beaded blouses and side-fastening, embroidered dresses for women. All is opulent, if slightly fussy, at Favourbrook. *favourbrook.com*

Very expensive *Amex/MC/V*

020 7493 5060
55 Jermyn Street (M)
London SW1

tube: Piccadilly Circus/Green Park
Mon-Wed 9:30-6:30
Thurs-Fri 9:30-7, Sat 10-6

020 7491 2331
18 & 19-21 Piccadilly Arcade
London SW1

tube: Piccadilly Circus/Green Park
(opening hours as above)

Feathers

Its VIP room is frequented by film stars (Mena Suvari), models (Mila Jovovich) and footballers' wives (Louise Redknapp). Culling from the collections of various high-end designers, Feathers offers nothing but the finest—and a sales staff that won't let you forget it. Trendy, chic and sophisticated, the colourful (and bountiful) stock of labels includes Antonio Marras, Alessandro Dell'Acqua and hot American Rick Owens. An alteration service is also offered.

Expensive *Amex/MC/V*

020 7243 8800
176 Westbourne Grove
London W11

tube: Notting Hill Gate
Mon-Sat 10-6
Sun 12-5

020 7589 5802
42 Hans Crescent
London SW1

tube: Knightsbridge
Mon-Sat 10-7

Fenn Wright Manson

Chandeliers, gold walls and designer wallpaper give their King's Road store (the first to be refurbished) a modern boudoir feel. Ever-versatile pashminas and vintage beaded bags accessorise the sometimes mumsy shapes, but quality is good and in a world of passing fashions and virtually disposable clothes how nice to have some wardrobe longevity. Look out for nautical knitwear and pretty chiffon dresses. *fennwrightmanson.com*

Moderate *Amex/MC/V*

020 7376 2404
Barkers Arcade
London W8

tube: High Street Kensington
Mon-Sat 10-7
Sun 12-6

020 7486 6040
95 Marylebone High Street
London W1

020 7730 7384
19 King's Road
London SW3

tube: Sloane Square
Mon-Sat 10-7 (Wed 10-7:30)
Sun 12-6

☆ Fenwick

A hotbed for new designers and with a fantastic personal shopping service and discreet beauty salon, Fenwick is the only department on Bond Street and continues to delight twentysomethings as well as their mothers. No wonder it's a firm favourite with fashionistas. Take your time on the ground floor as there is much to savour including Sara Berman and Orla Keily. The lingerie department has new collections from FrostFrench, Myla and Only Hearts, and (perhaps more importantly) has the most patient staff in town. Amongst the irresistible bag selection you'll find established names like Furla and newer designers Jamin Puech, Buba and Amy Morris. The beauty hall is the most un-intimidating in London and carries all the big names such as Shiseido and Clinique as well as lesser-known brands like Paul & Joe and Becca. Stop for a quick manicure at Nails Inc before heading upstairs. Be on the lookout for new designing talents because Fenwick is particularly good at importing names you'll hardly find anywhere else: Wayne Cooper, Calypso and Alannah Hill. When it comes to the classics, there's Nicole Farhi, Paul Smith, Armani Collezioni, Collette Dinnigan, Joseph and Kenzo, among others. New to the store: Anna Sui and Sonia Rykiel's very popular diffusion line Sonia. If you need to refuel, head to Joe's café or ride all the way down to the bottom level for a bowl of pasta (and much more) at Carluccio's; for a bit of pampering treat yourself to a Chantecaille facial on the third floor. *fenwick.co.uk*

Affordable to very expensive   *Amex/MC/V*

020 7629 9161
63 New Bond Street
London W1

tube: Bond Street
Mon-Sat 10-6:30 (Thurs 10-8)

Field & Trek

For those days when you feel like Lara from Tomb Raider (don't we all have them?) this specialist in outdoor wear and equipment offers high-performance clothing that is equally suitable for the street. The activewear comes from such top brands as The North Face, Columbia and Lowe Alpine, as well as the store's own label. Selection includes base clothing, polar fleece, waterproof outerwear and footwear, plus navigation equipment. *fieldandtrek.com*

Moderate   *Amex/MC/V*

020 7379 3793
42 Maiden Lane
London WC2

tube: Covent Garden
Mon-Fri 10-7 (Thurs 10-8)
Sat 9:30-6:30, Sun 11-5

Fifi Wilson

Here is a treasure trove of women's and children's wear, accessories and gifts, humming with yummy mummies during the week and city girls getting their girly fix at the weekend. Former actress Fi Lovett keeps this darling shop packed with an eclectic collection of treats from designers on their way up. West Village dresses sit alongside tops by Eucalyptus, Erotokritos jackets and Noa Noa clothes for children. Whatever your budget, you won't leave empty-handed. Ask about their interiors service—fabrics from Andrew Martin to Osborne & Little will have your house looking as fabulous as you. The Chelsea shop was about to open as we went to press. *wilsonslifestyle.co.uk*

Affordable to expensive MC/V

n/a at press time **tube: Sloane Square**
1 Godfrey Street Mon-Sat 10-6, Sun 12-5
London SW3

020 8675 7775 **tube: Clapham Common**
51 Abbeville Road (opening hours as above)
London SW4

Fiorelli

Canary Wharf is chain store central, convenient for the career girls and boys whose only shopping opportunity is a few snatched minutes at lunchtime, but hardly exciting. Fiorelli's colourful, sexy bags and shoes are a welcome diversion. *fiorelli.com*

Moderate MC/V

020 7519 6854 **tube: Canary Wharf**
Unit 28, 45 Bank Street Mon-Fri 9-7
London E14 Sat 10-6, Sun 12-6

Fogal

The future of the stock market may be uncertain but stockings have never been hotter. On high-designer Sloane Street you'll find the perfect pair to match any colour you want, even that particular shade of Prada plum. Socks, bodies and bustiers are also available. With over 20 years in the market, these folks really have a leg up. *fogal.com*

Moderate Amex/MC/V

020 7235 3115 **tube: Knightsbridge**
3a Sloane Street Mon-Sat 10-6:30 (Wed 10-7:30)
London SW1 Sun 12-5

Foot Locker

This most dependable of American sports chains offers a huge variety of athletic clothing, sneakers and accessories, aimed at teens looking for the latest brands rather than the bona fide athlete. We love the hold-and-browse system (tin drawers are provided to hold items while you keep shopping), but on a weekend afternoon you could wait hours for a member of staff to find your size. The range of choice—every conceivable shoe from Nike, Fila, Adidas, Reebok and New Balance—almost makes the wait worth while. *footlocker-europe.com*

Affordable to expensive *Amex/MC/V*

020 7491 4030 **tube: Oxford Circus**
363-367 Oxford Street Mon-Wed, Sat 10-7, Thurs-Fri 10-8
London W1 Sun 12-6

020 7734 5780 **tube: Tottenham Court Road**
309 Oxford Street (opening hours as above)
London W1

020 7379 9398 **tube: Covent Garden**
30-32 Neal Street Mon-Sat 10-7 (Thurs 10-8)
London WC2 Sun 12-6

Formes

If your idea of maternity-wear-from-hell is dungarees and your partner's shirts, head here. Formes is the freshest of the major maternity chains, but the staid selection is more French-mumsy than yummy-mummy. You'll find sleeveless tunics, turtlenecks, sweaters, jeans and long skirts, all in the requisite roomy cuts and deliberately cheery colours. The search is never-ending for maternity wear that's truly cool, but in the meantime you might find some suitable bits here. *formes.com*

Moderate to expensive *Amex/MC/V*

020 7493 2783 **tube: Bond Street**
33 Brook Street Mon-Wed 10-6, Thurs 10-7
London W1 Fri-Sat 10-6:30, Sun 12-5

020 7584 3337 **tube: Knightsbridge**
313 Brompton Road Mon-Tues, Thurs 10-6
London SW3 Wed, Fri-Sat 10-6:30, Sun 12-5

020 7240 4777 **tube: Covent Garden**
28 Henrietta Street Mon-Sat 10:30-6:30 (Thurs 10:30-7)
London WC2 Sun 12-5

020 7431 7770 **tube: Hampstead**
66 Rosslyn Hill Mon-Sat 10-6
London NW3 Sun 12-5

Fortnum & Mason

It's all too easy to be sidetracked on the ground floor by the handmade chocolates, English cheeses and gourmet treats like foie gras, but if you do manage to make it up the plush red-carpeted stairs to the shoes and accessories depart-ments, you'll find British stalwarts such as Lulu Guinness, Philip Treacy and Emma Hope. Sadly, they no longer carry any women's fashion but the shop is still a delight and well worth a visit, if only to see the window displays which are particularly beautiful at Christmas. All year round, the ele-gant surroundings and superlative service make a relaxing antidote to stressful city life, and the street-level restaurant at the back (opening on to Jermyn Street) has been a high-ly fashionable lunch venue as long as anyone can remem-ber. *fortnumandmason.co.uk*

Expensive   *Amex/MC/V*
020 7734 8040   **tube: Piccadilly Circus/Green Park**
181 Piccadilly   Mon-Sat 10-6:30, Sun 12-6
London W1   (for Food Hall and Patio restaurant only)

Foster & Son

Everything you would expect from a Jermyn Street shoe store. The atmosphere is peaceful and traditional with soft leather chairs, polished wooden floorboards and leather shoes, boots and luggage displayed in shiny glass cabinets. Bespoke and ready-to-wear both fetch high prices, but after trying on a pair of their soft-as-butter boots, you'll feel more inclined to reach for the plastic.

Expensive   *Amex/MC/V*
020 7930 5385   **tube: Piccadilly Circus/Green Park**
83 Jermyn Street   Mon-Fri 10-6, Sat 10-4
London SW1

Franchetti Bond

Conservative bags and shoes in styles that may appear stuffy to younger generations are Miss Marple classic. Made from the supplest Italian leather you will find mock croc loafers, ballerina pumps, bugatti bags and totes. All come in a basic palette of blacks, reds, racing greens and caramels. Reliable if unexciting.   *franchettibond.com*

Expensive   *Amex/MC/V*
020 7823 5550   **tube: Sloane Square**
12 Symons Street   Mon-Sat 10-6
London SW3

020 7629 0025   **tube: Green Park/Piccadilly Circus**
7 Burlington Arcade   Mon-Sat 10-6
London W1

Fratelli Rossetti

With a tradition of fine craftsmanship dating back to the Fifties, Fratelli Rossetti is the granddaddy of the brown loafer. The London headquarters are comfortable and refined, with a wide selection that features soft, leather slip-ons and lace-ups for women and men. The store also carries shoes from the casual line Flexa and an assortment of leather accessories.   *rosetti.it*

Moderate to expensive   *Amex/MC/V*
020 7491 7066   **tube: Green Park**
177 New Bond Street   Mon-Sat 10-6 (Thurs 10-7)
London W1

020 7259 6397   **tube: Knightsbridge**
196 Sloane Street   Mon-Sat 10-6 (Wed 10-6:30)
London SW1

Fred Perry

Known for dressing well (and playing even better) on the tennis court, Perry packaged his own brand for the masses when he became the last Englishman to win the men's singles at Wimbledon, in the Thirties. Today's collection includes retro and contemporary styles of street and sportswear. The polo shirts (now in a multitude of colours) are still the champions of the collection and have a loyal following. Check out the higher-end diffusion line, designed in collaboration with Comme des Garçons at the Seven Dials branch. *fredperry.com*

Moderate   MC/V

020 7836 3327	**tube: Covent Garden**
14 The Piazza	Mon-Sat 10-7, Sun 11-5
London WC2	

020 7836 4513	**tube: Covent Garden**
6-7 Thomas Neals Centre	Mon-Sat 10-7
London WC2	Sun 12-5

French Connection   👤👤👤

Although we tired of the mock-shock FCUK ad campaign a long time ago, French Connection is still a star of the British high street. With a 14,000 square foot flagship store at the heart of Oxford Circus, the chain covers all the basics: frilly skirts, button-down blouses, cashmere sweaters, T-shirts, tailored trousers and all things denim. Prices are highish, but on the whole the styles are worth it. The "concept store" on Westbourne Grove also has a café, in case it's all too much for you. *frenchconnection.com*

Affordable to moderate   Amex/MC/V

020 7493 3124	**tube: Oxford Circus**
249 Regent Street	Mon-Sat 10-7
London W1	Sun 12-6

020 7589 5560	**tube: Knightsbridge**
44 Brompton Road	Mon-Sat 10-7
London SW3	(Thurs 10-8), Sun 12-6

020 7379 6560	**tube: Covent Garden**
99-103 Long Acre	Mon-Sat 10-7 (Thurs 10-8)
London WC2	Sun 12-6

020 7629 7766	**tube: Bond Street**
396 Oxford Street	Mon-Fri 10-8 (Thurs 10-9)
London W1	Sat 10-7, Sun 11:30-6

020 7836 0522	**tube: Covent Garden**
11 James Street	Mon-Sat 10-7 (Thurs 10-8)
London WC2	Sun 12-6

020 7225 3302	**tube: Sloane Square**
140-144 King's Road	Mon-Sat 10-7
London SW3	Sun 12-6

020 7229 8325	**tube: Notting Hill Gate**
191 Westbourne Grove	Mon-Sat 10-6
London W11	Sun 12-5

020 7937 4665	**tube: High Street Kensington**
168-170 Kensington High Street	Mon-Sat 10-7
London W8	Sun 12-6

020 7287 2046	**tube: Oxford Circus**
10 Argyll Street	Mon-Sat 10-6:30
London W1	(Thurs 10-8, Fri 10-7)

020 7794 1115
29 Hampstead High Street
London NW3

tube: Hampstead
Mon-Sat 10-6, Sun 12-6

020 7512 9110
18 Jubilee Place
London E14

tube: Canary Wharf
Mon-Fri 9-7, Sat 10-6
Sun 12-6

French For Less

The name screams naff continental fashion, but although the selection is a bit hit-and-miss it's not as bad as all that. New styles arrive regularly from Paris: wool suits, silk shirts and sparkly eveningwear are available, as are scarves, handbags and a surprisingly cool selection of belts. The labels include Terry, Surabaya, Serena Kay and Cara Lotti. For those who appreciate classic French designs at decent prices, this might be worth a visit. *frenchforless.com*

Moderate *Amex/MC/V*

020 7629 9617
8 South Molton Street
London W1

tube: Bond Street
Daily 10-6 (Thurs 10-7)
Sun 12-6

French Sole

Dancing to the beat of the ballet, this shoe store offers every type of pump you can imagine. There are hundreds of them, in snakeskin, gingham and beaded styles, or just basic solid colours. They're more for pirouetting through Harvey Nicks than the Royal Opera House, but Sloaney ladies love them and they're certainly a lot more comfortable than third position. *frenchsole.com*

Moderate *Amex/MC/V*

020 7730 3771
6 Ellis Street
London SW1

tube: Sloane Square
Mon-Sat 10-6

Frockbrokers

Proprietor Merlyn Bignell prides herself on showcasing up-and-coming London designers. The store is an exciting mix of cutting-edge designer clothing, jewellery and accessories, with current designs from Fake London, Hunters & Gatherers and Gharani Strok among others, alongside end-of-season bargains. The friendly atmosphere is an added bonus.

Moderate *MC/V*

020 7247 4222
115 Commercial Street
London E1

tube: Liverpool Street
Mon-Fri 11-7 (Thurs 11-8)
Sat 11-5:30, Sun 11-6

Frontier

A plain, unpretentious shoe shop selling an exciting (and in some cases pretentious) range of shoes. This is a good place to find cutting-edge footwear: smarter shoes by Tsubo, trainers from Gola, Merrell walking shoes, skater shoes and ranges by PF Flyers, Onitsuka Tigers and limited-edition New Balance trainers. There is a great range of sizes to keep everyone happy, from size 3 twinkletoes to size 15 clodhoppers, along with beanie hats, and limited-edition Oakley sunglasses. *frontier-i.com*

Moderate to expensive   *Amex/MC/V*

020 7287 3555   **tube: Oxford Circus**
9 Brewer Street   Mon-Wed 10:30-8
London W1   Thurs-Sat 10:30-9, Sun 11-7

020 7433 1849   **tube: Hampstead**
18 Hampstead High Street   Mon-Sat 10-6 (Thurs 10-7)
London NW3   Sun 12-6

Furla

In classic shapes and lovely, supple leather these bags are the epitome of Italian style. Colours range from essential black and brown to indulgent tangerine and lemon sorbet, and drawers filled with matching wallets and fine watches will make you feel like you're shopping in a dream closet. *furla.com*

Expensive   *Amex/MC/V*

020 7629 9827   **tube: Green Park/Bond Street**
31 New Bond Street   Mon-Sat 10-6 (Thurs 10-7)
London W1

020 7823 5110   **tube: Sloane Square**
17 King's Road   Mon-Sat 10-6:30 (Wed 10-7)
London SW3   Sun 12-5

G.J.Cleverley & Co

This little jewel of a store is a relatively recent addition to the ranks of bespoke shoemakers but has a long tradition. Owner-managers George Glasgow and John Carnera worked for years with George Cleverley who, despite a huge weakness for playing the ponies, was universally acknowledged as a footwear magician. Working from the lasts and patterns they inherited, Carnera and Glasgow have recreated Cleverley's unique style and built a bespoke service that is now seen as one of the best in the world by insiders in the shoe trade. Despite this reputation, prices start from around £1,600, a snip compared to what you might pay elsewhere. Ready-to-wear from £320. *gjcleverley.co.uk*

Expensive   *Amex/MC/V*

020 7493 0443   **tube: Green Park**
13 The Royal Arcade   Mon-Fri 9-5:30
28 Old Bond Street   Sat 10-4
London W1

Gamba

If your feet were made for dancing, look no further. In the heart of London's theatre district Gamba is a small shop stocked with everything you could need to pirouette, tango or tap as well the "repetto", a new line of dance shoe that can be worn outside. Clothing starts at age five with adorable pink mini ballet pumps and white tulle tutus. For adults there are leotards, loose black jazz trousers, fold-over trousers in funky hip-hop styles, Lycra T-shirts and all sorts of different dance shoes. Whether you're a professional or a happy amateur, this is an essential stop for anyone seeking a dance wardrobe.

Affordable | *Amex/MC/V*

020 7437 0704 | **tube: Leicester Square**
3 Garrick Street | Mon-Sat 10:30-6
London WC2

Gant USA

The names of the ranges give the game away: University, Park Avenue, Hamptons… Gant offers different spins on classic American styles. Gant Madison attracts the 30-plus demographic with V-neck sweaters and tailored trousers, while Gant Ivy League aims for the younger preppy crowd with piqué and oxford cloth shirts. While the flagship store may be big and bright, the clothing is comfortable, practical and as timeless as *Love Story*. *gant.com*

Moderate | *Amex/MC/V*

020 7584 8077 | **tube: Knightsbridge**
47-49 Brompton Road | Mon-Sat 10-6:30 (Wed 10-7)
London SW3 | Sun 12-5

☆ Gap

Named after the generation gap, this reliable high street staple celebrated its 35th anniversary in 2004. The first store (opened in San Francisco in August 1969) was dedicated entirely to jeans, neatly organised by size and colour, and 35 years on there's still no better place to grab wardrobe basics like jeans, khakis and cotton tops. With the arrival of designer Pina Ferlisi, who worked on Marc by Marc Jacobs, expect an exciting new design element with more fitted shirts and separates. With a men's selection as varied as the women's, Gap is a consistent, dependable source of comfortable clothing. But American visitors beware, prices were about 30% higher here than in the US even before the dollar began to lose its value three years ago. Of course, there's always a sales rack, so search it out. *gap.com*

Affordable | *Amex/MC/V*

020 7225 1112 | **tube: Knightsbridge**
145-149 Brompton Road | Mon-Tues 9:30-7
London SW3 | Wed-Sat 9:30-8, Sun 12-6

020 7437 0138 | **tube: Piccadilly Circus**
1-7 Shaftesbury Avenue | Mon-Sat 10-8
London W1 | Sun 12-6

020 7734 3312 | **tube: Oxford Circus**
223-235 Oxford Street | Mon-Fri 10-8, Sat 10-7
London W1 | Sun 12-6

020 7493 3316 | **tube: Oxford Circus/Bond Street**
315 Oxford Street | Mon-Sat 10-7:30 (Thurs 10-8)
London W1 | Sun 10-6

020 7408 4500
376-384 Oxford Street
London W1

tube: Bond Street
Mon-Sat 9:30-8 (Fri 9:30-9)
Sun 11:30-6:30

020 7836 8148
2-3 James Street
London WC2

tube: Covent Garden
Mon-Sat 10-7 (Thurs 10-8)
Sun 12-6

020 7379 0779
30-31 Long Acre
London WC2

tube: Covent Garden
Mon-Sat 10-7 (Thurs 10-9)
Sun 12-6

020 7823 7272
122 King's Road
London SW3

tube: Sloane Square
Mon-Sat 9:30-7, Sun 12-6

020 7368 2900
99-101 Kensington High Street
London W8

tube: High Street Kensington
Mon-Wed 9:30-7
Thurs-Sat 9:30-8, Sun 12-6

020 7221 5828
132-136 Notting Hill Gate
London W11

tube: Notting Hill Gate
Mon-Sat 10-7
Sun 12-6

020 7485 4357
6-12 Parkway
London NW1

tube: Camden Town
(opening hours as above)

020 7489 0214
4 Poultry
London EC2

tube: Bank
Mon-Fri 8:30-7

020 7512 1335
16-17 Canada Square
London E14

tube: Canary Wharf
Mon-Fri 9-8
Sat 10-6, Sun 12-6

Gap Kids (& Baby Gap) ✉

Everything we love about Gap, but shrunk for children and in bright colours and fabrics that will last forever. The baby clothing is just as it should be—durable, cheap and cute, but never nauseatingly so. From outdoor weekend wear to back-to-school basics, Gap Kids has it all for your junior hipsters and babies-about-town. *gapkids.com*

Affordable   Amex/MC/V

020 7287 5095
208 Regent Street
London W1

tube: Oxford Circus
Mon-Sat 10-7 (Thurs 10-8)
Sun 12-6

020 7734 3312
223-235 Oxford Street
London W1

tube: Oxford Circus
Mon-Fri 10-8, Sat 10-7
Sun 12-6

020 7493 3316
315 Oxford Street
London W1

tube: Oxford Circus/Bond Street
Mon-Sat 10-7:30 (Thurs 10-8)
Sun 12-6

020 7408 4500
376-384 Oxford Street
London W1

tube: Bond Street
Mon-Sat 9:30-8 (Fri 9:30-9)
Sun 12-6

020 7836 0646
121-123 Long Acre
London WC2

tube: Covent Garden
Mon-Sat 10-7 (Thurs 10-8)
Sun 12-6

020 7368 2900   **tube: High Street Kensington**
99-101 Kensington High Street   Mon-Wed 9:30-7
London W8   Thurs-Sat 9:30-8, Sun 12-6

020 7225 1112   **tube: Knightsbridge**
147-149 Brompton Road   Mon-Tues 9:30-7
London SW3   Wed-Sat 9:30-8, Sun 12-6

020 7823 7272   **tube: Sloane Square**
122 King's Road   Mon-Sat 10-7, Sun 12-6
London SW3

020 7485 4357   **tube: Camden Town**
6-12 Parkway   Mon-Sat 10-7, Sun 12-6
London NW1

020 7586 6123   **tube: St John's Wood**
47-49 St John's Wood High Street   Mon-Sat 9:30-6
London NW8   Sun 11-6

020 7513 0241   **tube: Canary Wharf**
330-340 Cabot Place East   Mon-Fri 8:30-7, Sat 10-6
London E14   Sun 11-6

Gary Anderson

This spacious, modern store specializes in the sale and hire of formal menswear, especially for weddings, in both traditional and contemporary styles. This means that classic cuts mingle with colourful, funky waistcoats and all sorts of cravats and ties. They offer a full bespoke service and a range of 300 different silks, with fittings generally by appointment. *garyanderson.co.uk*

Expensive   *Amex/MC/V*

020 7287 6661   **tube: Piccadilly Circus/Oxford Circus**
34-35 Savile Row   Mon-Sat 10-6
London W1

020 7224 2241   **tube: Baker Street**
12-15 Chiltern Street   Mon-Sat 10-5:30
London W1

General Trading Company

In a contemporary setting—polished concrete floor and plaster walls—wooden fixtures showcase unique luxury homewares, accessories and gifts from global names such as Riedel and Biot, in addition to their clothes collections. Founded in Mayfair in 1920, GTC have all four royal warrants and furnish London's best-dressed homes from their unusual location in Sloane Square's former fire station. *general-trading.co.uk*

Moderate to expensive   *Amex/MC/V*

020 7730 0411   **tube: Sloane Square**
2 Symons Street   Mon-Sat 10-6:30 (Wed 10-7)
London SW3   Sun 12-5:30

Georgina Goodman

As you would expect of a former pupil of Manolo Blahnik, Georgina Goodman is turning out some of the most original designs this town has seen in ages. Joining the ranks of other lady bespoke shoe designers (Jane Brown and Olivia Morris), Goodman's craftsmanship and creativity do not disappoint. Each couture shoe is made from a single piece of vegetable-dyed, hand-painted leather and heels are carved from natural woods. A pair takes from four to six weeks to make (12-16 weeks for men's shoes). Organic and sculptural, she has slip-ons with the toe cut out, pretty wedge sandals with long woven ankle straps, a small selection of inspiring belts and bags and a limited collection of men's accessories. The part retro, part wacky look will appeal to young boho fashionistas.

Expensive	*Amex/MC/V*
020 7499 8599	**tube: Green Park**
12-14 Shepherd Street	Mon-Fri 10-6
London W1	Sat 10-6

Georgina von Etzdorf

Still going strong and relocated in a bright new store, von Etzdorf's hand-printed silk scarves truly are works of art, and her clothing expresses an equally powerful design sensibility. Many of this English designer's dark-toned designs (in brooding shades of aubergine, black and brown) are splashed, Jackson Pollock style, with streaks of fuchsia or gold. The results are more dramatic than cutting-edge.

Expensive	*Amex/MC/V*
020 7259 9715	**tube: Sloane Square**
4 Ellis St	Mon-Sat 10-6
London SW1	

Ghost

If Ophelia, barefoot with flowers in her hair, needed a new dress, this would be her best bet. Ethereal and bias-cut, the drapey viscose/rayon dresses in pale shades like rose, lilac and cream will make you want to wiggle your toes in the grass. The mood for men is more down-to-earth, offering colourful button-down shirts and suits. This simple, comfortable clothing with its generous sizing is machine-washable and makes great holidaywear.   *ghost.co.uk*

Moderate to expensive	*Amex/MC/V*
020 7229 1057	**tube: Notting Hill Gate**
36 Ledbury Road	Mon-Fri 10:30-6:30, Sat 10-6
London W11	
020 7486 0239	**tube: Bond Street**
14 Hinde Street	Mon-Sat 10-6 (Thurs 10-7)
London W1	

Gianfranco Ferré

Ferré is an Italian stalwart who seems to be treading younger and more dangerous ground lately, with tight leather trousers and tops that dare to bare, low-slung belts and high-riding heels. His older fans needn't fear, though—Ferré's classic sense of style is still present in his collection of cocktail dresses and tailored suits, so well cut they're an enduring reflection of his early training as an architect. *gianfrancoferre.com*

Very expensive   *Amex/MC/V*

020 7838 9576   **tube: Knightsbridge**
29 Sloane Street   Mon-Sat 10-6 (Wed 10-7)
London SW1

Gieves & Hawkes

Large, impressive premises at this rather special address—No.1 Savile Row—offer a balance of traditional solemnity and metropolitan cool that reflects the vast and excellent range of clothes within. Warm wood flooring, a chandelier made from antlers and an open fire give the shop a welcoming, hunting lodge feel. Displays mix numerous royal warrants with beautifully cut casual clothing and a huge selection of shirts, ties, belts, coats and ready-to-wear suits through a dozen different rooms. The company has been undergoing modernization under creative director James Wishaw, who has injected an edgy Sixties feel to many of the separates. For older, more established clients the bespoke service remains, as it always has been, second to none. *gievesandhawkes.com*

Expensive   *Amex/MC/V*

020 7434 2001   **tube: Piccadilly Circus/Oxford Circus**
1 Savile Row   Mon-Thurs 9:30-6:30
London W1   Fri 9-6, Sat 10-6

020 7730 1777   **tube: Sloane Square**
33 Sloane Square   Mon-Sat 9:30-6 (Wed 10-7)
London SW1   Sun 11-5

Gigi

Slick, clean-cut and the epitome of London chic, Gigi is the sister store to Joseph and an essential stop off for London's SW set. Labels like Prada, Plein Sud and Katharine Hamnett embody classic design with an edge. Luxurious sweaters, perfect black trousers, cute tailored shirts and the odd eccentricity make for a selection that is safe but still fun. Accessories, though limited, couldn't be better.

Expensive   *Amex/MC/V*

020 7584 1252   **tube: South Kensington**
124 Draycott Avenue   Mon-Sat 10-6:30 (Wed 10-7)
London SW3   Sun 1-6

Gina

Any shoe shopper worth her slingbacks will tell you there are few more tempting places to squander a fortune. Gina shoes are coveted by London party girls for their striking adornment and sexy styles, from jewelled toe-ring sandals to sleek sassy boots—most with hazardously high heels. Handbags are also available, for day and evening. For the ultimate indulgence, an extra £150 will get you Gina's couture service. Any shoe can be customised in a different colour or fabric, so never again will you have to hide at a cocktail party because you've spotted someone else wearing the same shoes.   *ginashoes.com*

Expensive to very expensive   Amex/MC/V

020 7235 2932   **tube: Knightsbridge**
189 Sloane Street   Mon-Sat 10-6 (Wed 10-7)
London SW1

020 7409 7090   **tube: Green Park**
9 Old Bond Street   Mon-Sat 10-6 (Thurs 10-7)
London W1

Ginka (formerly Neisha Crossland)

Neisha Crosland is going from strength to strength. She recently opened a new interiors shop in lovely Chelsea Green and textile experts will recognize her name from concessions in Harvey Nichols, Liberty and Harrods. Her magic touch yields many lovely results, from rich velvet shawls, floppy sunhats and handbags to colourful pillows, notebooks and bed throws. Bright, bold patterns are her signature, ranging from swirling flower prints to funky polka dots in orange and pink. Whether you are decorating yourself, or decorating your home, Crosland's designs are bound to inspire.   *neishacrosland.com*

Moderate   Amex/MC/V

020 7589 4866   **tube: South Kensington**
137 Fulham Road   Mon-Sat 10-6, Sun 12-5
London SW3

Giorgio Armani

His hallmark elongated silhouette draws Hollywood ladies for their red carpet dresses and lesser but equally loyal customers for the slimline trousers and fabulous jackets. Fashion-forward fans will be tempted by the trend for cropped trousers and his extra-long bermudas, which give the effect of a skirt. The Privé jewellery collection, accessories and fragrance are the cherry on top of a label synonymous with timeless elegance, and the designer's favourite stars Michelle Pfeiffer and Cate Blanchett wear them well. In Armani Jeans clean-cut Armani man sets aside his minimalist suit and takes a motorcycle trip in distressed denim. Even Armani ladies like a bit of rough sometimes.   *giorgioarmani.com*

Very expensive   Amex/MC/V

020 7235 6232   **tube: Knightsbridge**
37 Sloane Street   Mon-Sat 10-6 (Wed 10-7), Sun 12-6
London SW1

020 7491 8080   **tube: Bond Street**
51 New Bond Street   Mon-Sat 10-6 (Thurs 10-7)
London W1   Sun 12-6

The Gladys (formerly Justin Kara)

This Australian-designed womenswear is rife with vintage references: Hawaiian florals, girlish gingham, and bikinis made from recycled decal T-shirts. Jewellery and woven belts and bags capture the bohemian beach flavour of

Malibu circa 1976. Occasionally you will also find childrenswear here, if the owner has come across something she likes—it's very much about the personal touch.

Moderate   *MC/V*

020 7792 6920   **tube: Ladbroke Grove**
253 Portobello Road   Mon-Sat 11-6:30, Sun 12-5
London W11

Gloss

Plenty of glossy names and glamorous looks make this one of the best new boutiques on the King's Road. Designers stocked include FrostFrench, Anna Sui, Pringle and Tocca. The shelves are piled high with sleek jeans by Paper Denim, a great staple all year round. In winter there are fabulous fake furs; in summer you'll find diaphanous dresses and slinky skirts. The frilly silk knickers with "Saturday" inscribed on them should be saved for special occasions.

Expensive   *Amex/MC/V*

020 7351 9314   **tube: Sloane Square**
159 King's Road   Mon-Sat 10-7, Sun 11-6
London SW3

Golden Glow

This tiny gem used to be called Amiche (Italian for girlfriends) but now doubles as boutique and tanning salon (see Health & Beauty). Afy Naghibi sells the most delightful jewellery to complement her much coveted Kesslord bags from France, which start at a painless £59. And for only half that, you can get the 60-second tan. The Mayfair location is in what is now called Avery Village, would you believe.   *goldenglowuk.com*

Moderate   *Amex/MC/V*

020 7495 7677   **tube: Bond Street**
31 Avery Row   Mon-Sat 10-6
London W1

Gordon Scott

For anyone who was teased as Bigfoot at school this shoe store is a handy place to know. It specializes in wide fittings and extra large sizes for both women and men. The majority of styles are basic, made of leather and business-oriented. Sturdy English staples include Church's, Jones the Bootmaker and Barkers while Italian labels Stemar, Hugo Boss and Artioli are supple and soft. Sizes go up to an English 13 and there is also a made-to-measure and shoe repair service.   *gordonscott.com*

Moderate   *MC/V*

020 7495 3301   **tube: Bond Street**
29 New Bond Street   Mon-Sat 10-6:30
London W1   (Thurs 10-7), Sun 12-6

Graham & Green

This lovely boutique is bursting with beautiful booty. For the home, there are Venetian mirrors, Moroccan leather beanbags, and Indian bed linens. For your darling self: Orla Kiely bags, cashmere sweaters by Marilyn Moore, linen dresses in shades of summer and an inspired selection of pretty tops and skirts from such labels as Day. A must, even if you can only afford to browse. *grahamandgreen.co.uk*

Expensive *Amex/MC/V*

020 7352 1919 tube: **Sloane Square**
340 King's Road Mon-Sat 10-6
London SW3 Sun 12-6

020 7727 4594 tube: **Notting Hill Gate/Ladbroke Grove**
4 & 10 Elgin Crescent Mon-Sat 10-6
London W11 Sun 11:30-5:30

020 7586 2960 tube: **Chalk Farm**
164 Regent's Park Road Mon-Sat 10-6, Sun 11:30-5:30
London NW1

Great Expectations ♀

Hidden upstairs from Night Owls is a little shop for the stork watchers. If you're a mother-to-be searching for appealing maternity wear, have a look here. Great Expectations provides a smart selection of trousers, dresses, skirts and shirts that are more sympathetic than stylish. Colourful swimwear, maternity bras, cashmere cardigans and business suits with room to breathe will take you all the way to the delivery room.

Moderate *Amex/MC/V*

020 7584 2451 tube: **South Kensington**
78 Fulham Road Mon-Sat 10-6 (Wed 10-7)
London SW3

Gucci ♂♀♂

Gucci girls, fear not. Womenswear designer Alessandra Facchinetti (of Miu Miu and Prada fame) followed on where Tom Ford left off. Her second collection saw the world's best-dressed women from the boardroom to the nightclub with trademark sexy spray-on trousers and sharp pencil skirts. She cleverly managed to work a bit of ethnic charm into Tom Ford's raunchy legacy while John Ray designed the menswear with equal glamour. Facchinetti has now moved on and been replaced by Frida Giannini, but private jets still fly good-looking label shoppers into town to pay homage, and platinum cards are still ringing the tills. *gucci.com*

Expensive to very expensive *Amex/MC/V*

020 7629 2716 tube: **Green Park**
34 Old Bond Street Mon-Sat 10-6 (Thurs 10-7)
London W1

020 7235 6707 tube: **Knightsbridge**
17-18 Sloane Street Mon-Sat 10-6 (Wed 10-7)
London SW1

020 7623 3626 tube: **Bank**
9 Royal Exchange Mon-Fri 10-6
London EC3

Guys and Dolls

A shop for little adults with grown-up price tags. Sling-back Roberto Cavalli trainers, Cacharel pinstripe blazers and Sonia Rykiel cotton dresses hang from a curly rail that runs like a caterpillar along the wall. Brightly coloured pods contain a play area to keep the little ones amused and a dressing-room complete with a mirror for aspiring shopaholics. Look out for Lucy Sykes Baby (yes, fashionista Plum Sykes' sister) and Roberto Cavelli's new line Angels and Devils.

Moderate to expensive   *Amex/MC/V*

020 7589 8990   **tube: South Kensington**
172 Walton Street   Mon-Fri 10-6, Sat 11-6
London SW3

Gymboree

Gymboree offers casual clothing for kids (newborn to seven) in Fisher Price-style primary colours, with leopard-print jackets, whale-print wellies and cute bumble-bee slippers. A mix-and-match approach, with multiple possible combinations, makes expanding a child's wardrobe easy, expecially when the prices are so reasonable. Bikinis, sunglasses and tiny handbags add a tempting dose of fun for the girls, while boys will look cute in canvas hats and dungarees.   *gymboree.com*

Affordable to moderate   *Amex/MC/V*

020 7494 1110   **tube: Oxford Circus**
198 Regent Street   Mon-Sat 10-7 (Thurs 10-8)
London W1   Sun 11:30-5:30

H&M (Hennes & Mauritz)

A shopaholic's dream, H&M's formula is fashion and quality at the best price. Some might argue they haven't quite got the quality quotient yet, but this is still a great place to find the impulse-buy that you will wear only once or twice. With five collections for women, four for men and various other lines for teenagers and children, H&M cuts into the trendy cross-section of every market. The emphasis is on merchandise turnaround, so nothing lasts more than a few weeks and they will keep lowering the price, if necessary, until the stock has gone.   *hm.com*

Affordable   *Amex/MC/V*

020 8382 3262   **tube: Knightsbridge**
17-21 Brompton Road   Mon-Fri 10-8
London SW3   Sat 10-7, Sun 12-6

020 7493 4004   **tube: Oxford Circus**
261-271 Regent Street   Mon-Sat 10-8 (Thurs-Fri 10-9)
London W1   Sun 12-6

020 7493 8557   **tube: Marble Arch**
481 Oxford Street   (opening hours as above)
London W1

020 7518 1630
360-366 Oxford Street
London W1

tube: Oxford Circus
(opening hours as above)

020 7612 1820
174-176 Oxford Street
London W1

tube: Oxford Circus
(opening hours as above)

020 7368 3920
103-111 Kensington High Street
London W8

tube: High Street Kensington
Mon-Sat 10-7
(Thurs 10-8), Sun 12-6

020 7395 1250
27-29 Long Acre
London WC2

tube: Covent Garden
Mon-Fri 10-8
Sat 10-7, Sun 12-6

020 7313 7500
Whiteley's, Queensway
London W2

tube: Queensway/Bayswater
Mon-Sat 10-8, Sun 12-6

Hats Etc (formerly The British Hatter)

Pick your occasion, and Pamela Bromley will design a suitable lid, be it bright and wide-brimmed for Ascot or a tiny pillbox for lunching. Millinery may be fashion's most traditional medium but Bromley favours an unconventional approach. She's not a fan of wearing one colour head to toe, and many of her designs are more madcap than minimalist. If you love one of her hats, but know you could only get away with wearing it once, hire it for three days for half the cost of the purchase price. *hatsetc.co.uk*

Moderate   *Amex/MC/V*

020 7361 0000
36b Kensington Church Street
London W8

tube: High Street Kensington
Mon-Sat 11-6

Hackett

The face of Hackett is Jonny Wilkinson, heart-throb hero of English rugby. His clean-cut, down-to-earth image, his innate Englishness and his unwavering reliability make him the perfect model for this conservative, old-school brand. Corduroy trousers, linen shirts and tweed jackets please polite public school boys, while a somewhat predictable new range of sportswear, using the number 10 as worn by Jonny, appeals to action heroes everywhere. The brand's look is distinctly British and the sharp tailoring and attention to detail ensure Hackett is often the first kick-off for men seeking made-to-measure occasional wear. Even if you don't like the clothing you can admire the body that wears it. *hackett.co.uk*

Expensive   *Amex/MC/V*

020 7930 1300
87 Jermyn Street
London SW1

tube: Piccadilly Circus/Green Park
Mon-Sat 9:30-6:30 (Thurs 9:30-7)
Sun 12-5

020 7730 3331
136-138 Sloane Street
London SW1

tube: Sloane Square
Mon-Sat 9:30-6 (Wed 9:30-7)
Sun 12-6

020 7494 1855
143-147 Regent Street
London W1

tube: Piccadilly Circus
Mon-Sat 10-7
Sun 11-5

020 7626 0707
19 Eastcheap
London EC3

tube: Monument
Mon-Fri 8:30-6

020 7240 2040
31-32 King Street
London WC2

tube: Covent Garden
Mon-Sat 10-7
Sun 11-5

020 7379 5866
38 Floral Street
London WC2

tube: Covent Garden
(opening hours as above)

Hampstead Bazaar ♀

If you're a youthful size 8 you'll wonder why we've included this one. If, however, you're a lady of a certain age—and a certain size—this may be your retail nirvana: loose-fitting styles in jersey and velvet, with lots of swooshing drapery and batwing sleeves to hide those wobbly upper arms, accompanied by dramatic chunky jewellery. Comfort clothing for ageing drama queens. *hampsteadbazaar.com*

Moderate   *Amex/MC/V*

020 7431 3343
31 Heath Street
London NW3

tube: Hampstead
Mon-Sat 10-6
Sun 12-5

020 7629 2741
1 Gees Court
London W1

tube: Bond Street
Mon-Sat 10-6 (Thurs 10-7)
Sun 12-5

020 7637 2274
45 Charlotte Street
London W1

tube: Goodge Street
Mon-Fri 10-6

Hardy Amies ♂♀

Most famous perhaps as a women's couture house making formal, uncluttered designs for the great and good of a certain age (including the Queen), Hardy Amies has undergone a quiet revolution in recent years. With Ian Garlant at the helm, the traditional custom-made mens' suits and classic womenswear, from chiffon dresses to suits in silk and wool, have all benefited from subtle design updates. *hardyamies.com*

Expensive to very expensive   *Amex/MC/V*

020 7734 2436
14 Savile Row
London W1

tube: Piccadilly Circus/Oxford Circus
Mon-Fri 9:30-5

Harley-Davidson ♂♀

Beer guts, beards and tattoos are the images that spring to mind when you hear the name Harley-Davidson, a brand that has surely outlived its heyday. But this store means serious business for any kind of bike enthusiast. Genuine motorcycle clothes in all sizes (with or without the gut) are featured in styles tough enough to keep out the wind. Leather accessories are also available and, from the range of collectibles, there are logo'd T-shirts, sweatshirts and jackets. *warrs.com*

Expensive   *Amex/MC/V*

020 7376 7084   **tube: Sloane Square**
125 King's Road   Mon-Sat 10-6, Sun 12-5
London SW3

Harriet Gubbins

There's a strong dose of personality and colour to everything Gubbins designs. Her made-to-measure suits are tightly tailored and sharp in an Eighties "career gal" sort of way (think Melanie Griffiths's Working Girl wardrobe), with an emphasis on flared sleeves and strong, power colours. Mother-of-the-bride suits are less severe, if a bit mumsy. The bridal gowns are the best of the bunch, more understated and infinitely prettier.   *harrietgubbins.co.uk*

Expensive   *Cash/cheque only*

020 7736 0748   **tube: Parsons Green**
813b Fulham Road   (by appointment only)
London SW6

☆ Harrods

Harrods is still the grande dame of London department stores: big, bustling, bursting. The list of different departments is endless—antiques, contemporary furniture, home entertainment, pianos and musical instruments, outdoor living and even a Christmas World, and that's before we've even got to the fashion. There are 25 restaurants and bars, so whether you are after tapas or sushi you will find it here. Then there's a barber shop, a hamper service and a recently extended personal shopping service. There's even a Haute Parfumerie department and the Urban Retreat beauty salon offers the exclusive Crème de la Mer facial and hand treatment. Harrods is so huge that, like a museum, it offers an indoor map of the store. The enormous Food Hall is legendary and the arrival of the famous macaroons from Patisserie Ladurée has drawn in queues of little French piggies. On the fashion front you'll find one of the best men's departments anywhere and women's designer labels range from Fake London to Armani. New labels they now carry include Oscar de la Renta, Balenciaga, Emanuel Ungaro and Valentino. All in all, there is very little they have not thought of. There is a Harrods teddy bear, a Harrods bank, a Harrods on-line casino and you even can charter a Harrods helicopter. It's a shopping mecca and worth a visit if only for the experience.   *harrods.com*

Expensive to very expensive   *Amex/MC/V*

020 7730 1234   **tube: Knightsbridge**
87-135 Brompton Road   Mon-Sat 10-7
London SW1

Harvest

With every new season Harvest yields a mixed crop of international designers, but the list of featured labels, including

Kenzo, Plein Sud and Firenze, seems to promise more than it delivers. The style is confusingly hit-and-miss, from gypsy blouses to bland dresses that might suit a mother of the bride. Flamboyant details (on lacy skirts, ruffled blouses and feathered hats) keep the clothing from being too mainstream, but there's a dowdy flavour to the shop that makes the selection feel flat.

Moderate   *Amex/MC/V*

020 7581 9245   **tube: Sloane Square**
136 King's Road   Mon-Sat 10-7, Sun 12-5:30
London SW3

☆ Harvey Nichols

Harvey Nicks (no one ever says "Nichols"!) has pulled off the best possible marketing trick—it has wormed its way into people's affections. Londoners love Harvey Nicks. Refined, bright and buzzy, it pulls the ladies-who-lunch (and how well they lunch on the fifth floor!) with its fashionable names. Behind brilliant window displays the ground floor is devoted to beauty goodies and sensational accessories. You could happily spend an hour picking out some new jewellery, an outrageous hat by Cozmo Jenks or Philip Treacy, a lipstick by RMK or some sunglasses by Prada. Then, for a bit of eyebrow-tidying, head to Blink. The rest of the store is a temple to elegant urban design, from classics such as Ralph Lauren, Armani Collezioni and Paul Smith to hot young names such as Martin Grant, Thakoon and Proenza Schouler. The third floor has Maharishi, jeans by Paige and Superfine, Gwen Stefani's label LAMB and the slick Jimmy Choo salon. A refurbished homes department offers furniture and accessories by After Noah, Armani Casa, Lombok and Catherine Memmi, and a kitchen shop with the funkiest domestic goods around. When it comes to food, the ladies who shop here may be lettuce-only types but there are plenty of places to break this diet. The store has a space-age fifth floor restaurant, a branch of Wagamama in the basement and a jam-packed café where you can sit outside in summer and enjoy soups, risottos, or crunchy Caesars. The glistening food market is furiously expensive but beautiful to look at. The joy of Harvey Nicks is that it is small enough to manage. Get to know it and it will earn a place in your shopper's heart. Darlings, it's absolutely fabulous.   *harveynichols.com*

Expensive to very expensive   *Amex/MC/V*

020 7235 5000   **tube: Knightsbridge**
109-125 Knightsbridge   Mon-Tues, Sat 10-7
London SW1   Wed-Fri 10-8, Sun 12-6

Harvie & Hudson

In the rarefied atmosphere of Jermyn Street, Harvie & Hudson are major league players. The shop has been in the ownership of its two namesake families since 1949 and the in-store ambience is one of old-school splendour. Silk and cotton poplin shirts are the speciality here, with slightly cutaway Kent collars, and matching ties in traditional colours. They also sell mix-and-match suits so that customers with very different jacket and trouser measurements can buy off the peg; the sort of personalised service which gives Jermyn Street's family-run establishments their enduring appeal.   harvieandhudson.com

Expensive   *Amex/MC/V*

020 7930 3949   **tube: Piccadilly Circus/Green Park**
77 Jermyn Street   Mon-Sat 9-5:30
London SW1

020 7839 3578   **tube: Piccadilly Circus/Green Park**
97 Jermyn Street   Mon-Sat 9-5:30
London SW1

020 7235 2651   **tube: Knightsbridge/Hyde Park Corner**
55 Knightsbridge   Mon-Sat 9-5:30
London SW1

Hawes & Curtis

This friendly gentleman's outfitter offers the usual Jermyn Street range of plain, striped and check cotton shirts in a clubby, wood-panelled interior. Downstairs is the formal selection for tails (cutaways) and white-tie. Hawes & Curtis made clothes for the Duke of Windsor and bought part of his wardrobe at the famous Sotheby's auction in New York.   hawesandcurtis.com

Expensive   *Amex/MC/V*

020 7287 8111   **tube: Piccadilly Circus**
23 Jermyn Street   Mon-Sat 9:30-6:30 (Thurs 9:30-7)
London SW1   Sun 12-5

020 7730 0022   **tube: Sloane Square**
39 King's Road   Mon-Tues 9:30-6:30
London SW3   Wed-Sat 10-7, Sun 12-6

☆ Heidi Klein

A one-stop holiday shop with beachwear all year round. As you enter, you are greeted with the smell of coconut-scent-ed candles which instantly transports you to beach babe mode. Bikinis and bathing-suits by Melissa Odabash, Missoni, Dos Mares, Helen Kaminski and Cacharel are all in stock. Find cover-ups by Allegra Hicks for the more modest bunch, as well as a selection of cotton T-shirts, linen trousers and kidswear. Accessories are just as cool, includ-ing sunglasses by Chloé and Costume National, colourful Billy Bags and cuff bracelets by Johnny Loves Rosie. Best of all, there's a beauty spa with body brushing, fake tanning, waxing, manicures and pedicures for top-to-toe holiday preparation.   heidiklein.co.uk

Affordable to expensive   *Amex/MC/V*

020 7243 5665   **tube: Notting Hill Gate**
174 Westbourne Grove   Mon-Sat 10-6
London W11   Sun 12-5

020 7259 9418
257 Pavilion Road
London SW1

Directory

Henri Lloyd

This company has quite a prestigious history. First, it introduced the revolutionary fabric Bri-Nylon into the marine world and saw a century of oilskin-clad yachtsmen disappear. Then when Sir Francis Chichester undertook his epic single-handed voyage around the world in 1967 he chose Henri Lloyd clothing to protect him from the elements. Today the company remains the choice of yachting champions and the Carnaby Street shop is bursting with top technical boatwear and some fun forays into fashion too. Alongside waterproof, windproof, breathable jackets you'll find striped T-shirts, cotton piqué dresses and cable-knit sweaters. Looking sporty has never been so fashionable.

Moderate to expensive   *Amex/MC/V*

020 7287 4376
48 Carnaby Street
London W1

tube: Oxford Circus/Piccadilly Circus
Mon-Sat 10-6:30, Sun 11-5

Henry Maxwell

The original speciality of these bespoke shoemakers was riding boots, but today they will make any shoe or boot you desire at prices from £1,400 upwards. Initial fittings require a wooden last of your foot to be made, and this is kept for all future orders. Good things come to those who wait and patience is definitely a virtue here—it can take up to a year to complete a pair of riding boots and around five months to make a shoe from scratch. But your feet will be in good company—Charlie Chaplin and President Roosevelt were both customers here.

Very expensive   *Amex/MC/V*

020 7930 1839
83 Jermyn Street
London W1

tube: Piccadilly Circus/Green Park
Mon-Fri 10-6, Sat 10-4

☆ Henry Poole

As you might expect of a company that set the whole Savile Row ball rolling 150 years ago, that clothed the likes of Charles Dickens, Napoleon, Winston Churchill and Haile Selassie and that invented the tuxedo, Henry Poole is a busy, confident, friendly and firmly traditional business. Eschewing considerations of house style, it offers a popular, purely bespoke suit and shirt service for the high-waisted, slim-fitting look that is classic Savile Row.   *henrypoole.com*

Very expensive   *Amex/MC/V*

020 7734 5985
15 Savile Row
London W1

tube: Piccadilly Circus/Oxford Circus
Mon-Fri 9-5:15

Herbert Johnson
(see under Swaine Adeney Brigg/Herbert Johnson)

Herbie Frogg
The various locations of this privately-owned British outfitter offer different selections of menswear. Jermyn Street features the Herbie Frogg shirt and suit label, and accessories; the flagship, in Hans Crescent, offers a selection of leather as well as the Brioni label. Traditional designs are the unifying quality, made-to-measure service is available in all the stores and Swiss cotton shirts are a speciality. The slightly stuffy but friendly atmosphere is beloved of middle-aged tourists and British alike.   *herbie-frogg.co.uk*

Expensive   *Amex/MC/V*

020 7437 6069   **tube: Piccadilly Circus**
18-19 Jermyn Street   Mon-Sat 9:30-6 (Thurs 9:30-7)
London SW1

020 7439 2512   **tube: Piccadilly Circus**
21 Jermyn Street   (opening hours as above)
London SW1

020 7823 1177   **tube: Knightsbridge**
13 Lowndes Street   Mon-Sat 9:30-6 (Wed 9:30-7)
London SW1

Hermès
The luxury label more luxe than any other. Grown women have been known to cry over the elegant, indestructible leather handbags, and the lovely scarves and uniquely patterned ties are instantly recognisable and internationally coveted. Like its classic Birkin bag, the ready-to-wear for both sexes resides in its own sophisticated universe beyond flashy trends.   *hermes.com*

Expensive   *Amex/MC/V*

020 7499 8856   **tube: Bond Street**
155 New Bond Street   Mon-Sat 10-6
London W1

020 7823 1014   **tube: Knightsbridge**
179 Sloane Street   (opening hours as above)
London SW1

020 7626 7794   **tube: Bank**
2-3 Royal Exchange   Mon-Fri 10-6
London EC3

High & Mighty
It can be hard shopping for big friendly giants, but High & Mighty makes the task easy. Offering business and casual clothing for large and tall men, the selection here features designer suits, shirts, ties, jeans and jackets as well as underwear and accessories. Labels include Ben Sherman, Pierre Cardin and Animal. With sizes maxing out at 40 inches for trouser length, 60 for chest and 60 for waist, big boys have never looked so good.   *highandmighty.co.uk*

Moderate   *Amex/MC/V*

020 7589 7454
81-83 Knightsbridge
London SW1

tube: Knightsbridge
Mon-Fri 10-6:30, Sat 10-6

020 7723 8754
145-147 Edgware Road
London W2

tube: Marble Arch/Edgware Road
Mon-Sat 9-6 (Thurs 9-7)

020 7436 4861
The Plaza, 120 Oxford Street
London W1

tube: Oxford Circus
Mon-Sat 10-7
(Thurs 10-8)

High Jinks

This quintessential streetwear shop, thumping with bass, offers a formidable array of the latest in street and skateboard looks for moody teens and Peter Pan thirtysomethings. Guys can find cargo trousers, Hooch sweatshirts, decal T-shirts and nylon jackets. Girls have slightly fewer choices—distressed cords, ripped cargo skirts and baby tees. Labels include Tribal, Ringspun, Aemkei, The Criminal and Dickies.   *high-jinks.com*

Moderate   *Amex/MC/V*

020 7240 5580
25 Thomas Neals Centre
London WC2

tube: Covent Garden
Mon-Sat 10-7, Sun 12-6

020 7734 6644
13-14 Carnaby Street
London W1

tube: Oxford Circus
(opening hours as above)

☆ Hilditch & Key

Karl Lagerfeld buys over a hundred shirts a year from Hilditch & Key, thought by some to be the finest shirtmaker in the world. The beautiful wood-panelled interior is lined with every style a gentleman could need, and you can choose an off-the-peg classic or order bespoke. The attention to detail—single-needle seams, patterns that blend seamlessly at collar and cuff, highest quality fabrics—ensure the label's undisputed success. These shirts are made to last.   *hilditch.co.uk*

Expensive   *Amex/MC/V*

020 7734 4707
37 & 73 Jermyn Street
London SW1

tube: Piccadilly Circus/Green Park
Mon-Sat 9:30-6

020 7823 5683
131 Sloane Street
London SW1

tube: Sloane Square
Mon-Fri 9:30-5:45, Sat 10-5:45

The Hive

This boutique treads the fine line between cool, customised clothing and dubious eurotrash. T-shirts by Passepartout are trimmed with just the right type of decorative detail and sit among attire from the likes of Studds and Gatano Navaro. If the vibe were cooler (this hive was anything but buzzing) and the sales staff a bit less severe, this would probably be more fun.

Moderate to expensive   *Amex/MC/V*

020 7467 0799   **tube: Notting Hill Gate**
3 Lonsdale Road   Mon-Sat 11-6
London W11

Hobbs   ♀

For nice girls who like to play it safe, Hobbs brings stodgy
British style into the 21st century with a soothing atmosphere and a selection of smart women's suits in a palette
that borders on business-blah. Faultlessly crafted skirts,
dresses and coats come in simple styles. Some shoppers
stop by just for the shoes, which are equally unfussy with a
selection of sturdy high-heeled boots and smart court
shoes.   *hobbs.co.uk*

Moderate   *Amex/MC/V*

020 7437 4418   **tube: Oxford Circus**
217-219 Regent Street   Mon-Sat 10-7 (Thurs 10-8)
London W1   Sun 12-6

020 7629 0750   **tube: Bond Street**
47-49 South Molton Street   Mon-Sat 10-6:30
London W1   (Thurs 10-7:30), Sun 12-6

020 7836 9168   **tube: Covent Garden**
17 The Market   Mon-Fri 10-7 (Thurs 10-7:30)
London WC2   Sat 10:30-7, Sun 11-5

020 7581 2914   **tube: Sloane Square**
84-88 King's Road   Mon-Fri 10-7 (Wed 10-7:30)
London SW3   Sat 10-6:30, Sun 10-6

020 7225 2136   **tube: Knightsbridge**
37 Brompton Road   Mon-Sat 10-6:30
London SW3   (Wed, Fri 10-7), Sun 12-6

020 7937 1026   **tube: High Street Kensington**
63 Kensington High Street   Mon-Wed, Sat 10-6:30
London W8   Thurs 10-7:30, Fri 10-7, Sun 10-6

020 7836 0625   **tube: Covent Garden**
124 Long Acre   Mon-Sat 10:30-7 (Thurs 10:30-8)
London WC2   Sun 12-5

020 7431 2228   **tube: Hampstead**
9 & 15 Hampstead High Street   Mon-Sat 10-6:30
London NW3   Sun 12-5

020 7929 4900   **tube: Monument/Bank**
64-72 Leadenhall Market   Mon-Fri 10-6:30
London EC3

020 7628 6771   **tube: Liverpool Street**
135 Bishopsgate   Mon-Fri 9-6:30 (Thurs 9-7)
London EC2

020 7513 2763   **tube: Canary Wharf**
4 Canada Place Mall   Mon-Fri 9-7 (Thurs 9-8)
London E14   Sat 10-6, Sun 12-6

Hogan   ♂♀

The sporty sister of luxury leather goods giant Tod's, Hogan
makes casual shoes and handbags for European royalty, off-

duty celebrities and girls and guys looking for deluxe trainers to wear with their smart black trousers. This is their first store in the UK and we hope it won't be their last. It's Italian chic for people who value quality and don't want to make a statement. Just add sunglasses. *hogan.it*

Expensive *Amex/MC/V*

020 7245 6363
10 Sloane Street
London SW1

tube: Knightsbridge
Mon-Sat 10-6 (Wed 10-7)

Holland & Holland

The legendary gun company has been supplying Britain's green welly wearers since 1835. It celebrated its 165th anniversary a few years ago with the launch of a luxury clothing line, only to fire the designer a year later and retreat to its shooting roots. The focus is on its heritage as an outdoor brand, with only a small selection of ready-to-wear, so look for plenty of weatherproof and functional clothing: flat caps, tweeds, boots—you get the picture. Perfect for the country house or a ramble in Central (or Hyde) Park. *hollandandholland.com*

Expensive *Amex/MC/V*

020 7408 7921
31-33 Bruton Street
London W1

tube: Green Park
Mon-Fri 9-6, Sat 10-5

Hope + Glory

This casual, urban clothing store features dressed-down work- and weekendwear for men. Not quite statement-making, but still funky and smart, the clothing's character could be described as part Ted Baker, part Hackett. Pink ruffled pin-striped shirts and deconstructed Legolas T-shirts please the trend-hunters; chunky sweaters, rugby shirts and V-neck sweater vests cover the conventional end of the spectrum. A good option for grown-ups who still care about looking cool. *hopeandglory.com*

Moderate to expensive *MC/V*

020 7240 3713
Shorts Gardens
London WC2

tube: Covent Garden
Mon-Fri 10-6:30 (Thurs 10-7)
Sat 10-7, Sun 12-5

020 7628 3328
Broadgate Link
Liverpool Street Station
London EC2

tube: Liverpool Street
Mon-Fri 8-7:30

House of Cashmere

For years Barbour, makers of the oilskin coat that achieved icon status in the Eighties, was the House of Cashmere's most famous name. Now House of Cashmere has branched out with a line of cosy shawls, pashminas, sweaters, trousers, children's clothes and shoes. They might not keep the rain out, but they will deliver excellent quality in just about any colour you could want.

Expensive *Amex/MC/V*

020 7495 7385
8-9 Burlington Arcade
London W1

House of Fraser

This staid department store won't be one of the highlights on your fashion tour of London, but bring low expectations and you may be pleasantly surprised. There's a signature clothing range, Therapy, alongside such designers as Betty Barclay, DKNY, Nicole Farhi, Diesel, French Connection and Austin Reed, and new collections by Tara Jarmon and Quin Donnelly. It's more Macy's than Saks Fifth Avenue but, if nothing else, it's a reliable source of everyday basics from cosmetics to accessories to housewares. *houseoffraser.com*

Affordable to expensive   *Amex/MC/V*

020 7529 4700
318 Oxford Street
London W1

tube: **Oxford Circus/Bond Street**
Mon-Sat 10-8 (Thurs 10-9)
Sun 12-6

020 7937 5432
(Barkers of Kensington)
63 Kensington High Street
London W8

tube: **High Street Kensington**
Mon-Fri 10-7 (Thurs 10-8)
Sat 9-7, Sun 12-6

Hugo Boss

Bland but functional, this German juggernaut keeps rolling along. Once a hot menswear label, Boss is now more favoured by the wannabe than the truly smart dresser. The collection features suits, sportswear, formalwear and outerwear, all in great quality fabrics. Not a bad place to begin to build your wardrobe. *hugoboss.com*

Expensive   *Amex/MC/V*

020 7734 7919
184-186 Regent Street
London W1

tube: **Oxford Circus/Piccadilly Circus**
Mon-Sat 9:30-6:30 (Thurs 10-8)
Sun 12-5

020 7240 1020
47 Long Acre
London WC2

tube: **Covent Garden**
Mon-Fri 10-7 (Thurs 10-8)
Sat 9:30-6:30, Sun 12-6

020 7213 9717
85-90 Queen Street
London EC4

tube: **Mansion House/Bank**
Mon-Fri 9-6

Huntsman

One of Savile Row's most imposing premises is host to one of the street's longest established—and most expensive—tailors. The shop positively drips tradition, with stag heads and dark wood throughout. The quality of a Huntsman bespoke suit is undeniable, with 30% more hand work than anyone else's. Especially famous and popular for their exclusive Huntsman tweeds, the firm also offers a "special order" tailored service allowing less wealthy customers a choice of fabric and (factory) cut. Accessories include ties, cufflinks, umbrellas and dressing-gowns. They don't offer womenswear per se, but some well-known female New York socialites are fans of their blazers and suits and in England the Hon Daphne

Guinness (the woman Valentino most likes to dress) happily, and very elegantly, wears Huntsman.   *h-huntsman.com*

Expensive to very expensive   *Amex/MC/V*

020 7734 7441   **tube: Piccadilly Circus**
11 Savile Row   Mon-Fri 10-6, Sat 10-5
London W1

Iana

Speed-walkers beware: you can rarely walk this stretch of the King's Road without dodging mothers with prams. Now there is another children's store to distract you en route, offering cute practical clothing for boys and girls aged 0-14. The selection includes all the basics—cargo trousers, pinafores and polo shirts—topped off with mini red rain-coats, cream leather jackets and cool denim. With 40 shops worldwide and expansion plans for London, this family-owned Italian label might just be the next Petit Bateau.

Affordable to moderate   *Amex/MC/V*

020 7352 0060   **tube: Sloane Square**
186 King's Road   Mon-Fri 10-6 (Wed 10-7)
London SW3   Sat 10-6:30, Sun 11-6

IBlues

Businesswear is never meant to make a fashion statement but there's no question that outdated, ill-cut suits can dam-age your career. This division of MaxMara will keep you up to speed with smart, stylish suits that are appropriately understated but never frumpy. Pastel dresses, trousers and skirts are sold with coordinating jackets, and the few pat-terns are simple and sweet. A safe investment.

Expensive   *Amex/MC/V*

020 7824 8000   **tube: Sloane Square**
23 King's Road   Mon-Sat 10-7 (Wed 10-8), Sun 1-6
London SW3

Isabell Kristensen

Numerous luminaries, including Nicole Kidman, Joan Collins and Jerry Hall, have strutted their stuff in Kristensen's super-sophisticated couture dresses which embody old-world glamour and elegance. Long and struc-tured, bejewelled with trademark glitter and pearls—ordi-nary mortals will need an occasion to justify one. Even the bridal gowns are a bit too bold for the run-of-the-mill bride. Her hefty materials may induce a 19th-century swoon, but you'll undoubtedly be surrounded by amours eager to catch you.   *isabellkristensen.com*

Very expensive   *Amex/MC/V*

020 7589 1798   **tube: Knightsbridge**
33 Beauchamp Place   Mon-Fri 10:30-6
London SW3

Iselin

Whether you prefer a romantic fairytale look or something more modern and sassy, designer Iselin creates eveningwear for all occasions. Feminine, Cinderella-style skirts are chiffon puffy and delicate and look sensational teemed with fitted silk tops, while lace-trimmed short dresses are figure-hugging and sexy. There are long silk dresses with slits up to the thigh, colourful stoles for chilly evenings and stylish hats to top everything off.

Expensive   *MC/V*

020 8392 2418   **tube: South Kensington**
72 Fulham Road   Mon-Sat 10-6
London SW3

Issey Miyake

Welcome to high-concept fashion: skirts flare at odd angles, trousers have shoes attached and colours scream in bright red, yellow or blue. Miyake's patterned men's shirts may look outrageous, the womenswear fabrics a bit too sheer, but this is avant-garde style at its finest, where innovation means having a sense of humour. If you're too chicken to risk it, stick to rubber bags, T-shirts, socks, belts or the famous fragrances.   *isseymiyake.com*

Moderate to very expensive   *Amex/MC/V*

020 7851 4620   **tube: Oxford Circus**
52 Conduit Street   Mon-Sat 10-6
London W1

020 7581 3760   **tube: South Kensington**
270 Brompton Road   (opening hours as above)
London SW3

J&M Davidson

More Sloane Square than Notting Hill, this large shop caters to the risk-averse, with pretty womenswear, accessories and a home collection that whispers country-chic. Suede beanbags, zebra pillows and an assortment of lamps reflect a sense of easy living. Inoffensive, if a bit dull, particularly for a neighbourhood where quirky is the name of the game.   *jandmdavidson.com*

Expensive   *Amex/MC/V*

020 7313 9532   **tube: Notting Hill Gate**
42 Ledbury Road   Mon-Tues 10-6, Wed-Sat 10-7
London W11   Sun 12-5

J.W.Beeton

Owner Debbie Potts offers an egalitarian mix of trendy streetwear and more wearable feminine clothes. The range features fashion veterans Tracey Boyd and Comme des Garçons, as well as virtual unknowns like Ann-Louise Roswald whose lovely textile-inspired dresses sell like mad. There are also jeans, funky T-shirts and Fake London's recycled cashmere, plus safer linen pieces. A lot less stuffy than the name suggests.

Expensive to very expensive   *Amex/MC/V*

020 7229 8874   **tube: Notting Hill Gate**
48-50 Ledbury Road   Mon-Fri 10:30-6, Sat 10-6
London W11

The Jacksons

This out-of-the-way shop packs a pleasing punch with colourful accessories from Louise and Joey, the Jackson twins. Summer saw cow-print bags with leather straps, mules in white, camel and black and an assortment of their famous flip-flops. For winter, there are high-heeled leather boots, sweet embroidered skirts and a range of sheepskin boas—definitely worth a cold-weather detour. *thejacksons.co.uk*

Moderate to expensive — Amex/MC/V

020 7792 8336 — **tube: Ladbroke Grove/Notting Hill Gate**
5 All Saints Road — Mon-Sat 10-6
London W11

Jacques Azagury

For all those facing a dressy night out but bemoaning an uninspiring wardrobe, Jacques Azagury is a fairy godfather. His sophisticated daytime and evening clothes maintain a following among Knightsbridge ladies who favour classic creations and subtle cuts. To complete the look, head to brother Joseph's exquisite shoe boutique across the street.

Expensive — Amex/MC/V

020 7245 1216 — **tube: Knightsbridge/Hyde Park Corner**
50 Knightsbridge — Mon-Sat 9:30-5:30
London SW1

Jaeger

Jaeger's revamp continues, with the help of model Laura Bailey, the company's new face, and Belinda Earl, the new chief exec formerly boss at Debenhams. Earl wants to "do a Burberry", i.e. turn a sleepy fashion house into a global player, and when she took over there was certainly room for improvement. The collection does now have a younger feel with the odd bustier and floaty dress thrown in, but Jaeger, traditionally favoured by older professionals and country ladies, has some way to go to shed its staid and somewhat conservative image. *jaeger.co.uk*

Moderate to expensive — Amex/MC/V

020 7979 1100 — **tube: Oxford Circus**
200-206 Regent Street — Mon-Fri 10-6:30 (Thurs 10-8)
London W1 — Sat 10-7, Sun 12-5

020 7584 2814 — **tube: Knightsbridge**
16-18 Brompton Road — Mon-Sat 10-6 (Wed 10-8)
London SW1 — Sun 12-6

020 7352 1122 — **tube: Sloane Square**
145 King's Road — Mon-Tues 10-6, Wed-Fri 10-7
London SW3 — Sat 10-6, Sun 12-6

020 8944 7266 — **tube: Wimbledon**
27 High Street — Mon-Fri 9:30-6
Wimbledon Village — Sat 9:30-6, Sun 12-5
London SW19

James Lakeland

Catch an ocean wave at James Lakeland. If you don't have the money for a multimillion pound yacht to complete your summer holiday, it doesn't mean you can't afford the St Tropez-to-Monte-Carlo look. Lakeland offers sporty, sexy clothing with a nautical bent, but is as much about the evening drinks party as the picnic on the beach. Highlights include tie-dye separates, swimsuits and sexy out-on-the-town wear, from tight white trousers to a turquoise halter-neck dress. It is all a little flash and revealing, but when you are a sun-kissed goddess ready to party into the small hours, who cares?

Expensive   *Amex/MC/V*

020 7352 2480   **tube: Sloane Square**
113 King's Road   Mon-Sat 10-7
London SW3   Sun 12-6

James Levett

An experienced Savile Row tailor who set up his own shop about six years ago, James Levett offers traditional bespoke tailoring in everything from business suits to tails (cutaways) in his affable, unstuffy basement workshop. Low overhead costs mean that classic Savile Row looks and quality come at surprisingly reasonable prices, with a two-piece bespoke suit starting at £1,500 and taking between six and eight weeks to produce. Service here is exceptional.

Expensive   *MC/V*

020 7287 5995   **tube: Piccadilly Circus/Oxford Circus**
13 Savile Row   Mon-Fri 9-5:30
London W1

James Purdey & Sons

There's no more famous gunsmith in the world than James Purdey & Sons, and the imposing premises just south of Grosvenor Square and the US Embassy are a treat to visit. Guns remain the core business, but there is a vast range of ultra-high-quality, shooting-orientated clothes and accessories on offer, ranging from clay vests (special vests for clay pigeon—skeet to Americans—shooting) and heavy tweed field coats to padded knitwear, brightly checked shirts, scarves, boots, cufflinks and hi-tech shooting goggles. They have injected a bit more fashion into their menswear recently and have also launched a womenswear collection, including dramatic reversible cloaks in velvet and silk.   *purdey.com*

Expensive   *Amex/MC/V*

020 7499 1801   **tube: Bond Street**
57-58 South Audley Street   Mon-Fri 9:30-5:30
London W1   Sat 10-5

Jane Norman

Stretchy, strappy and sexy, Jane Norman's inexpensive selection is tarty fun for followers of casual fashion trends. Recent pieces include tight denim miniskirts, skinny white trousers and revealing halternecks. The quality leaves something to be desired, but there are times when a throwaway £20 top is just what you need.   *janenorman.com*

Affordable   *Amex/MC/V*

020 7225 3098   **tube: Knightsbridge**
59 Brompton Road   Mon-Tues 10-7, Wed-Fri 10-7:30
London SW3   Sat 10-7, Sun 12-6

Jane Shilton

Victoria Beckham, Denise van Outen and Dannii Minogue
are just a few of the well-heeled celebrities who have
stepped out in shoes by Jane Shilton. Designs are street-
style rather than classic, following the catwalks to the
minute, and affordable prices are a fair reflection of how
long looks will remain trendy. Here today, gone tomorrow,
but oh what fun we have. There are fuchsia-pink stilettos,
knee-high boots, slip-on loafers in pale pastels and
vibrantly hued flip-flops. If you feel like a cheap thrill this is
for you.   *janeshilton.com*

Affordable   *Amex/MC/V*

020 7352 9687   **tube: Sloane Square**
164 King's Road   Mon-Sat 10-6:30 (Wed 10-7)
London SW3   Sun 12-6

Janet Reger

Sexy, sensuous, seductive—nothing will get you (or your
other half) in the mood like Reger's luxury lingerie. The label
made it big in the Sixties with fans like Bianca Jagger, and
early pieces are now desirable collectors' items. Still going
strong with daughter Aliza Reger now at the helm, the selection ranges from clinging nightgowns and peignoirs to bras
sprinkled with Swarovski crystals (sizes go from 32A to 38D)
and the pearl and lace G-strings made famous in Sex and
the City. The window displays are as adventurous and
tongue-in-cheek as Agent Provocateur's; men driving past
find it hard to keep their eyes on the road. If the items are a
little too pricey for your budget, check out the Reger range
at Debenhams.   *janetreger.com*

Expensive   *Amex/MC/V*

020 7584 9368   **tube: Knightsbridge**
2 Beauchamp Place   Mon-Sat 10-6
London SW3

Jauko

Shoppers with a weakness for Asian fashion should stop by.
The designs are fresh and modern, with only a handful of
each piece in stock. You might find a ruffled linen skirt, a
casual colourful T-shirt or a chiffon dress sprinkled with flowers. If nothing takes your fancy, the pretty patterned fans are
perfection for hot summer days with no air-conditioning. If
your timing is right you'll leave with a free gift, a Japanese
gesture of good fortune.

Moderate   *Amex/MC/V*

020 7376 1408   **tube: High Street Kensington**
34c Kensington Church Street   Mon-Sat 10-6
London W8

Jean Paul Gaultier Boutique

From the man who first gave us corsets as outerwear comes this cutting-edge boutique, where a huge plasma screen framed with purple glass in the window displays the Gallic Gaultier catwalks and reveals the fast-forward fashion awaiting inside. Shirts that look like they've been slashed with a knife might startle the traditionalist, but don't be scared off: Gaultier also has a classic side, expressed in the sharply tailored suits and sexy short dresses that pop up season after season. Still, it's his outlandish sensibility—who else has spun spider-web print trousers?—that keeps his devotees coming back for more. *jpgaultier.com*

Expensive   *Amex/MC/V*

020 7584 4648   **tube: South Kensington**
171-175 Draycott Avenue   Mon-Sat 10-6 (Wed 10-7)
London SW3

Jeans West

If you don't want to drop serious cash on the newer crop of über-brands like Earl and Paper Denim, come here. It's self-explanatory: jeans, jeans and more jeans. All types and all brands. Levi's, Pepe, Wrangler, Diesel or Lee; basic blue, stone-washed or dirty denim...Jeans West is an essential source for these essential trousers. They may be stacked from floor to ceiling, but don't be daunted. The sales staff know their stuff and can save you hours of digging. With casual shirts, belts, hats, and backpacks Jeans West takes care of your top half, too.

Affordable   *Amex/MC/V*

020 7637 1892   **tube: Oxford Circus**
The Plaza, 120 Oxford Street   Mon-Sat 10-7 (Thurs 10-8)
London W1   Sun 10-6

020 7491 4839   **tube: Oxford Circus**
5 Harewood Place   Mon-Sat 10-7 (Thurs 10-8)
London W1   Sun 12-6

Jenesis

Sadly there is a eurotrash feel to some of Jennifer Stuart-Smith's hand-picked Italian imports: a bit too much gold and too many synthetic fabrics for our taste, which seems a shame when Italian fashion has so much to offer. The pretty fitted blouses and flower-print dresses are the best of the bunch, so make this a summer break shop and you'll be less disappointed.

Moderate   *MC/V*

020 7371 5903   **tube: Parsons Green**
52 New King's Road   Mon-Sat 10-6
London SW6

Jesiré

Don't make a special trip. There is nothing fancy, trendy or unique about the clothing in this store, but its City location makes it a useful source of officewear for working girls. If we had these clothes in our wardrobe, we'd wear 'em; if we didn't, we could live without them. *jesire.net*

Moderate *Amex/MC/V*

020 7588 9141 **tube: Liverpool Street**
Unit 9, Bishopsgate Arcade Mon-Fri 10-6:30
London EC2

020 7240 6290 **tube: Covent Garden**
28 James Street Mon-Sat 10:30-7:30 (Thurs 10:30-8)
London WC2 Sun 12-6

Jesus Lopez 👤
This small boutique offers an extensive and creative array of heels, handbags and accessories. Lime-green snakeskin slip-ons and gold mules fringed in beads are just some of the highlights on the Lopez list. *jesuslopez.com*

Moderate to expensive *Amex/MC/V*

020 7486 7870 **tube: Baker Street/Bond Street**
69 Marylebone High Street Mon-Sat 10-6 (Thurs 10-7)
London W1

Jigsaw 👤👤
Ask any London girl and she's likely to tell you that this is a store she holds close to her heart. There's a real flair to the collection, where just about everything strikes the perfect note—not too mainstream, not too offbeat. It's a perfect solution for the last-minute party or the work wardrobe that's gone stale, with a design sensibility that mixes modern edge with vintage romance, from cropped tweed jackets to floral chiffon dresses to slouchy suede boots. Accessories and junior lines (see Jigsaw Junior) are sold at select stores—perfect for a mother-daughter shopping day. *jigsaw-online.com*

Moderate *Amex/MC/V*

020 7730 4404 **tube: Sloane Square**
6 Duke of York Square Mon-Fri 10:30-7 (Wed 10:30-7:30)
London SW3 Sat 10-7, Sun 12-6

020 7499 3385 **tube: Bond Street**
49 South Molton Street (accessories only) Mon-Sat 10-6:30
London W1 (Thurs 10:30-7:30), Sun 12-6

020 7491 4484 **tube: Bond Street**
126-127 New Bond Street Mon-Sat 10-6:30
London W1 (Thurs 10-7:30), Sun 12-6

020 7437 5750 **tube: Oxford Circus**
9 Argyll Street Mon-Fri 10:30-7 (Thurs 10:30-8)
London W1 Sat 10:30-6:30, Sun 12-6

020 7493 9169 **tube: Oxford Circus**
St. Christopher's Place Mon-Sat 10-6:30
London W1 (Thurs 10:30-8), Sun 12-6

020 7929 2361 **tube: Monument/Bank**
31 Leadenhall Market Mon-Fri 10-6:30
London EC3

020 7240 3855
21 Long Acre
London WC2

tube: Covent Garden
Mon-Fri 10:30-8
Sat 10:30-7, Sun 11-6

020 7497 8663
449 The Strand
London WC2

tube: Charing Cross
Mon-Fri 10-7 (Thurs 10-8)
Sat 10-6:30, Sun 12-6

020 7937 3573
65 Kensington High Street
London W8

tube: High Street Kensington
Mon-Fri 10:30-7
(Thurs 10:30-7:30), Sat 10-7, Sun 12-6

020 7584 6226
31 Brompton Road
London SW3

tube: Knightsbridge
Mon-Fri 10:30-7 (Wed 10:30-7:30)
Sat 10-7, Sun 12-6

020 7589 9530
91-97 Fulham Road
London SW3

tube: South Kensington
Mon-Sat 10-7 (Wed 10-7:30)
Sun 12-6

020 7727 0322
190-192 Westbourne Grove
London W11

tube: Notting Hill Gate
Mon-Wed 10:30-6:30
Thurs-Fri 10:30-7, Sat 10:30-6, Sun 12-6

020 7794 3014
58 Heath Street
London NW3

tube: Hampstead
Mon-Sat 10-6, Sun 12-6

020 8785 6731
114 High Street
London SW15

tube: East Putney/Putney Bridge
Mon-Sat 9:30-6, Sun 12-5

020 7329 5752
44 Bow Lane
London EC4

tube: Mansion House/St. Paul's
Mon-Wed 10-6:30, Thurs-Fri 10-7

Jigsaw Junior   ♀

Clothes so adorable, you'll wish, like the ugly sisters, that you could squeeze yourself into them. On the first floor of the massive new King's Road store, Jigsaw Junior offers a multitude of mini styles for budding young shoppers, with looks that are modern, girlish and perfectly in tune. Find sweet beaded dresses, frilly-trimmed skirts, flowered capri trousers and tiny tees. With sizes that range from a tender age two to a dangerous 13, Jigsaw Junior could be your daughter's undoing.   *jigsaw-online.com*

Moderate to expensive   Amex/MC/V

020 7730 4404
6 Duke of York Square
London SW3

tube: Sloane Square
Mon-Fri 10:30-7
(Wed 10:30-7:30) Sat 10-7, Sun 12-6

020 7491 4484
126-127 New Bond Street
London W1

tube: Bond Street
Mon-Sat 10-6:30
(Thurs 10-7:30) Sun 12-6

020 7823 8915
97 Fulham Road
London SW3

tube: South Kensington
Mon-Sat 10-7 (Wed 10-7:30)
Sun 12-6

020 7229 8654
190 Westbourne Grove
London W11

tube: Notting Hill Gate
Mon, Sat 10:30-6:30
Tues-Wed 10-6:30
Thurs-Fri 10-7, Sun 12-6

020 7431 0619   **tube: Hampstead**
83 Heath Street   Mon-Sat 10-6, Sun 12-6
London NW3

Jil Sander

Housed in what was once an impressive bank, with giant windows and a glass atrium, this elegant store is impressive and flooded with natural light. The more unusual of the designs come with bits of unexpected detail (a shoulder ruffle, a sprinkling of beading) but the majority of the collection is decidedly simple: a scooped-neck dress in vivid purple, a velvet double-breasted coat, a billowing knee-length skirt in inky blue satin. Even if you can't afford to buy, it's worth popping in just to feel the lovely fabrics.

Expensive to very expensive   *Amex/MC/V*

020 7758 1000   **tube: Green Park/Piccadilly Circus**
7 Burlington Gardens   Mon-Sat 10-6 (Thurs 10-7)
London W1

☆ Jimmy Choo

"Tread softly because you tread on my dreams" wrote W.B.Yeats, clearly anticipating a visit to Jimmy Choo's new Sloane Street store. This is shoe heaven. Daring heights and dagger-sharp toes make some styles dangerous for walkers, and cumulative cab fares should probably be factored into the price. Still, few shoes come sexier than these and, short of Manolos, there's no quicker way to earn a fashion editor's undying respect. Tulita handbags come in sizes from clutch to traveller and have quickly become the only bag for a self-respecting Bond Street girl to be seen with. The new Ross bag range is made from cashmere leather and available in gorgeous colours from blood orange to mustard—the ultimate arm candy. You know you want one… *jimmychoo.com*

Expensive to very expensive   *Amex/MC/V*

020 7493 5858   **tube: Bond Street**
27 New Bond Street   Mon-Sat 10-6 (Thurs 10-7)
London W1   Sun 12-5

020 7823 1051   **tube: Sloane Square**
32 Sloane Street   Mon-Sat 10-6 (Wed 10-7)
London SW1   Sun 12-6

Jimmy Choo Couture

Indulge in the ultimate bespoke service with a pair of hand-crafted shoes by the man himself. Visit the small, intimate boutique to choose the material, colour and trimmings, then return three to four weeks later for a final fitting. A refreshing change from the conveyor-belt world of fashion, for those lucky enough to be able to afford it.

Very expensive   *MC/V*

020 7262 6888   **tube: Marble Arch**
18 Connaught Street   Mon-Fri 10-6 (by appointment)
London W2

Jitrois

French company Jitrois is best known for its line of stretch leather, predominantly in black and brown with a bit of beige suede thrown in for a softer look. From bustiers to halternecks, with trousers that lace up the legs, the effect can be dangerous dominatrix or cool cowgirl.   *jitrois.com*

Expensive   *Amex/MC/V*

020 7245 6300   **tube: Knightsbridge**
6f Sloane Street   Mon-Sat 10-7
London SW1

Johanna Hehir

A small shop specializing in made-to-measure eveningwear and bridalwear, this store offers a more personalized level of service than most people under 40 are accustomed to. Designs are inspired by the craftsmanship and detail of the Twenties and Thirties, from flapper-style cocktail dresses to bridal gowns with accessories to match. Pinks and purples predominate and prices start at £250. Someone else will have to teach you the Charleston.   *johanna-hehir.com*

Expensive   *MC/V*

020 7486 2760   **tube: Baker Street**
10-12 Chiltern Street   Mon-Fri 11-7
London W1   Sat 10-6 (by appointment only)

John Bray

Renowned for its own-label off-the-peg suits, made from the finest Italian cloth. Styles are fashionable enough for the thirtysomething customer who prefers to steer away from the stiff old-school look, and the super-lightweight suits are particularly popular. They also sell a huge range of ties and shirts.

Expensive   *Amex/MC/V*

020 7839 6375   **tube: Green Park**
78-79 Jermyn Street   Mon-Sat 9-6 (Thurs 9-7)
London SW1

John Lewis

Londoners would be lost without their beloved John Lewis. Where else can you buy a stereo, a new pair of shoes, a backgammon board and a box of detergent, all in one go? This sister department store to Peter Jones in Sloane Square has been around since 1864. Renowned for its good value, the store promises that if you see something you've bought priced for less elsewhere, they'll match it or refund the difference. It's a safe place to take your mother-in-law shopping: she can check out the haberdashery department while you stroke Joseph sheepskin. Other chic collections from the likes of Gérard Darel, Betty Barclay and MaxMara attract the Sloane Ranger crowd (and some very discerning boys and girls from Vogue House, only a couple of blocks away).   *johnlewis.co.uk*

Affordable to expensive   *MC/V*

020 7629 7711
278-306 Oxford Street
London W1

tube: Oxford Circus/Bond Street
Mon-Sat 9:30-7 (Thurs 9:30-8)
Sun 12-6

John Lobb

Gentleman with a penchant for serious shoes should head to John Lobb, all of whose stores, with one exception (see below), are owned by Hermès. That means three in Tokyo, three in Paris, the Rodeo Drive store in Beverly Hills and the Madison Avenue store in Manhattan. Plus, of course, this airy store in Jermyn Street where you'll find ready-made classical English footwear like you never imagined and a wonderfully gracious, old-world atmosphere. *johnlobb.co.uk*

Very expensive   *Amex/MC/V*

020 7930 8089
88 Jermyn Street
London SW1

tube: Piccadilly Circus/Green Park
Mon-Sat 10-6 (Thurs 10-7)

John Lobb (private)

The exception to the above is the shop round the corner from Jermyn Street in St James's Street. This more traditional-looking store is independent (dating from 1849) and still family-owned, and is the bespoke specialist, often referred to as the world's finest bespoke shoemaker. Some styles might be a bit too dressy, but if you want to be shod in the same quality as royalty and celebrities the world over, this is the shop for you. Remember to go to the bank first, though. A pair of made-to-measure gentleman's shoes (plus their shoe trees) starts at £1,900—that'll be for the basic, cheapest leather—and a pair of riding boots at £2,500...before VAT, of course.

Very expensive   *Amex/MC/V*

020 7930 3664
9 St James's Street
London SW1

tube: Green Park
Mon-Fri 9-5:30, Sat 9-4:30

John Richmond

A British designer with Italian influences, John Richmond claims to be inspired by music (he has dressed Madonna, Mick Jagger and George Michael) and street chic. His first London store has black stone interiors, a glass-floored entrance and projectors screening a fashion show—it's all very catwalk, darling. Clothing includes beaded tank tops, satin slashed jackets, ruffled skirts and embroidered white shirts. Bags, belts and kitten heels complete the clubbing look. *johnrichmond.com*

Moderate to expensive   *Amex/MC/V*

020 7287 1860
54 Conduit Street
London W1

tube: Oxford Circus
Mon-Sat 10-6

John Smedley

It's a bit like an upmarket Gap for the seriously loaded. John Smedley is known for his fine merino wool, and specialises in sweaters, turtlenecks and twinsets that are beloved by everyone from Madonna to Tom Cruise. Cashmere, woollen silk and sea-island cotton also feature. Classic with the occasional twist, the styles are as universally pleasing as the quality. We would shop here every day if we could afford to. *johnsmedley.com*

Expensive   *Amex/MC/V*

020 7495 2222   **tube: Bond Street**
24 Brook Street   Mon-Sat 10-6 (Thurs 10-7)
London W1

Jones

Featuring creations from a legion of top cutting-edge designers—Raf Simons, Martin Margiela, Helmut Lang, Hussein Chalayan—Jones has a brilliantly funky menswear selection and attracts arty late twenty- and early thirtysomethings with impeccable taste. For Notting Hill wannabes savouring the starving-artist-cum-punk-rocker look, this is the place to find Alexander McQueen's jeans collection and a bevy of other looks to flatter that bed head. The staff are a bit too cool for skool, but know their stuff. *jones-clothing.co.uk*

Expensive   *Amex/MC/V*

020 7240 8312   **tube: Covent Garden**
13 Floral Street   Mon-Sat 10-6:30, Sun 1-5
London WC2

Jones the Bootmaker

Affordable, durable and wearable, the dull styles churned out by this long-established shoe label are perfect for young professionals or those with a conservative sensibility. From classic leather wingtips and square-toed office shoes to Camper lace-ups and Church's loafers, nothing will make your heart skip a beat. But for a solid pair of winter boots, you could do worse than come here—they don't call themselves "the Bootmaker" for nothing. We hate to admit it, but sometimes reliability is a better bet than frivolous excitement. *jonesbootmaker.com*

Moderate   *Amex/MC/V*

020 7930 8864   **tube: Piccadilly Circus/Green Park**
112 Jermyn Street   Mon-Sat 9:30-6
London SW1

020 7408 1974   **tube: Bond Street**
15 South Molton Street   Mon-Sat 10-6:30 (Thurs 10-7)
London W1   Sun 11:30-5:30

020 7823 8024   **tube: Knightsbridge**
187 Brompton Road   Mon-Fri 10-6:30 (Wed 10-7)
London SW3   Sat 10:30-6:30, Sun 12-6

020 7240 6558   **tube: Covent Garden**
16 New Row   Mon-Sat 10-6:30 (Thurs 10-7)
London WC2   Sun 12-5

020 7734 2351   **tube: Oxford Circus**
15 Foubert's Place   Mon-Fri 10-7, Sat 10-6:30
London W1   Sun 11:30-5:30

020 7836 5079 (M)
7-8 Langley Court
London WC2

tube: Covent Garden
(opening hours as above)

020 7937 5440
26 Kensington Church Street
London W8

tube: High Street Kensington
(opening hours as above)

020 7730 1545
57-59 King's Road
London SW3

tube: Sloane Square
Mon-Sat 10-7, Sun 12-6

020 7929 2732
15 Cullum Street
London EC3

tube: Monument
Mon-Fri 9-5:30

020 7248 1828
70-71 Watling Street
London EC4

tube: Mansion House
Mon-Fri 9-6
(Thurs 9-6:30)

020 7831 1850
320 High Holborn
London WC1

tube: Chancery Lane
Mon-Fri 9-6

020 7531 1677
Cabot Place East
London E14

tube: Canary Wharf
Mon-Fri 9-7
Sat 10-6, Sun 12-5

020 7626 3773
119 Cannon Street
London EC4

tube: Cannon Street
Mon-Fri 9-6

☆ Joseph 👫

Joseph Ettedgui is master of his own style empire with a ubiquitous signature label which has won him legions of fans. His subtly stylish boot-cut, hip-hugging trousers are a flattering wardrobe essential, sexy yet reliable; slick urban separates, in sophisticated neutral tones, feed a fashionista's craving for trends with a twist. Little details, such as coloured piping down the side seams of trousers, or pearly buttons on fitted T-shirts ensure a look classic enough to last more than one season. The Brompton Cross flagship carries other designers as well, including Prada, Gucci and Helmut Lang. Don't let limited cash flow deter you: the King's Road discount shop offers last season's stock at joyously low prices.

Expensive

Amex/MC/V

020 7730 2395
76 Duke of York Square
London SW3

tube: Sloane Square
Mon-Sat 10-6:30
Sun 12-5

020 7823 9500 (W)
77 Fulham Road
London SW3

tube: South Kensington
Mon-Sat 10-6:30 (Wed 10-7)
Sun 12-5

020 7352 6776
299 Fulham Road
London SW3

tube: South Kensington
Mon-Fri 11-8
Sat 10-6:30, Sun 12-5

020 7591 0808 (M)
74 Sloane Avenue
London SW3

tube: South Kensington
(opening hours as above)

020 7225 3335
315 Brompton Road
London SW3

tube: South Kensington
(opening hours as above)

020 7730 7562
53 King's Road
London SW3

tube: Sloane Square
Mon-Sat 10:30-6:30
(Wed 10:30-7), Sun 12-5

020 7235 1991
16 Sloane Street
London SW1

tube: Sloane Square
Mon-Sat 10-6:30 (Wed 10-7)

020 7629 3713
23 Old Bond Street
London W1

tube: Green Park
Mon-Sat 10-6:30 (Thurs 10-7)
Sun 12-5

020 7629 6077 (W)
28 Brook Street
London W1

tube: Bond Street
(opening hours as above)

020 7240 1199
15 Floral Street
London WC2

tube: Covent Garden
Mon-Sat 10:30-7 (Thurs 10:30-7:30)
Sun 12:30-5:30

020 7243 9920
236 Westbourne Grove
London W11

tube: Notting Hill Gate
Mon-Sat 10-6:30
Sun 1-6

020 8946 5880
64 High Street
London SW19

tube: Wimbledon
Mon-Sat 10-6, Sun 12:30-5

020 7722 5883
21 St John's Wood High Street
London NW8

tube: St John's Wood
Mon-Fri 10-6
Sat 10-6:30, Sun 12-5

Joseph Azagury   ♀

Across the street from brother Jacques' clothing store, Joseph Azagury offers a refined selection of shoes well worthy of their Knightsbridge address. Strappy sandals and high-heeled boots are favourites, chic but still delicate enough for ladies who lunch.

Expensive   *Amex/MC/V*

020 7259 6887
73 Knightsbridge
London SW1

tube: Knightsbridge/Hyde Park Corner
Mon-Sat 10-6 (Wed 10-7)

Joujou & Lucy   ♂

This pint-size Little Venice boutique will have grown-up girls wishing for Alice in Wonderland's "Drink Me" shrinking formula. Exquisite frilled dresses by Trussardi Junior, bold Kenzo jungle prints, tough-nut gear from Timberland… if only we could squeeze into it. Joujou Lucy is particularly perfect for the novice uncle or godparent in search of presents: the charming Iranian owner will steer you through the choice of international labels while soothing opera plays in the background. Sizes go up to age 12 for girls and around four for boys.

Expensive   *MC/V*

020 7289 0866
32 Clifton Road
London W9

tube: Warwick Avenue
Mon-Sat 10-6 (Sun 12-4)

Jungle

A specialist in army and other government clothing, Jungle is a dense wilderness of sweaters, rucksacks and shirts, as well as camouflage trousers in a mind-boggling range of colours, including ones which can't be detected by night vision goggles—how have we lived without them? Staff are friendly and informative. Not a destination for the fashion-conscious, but this place offers plenty of sturdy gear at low prices.   *jungleclothing.com*

Affordable   *Amex/MC/V*

020 7379 5379   **tube: Covent Garden/Leicester Square**
7 Earlham Street   Mon-Wed 10-6:30, Thurs-Sat 10-7
London WC2   Sun 12-5:30

Kamara

Classic Italian fashion is the speciality at this cosy, inviting boutique. We particularly liked the structured black silk jackets embroidered with green flowers, while studded handbags in pink, black and white are fun but not to everyone's taste. They also sell jewellery by Otazu, who designed the pieces for the film Moulin Rouge.   *kamara.co.uk*

Moderate to expensive   *Amex/MC/V*

020 7493 9222   **tube: Bond Street**
3 Gees Court   Mon-Sat 10:30-7
London W1   Sun 11:30-5:30

Kanves

This mens' boutique stocks great labels for the preppy-allergic, including John Paul Gaultier, Dirk Bikkemberg, Viktor & Rolf and a small DSquared2 selection for women. The look is urban and simple, accessorised with shoes by Puma, Costume National and Roberto Cavalli. A fan contacted us to commend the staff: "They're friendly and try to be helpful, especially difficult when the supply of arty clothes is as unpredictable as the sizing."   *kanves.co.uk*

Expensive   *Amex/MC/V*

020 7734 7300   **tube: Piccadilly Circus**
19 & 20 Brewer Street   Mon-Sat 11-8, Sun 1-6
London W1

Karen Millen

A typically (and infuriatingly) unpredictable high street chain. One week you might discover a hugely desirable collection, the next week nothing will catch your eye. On a good day, sharp suits, sexy shoes and dramatic dresses are perfect for confident women looking for feminine fashion at an upper-mid price range. On a bad day, the bold designs are too far-fetched and sexy veers the wrong side of tarty. Cuts tend to suit the more petite figure and sizes only go up to a diminutive 14. A small selection of footwear is available in all stores, but if you want more the 46 South Molton Street branch carries only bags and shoes. Here you can find the perfect Millen complement,

be it a clutch bag, purple snakeskin knee-high boot or pink
gemstone sandal. *karenmillen.com*

Moderate   *Amex/MC/V*

020 7495 5297   **tube: Bond Street**
46 South Molton Street   Mon-Sat 10-6:30 (Thurs 10-7:30)
London W1   Sun 12-6

020 7629 5539   **tube: Bond Street**
57 South Molton Street   Mon-Sat 10-6:30 (Thurs 10-7:30)
London W1   Sun 12-6

020 7287 6158   **tube: Oxford Circus**
262-264 Regent Street   Mon-Fri 10-8 (Thurs 10-8:30)
London W1   Sat 10-7:30, Sun 12-6

020 7938 3758   **tube: High Street Kensington**
4 Barkers Arcade   Mon-Sat 10-6:30 (Thurs 10-7:30)
London W8   Sun 12-6

020 7730 7259   **tube: Sloane Square**
33e King's Road   Mon-Sat 10-6:30 (Wed 10-7)
London SW3   Sun 12-6

020 7225 0174   **tube: Knightsbridge**
33 Brompton Road   Mon-Sat 10-7
London SW3   Sun 12-6

020 7836 5355   **tube: Covent Garden**
22-23 James Street   Mon-Sat 10:30-7:30, Thurs 10:30-8
London WC2   Sun 12-6

020 7229 6924   **tube: Queensway/Bayswater**
Whiteley's, Queensway   Mon-Sat 10-8
London W2   Sun 12-6

020 7256 6728   **tube: Liverpool Street**
135 Bishopsgate   Mon-Fri 10-6:30
London EC2   (Thurs 10-7)

020 7626 2782   **tube: Bank**
1-2 Royal Exchange Buildings   Mon-Fri 8-6
London EC3   (Thurs 8-7)

020 7794 3686   **tube: Hampstead**
4 Hampstead High Street   Mon-Sat 10-6
London NW3   Sun 12-6

Katch   👤

Yummy mummies and the Harrods crowd flock to this shoe
emporium. The selection isn't extensive—it's more about
the frightfully good-taste display. Emanuel Ungaro,
Givency, Christian Lacroix and Valentino sit in pairs on top
of a mirrored Georgian table and in glass cases. There are
lots of heels but if you do fancy some casual flats think
exotic Emilio Pucci thong sandals or Marc Jacobs floral
pumps. Rock & Republic bootleg jeans and party dresses
by Sanimi are at hand if you haven't come in the right
attire. *katchfashion.com*

Expensive   *Amex/MC/V*

020 7052 9200   **tube: South Kensington**
91 Walton Street   Mon-Sat 11-7
London SW3   Sun 12-6

020 7467 0777
185 Westbourne Grove
London W11

tube: Notting Hill Gate
Mon-Sat 11-7
Sun 12-6

Kate Kuba

Once you get past the slightly intimidating atmosphere of this shoe shop, you'll find hot pink clogs, gold high-heeled slingbacks and pretty flat sandals. Handbags are also available, from small yellow crescent shapes for day to bejewelled evening creations. You'll be pleasantly surprised by the reasonable prices too. *katekuba.com*

Moderate to expensive   *Amex/MC/V*

020 7499 2626
26 Brook Street
London W1

tube: Oxford Circus
Mon-Sat 10-6:30
Sun 12-6

020 7259 0011
22-23 Duke of York Square
London SW3

tube: Sloane Square
(opening hours as above)

Ken Smith Designs

It's possible that the obscure location, on an inconspicuous side street off Goodge Street, has limited the profile of this pleasing little plus-size boutique. There's no reason it should remain a secret, though. Selection is particularly chic for sizes 16-32, from jeans and casual tops to eveningwear. Colour reigns supreme—no black to hide behind here. If you're lucky, Ken himself will be there to offer his expert eye.

Moderate to expensive   *Amex/MC/V*

020 7631 3341
6 Charlotte Place
London W1

tube: Goodge Street
Mon-Fri 10-6, Sat 10-2
(some Sundays 11-2)

Kenneth Cole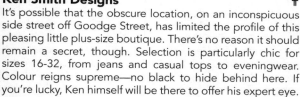

Cole is best known for his smart functional shoes, from suede heels to leather loafers, but his accessible ready-to-wear lines for men and women are proving equally appealing. The look is clean-cut and urban—leather jackets, tailored trousers, fitted shirts—smarter than Next but not as interesting as Karen Millen. The shop on Sloane Street sells accessories, luggage, watches and outerwear. *kennethcole.com*

Moderate   *Amex/MC/V*

020 7235 0564
3 Sloane Street
London SW1

tube: Knightsbridge
Mon-Sat 10-7, Sun 12-6

020 7730 4360
33 King's Road
London SW3

tube: Sloane Square
Mon-Sat 10-7 (Wed 10-7:30), Sun 12-6

Kenzo

Kenzo Takada has retired but his Japanese design aesthetic continues to flourish under the ownership of the LVMH group. Bright colours, wonderful patterns and avant-garde cuts are not for the meek, but if you like to forge your own

117

style with a mixture of bohemian and classic pieces then Kenzo should take a starring role in your wardrobe. The label is loved by the French for its neat petite shapes with feminine flourishes and for its historical detailing, from billowing puffed sleeves to ruffled necklines. If you prefer to invest in just one "Wow" item, pick from the stunning array of scarves in silk, chiffon or woven wool. Some are reversible and all are eye-catchingly pretty. Once you have got your eye in, you will be able to spot a Kenzo ensemble a mile off. They are invariable stylish, adventurous and lively.   kenzonet.com

Expensive   *Amex/MC/V*

020 7225 1960   **tube: South Kensington**
70 Sloane Avenue   Mon-Sat 10-6:30 (Wed 10-7)
London SW3   Sun 1-6 (summer), 12-5 (winter)

☆ Kew

Kew is a bold new brand which successfully brings comfortable, affordable clothing to the high street. Owned by the same company as Jigsaw, you can spot the similarities—a natural-coloured palette, plenty of useful separates (including a huge variety of T-shirts), flattering A-line skirts and sturdy coats. Like Jigsaw, the look combines country-style clothing with a sleek urban edge. Blue and brown striped V-neck jumpers are lined with a ruffle trim and casual cord trousers are low slung and curve-hugging. You won't find anything cutting-edge here, but you will find familiar favourites that will blend seamlessly into your wardrobe   kew-online.com

Affordable   *MC/V*

020 7823 7304   **tube: Sloane Square**
124 King's Road   Mon-Fri 10-7
London SW3   Sun 12-6

020 7937 8850   **tube: High Street Kensington**
123c Kensington High Street   Mon-Sat 10-7
London W8   (Thurs 10-7:30) Sun 12-6

020 7229 7609   **tube: Queensway/Bayswater**
Whiteley's, Queensway   Mon-Sat 10-8
London W2   Sun 12-6

Kilgour French Stanbury

Probably the trendiest and savviest of the traditional Savile Row tailors, Kilgour French Stanbury has revamped a brand that had long been cool enough for the likes of Cary Grant and various James Bonds. Cashmere jumpers, sheepskin coats and corduroy blazers are the highlights of the ready-to-wear collection, and there are also plans for a new luggage collection. With its traditional bespoke service (and a semi-bespoke service) still thriving, KFS pulls a wide clientele of celebrities, hip young men about town and more seasoned clients. It's a particular favourite with the style-setters at *GQ* magazine, two blocks away in Vogue House.   8savilerow.com

Expensive   *Amex/MC/V*

020 7734 6905   tube: Piccadilly Circus/Oxford Circus
8 Savile Row   Mon-Fri 9-6, Sat 10:30-6
London W1

Directory

King's Road Sporting Club

This store leads the way in cutting-edge sportswear, and a major refurbishment has modernized the environment too. The staff are knowledgeable and helpful, and the range strikes the perfect balance between athletic and fashionable, from stylish yoga trousers to colourful men's swimming trunks. Season permitting you'll find bikinis, sports bras, T-shirts, running shorts and jackets. Big brands like Nike, Quiksilver, O'Neill, Nautica and Billabong are stocked alongside the store's reliable signature collection. *krsc.co.uk*

Moderate   *Amex/MC/V*

020 7589 5418   tube: Sloane Square
38-42 King's Road   Mon-Sat 10-6:30 (Wed 10-7)
London SW3   Sun 12-6

Kit Clothing/Twentieth Century Frox

Spring has sprung at this colourful shop where the racks are grouped in pinks, blues and greens with a splash of white thrown in. There are some lovely casual pieces including NafNaf cardigans, linen dresses by Out of Exile and knitwear by Anthology. Other girly bits include beaded flip-flops and baskets with bows. A secret surprise awaits at the back of the store where you'll find a brilliant dress-for-hire service, Twentieth Century Frox, featuring sparkling eveningwear for those more glamorous occasions.

Moderate   *MC/V*

020 7731 3242   tube: Parsons Green
614 Fulham Road   Mon, Wed-Thurs 10-7
London SW6   Tues, Fri-Sat 10-6

Knickerbox

If you're running low on underwear, and you've already tried Marks & Spencer, Knickerbox is the natural next stop. From sheer to lacy, eye-catching colours and comfortable designs are the key ingredients of this chain's success. Selection includes bras (up to an E cup), panties, T-shirts and tanks, featuring a mix of intricate patterns and simpler sporty styles. They also have matching pyjama sets.   *knickerbox.com*

Affordable   *Amex/MC/V*

020 7499 6144   tube: Oxford Circus
281a Regent Street   Mon-Sat 9-6 (Thurs 9-7)
London W1   Sun 12-5

020 7823 4437   tube: Sloane Square
28 Sloane Square   Mon-Sat 9:30-7 (Wed 9-8)
London SW1   Sun 12-6

020 7937 8887   tube: High Street Kensington
Kensington Arcade   Mon-Sat 9-7 (Thurs 9-8)
London W8   Sun 12-6

020 7353 5965   **tube: Temple**
69 Fleet Street   Mon-Fri 8:30-6
London EC4

Koh Samui

Rub shoulders with celebs and their stylists, as well as die-hard followers of fashion. A seriously savvy boutique, Koh Samui offers some of the season's finest and most eclectic pieces. Clothing tends towards the avant garde and consistently features the hottest British labels. Shoppers can head straight for their favourite colours, as the store is organized by shade: bright and baby pinks in one corner, mossy green and turquoise in another. Only one of each item is displayed, creating the impression that each piece is a one-off. Below the racks of dresses, skirts, and tops rest rows of matching shoes. Designers include Chloé, Matthew Williamson, Dries Van Noten, Marc Jacobs, Vanessa Bruno and Jimmy Choo. Jewellery and handbags are also available. Paradise for the hardcore shopper.

Expensive   *Amex/MC/V*

020 7240 4280   **tube: Covent Garden**
65-67 Monmouth Street   Mon-Tues, Sat 10-6:30
London WC2   Wed, Fri 10:30-6:30
      Thurs 10:30-7, Sun 11:30-5:30

Kokon to Zai

This finger-on-the-pulse boutique sells a could-not-be-cooler mix of progressive dance music and fashion. Funky new talents top the rails—Marjan Pejoski, Viktor & Rolf, Bernard Willhelm—and new pieces quickly replace the old. New too is the shop's own label, K-Z, which is equally cutting-edge. Hip accessories like beaded chokers, soft leather bags, diamond gecko pins and extra-wide leather belts are straight out of the fashion pages. Extra points if you can figure out what the name means.

Affordable to expensive   *Amex/MC/V*

020 7434 1316   **tube: Piccadilly Circus**
57 Greek Street   Mon-Sat 11-7:30, Sun 12-6
London W1

Kookaï

Trendy Kookaï brings Parisian disco-style to the masses. Prices are low and colours all over the spectrum, from a pink baby-doll T-shirt to trousers in basic black. Quality, on the other hand, is consistently mediocre. Embellishments like rhinestones and stripes are used liberally, and synthetic skirts, dresses and casual T-shirts are popular pieces. If you're between 14 and 23, Kookaï, Oasis and Warehouse (all cheap and fun) should be on your list.   *kookai.co.uk*

Moderate   *Amex/MC/V*

020 7938 1427   **tube: High Street Kensington**
123d Kensington High Street   Mon-Sat 10-7 (Thurs 10-8)
London W8   Sun 12-6

020 7581 9633
5-7 Brompton Road
London SW3

tube: Knightsbridge
Mon-Fri 10-7 (Wed 10-7:30)
Sat 10-7, Sun 12-6

020 7408 2391
257-259 Oxford Street
London W1

tube: Oxford Circus
Mon-Wed 10-7, Thurs-Sat 10-8
Sun 12-6

020 7730 6903
27a Sloane Square
London SW1

tube: Sloane Square
Mon-Sat 10-7 (Wed 10-7:30)
Sun 12-6

020 7240 0997
39 Long Acre
London WC2

tube: Covent Garden
Mon-Sat 10-7 (Thurs 10-8)
Sun 12-6

Krizia

Mariuccia Mandelli, Krizia's creator, so effectively grasps the relationship between fashion and physical form that her designs seem sculpted for the body. From tailored suits to T-shirts the collection is made mostly of cashmere and wool in fall and winter, linen in spring and summer. Her crowning glory is her bright knitwear. Men will find linen shirts and immaculately sharp business suits. It's all perfectly wearable, although the leather skirts and chi-chi sunglasses might seem scarily Italian.

Expensive

krizia.net

Amex/MC/V

020 7491 4987
24-25 Conduit Street
London W1

tube: Oxford Circus
Mon-Sat 10-6

Kruszynska

You're Daddy's little princess, but can you charm him into splashing out £15,000 for your wedding dress? If so, a pale pink tulle gown sprinkled with tiny pink stars and finished with a scallop-edged three-metre train could be yours. Since not all blushing brides want to make their guests gasp, the Polish-born Kruszynska sisters also do understated (and more moderately priced) wedding gowns, as well as subtly coloured eveningwear elaborately detailed with Swarovski crystals, hand embroidery or trails of chantilly lace.

Very expensive

MC/V

020 7589 0745
35 Beauchamp Place
London SW3

tube: Knightsbridge
Mon-Fri 9:30-6:30, Sat 10-6:30

Kurt Geiger

The South Molton Street store has wide-ranging appeal: strappy high heels for the teenage clubber, the KG diffusion line for the catwalk-conscious, and leather ankle boots and kitten heels with buckles and bling for everyone else. The store also offers a wide variety of other brands from Marc Jacobs to Gucci.

Moderate to expensive

kurtgeiger.com

Amex/MC/V

020 7546 1888
65 South Molton Street
London W1

tube: Bond Street
Mon-Sat 10-7 (Thurs 10-8)
Sun 12-6

020 7937 3716   tube: **High Street Kensington**
133 Kensington High Street   (opening hours as above)
London W8

The L Boutique

This is a one-stop shop for rich women seeking an opulent look unique to them. If you're tired of trends or want to transform a simple black dress into something unforgettable, Lucia Silver's boudoir boutique could be the answer. Lucia offers a personal styling service to help customers develop a signature look and her feminine, theatrical clothing makes a strong statement. There are Moroccan Thirties-style organza coats, intricate brocade jackets, pretty bias-cut dresses, silk kimonos and masses of accessories from butterfly hairclips and semiprecious chokers to ostrich feather headpieces. If you can afford to shop here, rest assured your clothing will help you stand out in a crowd.   *l-boutique.com*

Expensive   *MC/V*

020 7243 9190   tube: **Notting Hill Gate**
28 Chepstow Corner   Tues-Sat 10:30-6
London W2

L.K.Bennett

Go to an English country wedding and we guarantee that at least half the girls will be shod by L.K.Bennett. (To make yourself popular, offer elastoplast—these beautiful shoes can be blisteringly uncomfortable.) Feminine sophistication is the ongoing theme here, with simple silhouettes often lightly embellished with a tiny bow or a bit of embroidery. Kitten heels are the shape of every season. They also do a hit-and-miss clothing line—Jackie O-style suits and dinky bags to see you through Ascot week, an imaginative selection of coats, and a workwear line which is workably wearable.

Expensive   *Amex/MC/V*

020 7491 3005 & Mail Order   tube: **Bond Street**
31 Brook Street   Mon-Sat 10-7 (Thurs 10-8)
London W1   Sun 11-6

020 7499 7949   tube: **Bond Street**
25 Brook Street   (opening hours as above)
London W1

020 7881 0766   tube: **Sloane Square**
20-23 Duke of York Square   Mon-Sat 10-7
London SW3   Sun 11-6

020 7352 8066 (shoes only)   tube: **Sloane Square**
83 King's Road   Mon-Sat 10-7 (Wed 10-8)
London SW3   Sun 11-6

020 7351 1231   tube: **Sloane Square**
97 King's Road   (opening hours as above)
London SW3

020 7376 4108 (sale shop)   tube: **Sloane Square**
239 King's Road   (opening hours as above)
London SW3

Directory

020 7376 7241
219 King's Road
London SW3

tube: Sloane Square
Mon-Sat 10-6:30, Sun 11-6

020 7379 1710
130 Long Acre
London WC2

tube: Covent Garden
Mon-Sat 10:30-7:30 (Thurs 10:30-8)
Sun 11-6

020 7937 6895
1 Kensington Church Street
London W8

tube: High Street Kensington
Mon-Sat 10-7
Sun 11-6

020 7792 4678
220 Westbourne Grove
London W11

tube: Notting Hill Gate
Mon-Sat 10-6:30
Sun 11-6

020 7431 1977
23 Hampstead High Street
London NW3

tube: Hampstead
Mon-Sat 9:30-6
Sun 11-6

020 7283 4744
1-2 Royal Exchange Buildings
London EC3

tube: Bank
Mon-Fri 9-7

020 7719 0090
31 Jubilee Place
London E14

tube: Canary Wharf
Mon-Fri 9-7, Sat 10-6
Sun 12-6

La Perla

If women could pick one underwear shop to go wild in, you can bet money they would choose La Perla. Exquisitely delicate and decadently expensive, this Italian label offers what is arguably some of the finest lingerie in the world. From elegant to demure to downright seductive, the whole range of boudoir sensibilities is represented here. Practicality comes into play as well, with multi-functional bras and slimming panties. Don't forget to check out the sleepwear and swimwear. *laperla.com*

Expensive *Amex/MC/V*

020 7245 0527
163 Sloane Street
London SW1

tube: Knightsbridge
Mon-Sat 10-6 (Wed 10-7)

La Scala

In lovely Chelsea Green, this secondhand store is refreshingly bright and offers a great selection of top-notch, nearly new designer clothing and accessories. Browse and find a linen dress by Ralph Lauren or some perfectly cut Joseph trousers for less than half their original price. Throw in shoes by Jimmy Choo, Gucci or Prada and you're ready to start dancing.

Moderate *Amex/MC/V*

020 7589 2784
39 Elystan Street
London SW3

tube: South Kensington
Mon-Sat 10-5:30

La Senza

If you're like most women, shopping for underwear is one excursion you're not dying to make. But when it's got to be done, this is a great place to do it. La Senza could be seen as a cheaper version of La Perla or Rigby & Peller. Granny pants or a lace teddy, no matter what your heart (or sweetheart) fancies this store has a wide selection of reasonable quality, affordably priced lingerie, from matching bra-and-knicker sets to provocative silk and satin sleepwear. *lasenza.com*

Affordable   *Amex/MC/V*

020 7580 3559   **tube: Oxford Circus**
162 Oxford Street   Mon-Sat 10-7 (Thurs 10-8)
London W1   Sun 12-6

020 7630 6948   **tube: Victoria**
8 Kingsgate Parade   Mon-Fri 9-6 (Thurs 9-7)
London SW1   Sat 9:30-5:30

Lacoste

The embroidered alligator logo will never quite reach the status it achieved in the Eighties when the Lacoste polo shirt, collar up, was de rigueur with the sloaney, yuppie crowd. However, a groovy modern shop, complete with mini video screenings of sports events and ambient lighting, shifts the label into the contemporary limelight. The knit piqué shirt comes in over 40 colours, from bright white to dusty rose, and more sporting styles include soft shirts and jersey dresses. *lacoste.com*

Moderate   *Amex/MC/V*

020 7225 2851   **tube: Knightsbridge**
52 Brompton Road   Mon-Sat 10-7
London SW1   Sun 12-6

020 7491 8968   **tube: Oxford Circus**
233 Regent Street   Mon-Sat 10-7 (Thurs 10-8)
London W1   Sun 12-6

Laden Showroom

Packed to the rafters with vintage finds and new designers, the Laden Showroom offers racks and racks of funky clothing. Hidden treasures include Charles of London T-shirts, Escape Velocity's one-off lace dresses and the full range from Red Mother. Give yourself time to browse around. *laden.co.uk*

Affordable to moderate   *Amex/MC/V*

020 7247 2431   **tube: Aldgate East**
103 Brick Lane   Mon-Sat 12-6
London E1   Sun 10:30-6

Lanvin

This French label, established in 1889, is trying to reposition itself as a world-class couture house. The clothing is traditional, simple (though in the most sophisticated sense) and of the highest quality. Known for its fine fabrics and tailored suits, Lanvin takes subtle elegance down to the last stitch. *lanvin.com*

Expensive *Amex/MC/V*

020 7499 2929 **tube: Bond Street**
108 New Bond Street Mon-Sat 10-6:30 (Thurs 10-7)
London W1

Laundry Industry

It sounds progressive and, in terms of decor, it certainly is, with minimalist space and a stone floor that slopes. The clothing, on the other hand, is quite conventional: cotton and silk tops in seasonal colours, linen suits and a limited selection of bags, perfumes and belts are on offer. Three Dutch owner/designers based in Amsterdam have created a wearable selection of clothing that is practical and generation-free. Useful though it may be, ultimately this shop offers more style than substance.

Affordable to moderate *Amex/MC/V*

020 7792 7967 **tube: Notting Hill Gate**
186 Westbourne Grove Mon-Sat 10-6
London W11 Sun 11-6

Laura Tom

It's summer all year long at this hidden holidaywear shop in Fulham. You'll find bikinis, swimsuits, cotton capri pants and long linen trousers, sweet floaty dresses, plenty of T-shirts and a pretty selection of cashmere cardigans for chilly evenings. Other highlights include Thai wraparound trousers made in contrasting shades of shot silk, and clever halterneck tops with built-in bras to be worn with trousers or matching bikini bottoms. Dotted around the store are beach bags embellished with embroidered butterflies, wide-brimmed straw hats and sequined sandals. There are also a few pickings from abroad to get you in the mood—kikoys from Kenya and Chinese floral fans. The perfect stop-off when you're heading for the sun and all the shops are filled with depressing heavy winter stuff. *lauratom.com*

Moderate *MC/V*

020 7736 3393 **tube: Fulham Broadway**
The Gasworks Mon-Fri 10-6, Sat 10-4
Redloh House
2 Michael Road
London SW6

Laurence Tavernier

Ladies of leisure be careful. The traditional French nightwear by Tavernier is so soft and comfortable you'll want to stay in bed all day. From silk nightgowns to striped cotton pyjamas, the effect is old-fashioned and homely. Tavernier's bathrobes and cotton dressing-gowns are also perfect for lounging at the weekend, though the prices may not make you feel so relaxed.

Expensive Amex/MC/V
020 7823 8737 **tube: South Kensington**
77 Walton Street Mon-Sat 10-6
London SW3

Le Silla

Sexy shoes straight from Milan create a stiletto-strong collection for women who like their shoes to stand out. Silver, gold and fuchsia pink are the colours of the moment and the designs are determinedly individual. There are pink and blue snakeskin boots, and gold slingbacks are embellished with diamanté stars and the word "rock". Not for the conservative, these shoes are made for dancing all night. *lesilla.com*

Expensive Amex/MC/V
020 7589 5717 **tube: South Kensington**
133 Fulham Road Mon-Sat 10-6:30
London SW3 Sun 12-5

Levi's

Founded in 1853, this American jeans company has revolutionized its selection beyond the 501, creating innovative "twisted" styles and loose cuts with back pockets turned on a bias and dropped a few inches below the waist. The store, which has been given a new airy look, is a denim wonderland, with a few T-shirts, jackets and accessories thrown in. And if you can't find that perfect pair off the rack, you can customise your own. *levi.com*

Affordable Amex/MC/V
020 7292 2500 **tube: Oxford Circus**
174-176 Regent Street Mon-Wed, Fri 10-7, Thurs-Sat 10-8
London W1 Sun 12-7

020 7409 2692 **tube: Oxford Circus**
269 Regent Street Mon-Sat 10-7 (Thurs 10-8)
London W1 Sun 12-6

020 7497 0566 **tube: Covent Garden**
117a Long Acre Mon-Tues 10-7, Wed-Sat 10-7:30
London WC2 (Thurs 10-8), Sun 12-6

020 7938 4254 **tube: High Street Kensington**
171 Kensington High Street Mon-Sat 10-7
London W8 (Thurs 10-7:30), Sun 12-6

☆ Liberty

Not so much a shop as a fashion institution, this landmark Tudor mansion perfectly placed between Mayfair and Soho was once Arthur Liberty's warehouse for goods shipped from the Orient. Liberty is recognized for carrying hip names from Roland Mouret to Ann Demeulemeester as well as its own famous floral prints. There's an astonishing beauty department and separate areas for jewellery, gifts, linens, homewares and Arts and Crafts antiques. The refurbished western wing offers cosmetics, menswear and accessories. Don't miss this place at sale time. *liberty.co.uk*

Expensive   *Amex/MC/V*

020 7734 1234   **tube: Oxford Circus**
210-220 Regent Street   Mon-Sat 10-7 (Thurs 10-8)
London W1   Sun 12-6

The Library   �

Shhh…don't be fooled by the name. The small selection of decorative books on these shelves is only a subplot, the real story being trendsetting menswear. The protagonists are edgy designers like Dirk Schönberger, Alexander McQueen and Maharishi and you'll find all styles of casualwear from jeans and cords to funky sweaters. More formal business attire from luminaries like Dries Van Noten can be found downstairs. The staff look super-cool in their street-style clothing, but don't be intimidated: they are friendly and attentive.

Expensive   *Amex/MC/V*

020 7589 6569   **tube: South Kensington/Knightsbridge**
268 Brompton Road   Mon-Sat 10-6:30 (Wed 10-7)
London SW3   Sun 12:30-5:30

Lilli Diva   ♀

A tempting oasis of fashion on an otherwise bleak street, Lilli Diva is one of the few cool boutiques in Clapham. Amongst the girly goodies there are ever-cheery Orla Kiely bags, chic Sportmax separates, tops by Antik Batik, pretty dresses by Omnia and high heels by Bocaccini and L'Autre Chose. The soothing interior, lit with a pretty glass chandelier and decorated with Venetian mirrors, makes for a lovely shopping environment.

Moderate   *MC/V*

020 7801 9600   **tube: Clapham Common**
32 Lavender Hill   Mon-Sat 10-6 (Wed 10-7)
London SW11

Lillywhites   ♂♀♂

Founded in 1863, Lillywhites is England's only sports department store but you won't need another. Staff members are sports men and women themselves and can help you make precisely the right choice. You won't find the kit for horse-riding or fencing here, but pretty much everything else is catered for. The equipment has evolved quite a bit since the early days—tennis rackets are made of titanium and ladies don't have to play in long skirts, thank god. Whatever comes into sports fashion, you can count on Lillywhites to keep up. (Tourist tip: the main staircase gives you a great view of the fascinating maelstrom that is Piccadilly Circus.)

Affordable   *Amex/MC/V*

0870 333 9600   **tube: Piccadilly Circus**
24-36 Lower Regent Street   Mon-Sat 10-9
London SW1   Sun 12-6

Linea

Full marks for labels here (Etro, Missoni, Juicy Couture, Celine, Jimmy Choo for women; Gianfranco Ferré, Dirk Bikkemberg, Christian Lacroix, Cesare Paciotti for men) but minus points for the slightly frosty atmosphere. Serious clothing in a serious environment for the serious spender. Funseekers should possibly go elsewhere. *lineaofhampstead.com*

Expensive   *Amex/MC/V*

020 7794 1775   **tube: Hampstead**
8 Heath Street   Mon-Fri 10-7, Sat 11-6
London NW3   Sun 12-6

Links of London

Looking for a present and short on time or inspiration? Head to Links, a one-stop luxury shop for fine gifts. The brand was build around its silver charm bracelets and other charms—perfect for 21st birthdays—and now you can buy everything from silver baby trains, quality leather goods, cufflinks and watches to pearls and 18-carat gold jewellery. Make sure you indulge yourself with a charm on the way out—at £24 it would be rude not to. You can also find Links in Harrods, and there are several branches in the City.*linksoflondon.com*

Moderate to expensive   *Amex/MC/V*

020 7499 7909   **tube: Bond Street**
32 Brook Street   Mon-Sat 10-6 (Thursday 10-7)
London W1

020 7930 0400   **tube: Piccadilly Circus**
94 Jermyn Street   Mon-Sat 9:30-6 (Thurs 9:30-7)
London SW1

020 7730 3133   **tube: Sloane Square**
16 Sloane Square   Mon-Sat 10-6 (Wed 10-7), Sun 12-6
London SW1

Liola

Liola offers the softest jersey clothing, made in Italy, with comfort and stretch being the main appeal. The designs give the impression of being put together but with room to move. Separates coordinate seamlessly in bold shades and patterns, from blues and greens to a wilder tiger print, with chunky jewellery to complete the effect. In crease-free fabric that's perfect for packing, the collection will strike well-travelled women as both forgiving and chic. Think contemporary earth mother with a sense of style.

Moderate   *Amex/MC/V*

020 7581 5677   **tube: South Kensington**
69 Walton Street   Mon-Fri 10-5:30, Sat 11-5
London SW3

Liz Claiborne

A fashion mainstay in America, Liz Claiborne remains ever-attuned to dependable comfort with a bit of style. The selection sticks to the basics, using practical wash-and-wear fabrics, solid colours and loose cuts to suit the over-40 crowd. A more casual, younger-feeling line features knitwear, dresses, trousers and skirts, and there's a collection just for petites and larger sizes ranging from 16-24. *lizclaiborne.com*

Moderate *Amex/MC/V*

020 7734 4987 **tube: Oxford Circus**
211-213 Regent Street Mon-Wed 10-6, Thurs 10-8
London W1 Fri-Sat 10-7, Sun 12-6

Liza Bruce

Her sexy swimwear, available in every desirable colour and cut, is a tour de force but equal airtime should be given to Bruce's holiday clothing. Summer tops, sarongs and slip dresses are set against a bright minimalist interior and modern furniture designed by Bruce's husband, Nicholas Alvis Vega. The atmosphere is enhanced by its location on one of the prettiest little streets in London. *lizabruce.com*

Expensive *Amex/MC/V*

020 7235 8423 **tube: Knightsbridge**
9 Pont Street Mon-Sat 11-6
London SW1

Lock & Co

It's like stepping into a time machine and finding yourself in early 19th-century London. In fact the most famous hatters in the world have been in business since 1676, and their impressive list of past customers includes Winston Churchill, Oscar Wilde and Frank Sinatra. There is a vast selection of styles for men and women—felt hats including homburgs, fedoras, and trilbies; tweeds including flat caps and deerstalkers; waxed fishing hats; panamas and riding hats. There is also a small range of country clothing. *lockhatters.co.uk*

Expensive *Amex/MC/V*

020 7930 8874 **tube: Green Park**
6 St James's Street Mon-Fri 9-5:30, Sat 9:30-5:30
London SW1

Loewe

The smell of leather that permeates this store leaves no doubt about Loewe's stock in trade. This Spanish institution has a history of producing fine leather products since 1846. Best known for its luxurious handbags and luggage, the store also carries a sophisticated women's ready-to-wear designed by Jose Enrique Oña Selfa. Leather biker jackets, slate-hued belted dresses, fur gilets and most elegant trenches are the highlights of this sleek collecton. The label may not have reached the dizzy heights of Louis Vuitton, but is a definite player in the luxury league. *loewe.com*

Expensive *Amex/MC/V*

020 7493 3914
130 New Bond Street
London W1

The Loft

If you dream of a designer wardrobe to rival Gwyneth's but lack the dough, come to the loft for secondhand clothing sourced from magazine shoots or ex-fashion house samples. The space is somewhat cramped and often busy, but don't let that stop you digging through the racks. Womenswear, found downstairs, is organized by colour, from evening dresses to Earl jeans. Gucci, Joseph, Nicole Farhi, Paul Smith, Comme des Garçons…and shoes by Prada and Jimmy Choo. It's a label lover's dream.   *the-loft.co.uk*

Affordable to moderate   *MC/V*

020 7240 3807
35 Monmouth Street
London WC2

tube: **Covent Garden**
Mon-Sat 11-6, Sun 12:30-5:30

Long Tall Sally

Women topping the tape measure at five foot nine will find an assortment of casualwear, suits, eveningwear and accessories. Sizes range from 10-20, with a separate maternity collection available if you order it. Cuts are modern, if not quite cool, but traces of denim and diamanté add a spark of style. Accessories like knee-high socks are a godsend for those afflicted with exceptionally long limbs.   *longtallsally.co.uk*

Moderate to very expensive   *Amex/MC/V*

020 7487 3370
21-25 Chiltern Street
London W1

tube: **Baker Street**
Mon-Sat 9:30-5:30 (Thurs 10-7)

Look Who's Walking

If you don't break your leg on the bench immediately inside the door (or are we just particularly clumsy?), you'll find plenty to please in this children's clothing shop. Although they stock their fair share of labels (a line of Dior dresses and cardies here, a diminutive Prada shoe there), the emphasis is on discreet luxury and good quality rather than big names: a refreshing change in this mad world of miniature designer branding. A line of tiny shoes at adult eye height is guaranteed to make you go goo-gooey.

Expensive   *Amex/MC/V*

020 7433 3855
78 Heath Street
London NW3

tube: **Hampstead**
Mon-Sat 10-5:30
Sun 12-6

Loro Piana

This is the ultimate in Italian cashmere, with lush sweaters, cosy shirts and shawls in colours from delicate pastels to deep blues and browns. Patterns remain simple, with stripes at the decorative extreme. Trousers, shirts and twinsets are also available in linen, cotton and silk. Buttery soft leather and suede add a true sense of luxury. A new store was due to open in Bond Street as we went to press.

Very expensive   *Amex/MC/V*

020 7235 3203   **tube: Knightsbridge**
47 Sloane Street   Mon-Sat 10-6 (Wed 10-7)
London SW1

Louis Féraud

Elegance and desk-to-dinner versatility draw moneyed, sophisticated shoppers to this boutique. French painter-cum-designer Féraud brings bright colours and flattering cuts to tailored suits, blouses, sweaters and skirts, in a collection that stays safely away from trend. Corporate ladies love Féraud's clothes, including scarves inspired by his own paintings.

Moderate to expensive   *Amex/MC/V*

020 7493 1684   **tube: Bond Street**
68 New Bond Street   Mon-Sat 9:30-6:30 (Thurs 9:30-7)
London W1

Louis Vuitton

Marc Jacobs keeps this French luxury luggage label on the top tier of fashion must-haves with one of the most sought-after collections on the catwalk. This year he has also created their first line of blue denim, the Icon range. A new generation of Vuitton lovers can buy jeans, skirts and capri pants alongside his beautifully handcrafted rtw collection. The coveted logo emblazoned on everything from bags to ballet pumps keeps his loyal customers and Japanese tourists flocking, and the waiting lists are long for the latest accessories. Whatever you find here, it will be as plain as the logo on your bag: impeccable quality at any price.   *vuitton.com*

Expensive to very expensive   *Amex/MC/V*

020 7399 4050   **tube: Green Park**
17-18 New Bond Street   Mon-Sat 10-6:30
London W1   (Thurs 10-7:30)

020 7399 4050   **tube: Knightsbridge**
190-192 Sloane Street   Mon-Sat 10-6:30, Sun 12-5
London SW1

020 7399 4050   **tube: Bank**
5-6 Royal Exchange   Mon-Fri 10-6:30
London EC3

Louise Kennedy

For those in the know, Louise Kennedy is a secret gem worth keeping quiet about. Her London shop is tiny compared with her Dublin flagship, a grand Georgian house that also functions as her home, but this quiet Belgravia block serves the Irish designer well. She offers beautifully made wool suits, hand-beaded cocktail dresses, cashmere sweaters and coats. Her bestsellers are the wide-legged palazzo pants in jersey which are ideal for travelling.

Kennedy's crisp cotton button-down shirts put nearby Thomas Pink to shame and the ruffle-fronted silk shirts are delicious. *louisekennedy.com*

Moderate *Amex/MC/V*

020 7235 0911 **tube: Knightsbridge**
11 West Halkin Street Mon-Sat 10-6
London SW1

Lulu Guinness

Lulu's adorable flowerpot bags have blossomed onto the fashion scene with a typically English mix of colour, creativity and wit. Her signature style is inspired by the Fifties: dinky bags decorated with summer flowers, pictures of ice cream sundaes and lipsticks. Such is their inventiveness that some are even on display at the wonderful fashion department in the Victoria & Albert museum (well worth a visit), but Lulu's bags are best seen in their element at her Chelsea shop, where a montage of vintage fashion pages reflects the kitsch spirit of her wacky collection. Madonna, Liz Hurley and Björk are just some of the celebrities who carry her bags. *luluguinness.com*

Expensive *Amex/MC/V*

020 7823 4828 **tube: Sloane Square**
3 Ellis Street Mon-Fri 10-6, Sat 11-6
London SW1

020 7626 5391 **tube: Bank**
23 Royal Exchange Mon-Fri 10-6:30
London EC3 (Thurs 10:30-7)

Machiko Jinto

An appealing mixture of new and vintage. Japanese designer Jinto's denim skirts, trousers, fitted coats and shirts have a Fifties flavour and come in a range of colours from orange and pink to blue and brown. The vintage collection includes bags from the Fifties, cute Thirties hats (think pillar boxes with quiffs of net) and jewellery by Mariam Haskell and Stanley Hagler—a favourite of Marilyn Monroe. This is a cool label for people who are looking for something a little different.

Moderate to expensive *MC/V*

020 7792 9772 **tube: Westbourne Park**
77 Westbourne Park Road Mon-Sat 10-6
London W2

Madeleine Press

An urban girl's dream. The designer behind the Press & Bastyan duo has opened her first boutique and created a chic space which is a favourite with Dido, Bond girl Rosamund Pike and Natalie Imbruglia. Her formula is elegant daywear with a simple attention to detail – you'll find pleated skirts and denim and a lovely new range of leather accessories. *mpress.com*

Moderate to expensive   MC/V

020 7935 9301   **tube: Bond Street**
90 Marylebone High Street   Mon-Sat 10:30-6:30
London W1   (Thurs 10:30-7) Sun 11:30-4:30

M-A-G Europe

When you crave stylish cashmere, M-A-G will satisfy. From V-necks to crew necks, baby pink to basic black, this sweater shop offers top-notch cashmere worth seeking out. Simple designs come in seasonal shades with decorative highlights like stripes, beading and speciality stitches. But the general feeling is that the knits border on the too expensive, even if they are cashmere. Pretty belts and bags are also available.

Expensive   Amex/MC/V

020 7591 0552   **tube: Knightsbridge**
20 Beauchamp Place   Mon-Sat 10-6
London SW3

Maharishi

If you know the name, you probably know the cargo pants. Delicately embroidered with fire-breathing dragons, red poppies and other Asian motifs, their combination of casual comfort and beautiful decoration has been a hit with fashion followers and celebs such as Jennifer Aniston. Not a designer per se, the man behind Maharishi, Hardy Blechman, is more of a concept creator. His diffusion line and varying interests in Asian spirituality, technology and the military are all apparent at the streetwear store called Dpmhi in Great Pulteney Street, where Bruce Lee dolls and limited-edition vinyl figures by Michael Lau sit beside recycled US army fatigues and vacuum-packed T-shirts designed by graffiti artist Futura. Check out the diffusion range, Mi-fi, for a more sporty look. Worth a look, even if you're not planning to buy.   *emaharishi.com/dpmhi.com*

Expensive   Amex/MC/V

020 7836 3860   **tube: Covent Garden**
19a Floral Street   Mon-Sat 10-7, Sun 12-5
London WC2

0871 218 0260   **tube: Piccadilly Circus**
2-3 Great Pulteney Street (Dpmhi) (opening hours as above)
London W1

Mandy

Trashy meets trendy at this small shop where glittery T-shirts and studded denim feed a Madonna wannabe crowd. Find skin-baring clubwear, leather trousers and colourful vest tops with velvet piping. More than one purchase might send you into trend overdrive—choose carefully.

Moderate   Amex/MC/V

020 7376 7491   **tube: Sloane Square**
139 King's Road   Mon-Sat 10-7, Sun 12-6
London SW3

Mango/MNG

A great place for cheap treats. In the same vein as Zara and H&M, this Spanish chain targets young women with knock-offs of the season's catwalk trends. Selection ranges from weekendwear to suits and businesswear, with a good range of accessories. But don't forget, this is fashion at its most mass, so you might be better off sticking to the casual stuff. *mango.com*

Affordable   *Amex/MC/V*

020 7434 1384   **tube: Piccadilly Circus**
106-112 Regent Street   Mon-Sat 10-8 (Thurs 10-9)
London W1   Sun 12-6

020 7240 6099   **tube: Covent Garden**
8-12 Neal Street   Mon-Sat 9:30-8, Sun 11-5
London WC2

020 7535 3505   **tube: Oxford Circus**
233 Oxford Street   Mon-Sat 10-8 (Thurs 10-9)
London W1   Sun 11-6

Manolo Blahnik

Loyal subjects flock to Manolo Blahnik's secret kingdom down a quiet side street in Chelsea where you have to ring a doorbell to be granted entry. Blahnik is the undisputed king of the stiletto and shows no signs of abdicating his throne. Fashion fanatics can spot Manolos a mile off—the three-inch heel, the curve of the instep, the point of the toe. From an indispensable black pump to a turquoise stiletto, he anticipates a woman's every step: sometimes practical, sometimes fanciful but, alas, almost always painful. They've been described as better than sex and sample sales drive Vogue girls to fisticuffs.

Very expensive   *Amex/MC/V*

020 7352 3863   **tube: Sloane Square**
49 Old Church Street   Mon-Fri 10-5:30, Sat 10:30-5
London SW3

Manucci

Yet another transplanted Italian selling suits, shirts and ties plus a few pieces of smart/casual menswear including the Jaguar Cars line and the Pal Zileri formal and casual collections. In a stark wood-floored interior Manucci offers alterations and free delivery, and rightly advertises its friendly service.

Moderate   *Amex/MC/V*

020 7930 7315   **tube: Piccadilly Circus/Green Park**
108 Jermyn Street   Mon-Sat 10-7, Sun 12-5
London SW1

Margaret Howell

Howell's understated style is typical of English country chic. The collection invariably includes stylish sheepskin coats, sloppy corduroy trousers and structured tweed jackets. Soft earthy colours—khaki, slate, chalk, damson—and fine British fabrics—Irish linen, flannel and soft knitwear—ensure Howell's pieces remain classics season after season. Don't be surprised if you too are bitten by the Howell bug. It is all too easy to accumulate a wardrobe of her well-loved designs without even realising it. *margarethowell.co.uk*

Expensive   *Amex/MC/V*

020 7009 9000   **tube: Oxford Circus**
34 Wigmore Street   Mon-Sat 10-6 (Thurs 10-7)
London W1

Margaretta

A tiny gem of a shop on the former site of The Corridor, a disappointing secondhand store. Now you will find a range of exciting accessories chosen by the lovely Margaretta. Handwoven mohair scarves, colourful pashminas and hand-made Italian belts adorned with crystals are just some of the highlights. The Fifties diamanté evening bags are very Grace Kelly—get here quickly before someone else does.

Moderate   *Amex/MC/V*

020 7823 3434   **tube: Sloane Square**
309 King's Road   Mon-Sat 10:30-7, Sun 1-5
London SW3

Maria Grachvogel

Known for dressing the rich and famous in red-carpet dress-es—think Liz Hurley in a slip dress—her trademark is spiral cutting on the bias and asymmetric shapes which hang well on all body types. However, not a lot of people are familiar with her ready-to-wear collection. If you overlook the unin-spiring decor you will find a grown-up classic collection of well-cut trousers and knitwear. Her best selling pieces are her size 14 trousers and, good news for taller ladies, they come in a longer 34-inch leg. *mariagrachvogel.com*

Expensive   *Amex/MC/V*

020 7245 9331   **tube: Sloane Square**
162 Sloane Street   Mon-Sat 10-6 (Wed 10-7)
London SW1

☆ Marie-Chantal

Marie-Chantal is aka Crown Princess Pavlos of Greece and, even more importantly, a mother of four. She became so tired of dashing from shop to shop looking for children's clothing that she decided to create her own line, ranging from play to party. The results are enchanting, classic yet full of colour, and range from three months to 12 years. For girls there are little tartan skirts and cream cashmere jumpers, for boys corduroy trousers and check shirts. The baby-grows with angel wings sewn onto the back sound a bit naff, but they are utterly adorable. Everything is made from the soft-est fabrics and with the utmost care. *mariechantal.com*

Moderate   *Amex/MC/V*

020 7838 1111   **tube: South Kensington**
148 Walton Street   Mon-Sat 10-6
London SW3

Marilyn Moore

Feminine and fun, Marilyn Moore designs are what every girl needs to cheer up a drab wardrobe. The renowned cashmere-silk knitwear is soft and affordable and comes in summery shades of pale blue, sea-green and pretty pink. Details like ruffled sleeves, appliqué flowers, colourful stripes or ribbons and, on one sweater, an image of a temptingly sweet cupcake, add character and style. You'll also find handbags decorated with little ladybirds, fitted shirts and skirts and a few pieces by Omnia.

Moderate to expensive   *Amex/MC/V*

020 7727 5577   **tube: Ladbroke Grove/Notting Hill Gate**
7 Elgin Crescent   Mon-Sat 10-6, Sun 12-5
London W11

Marina Rinaldi

This division of MaxMara specializes in understated styles in soft fabrics that don't cling for the bigger woman (sizes 12-26). Suits, trousers, knitwear and outerwear are spread throughout this three-floor store, which is typical Italian minimalism. Navy and white is a strong theme for summer, and they also do elegant eveningwear. Marina Sport is their more relaxed casual line.

Expensive to very expensive   *Amex/MC/V*

020 7629 4454   **tube: Green Park**
39 Old Bond Street   Mon-Sat 10-6 (Thurs 10-7)
London W1

Marks & Spencer

Having survived a highly publicised takeover attempt by Philip Green, clothing retail's most aggressive mogul, this British institution is putting its all into reviving the public's confidence in their once favourite department store. The Limited Collection Trend range, Autograph and Per Una keeps M&S on the fashion pages, while the main label with its linen blouses and washable skirts in sizes 10 to 22 supplies their loyal customers. You can certainly find something for a wedding in Piece by Piece, and Per Una will keep the teens happy. Bright lingerie by Cerise and fun pants by Spoilt for Choice give Top Shop a run for their money, while an ever-expanding beauty department stocks everything from luxurious salon-tested products by celebrity stylist Daniel Galvin Junior to nail varnishes to go with the Cerise lingerie collection.   *marksandspencer.com*

Affordable to moderate   *Amex/MC/V*

020 7935 7954   **tube: Marble Arch**
458 Oxford Street   Mon-Fri 9-9, Sat 9-8
London W1   Sun 12-6

020 7437 7722
173 Oxford Street
London W1

tube: Oxford Circus
Mon-Sat 9-8 (Thurs 9-9)
Sun 12-6

020 7376 5634
85 King's Road
London SW3

tube: Sloane Square
Mon-Fri 9-8:30, Sat 8:30-8
Sun 12-6

020 7938 3711
113 Kensington High Street
London W8

tube: High Street Kensington
Mon-Sat 9-8, Sun 12-6

020 7229 9515
Whiteley's, Queensway
London W2

tube: Queensway/Bayswater
Mon-Sat 9-10
Sun 12-6

020 7267 6055
143 Camden High Street
London NW1

tube: Camden Town
Mon-Fri 8:30-8
Sat 8:30-7, Sun 11-5

020 7786 9494
70 Finsbury Pavement
London EC2

tube: Moorgate
Mon-Fri 7-8
Sat 8:30-6

Mark Stephen Marengo

Understated modern classics are the core of this collection. Mark Stephen Marengo's primary focus is on mens' suits but there is also a small selection for women. Shirts and ties are neatly showcased in this clean, streamlined store, but nothing here will set your world on fire.

mark-stephen-marengo.com

Moderate   *Amex/MC/V*

020 7377 5802
32 Artillery Lane
London E1

tube: Liverpool Street
Mon-Sat 10:30-7, Sun 12-5:30

020 7987 4900
Lower Level, Port East
West India Quay
London E14

tube: West India Quay (DLR)
Daily 11-5

020 7439 4714
9 Quadrant Arcade
80-82 Regent Street
London W1

tube: Piccadilly Circus
Mon-Sat 10:30-7

020 7351 7597
287 Fulham Road
London SW10

tube: South Kensington
Mon-Sat 11-7:30
Sun 12-5:30

Marni

A favourite of *Vogue*'s Lucinda Chambers (long before a certain celebrity made boho de rigueur and then out of fashion again), Marni has no competitors in its deluxe hippy world. A red ceiling and a shiny white floor with octopus tentacle rails and silver daisy picnic tables perfectly complement the label we love, and a small children's collection upstairs includes necklaces just like mummy's.

Very expensive   *Amex/MC/V*
020 7245 9520   **tube: Knightsbridge**
26 Sloane Street   Mon-Fri 10-6 (Wed 10-7)
London SW1   Sat 10-6

Mash

Streetwear punters striving to look as if they don't care (even when they care very much) find the latest brands at this wannabe underground boutique. On Saturdays, a DJ spins the decks to add to the urban hip-hop atmosphere. Racks are packed with cool names like Carhartt and Ringspun and G-Star Raw denim jeans that look like they've been rolled in the dirt. The huge selection of baseball and ski caps will help you go low-pro.

Affordable   *Amex/MC/V*
020 7434 9609   **tube: Oxford Circus**
73 Oxford Street   Mon-Sat 10-7 (Thurs 10-8)
London W1   Sun 12-6

Massimo Dutti

There are armchairs and magazines for tired partners, but with a strong and very wearable collection of men's and womenswear, don't make it your last stop. Think grown-up Zara with a few directional gems thrown in. The quality is high street but you'll certainly find all the classic shapes dripping with the European chic we've come to expect of the Spanish invaders (it's owned by Zara), and some colourful knitwear and accessories to play with as well.   *massimodutti.com*

Affordable   *Amex/MC/V*
020 7851 1280   **tube: Oxford Circus**
156 Regent Street   Mon-Sat 10-7 (Thurs 10-8)
London W1   Sun 12-6

020 7225 4780   **tube: Knightsbridge**
71 Brompton Road   Mon-Sat 10-7
London SW3   Sun 12-6

☆ Matches

Expect a lot of posing in this A-list fashion hangout. The staff are experts who know their stuff about labels from Chloé and Gharani Strok to Marc Jacobs and Missoni (check out the tiny Missoni swimwear.) Customers can sip chardonnay while they sift through the racks of Lanvin trousers, Roland Mouret coats and all sorts of attire from Alexander McQueen. Other highlights include a stellar shoe selection, a VIP shopping area with a full bar. Hurrah!

Expensive to very expensive   *Amex/MC/V*
020 7221 0255   **tube: Notting Hill Gate**
60-64 Ledbury Road   Mon-Sat 10-6, Sun 12-6
London W11

020 7221 2334   **tube: Notting Hill Gate**
85 Ledbury Road   (opening hours as above)
London W11

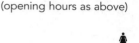
020 8947 8707 (W)
34 High Street
London SW19

tube: Wimbledon
(opening hours as above)

020 8946 8218 (M, casual)
38 High Street
London SW19

tube: Wimbledon
(opening hours as above)

020 8944 5366 (M)
39 High Street
London SW19

tube: Wimbledon
(opening hours as above)

020 8944 5995 (W, casual)
56b High Street
London SW19

tube: Wimbledon
(opening hours as above)

☆ Matthew Williamson

Williamson's first stand-alone store is a homage to "virtual nature": a huge box of tropical plants is suspended at the back of the shop, in which original Georgian panelling is mixed with Turkish stone flooring and neon rails. Kates Moss and Hudson are big fans of these rainbow-coloured clothes, as are Sadie Frost and Gwyneth Paltrow. You'll find beaded dresses to skim over the tiniest of figures, cropped trousers, prairie style tops and sheer, lacy shirts. It's all fairly spectacular and very, very pretty. *matthewwilliamson.com*

Expensive to very expensive   *Amex/MC/V*

020 7629 6200
28 Bruton Street
London W1

tube: Green Park
Mon-Sat 10-6

Maurice Sedwell

Don't be put-off by the "ring to enter" sign at the door. Despite its instantly apparent and strong sense of tradition, Maurice Sedwell prides itself on being one of the most creative tailors on Savile Row. This urge to stand out from the crowd manifests itself most obviously in its unique bespoke leather suit service as well as a willingness to mix a wide range of traditional fabrics with leather in all sorts of surprising combinations. *savilerowtailor.com*

Very expensive   *Amex/MC/V*

020 7734 0824
19 Savile Row
London W1

tube: Piccadilly Circus/Oxford Circus
Mon-Fri 9-6, Sat 9-1

Mayfair Rat (formerly Leather Rat Classics)

Head here to satisfy your leather craving. Leather Rat offers a range of colours and models, from biker to blazer, as well as any cut of trousers. It might look like a dump but trust us, it's a treasure-house. Don't be discouraged by the treacherous, winding staircase that leads to the lower floor, where such brands as Redskins and Chevignon await.

Expensive   *MC/V*

020 7491 9753
37 South Molton Street
London W1

tube: Bond Street
Mon-Sat 10:30-6:30
(Thurs 10:30-7), Sun 12:30-5:30

MaxMara

Fans of well-groomed, classic clothing will love this look: in the relaxed atmosphere of MaxMara all racks lead to simplicity. The understated collection avoids passing fads with a perennial devotion to high quality and style. Soft feminine fabrics in the safe shades of taupe, beige, navy and black are prominent, along with the occasional print. Their beautiful overcoats add the perfect finish. These investment buys will stand the test of time.

Expensive   *Amex/MC/V*

020 7499 7902   **tube: Green Park**
19-21 Old Bond Street   Mon-Sat 10-6 (Thurs 10-7)
London W1

Mexx

If you were a fan of the Eighties pop groups Aha and Duran Duran (pre-revival), you'll remember this brand from the Netherlands. Mexx still features affordable wardrobe staples with a fashion edge. The selection is dominated by casual mix-and-match separates, with an emphasis on skirts, trousers and shirts. From long-sleeved cotton T-shirts to sporty capris, Mexx covers all the bases, including accessories. *mexx.com*

Affordable   *Amex/MC/V*

020 7836 9661   **tube: Covent Garden**
112-115 Long Acre   Mon-Sat 10:30-7:30 (Thurs 10:30-8)
London WC2   Sun 12:30-6:30

020 7225 2993   **tube: Knightsbridge**
75 Brompton Road   Mon-Sat 10:30-7
London SW3   Sun 12-6

☆ Microzine

When this super-cool mens' store opened on an Islington back street in 2003, the fuss was huge. It's a paradise for the gadget fiend, the fashion victim or the affluent GQ reader who has to surround himself with the latest boys' toys and bachelor-pad accessories. Clothes by Gieves, Oliver Spencer, Griffin, Reebok, Kim Jones, Dirty Youth and G-Star line the walls, and even the shelving units are for sale—with the £3,000 price tag being loose change to their target customer. Even if you don't have the readies, it's still fun—and a useful source of presents for The Man Who Has Everything. *microzine.co.uk*

Expensive   *Amex/MC/V*

020 7704 6667   **tube: Angel**
66-67 Colebrooke Row   Mon-Fri 11-6
London N1   Sat 10-7, Sun 12-6

MiMi

Holding court at the western end of the King's Road, MiMi maintains royal status among London's fashion devotees, including Yasmin Le Bon and Madonna. No wonder. The store is popping with colour and an energetic mix of designer labels—Marc Jacobs, Gharani Strok, Collette Dinnigan, Vanessa Bruno, Christian Louboutin and Jimmy Choo. A refreshing reprieve from the usual high street chains, this is a great place to go when you feel like treating yourself.

Expensive   *Amex/MC/V*

020 7349 9699   **tube: Sloane Square**
309 King's Road   Mon-Sat 10:30-6:30, Sun 1-6
London SW3

Mimi

Searching for the perfect handbag can be a painstaking endeavour. The soft leather bags and purses at Mimi's little boutique, off Brick Lane, are real eye-catchers and come in a selection of colours from red and orange to black and brown. As befits a graduate of Central St Martins College of Art and Design, Mimi's designs are understated and cool. Cheshire Street is quickly becoming the latest address for style gurus, so don't be surprised if Mimi's appointment diary is fully booked. Try leaving the store with just one purchase—easier said than done.   *mimimika.com*

Expensive   *MC/V*

020 7729 6699   **tube: Shoreditch**
40 Cheshire Street   Tues-Thurs by appointment only
London E2   Fri-Sun 10:30-6

Mimmo

Affluent Fulham is bursting with smartly turned-out designer mums. Now they can dress their little darlings in style too. Mimmo is a temple of A-label childrenswear up to eight years old, with pieces by Christian Lacroix Junior, Juicy and Nolita. Styles range from a classic soft beige coat with creamy collar—very Little Lord Fauntleroy—to funky T-shirts splashed with fluorescent paints—very rock chic. It seems dangerous to foster an affinity with high-end fashion at such an early age, but with such an exciting collection it's not surprising mothers are tempted—after all, it's still much cheaper than shopping for themselves.   *mimmo.co.uk*

Moderate   *Amex/MC/V*

020 7731 4706   **tube: Parsons Green**
602 Fulham Road   Mon-Sat 10-6
London SW6

Mirage

Understated French style: plain clothes in quality fabrics. Block colours predominate and white, black and navy blue are firm favourites. Chic white suits for summer from Teenflo; tailored yet feminine jackets by Sylvie Schimmel; handbags and shoes by Barbara Bui and accessories by Richard Gampel. You will also find soft cashmere knits and conservative shoes by the store's own label. Nothing dramatic, nothing special. Pop in if you are investigating the slick new Duke of York developments, but don't make a special trip.   *mirage.com*

Moderate to expensive   *Amex/MC/V*

020 7730 2070   **tube: Sloane Square**
73 Duke of York Square   Mon-Sat 10-6:30
London SW3   Sun 12-6

020 7581 9787   **tube: Knightsbridge**
193-195 Brompton Road   (opening hours as above)
London SW3

020 7433 8113   **tube: Hampstead**
76 Hampstead High Street   (opening hours as above)
London NW3

☆ Miss Selfridge   👫

Part of Philip Green's retail empire, this High Street darling bud has blossomed into a brand of its own, no longer in the shadow of neighbours Top Shop and American import Urban Outfitters. Having homed in on quality, Miss Selfridge now attracts an older clientele of twentysomethings who flock to the boutique for its fantastic clothing and accessory collections hot off the catwalk, plus its vintage range. *missselfridge.co.uk*

Affordable   *Amex/MC/V*

020 7927 0188   **tube: Oxford Circus**
214 Oxford Street   Mon-Sat 9-8 (Thurs 9-9)
London W1   Sun 11:30-6

Miss Sixty   👬👩

With red leather trousers, tiny halter tops and jeans that lace at the waist this Italian chain has swept young girls off their feet. They come by the gaggle to stock up on the trademark trash-glamour gear: flared, boot-cut and low-waisted denim, micromini skirts, fuchsia hotpants and cowgirl shirts that tie at the waist. This label has lately become a hit with twentysomethings, too, for its low prices and keen trendspotting. Anyone over size 14 should beware, though—Miss Sixty suits tiny sizes best. Also check out the new men's store, Energy, in Covent Garden. *misssixty.com*

Affordable   *Amex/MC/V*

020 7376 1330   **tube: High Street Kensington**
42 Kensington High Street   Mon-Sat 10-7
London W8   (Thurs 10-7), Sun 12-6

020 7434 3060   **tube: Oxford Circus**
31-32 Great Marlborough Street   Mon-Sat 10-7, Sun 12-5
London W1

020 7836 3789 (W)   **tube: Covent Garden**
39 Neal Street   Mon-Sat 10-6:30
London WC2   (Thurs 10-7:30), Sun 12-6

020 7836 7719 (M)   **tube: Covent Garden**
47-49 Neal Street   (called Energy)
London WC2   (opening hours as above)

Miu Miu

It might be Prada's cute younger sister, but this is hardly a bargain-basement brand. Miu Miu's character tends to be a bit more girlish than super-sophisticated big sis, with shift dresses, pleated skirts and sheer, frilly tops. Shoes and handbags are playfully innovative. Part headmistress, part schoolgirl, sophistication plus whimsy is the Miu Miu style.

Expensive   *Amex/MC/V*

020 7409 0900   **tube: Bond Street**
123 New Bond Street   Mon-Sat 10-6 (Thurs 10-7)
London W1

Monogrammed Linen Shop

If you can't picture your bed linens, kitchen towels and throws without embroidered initials, make your way here, where lovely linen is personalized to order. When it comes to clothes there is a small but traditionally appealing selection of Victorian style nightdresses, adorable smock frocks for little girls and, for babies, christening dresses and rompers too cute to resist.   *monogrammedlinenshop.co.uk*

Moderate   *Amex/MC/V*

020 7589 4033   **tube: South Kensington**
168 Walton Street   Mon-Sat 10-6
London SW3

☆ Monsoon

Monsoon expertly blends an eastern aesthetic with modern trends to bring hippy chic to the high street. The fluttery, feminine creations appeal most in the hot days of summer when lightweight silk, sexy chiffon and the softest cottons come into their own. And, a rare bonus, they have the best selection of those impossible-to-find bridesmaids' dresses for grown-ups. Fear not, there's no pink meringue here. Flower-power children can enjoy the boho collection too: the mini separates are beautifully embellished with beading, embroidery and appliqué. Best of all, boys and girls alike can be inexpensively kitted out for a wedding in white linen Nehru jackets or butterfly-embroidered dresses. If you haven't visited this store for a while, check out the new, albeit small, men's collection—all in all, it really is worth popping in.   *monsoon.co.uk*

Moderate to expensive   *Amex/MC/V*

020 7581 1408   **tube: Knightsbridge**
48 Brompton Road   Mon-Sat 9:30-7 (Wed-Thurs 9:30-9)
London SW3   Sun 12-6

020 7499 2578   **tube: Oxford Circus**
264 Oxford Street   Mon-Fri 9:30-8 (Thurs 9:30-8)
London W1   Sat 9:30-6:30, Sun 11-6

020 7491 3004   **tube: Marble Arch**
498-500 Oxford Street   Mon-Sat 10-8
London W1   Sun 12-6

020 7836 9140
23 The Piazza
London WC2

tube: Covent Garden
Mon-Sat 10-8, Sun 11-6

020 7379 3623
5-6 James Street
London WC2

tube: Covent Garden
(opening hours as above)

020 7730 7552
37 King's Road
London SW3

tube: Sloane Square
Mon-Sat 10-7 (Wed 10-7:30)
Sun 12-6

020 7376 0366
5 Barkers Arcade
Kensington High Street
London W8

tube: High Street Kensington
Mon-Sat 10-7 (Thurs 10-8)
Sun 12-6

020 7512 9543
21-22 Canada Square
London E14

tube: Canary Wharf
Mon-Fri 8:30-7 (Thurs 8:30-8)
Sat 10-6, Sun 12-5

020 7623 3774
87 Gracechurch Street
London EC3

tube: Monument
Mon-Fri 8-6:30

020 7435 1726
1 Hampstead High Street
London NW3

tube: Hampstead
Mon-Sat 10-6, Sun 11-6

020 7486 8466
96 Marylebone High Street
London W1

tube: Baker Street/Bond Street
Mon-Sat 10-7
Sun 12-5

020 8788 1286
Unit 25 Putney Exchange
High Street
London SW15

tube: Putney Bridge
Mon-Sat 9-6 (Thurs-Fri 9-7)
Sun 11-5

020 8944 8920
220-221 Centre Court Shopping Centre
London SW19

tube: Wimbledon
Mon-Fri 9-7
(Thurs 9-8), Sat 9-6, Sun 11-5

020 7704 6386
N1 Shopping Centre
10 Parkfield Street
London N1

tube: Angel
Mon-Sat 10:30-7
Sun 11-6

Morgan

Like many chains, the ongoing theme here has been inspired by young, sexy Eighties-style trash-glamour. But the prevailing grown-up glamour theme has taken hold even at Morgan, and former Britney Spears wannabes will find themselves coerced into drop-waisted beaded dresses in chiffon, floaty blouses and buckled heels, with ruffled tops and rose prints continuing the vintage boho theme. Luckily the new fragrance is reassuringly cheeky. *morgandetoi.com*

Affordable   *Amex/MC/V*

020 7499 4101
391-393 Oxford Street
London W1

tube: Bond Street/Marble Arch
Mon-Sat 10-7 (Thurs 10-8)
Sun 12-6

020 7491 1883
270 Oxford Street
London W1

tube: Oxford Circus
Mon-Sat 10-8
Sat 10-8, Sun 11-6

Moschino

It's high-designer but down to earth, with splashes of bright colour and playful details—Kylie is a fan. Stop by for a dose of good fashionable fun: frilly, floaty green shirts, lilac tights and Fifties-style gloves in bright orange or moss-green suede. Flirty cap-sleeved tops sit next to black ruffled shirts, brightly printed dresses, pink furry stoles and cheeky suits. If the signature label is out of reach, their bridge line, Cheap & Chic, offers similar flavour at a lower (but not much) price.   *moschino.it*

Expensive   *Amex/MC/V*

020 7318 0555   **tube: Oxford Circus**
28-29 Conduit Street   Mon-Sat 10-6 (Thurs 10-7)
London W1

Moss Bros

If the invitation arrived months ago but he's only just noticed the words "black tie", tell your date to hotfoot it over here. Moss Bros is the place to rent, or buy, men's formalwear: a complete package—jacket, trousers, shirt, cummerbund and bow tie—will set him back £69 a day for a morning suit and £53 for eveningwear. If he's looking to buy, there are several designers for sale, including Pierre Cardin, Canali, Hugo Boss and the Moss Bros label itself. For a more casual look, there are beige linen jackets, jeans and linen drawstring trousers. Periodically, quite often actually, they have serious value-for-money sales...designer shirts in every desirable colour reduced to £10-15, for example. (The Strand, Blomfield Street, Cheapside and Gracechurch Street addresses are also the Savoy Tailors Guild, all part of the same group.)   *mossbros.com*

Moderate to expensive   *Amex/MC/V*

020 7494 0665   **tube: Piccadilly Circus**
88 Regent Street   Mon-Fri 9:30-6:30 (Thurs 9-7)
London W1   Sat 9-7, Sun 12-6

020 7632 9700   **tube: Covent Garden**
27 King Street   Mon-Sat 9-6 (Thurs 9-7)
London WC2   Sun 11-5

020 7629 7371   **tube: Oxford Circus**
299 Oxford Street   Mon-Fri 10-8, Sat 9:30-7
London W1   Sun 12-6

020 7836 7881   **tube: Charing Cross**
92-93 The Strand   Mon-Sat 9-6 (Thurs 9-7)
London WC2   Sun 11-5

020 7588 8038   **tube: Liverpool Street (Eldon Street exit)**
35 Blomfield Street   Mon-Fri 8:30-6
London EC2

020 7600 7366   **tube: Bank (exit 9)**
83 Cheapside   Mon-Fri 9-6
London EC2

020 7929 0838   **tube: Monument**
81 Gracechurch Street   Mon-Fri 9-6
London EC3

Muji

This Japanese chain has made a name for itself by selling neutral-looking, unbranded products. The highlights of their selection are the no-frills cardboard, plastic, metal and wood homewares but their small collection of clothing is definitely worth a glance. Staying true to the ethos of practical, anonymous style, design remains minimalist, featuring muted monotones and simple patterns. Woollen sweaters, cotton shirts, underwear and linen trousers are all reasonably well made and equally well priced. Sizing tends to be on the small side—try before you buy.   *muji.co.uk*

Affordable   *Amex/MC/V*

020 7437 7503   **tube: Oxford Circus**
187 Oxford Street   Mon-Wed, Sat 10-7, Thurs 10-8
London W1   Fri 10-7:30, Sun 12-6

020 7379 0820   **tube: Covent Garden**
135 Long Acre   Mon-Sat 10:30-7:30
London WC2   (Thurs 10:30-8), Sun 12-6

020 7436 1779   **tube: Tottenham Court Road**
6 Tottenham Court Road   Mon-Sat 10:30-8
London W1   Sun 12-6

020 7376 2484   **tube: High Street Kensington**
157 Kensington High Street   Mon-Fri 10-7
London W8   (Thurs 10:30-7:30), Sat 10-7, Sun 12-6

020 7287 7323   **tube: Oxford Circus**
41 Carnaby Street   Mon-Sat 10-7 (Thurs 10-7:30)
London W1   Sun 12-6

020 7823 8688   **tube: Knightsbridge**
118 King's Road   Mon-Sat 10-7
London SW3   Sun 12-6

020 7792 8283   **tube: Queensway/Bayswater**
Whiteley's, Queensway   Mon-Thurs 10-8:30
London W2   Fri, Sat 10-9:30, Sun 12-6

Mulberry

What began in 1971 with Robert Saul's modest leather goods and jewellery collection has blossomed into an institution for the British country set. The relaunched brand is now a Bond Street institution, with an impressive flagship store and covetable clothing collections for women and men. Featuring soft suede trousers, flower-patterned shirts and double-breasted rain jackets, the women's line gives classic tailoring a trendy twist. The cosy Mulberry Home collection includes lovely furniture, crisp linens and floral fabrics, while the leather accessories are still a highlight.   *mulberry.com*

Moderate to expensive   *Amex/MC/V*

020 7491 3900   **tube: Bond Street**
41-42 New Bond Street   Mon-Sat 10-6 (Thurs 10-7)
London W1

020 7838 1411
171-175 Brompton Road
London SW3

tube: Knightsbridge
Mon-Fri 10-6 (Wed 10-7)
Sat 10-6:30

020 7493 2546 (accessories)
11-12 Gees Court
London W1

tube: Bond Street
Mon-Sat 10-6 (Thurs 10-7)

Musa

This tiny shop is a real find. Girly and romantic, it features two armoires filled with vintage and one-off pieces. Contemporary selection encourages a mix-don't-match approach, with denim by Sass & Bide, dresses by Roland Mouret, Megan Park, Gharani Strok and their own-label. Shoes, jewellery and separates are also available, including Fifties Trifari earrings, kaftans, sarongs and camisoles. A lovely little oasis.   *musalondon.com*

Moderate   *MC/V*

020 7937 6282
31 Holland Street
London W8

tube: High Street Kensington
Tues-Sat 11-6

Myla

Kate Moss had her maternity underwear handmade by this "sex shop with style" which specializes in super-luxe lingerie as well as a tasteful collection of sex toys, erotic literature, massage products and "after dinner mix condoms". The delicate underwear, in all manner of styles, is made from the finest laces, silks and satins and comes in cup sizes A-F. There are romantic rose tulle camisoles, pearl G-strings, Forties-style French knickers and raunchy hipster thongs. Whatever you desire, the professional fitters in the shop will help you find your perfect fit and such is their success they have opened three more stores in London and one in New York in the past year.   *myla.com*

Expensive   *Amex/MC/V*

020 7221 9222
77 Lonsdale Road
London W11

tube: Notting Hill Gate
Mon-Sat 10-6

020 7581 6880
166 Walton Street
London SW3

tube: South Kensington
Mon-Sat 10-6:30

020 7730 0700
74 Duke of York Square
London SW3

tube: Sloane Square
Mon-Sat 10-6:30
Sun 12-5

020 7491 8548
4 Burlington Gardens
London W1

tube: Bond Street
Mon-Sat 10-6

N.Peal

If it's cashmere you're craving, this label has some of the best. The tiny men's shop by the entrance to the famous Burlington Arcade offers a wide variety of styles in colours from navy to bright purple. The women's shop at the other end of the arcade sells equally colourful cardigans embellished with embroidery and sequins, as well as knit halters, scoop-necked twinsets, slippers and shawls. Cashmere is taken very seriously here: they offer a special shampoo to keep your favourite pieces at their finest, and (if hand-washing is just too much like hard work) they will send your precious woollies all the way to the Scottish border to be cleaned. A specialist repair service is also available. *npeal.com*

Expensive *Amex/MC/V*

020 7499 2952 (M)   **tube: Green Park/Piccadilly Circus**
71-72 Burlington Arcade   Mon-Sat 9:30-6
London W1

020 7493 9220 (W)   **tube: Green Park/Piccadilly Circus**
37 Burlington Arcade   Mon-Sat 9:30-6
London W1

The Natural Shoe Store

They're not the sexiest shoes on the market but they won't leave you crying with pain at the end of a hard day's pave-mount-pounding. Among the wide variety of well-made brands you'll find Arche, Birkenstock, Trippin and Nature Sko. Basic leather and suede lace-ups from classic brands like Cheaney are the most exhilarating items in a selection short on fashion but long on comfort. *naturalshoestore.com*

Affordable *Amex/MC/V*

020 7836 5254   **tube: Covent Garden**
21 Neal Street   Mon-Tues 10-6, Wed, Fri 10-7, Thurs 10-8
London WC2   Sat 10-6:30, Sun 12-5:30

020 7240 2762   **tube: Covent Garden**
37 Neal Street   Mon-Wed 10-6, Thurs-Fri 10-7
London WC2   Sat 10-6:30, Sun 12-5:30

020 7351 3721   **tube: Sloane Square**
325 King's Road   Mon-Fri 10-6, Sat 10-6:30
London SW3   Sun 12-5:30

020 7727 1122   **tube: Notting Hill Gate**
181 Westbourne Grove (called Issues)   Mon-Fri 10-6
London W11   Sat 10-6

Neil Cunningham

He has been called a master in the art of female flattery, and with a signature style that combines elegant tailoring with glamorous retro styles Neil Cunningham is one of London's most popular bridal couturiers. A strong Hollywood influence is evident in strapless bias-cut columns, simple sheath dresses and empire and A-lines. Detail is kept to a minimum, perhaps just a twinkle of Swarovski crystal or an eye-catching line of buttons. Classic, sexy and very grown-up. Audrey Hepburn and Jackie O would definitely approve. *neilcunningham.com*

Expensive *Amex/MC/V*

020 7437 5793
28 Sackville Street
London W1

tube: Piccadilly Circus
Mon-Sat 10-5:30 (every second Sat)
(by appointment)

Net-a-Porter

No snooty shop assistants, no scary changing rooms—you can even shop in your pyjamas. You won't find this shop on any high street—it's the world's best virtual boutique, created by a gang of brilliant alumnae from that stylish and unique magazine *Tatler*. The original concept was to create an online magazine with fashion features just like the glossies, but which visitors could buy from (see Gisele in a stunning Missoni bikini, double-click and it's yours). The idea has since expanded into an online emporium of hot designer names, featuring...well, virtually every label you can think of: Marc Jacobs, Miu Miu, Chloé, Rick Owens, Diane von Furstenberg, Temperley—do we need to go on? Shoes by luminaries like Christian Louboutin and Jimmy Choo, and separate sections for beauty, jewellery and music make this a chic one-stop-shop for those who prefer logging on to trekking about. Your order will come beautifully wrapped, like a present—as any savvy shopper knows, the best presents are always the ones you give yourself. You know you deserve it!   *net-a-porter.com*

Moderate to very expensive   *Amex/MC/V*

New & Lingwood

Two stores sit at the Jermyn Street entrance to the charming Piccadilly Arcade. Beautiful, curved windows display a wonderful selection of shirts, shoes, ties and accessories. A Jermyn Street establishment since 1865, New & Lingwood's gorgeous interior must be one of few in the world to feature chandeliers and coats of arms...perhaps it's not surprising that they are traditional outfitters to the boys of Eton College (most famous recent alumni: the late Diana's two sons, Princes William and Harry). Friendly service, plus bespoke shirts in addition to off-the-peg. Great selection of cufflinks, suspenders, socks, dressing-gowns and the rest.   *newandlingwood.com*

Expensive   *Amex/MC/V*

020 7493 9621
53 Jermyn Street
London SW1

tube: Piccadilly Circus/Green Park
Mon-Fri 9-6, Sat 10-6

New Look

A thumping sound system and futuristic aluminium steps leading up to the 15,000 square foot Oxford Street store will make teenagers squeal with delight and others think they have entered the spaceship from Brief Encounters of the Third Kind. This new flagship store is aiming for the TopShop touch with its fast turnover of catwalk-inspired styles, from Kelly Osborne-ish Eighties skirts and batwing tops to Fifties ladylike chic to more casual wear and lingerie.

A plus-size range is also available. The quality is cheap and cheerful. It's worth popping in for the funky accessories: charm bracelets by Tatty Devine or pieces from guest designers Pamela Blundell and Karen Walker which will leave your friends guessing. *newlook.co.uk*

Affordable　　　　　　　　　　　　　　　　　　　*MC/V*

020 7290 7860　　　　　　　　**tube: Marble Arch**
500-502 Oxford Street　　　　　　　　Mon-Sat 10-9
London W1　　　　　　　　　　　　　　　Sun 12-6

020 7629 6960　　　　　　　**tube: Covent Garden**
233 High Holborn　　　　　　　Mon-Fri 8-8, Sat 9-6
London WC1

020 7534 2005　　　　　　　**tube: Oxford Circus**
175-179 Oxford Street　　　　Mon-Fri 9-8, Thurs 9-9
London W1　　　　　　　　　Fri-Sat 9-7, Sun 11-6

020 7802 9768　　　　　　　　　**tube: Victoria**
Upper Concourse, Victoria Station　　Mon-Fri 8-8, Sat 9-7
London SW1　　　　　　　　　　　　　Sun 11-5

020 8946 5895　　　　　　　　**tube: Wimbledon**
Centre Court Shopping Centre　　　　Mon-Fri 10-7
London SW19　　　(Thurs 10-8), Sat 9-6, Sun 11-5

Next　　　　　　　　　　　　　　　👤👤👤

This store has less style and spunk than chains like Oasis and Zara (think practical big sister), but it can provide an adequate supply of trend-led essentials. The selection ranges from business blouses in pretty patterns to comfy cords and colourful sportswear. Designs remain generally unremarkable but you might find some stylish staples—raincoats, shoes and maternitywear, for example. *next.co.uk*

Affordable　　　　　　　　　　　　　　　*Amex/MC/V*

020 7434 0477　　　　　　　**tube: Oxford Circus**
201-203 Oxford Street　　　　　　　Mon-Sat 10-8
London W1　　　　　　　(Thurs 10-9), Sun 12-6

020 7659 9730　　　　　　　**tube: Marble Arch**
508-520 Oxford Street　　　　　　　Mon-Sat 10-8
London W1　　　　　　　(Thurs 10-9), Sun 12-6

020 7409 2746　　　　　　　**tube: Bond Street**
325-329 Oxford Street　　　Mon-Fri 10-8 (Thurs 9-9)
London W1　　　　　　　　Sat 9:30-8, Sun 12-6

020 7434 2515　　　　　　　**tube: Oxford Circus**
160 Regent Street　　　　　　　Mon-Sat 10:30-7
London W1　　　　　　(Thurs 10:30-9), Sun 12-6

020 7420 8280　　　　　　**tube: Covent Garden**
15-17 Long Acre　　Mon-Sat 10-8 (Thurs 10-9, Fri 11-8)
London WC2　　　　　　　　　　　　Sun 12-6

020 7938 4211　　**tube: High Street Kensington**
54-56 Kensington High Street　　Mon-Fri 10-7 (Thurs 10-8)
London W8　　　　　　　　Sat 10-7, Sun 12-6

020 7715 9410　　　　　　　**tube: Canary Wharf**
11-12 Canada Place　　　　　Mon-Fri 8-8, Sat 10-6
London E14　　　　　　　　　　　　Sun 11-6

Nicole Farhi

This darling of British design has been revered for some time. Her key to lasting fashion success: classic design, beautiful fabrics and creations that are simple but striking. Soft sweater sets, crisp oxford shirts and sleek trousers dominate the women's collection, while a similar selection of menswear reinforces the sense of understated style. Staff are exemplary, and the laid-back funk muzak adds to the relaxed atmosphere. Farhi's Home collection is increasingly popular and can be seen at the Fulham Road store where chunky wooden tables are set with heavy wine glasses, simple vases of flowers and lovely white china as well as at her dedicated homewear store at 17 Clifford Street, just off Bond Street. *nicolefarhi.com*

Expensive   *Amex/MC/V*

020 7499 8368   **tube: Bond Street**
158 New Bond Street   Mon-Fri 10-6 (Thurs 10-7)
London W1   Sat 10-6:30, Sun 11-5

020 7235 0877   **tube: Knightsbridge**
193 Sloane Street   Mon-Sat 10-6 (Wed 10-7)
London SW1

020 7497 8713 (M)   **tube: Covent Garden**
11 Floral Street   Mon-Sat 10:30-6:30
London WC2   (Thurs 10:30-7), Sun 11-6

020 7240 9983 (W)   **tube: Covent Garden**
15 The Piazza   Mon-Sat 10:30-6:30
London WC2   (Thurs 10:30-7), Sun 12-6

020 7838 0937   **tube: South Kensington**
115 Fulham Road   Mon-Sat 10-6 (Wed 10-7)
London SW3   Sun 12-5

020 7792 6888   **tube: Notting Hill Gate**
202 Westbourne Grove   Mon 10-6, Tues-Sat 8:30-6
London W11   Sun 10-5

020 7435 0866   **tube: Hampstead**
27 Hampstead High Street   Mon-Sat 10-6 (Thurs 10-6:30)
London NW3   Sun 12-6

Nigel Hall

The recent refurbishment means that this once small boutique is now a larger, cleaner space. Nigel Hall offers sleek designs for the slightly fashion-forward male. The simple, modern selection features fine knitwear, shirts, trousers and jackets. This otherwise unremarkable shop scores high marks for decent prices and nice detail.

Moderate to expensive   *Amex/MC/V*

020 7836 8223   **tube: Covent Garden**
18 Floral Street   Mon-Wed 10:30-6:30
London WC2   Thurs-Sat 10:30-7, Sun 12-5

Night Owls

As different from Agent Provocateur as your granny is from Kate Moss, this high-class but slightly fusty shop offers lacy lingerie, see-through chemises and linen loungewear. On the suggestive side there are plenty of pretty thongs with matching garter belts and bras. The pink polka-dot panties are cute, though like most of their pieces they are too elaborate in texture or pattern to be concealed by anything but the thickest trousers.

Moderate   *Amex/MC/V*

020 7584 2451   **tube: South Kensington**
78 Fulham Road   Mon-Sat 10-6 (Wed 10-7)
London SW3

Niketown London
Nike-philes should make a dash for this store, a massive, sleek emporium offering every imaginable piece of swish paraphernalia from coordinating water bottles and key-chains to the latest and lightest-weight running shoe. Organized by clothing category and sport, the wide selection of activewear is easy to navigate. But beware: these trademarked stay-dry fabrics and high-tech trainers come at a higher-than-average price—and avoid weekend visits if you're allergic to over-excited teenagers.   *nike.com*

Moderate   *Amex/MC/V*

020 7612 0800   **tube: Oxford Circus**
236 Oxford Street   Mon-Wed 10-7, Thurs-Sat 10-8
London W1   Sun 12-6

Nine West
American import Nine West retains a reputation for affordable, fashionable leather shoes and accessories. Lately the brand has expanded, offering everything from strappy sandals to towering boots to practical flats. The colours on offer have evolved too, reaching brightly beyond basic black and brown to seasonal pastels and braver brights. Sunglasses, handbags, jewellery and outerwear are also available.   *theshoestudio.com*

Affordable   *Amex/MC/V*

020 7629 3875   **tube: Bond Street**
9 South Molton Street   Mon-Sat 10-7 (Thurs 10-8)
London W1   Sun 12-6

020 7229 8208   **tube: Queensway/Bayswater**
Whiteley's, Queensway   Mon-Sat 10-8, Sun 12-6
London W2

020 7836 8485   **tube: Covent Garden**
1 James Street   Mon-Sat 10-8 (Thurs 10-9)
London WC2   Sun 12-6

020 7937 1479   **tube: High Street Kensington**
155 Kensington High Street   Mon-Sat 10-7
London W8   (Thurs 10-8), Sun 12-6

020 7581 7044   **tube: Sloane Square**
90 King's Road   Mon-Sat 10-7 (Wed 10-7:30)
London SW3   Sun 12-6

Nitya

Offering a comforting alternative to the sleek Bond Street boutiques, the French brand Nitya features Indian-inspired tunics, skirts, loose trousers and scarves that express a body-modest sensibility. Flowing, natural fabrics elegantly drape the body in subtle tones of grey, rust, cream, black, white and beige. Styles are dressy and some are intricately stitched with simple floral patterns. Perfect for the non-traditional mother of the bride.

Moderate to expensive   *Amex/MC/V*

020 7495 6837   **tube: Bond Street**
118 New Bond Street   Mon-Sat 10-6
London W1   (Thurs 10-7)

Noa Noa

This is a real hit-and-miss Danish label. With wool V-neck cardigans, soft felt handbags and wide-leg corduroys, it's hardly clothing you can find fault with—provided it doesn't put you straight to sleep. The colour palette is frequently dominated by uninspired shades of sludge, and the loose cuts hover dangerously close to frumpy. Among the few memorable pieces: crushed silk harem pants, quilted coats and long, ruffled-hem skirts.   *noa-noa.com*

Moderate   *Amex/MC/V*

020 7704 2131   **tube: Highbury & Islington/Angel**
146 Upper Street   Mon-Sat 9:30-6 (Thurs-Fri 10:30-7)
London N1   Sun 11-5

☆ Oasis

It's all going on at Oasis. Capitalising on the current fad for all things retro, the "New Vintage" collection comprises beautiful, limited-edition replicas of vintage designs, sourced globally: our favourites are a Sixties sequined cocktail dress picked up in LA and a delicately beaded Fifties dress from a flea market in Florence. There's also a fab new lingerie collection designed by the founder of Knickerbox, and a stand-alone clothing collection by Ann-Louise Roswald. Oasis has always been among the leaders of London's catwalk-to-sidewalk interpreters, and its individually styled stores—a chandelier here, a Venetian mirror there—are a refreshing change from the pile 'em high, sell 'em cheap high street norm. (The New Vintage and lingerie collections are only stocked in the flagship London stores: Argyll Street and James Street.)   *oasis-stores.com*

Affordable   *Amex/MC/V*

020 7323 5978   **tube: Oxford Circus**
292 Regent Street   Mon-Sat 10-7 (Thurs 10-8)
London W1   Sun 12-6

020 7434 1799   **tube: Oxford Circus**
12-14 Argyll Street   Mon-Sat 10-7 (Thurs 10-8)
London W1   Sun 12-6

020 7580 4763
The Plaza, 120 Oxford Street
London W1

tube: Oxford Circus
Mon-Sat 10-7(Thurs 10-8)
Sun 12-6

020 7240 7445
13 James Street
London WC2

tube: Covent Garden
Mon-Sat 10-7 (Thurs 10-8)
Sun 12-6

020 7584 5269
76-78 King's Road
London SW3

tube: Sloane Square
Mon-Sat 9:30-6:30 (Wed 9:30-7:30)
Sun 12-5

020 7512 9715
19 Canada Square
London E14

tube: Canary Wharf
Mon-Fri 8:30-7, Sat 9-6
Sun 12-6

020 7938 4019
28a Kensington Church Street
London W8

tube: High Street Kensington
Mon-Sat 9:30-6
(Thurs-Fri 9:30-7:30), Sun 12-6

020 7359 5620
10 Upper Street
London N1

tube: Angel
Mon-Sat 10-7, Sun 11-5

020 7256 8608
85-86 Old Broad Street
London EC2

tube: Liverpool Street
Mon-Fri 8-6
(Thurs 8:30-6:45)

020 7248 2922
4 Queen Victoria Street
London EC4

tube: Bank
Mon-Fri 8:30-6:15
(Thurs 8:30-6:45)

020 7243 2795
Whiteley's, Queensway
London W2

tube: Queensway/Bayswater
Mon-Sat 10-8, Sun 12-6

Office ♟♟♟

The name might fool you with its suggestion of corporate blandness but the majority of the shoes here are far too edgy for an average day at the office. Though not out-landish, the selection puts its own eccentric spin on season-al basics like crocodile boots, stiletto heels and colourful mules. You'll also find trendy sneakers and, in summer, a far-rago of flip-flops. If you fancy yourself as a girl-about-town, you'll love it. *office.co.uk*

Affordable   *Amex/MC/V*

020 7491 8027 (W)
55 South Molton Street
London W1

tube: Bond Street
Mon-Sat 10-7, Sun 12-6

020 7379 1896
57 Neal Street
London WC2

tube: Covent Garden
Mon-Fri 10-7:30 (Thurs 10:30-8)
Sat 10:30-7, Sun 12-6

020 7497 0390
60 St Martin's Lane
London WC2

tube: Covent Garden
Mon-Sat 10-7
Sun 12-6

020 7589 7286
61 Brompton Road
London SW3

tube: Knightsbridge
Mon-Sat 10-7
Sun 12-6

020 7229 3576   **tube: Notting Hill Gate/Ladbroke Grove**
206 Portobello Road   Mon-Fri 9-6, Sat 9:30-6:30
London W11   Sun 11-5

020 7584 5611   **tube: Sloane Square**
58 King's Road   Mon-Sat 10-7
London SW3   Sun 12-6

020 7434 2530   **tube: Oxford Circus**
35 Carnaby Street   Mon-Sat 10:30-7 (Thurs 10:30-8)
London W1   Sun 12-6

Offspring

This sporty sibling to Office swaps slingbacks for sneakers, offering a wide selection: Prada, Caterpillar, Timberland and Pumas. Workout enthusiasts and posers alike will flip for the hip styles from Nike, Adidas, New Balance and Converse. The store is perfect for sporty posers, but with its small dimensions and thumping music it may seem a bit claustrophobic for a casual drop-in.   *offspring.co.uk*

Affordable   *Amex/MC/V*

020 7497 2463   **tube: Covent Garden**
60 Neal Street   Mon-Sat 10-7 (Thurs 10-8)
London WC2   Sun 12-6

020 7267 9873   **tube: Camden Town**
221 Camden High Street   Daily 10-6:30
London NW1

020 7287 5200   **tube: Leicester Square**
49 Old Compton Street   Mon-Sat 10-7
London W1   Sun 12-6

OG2

This popular boutique on bustling Portobello Road has a new name (formerly Olowu Golding) but has stuck to its modern mix of sharp tailoring and offbeat detail. The clothing merges Duro Olowu's West African heritage with Elaine Golding's classic East Coast influence. Handmade shoes come with stained wooden heels and in fine materials like calf and snakeskin. Heart-stopping prices may put you off (shoes start at £350), but cool creativity comes at a cost.

Expensive   *Amex/MC/V*

020 8960 7570   **tube: Ladbroke Grove**
367 Portobello Road   Mon-Sat by appointment
London W10

Oilily

This 40-year-old Dutch line offers just what a dreary London day demands: colour, and the brighter the better. Orange, red, yellow and blue are combined in patterns of eye-crossing intricacy in knitwear, trousers and skirts. The children's line is delightful—dresses, sweaters, trousers and shirts splashed with patterns. Be warned, though: these aren't Gap prices.   *oilily.nl*

Expensive   *Amex/MC/V*
020 7823 2505   **tube: Knightsbridge**
9 Sloane Street   Mon-Sat 10-6 (Wed 10-7)
London SW1

Old Spitalfields Market

One of London's coolest markets, Old Spitalfields has over 250 stalls selling all things vintage, avant-garde designs by talented new names and every accessory you could ever wish for. A fashion market is held every Thursday and is a favourite with tourists, stylists and celebrities. We particularly liked the striped halterneck tops at Ami Ogundehin's stall, Oluremi. (She can also be found at Portobello market.) When you're shopped off your feet, stop for pie and mash, a crepe or an enchillada at one of the many international food stalls.   *oldspitalfieldsmarket.com*

Affordable   *Cash/cheque preferred*
(no phone)   **tube: Liverpool Street**
Brushfield Street   Market stalls: Mon-Sat 10-4, Sun 9-5
London E1   (Fashion market every Thursday)

Oliver Sweeney

Oliver Sweeney shoes combine the design of a classic British gentleman's shoe with a modern twist: his trademark look is an isometric toe. All shoes are manufactured with the utmost expertise in Italy; the pièce de résistance is a handmade shoe made from sting-ray. Brad Pitt is a Sweeney connoisseur and the store also stocks stylish sneakers and casual footwear.   *oliversweeney.com*

Expensive   *Amex/MC/V*
020 7626 4466   **tube: Liverpool Street**
133 Middlesex Street   Mon-Fri 10-7, Sat 10-6
London E1   Sun 10-4

020 7730 3666   **tube: Sloane Square**
29 King's Road   Mon-Sat 10-7
London SW3   (Wed 10-8), Sun 12-6

Olivia Morris

Having outgrown her tiny shop (and price point) at the Portobello Market, Morris packed up her pumps and moved a few blocks north. Her first collection was high-concept but fun, featuring do-it-yourself "blank canvas" heels which come in white with paint kit included. Now you'll find feminine high heels, sandals, pumps, slingbacks and softly rounded toes, and pretty flowered designs as well as bridal shoes. Olivia worked with Patrick Cox before launching her own collection and is now an established star in the footwear firmament.   *oliviamorrisshoes.com*

Expensive   *Amex/MC/V*
020 8962 0353   **tube: Ladbroke Grove**
355 Portobello Road   Mon-Tues by appointment
London W10   Wed-Thurs 11-6, Fri-Sat 10-6

One Night Stand

Who needs a fairy godmother? Frockless Cinderellas should direct the pumpkin straight to One Night Stand, London's original dress hire agency. With a constantly updated collection of over 400 dresses in sizes 6-18, and dress hire, at around £130, costing a fraction of the original, Cinders will find everything from ballgowns and chiffon floaty dresses to long satin evening gowns and corsets with skirts by designers like Robinson Valentine, Jenny Packham and David Fielden. If you're not the one-night type and you're heading off for a minibreak, don't panic, your hire lasts up to four days and is guaranteed not to turn to rags at midnight. Next day delivery is available in the UK and jewellery and accessories can also be hired.

Moderate   *Amex/MC/V*

020 7352 4848   **tube: Sloane Square**
8 Chelsea Manor Studios   (by appointment)
Flood Street
London SW3

One of a Kind

Sometimes secondhand doesn't come cheap, even in Notting Hill. They may be pre-worn, but the designer goods here—from the likes of Pucci, Gucci and Vivienne Westwood—are regarded more like a rare vintage Scotch, to be savoured and respected. No Seventies polyester here, just quality fabrics from the Victorian age to the Eighties. Surrounding walls are covered in every cornerstone style of shoe, from peep toes to platforms to pumps. It must be good—top designers have been known to pop in for inspiration.   *1kind.com*

Moderate to expensive   *Amex/MC/V*

020 7792 5284   **tube: Ladbroke Grove**
253 Portobello Road   (by appointment)
London W11

020 7792 5853   **tube: Ladbroke Grove**
259 Portobello Road   Mon-Sat 11-6, Sun 12-5
London W11

O'Neill

Straight from the beaches and boardwalks of Southern California, O'Neill brings sun-streaked surf style to London's streets. Grab some hot-pink flip-flops with tropical flowers printed on them or some jumbo Hawaiian printed luggage bags as well as bright T-shirts, long shorts, swimsuits and the inevitable wetsuit. Stop here for a heavy dose of the West Coast.   *oneilleurope.co.uk*

Affordable   *Amex/MC/V*

020 7836 7686   **tube: Covent Garden**
9-15 Neal Street   Mon-Sat 10-7 (Thurs 10-8)
London WC2   Sun 12-6

020 7734 3778
5-7 Carnaby Street
London W1

tube: Oxford Circus
Mon-Fri 10-7 (Thurs 10-8), Sun 12-6

Orvis

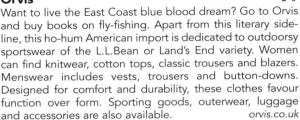

Want to live the East Coast blue blood dream? Go to Orvis and buy books on fly-fishing. Apart from this literary side-line, this ho-hum American import is dedicated to outdoorsy sportswear of the L.L.Bean or Land's End variety. Women can find knitwear, cotton tops, classic trousers and blazers. Menswear includes vests, trousers and button-downs. Designed for comfort and durability, these clothes favour function over form. Sporting goods, outerwear, luggage and accessories are also available. *orvis.co.uk*

Affordable to moderate   *Amex/MC/V*

020 7499 7496
36a Dover Street
London W1

tube: Green Park
Mon-Fri 9:30-6 (Tues 10-6), Sat 10-4

Osprey

Their plethora of purses, pocketbooks and planners at prices within reason should feed your accessories needs. Gentle pink, brown and navy leather keep many pieces looking simple. For the bolder bunch, there's crocodile, lizard and other styles straight from the wild. The range is promising and the quality top-notch.

Moderate to expensive   *Amex/MC/V*

020 7935 2824
11 St Christopher's Place
London W1

tube: Bond Street
Mon-Sat 11-6 (Thurs 11-7)

Ozwald Boateng

Perfect for the tall and trim build, but not for the slim wallet. Boateng is the most high-profile of the new breed of Savile Row tailors, bringing a touch of flash and a high celeb count to the Row. His razor-sharp suits in bright colours, or more sombre with bright linings, are instantly identifiable for their long slim lines. The staff all look as though they should be on the catwalk and are friendly with it. In addition to bespoke suits the store sells off-the-peg suits and brightly coloured shirts and ties, and a more informal diffusion line, Boateng, which claims to be inspired by British public schools and their sporting heritage. This says muddy knees and smelly rugby socks to us, but that's probably not what they mean. *ozwaldboateng.com*

Very expensive   *Amex/MC/V*

020 7437 0620
9 Vigo Street
London W1

tube: Piccadilly Circus
Mon-Sat 10-6 (Thurs 10-7)

Paddy Campbell

Whatever the trends, "ladylike" will never be out of fashion. Campbell's chic, understated seasonal pieces will bring to mind fashion clichés like "Jackie O" and "timeless"—there's no helping it once you've seen the classic, no-frills selection of predominantly pastel dresses, skirts and suits. Best for mature audiences. *paddycampbell.co.uk*

Expensive *Amex/MC/V*

020 7225 0543 **tube: Knightsbridge**
17 Beauchamp Place Mon-Fri 10-6 (Wed 10-7)
London SW3 Sat 10:30-6

020 7493 5646 **tube: Bond Street**
8 Gees Court Mon-Fri 10-6 (Thurs 10-7)
London W1 Sat 10:30-6

Pamela Shiffer

Jammed with floral skirts, linen dresses in warm earth tones and classic white shirts, this small boutique in Primrose Hill seems more geared towards the comfort-driven older lady than the trendy North London gal who is more likely to be found across the street at Anna's or Spice. Delicate silky wraps are beautifully displayed. *pamelashiffer.com*

Moderate *Amex/MC/V*

020 7483 4483 **tube: Chalk Farm**
75 Regent's Park Road Mon-Sat 10-6
London NW1 (Thurs 10-7), Sun 12-6

020 7243 1222 **tube: Notting Hill Gate**
25 Kensington Park Road (opening hours as above)
London W11

Pantalon Chameleon

It's neither trendy nor cutting-edge, but if you are looking for chic casual daywear or something special for Ascot, Pantalon Chameleon is well worth a look-in. Bright colours dominate the collection with linen halterneck dresses in tomato red and smart, tailored summer suits in hot pink. Relaxed pieces such as the jeans and wraparound shirts are perfect for everyday wear and the Brazilian-style flip-flops in turquoise, white and scarlet are a bestseller. In fact, Pantalon Chameleon's shoe collection is the principal signature of the brand and includes everything from traditional mules and black ankle boots to sorbet-coloured moccasins. They shine in winter, too—just check out their wonderful suede and velvet coats. *pantalonchameleon.com*

Moderate *Amex/MC/V*

020 7384 2909 **tube: Parsons Green**
28 New King's Road Mon-Sat 10-6 (Wed-Thurs 10-7)
London SW6 (clothes only)

020 7751 9871 **tube: Parsons Green**
187 New King's Road (opening hours as above)
London SW6 (shoes only)

020 7730 0200 **tube: Sloane Square**
50 Duke of York Square Mon-Sat 10-6 (Wed, Thurs 10-7)
London SW3 Sun 12-5

020 8767 3131   station: **Wandsworth Common (mainline)**
14 Bellevue Road   Mon-Sat 10-6
London SW17   Sun 12-5

Paraboot

A long-established French shoe company famous for its quietly stylish, ultra-durable, hand-stitched styles. The company's casual, two-hole lace-up leather shoe, known as the
Michael, lays claim to being the most copied shoe in the
world. Its simplicity and elegance is hard to beat. Prices
range from £125 to £250, reasonable in comparison with
some of London's other stalwart shoe labels. *paraboot.com*

Moderate   *Amex/MC/V*

020 7494 3233   tube: **Piccadilly Circus/Oxford Circus**
37 Savile Row   Mon-Fri 10-6, Sat 10-5
London W1

Parallel

Here's another reason to go shoe shopping in London. The
store has a boudoir feel and offers an ambitious range of
styles, from a ruthless high heel to a sympathetic loafer.
European designers include Sergio Rossi, Luc Berjen,
Baldinini and D'Allesandro. Best of all, at sale time, they've
banished the long waits to try on, opting instead for self-
service which means you can just grab your size and go.

Moderate   *Amex/MC/V*

020 7224 0441   tube: **Baker Street/Bond Street**
22 Marylebone High Street   Mon-Sat 10-6:45
London W1   Sun 12-6

Parallel Intimo

Just down the block from the shoe shop, Parallel Intimo
stocks some top labels to cover your bottom, including
Argentovivo and Andrea Sarda. Bra-and-panty sets, bust-
boosting lace corsets, swimwear and men's boxer briefs are
all available. Sexy nightgowns that drape to the floor are no
more mumsy than a lace teddy, while leaving plenty more to
the imagination with the help of their boudoir range of candles and body oils. New to the shop is a small collection of
womenswear which includes Seven Jeans, Essential and
Nocturne.

Moderate   *Amex/MC/V*

020 7486 7300   tube: **Baker Street/Bond Street**
13 Marylebone High Street   Mon-Sat 10-6:45
London W1

Patricia Roberts

Young hipsters might think (wrongly) that this shop is a bit
sad, but international knitting junkies cross the ocean to
come to Roberts's 30-year-old shop where bright-coloured
sweaters for women and kids are displayed amidst yards of
yarn. Her 12 published books on the subject are a testament
to her cult following, though fans will be hard-pressed to

recreate her charming hand-knits. Tiny blue sweaters with angora teddy bears and matching mittens are lovely for little ones.

Expensive   *Amex/MC/V*

020 7235 4742   **tube: Knightsbridge**
60 Kinnerton Street   Mon-Fri 10-6, Sat 11-3
London SW1

Patrick Cox

Cox is an alpha cobbler and is now moving into accessories with suitcases, day bags and wallets. He's worked with Vivienne Westwood, John Galliano and Anna Sui. His soft-soled, square-toed Wannabe loafer became the It-shoe of the Nineties and hit the one million mark a couple of years ago. He custom-makes diamanté-studded sandals for Madonna and counts Elizabeth Hurley and Elton John amongst his clients. So what's the big deal? Well, his stellar shoes are renowned for their distinctive shapes, whether they are square or pointy, slip-on or knee-high, and he uses luscious materials, from handmade leather to sexy skins.   *patrickcox.co.uk*

Expensive   *Amex/MC/V*

020 7730 8886   **tube: Sloane Square**
129 Sloane Street   Mon-Sat 10-6 (Wed 10-7)
London SW1   Sun 12-5

Patrizia Wigan Designs

London's yummy mummies have shopped here for close to 20 years because there's no other children's store quite like it. Specializing in traditional English clothing, Wigan's hand-embroidered smocked dresses and boy's breeches look as if they have just stepped out of Frances Hodgson Burnett's *The Secret Garden*. The store is one of the few to cater for pageboys as well as bridesmaids and for the best in baby couture there are Swiss cotton and French lace christening gowns. It's all a brilliant blast to the past. *patriziawigan.com*

Expensive   *Amex/MC/V*

020 7823 7080   **tube: Knightsbridge**
19 Walton Street   Mon-Fri 10:30-6:30, Sat 10:30-6
London SW3

Paul & Joe

The chilly staff might size you up like you're not quite cool enough, but don't be deterred. French designer Sophie Albon (who named the label after her sons) spins a beautifully cut, eclectic collection of inspired, wearable pieces and intricate prints...floaty organza tops, crisp cotton button-downs, hip-hugging trousers and tattered chiffon skirts sprinkled with dots of gold glitter. It's classic French tailoring with a twist, and a side order of pretty high heels and one-off jewellery pieces. The funky mood is enhanced by an assortment of colourful gift items, including bath products, cute lacy thongs and their own line of perfume, cosmetics and skincare. *paulandjoe.com*

Moderate to expensive Amex/MC/V

020 7243 5510 **tube: Notting Hill Gate**
39-41 Ledbury Road Mon-Fri 10-6 , Sat 10-6:30
London W11 Sun 12-5

020 7589 2684 **tube: South Kensington**
309 Brompton Road Mon-Fri 10-6:30 (Wed 10-7)
London SW3 Sat 10-7, Sun 1-6

020 7836 3388 (M) **tube: Covent Garden**
33 Floral Street Mon-Fri 10-6:30, Sat 10-7
London WC2 Sun 12-5

020 7824 8844 (W) **tube: Sloane Square**
134 Sloane Street Mon-Sat 10-6 (Wed 10-7)
London SW1

☆ **Paul Smith** 👤👥

If Alexander McQueen is London fashion's bad boy, Smith is its reigning knight—literally. Sir Paul brings his own quirky spin to classic English tailoring, with madcap collections that offer everything from purple oxfords with red polka dots for men to women's bright turquoise corduroys. Colours are confidently bright and patterns eye-catching. Smith's personality seems especially present in the details—suits with stand-out stitching, bright green belts with pink undersides and cufflinks shaped like manual typewriter keys. The children's line is adorable, featuring football club sweatshirts and pink glittered tees. Check out his fragrances too, which are equally playful, and the new pen and watch collection. His fabulously distinctive rug collection is available at The Rug Company on 124 Holland Park Avenue, London W11—definitely worth a visit for PS groupies. And—while we're singing his praises—the website is one of our all-time favourites for its funky graphics, clear illustrations and happy, foot-tappy soundtrack. Sir Paul, we salute you. *paulsmith.co.uk*

Moderate to expensive Amex/MC/V

020 7379 7133 **tube: Covent Garden**
40-44 Floral Street Mon-Sat 10:30-6:30
London WC2 (Thurs 10:30-7), Sun 12:30-5:30

020 7379 7133 (PS) **tube: Covent Garden**
9-11 Langley Court Mon-Wed 10:30-6:30, Thurs 10:30-7
London WC2 Fri, Sat 10:30-6:30, Sun 12-5:30

020 7589 9139 (W) **tube: South Kensington**
84-86 Sloane Avenue Mon-Fri 10:30-6:30 (Wed 10:30-7)
London SW3 Sat 10-6:30, Sun 1-5

020 7727 3553 **tube: Notting Hill Gate**
122 Kensington Park Road Mon-Thurs 10:30-6:30
London W11 Fri-Sat 10-6:30

020 7626 4778 **tube: Bank**
7 The Courtyard Mon-Fri 10-6
Royal Exchange
London EC3

Paule Ka

Harking back to the days when ladies wore white gloves on airplanes, this French label maintains an unerring devotion to detail. From a timeless gabardine check suit to a taffeta evening gown, every creation has its own set of accessories (a matching cloche hat or billowing tulle muffs). Designer Serge Cajfinger has reincarnated the total-look approach to dressing once maintained by style icons like Audrey Hepburn and Jackie O. These first ladies of fashion would certainly have approved of the pale fitted jackets with empire line bows, but might have spluttered over the cheeky ruffled micromini and matching bikini top. *pauleka.com*

Expensive   *Amex/MC/V*

020 7647 4455   **tube: Green Park**
13a Grafton Street   Mon-Sat 10-6 (Thurs 10-7)
London W1

020 7823 4180   **tube: Sloane Square**
161 Sloane Street   Mon-Sat 10-6 (Wed 10-7)
London SW1

Pegaso

Italian Pegaso stocks nothing out of the ordinary but is still likely to please, with top-end designers like Gucci, Versace and Calvin Klein. There's every cut and colour of men's suit, from double-breasted black to more contemporary (and frightening) straight-cut green. The helpful staff might tempt you into finishing the look with collared shirts, cuff-links and shiny leather loafers. If you can't get to the shop, fittings and deliveries can also be arranged at your home or office. *pegaso.co.uk*

Expensive   *MC/V*

020 7602 5225   **tube: High Street Kensington**
275 Kensington High Street   Daily 10-6:30
London W8

020 7379 7978   **tube: Covent Garden**
33 Neal Street   Mon-Sat 10-7
London WC2   Sun 12-6

Pepe Jeans

Gum-poppers come here for the casual selection of denim jeans, jackets and shirts. The new Portobello store has wooden floorboards which give a laid-back homely feel, and there's an in-store team dedicated to customising jeans and jackets. The diffusion line is updated every two or three months in an attempt to keep up with denim big boys Levi and Diesel. Keep trying, little brother. *pepejeans.com*

Affordable to moderate   *Amex/MC/V*

020 7439 0523   **tube: Oxford Circus**
42 Carnaby Street   Mon-Fri 10-7, Sat 10-7
London W1   Sun 12-6

020 7221 9287   **tube: Notting Hill Gate**
172 Westbourne Grove   Mon-Sat 10-6:30
London W11   Sun 12-5

163

020 8960 7001 tube: **Ladbroke Grove**
309 Portobello Road Mon-Sat 10-6
London W10

Peter Jones

Every self-respecting London girl has a place in her heart for this venerable department store, part of the John Lewis chain. If not for the fashion, which can be a bit mumsy, then for the prolific household essentials—from powerful Dyson vacuum cleaners to lavender candles to Nigella Lawson's kitchen utensils. Where can I get some cheap curtains made? How can I remove the scratch on my wooden floor? Where can I buy the best value bed? Whatever your domestic conundrum, Peter Jones has the answer. The store has recently undergone a massive £100 million renovation and transformed itself into a bright modern space with a skylit central atrium, shiny escalators and a much loved top floor café. Fashionwise you will find a host of familiar labels, from Kenzo to Ted Baker, and the children's wear is fantastic value. *peterjones.co.uk*

Affordable to expensive MC/V

020 7730 3434 tube: **Sloane Square**
Sloane Square Mon-Sat 9:30-7
London SW1

Petit Bateau

For over 100 years Petit Bateau has been France's leading manufacturer of children's undershirts, tees and sleepwear. Their design is comfortingly simple, based on the classic snug, scoop-necked cotton model with long or short sleeves, in softly muted colours, as well as more fun shades of burnt orange and cerise. So well loved are they that when they branched out to include tiny women's tees in 1994 it was only a minute before they were in the closets of just about every petite Parisienne. London girls have been quick to follow. *petit-bateau.com*

Affordable to moderate Amex/MC/V

020 7838 0818 tube: **Sloane Square**
106-108 King's Road Mon-Sat 10-6 (Wed, Thurs 10-7)
London SW3 Sun 12-6

020 7491 4498 tube: **Bond Street**
62 South Molton Street Mon-Sat 10-6:30 (Thurs 10-7)
London W1 Sun 11-5

020 7243 6331 tube: **Notting Hill Gate**
73 Ledbury Road Mon-Sat 10-6
London W11 Sun 12-5

Phase Eight

Phase Eight is high street for grown-ups. First impressions might not be great: the clothing can seem conservative and mumsy, from neutral suits to sturdy work shoes. But look a bit closer and you'll also find some more interesting pieces—patterned floaty dresses in summer, co-ordinating twinsets in winter. Nothing is liable to leap out at you but good quality basics with feminine flair make the label popular with corporate ladies. *phase-eight.co.uk*

Moderate   *Amex/MC/V*

020 7352 9025   **tube: South Kensington**
345 Fulham Road   Mon-Sat 9:30-6
London SW10   Sun 11-5

020 7229 7445   **tube: Notting Hill Gate**
164 Notting Hill Gate   (opening hours as above)
London W11

020 8947 4140   **tube: Wimbledon**
31 High Street   (opening hours as above)
London SW19

020 7823 4094   **tube: Sloane Square**
97 Lower Sloane Street   Mon-Sat 9:30-6
London SW1

020 7226 1904   **tube: Angel**
211-212 Upper Street   Mon-Fri 10-6:30
London N1   Sat 9:30-6, Sun 11-5

020 7730 5921   **tube: Sloane Square**
34 Duke of York Square   Mon-Sat 10-6:30 (Wed 10-7)
London SW3   Sun 11-5

Philip Somerville

London is arguably the last cosmopolitan city where women still love to wear hats. Widely considered among the best made-to-order milliners in the world, Somerville's clientele is unsurprisingly A-list. Diana, Princess of Wales was a devotee, and Somerville still holds a royal warrant. The design philosophy combines simple, striking shapes with bold colours and a traditional English feel. Every hat is handmade (this takes 3-4 weeks) and every last detail double-checked. For a quick fix, Fortnum & Mason and Selfridges stock some of his ready-to-wear.

Expensive   *Amex/MC/V*

020 7224 1517   **tube: Baker Street**
38 Chiltern Street   Mon-Fri 9-5:30
London W1

Philip Treacy

If your aim in life is to be noticed, you need a Philip Treacy hat. His millinery masterpieces top the lot, and are coveted by attention-seekers the world over for their bright colours, sharp, quirky shapes and extravagant details (e.g., feathers and veils). No matter how crazy, they're still entirely proper and so distinctive you won't get away with wearing one twice. His couture service will force you into a mortgage but don't lose heart—the ready-to-wear is more reasonable. These hats are special enough for your best friend's wedding—just be careful you don't upstage the bride. *philiptreacy.co.uk*

Expensive   *Amex/MC/V*

020 7730 3992
69 Elizabeth Street
London SW1

tube: **Sloane Square/Victoria**
Mon-Fri 10-6, Sat 11-5

Phillipa Lepley

Here comes the bride, and if Lepley has designed her dress it's liable to be sprinkled with freshwater pearls, sparkling with Austrian crystals or planted with embroidered peonies. Classic brides can always opt for a gown that's beautifully sculpted but unadorned. All lined in silk, Lepley's simple designs are cut to emphasize assets—A-line skirts and nipped waists give every woman an hourglass. The store itself is a lovely light space and the staff are renowned for being helpful, guiding nervous brides through every important decision.   *phillipalepley.com*

Very expensive   MC/V

020 7386 0927
494 Fulham Road
London SW6

tube: **Fulham Broadway**
Mon-Sat 10-6 (for browsing; otherwise best to make an appointment)

Phlip

With a slogan that boasts "original American clothing" come few surprises: loads of jeans and cargo pants, baseball caps and messenger bags. Labels like Carhartt, Schott, Eastpak and Converse sit happily in the streetwise atmosphere of the store. Rap music rattles out a cool vibe and the staff display a suitably rough attitude.

Expensive   MC/V

020 7352 4332
191 King's Road
London SW3

tube: **Sloane Square**
Mon-Sat 10:30-7, Sun 12-6

Pickett

If you relish the finer things in life, this store offers plenty of them. The Burlington Arcade shops have a Dickensian feel, with their dark wood interiors making the perfect backdrop for the lovely luxury gifts on offer. On one side of the arcade, you'll find sewn briefcases, exotic hide handbags, leather gloves, stud boxes and wallets; on the other, suede-covered A-Z London guides, trendy Turkish slippers, lovely shawls, and an expanding selection of colourful, chunky jewellery. Pickett also offers a custom-made service for everything from desk blotters to luggage sets.   *pickett.co.uk*

Moderate   Amex/MC/V

020 7493 8939
41 Burlington Arcade
London W1

tube: **Green Park/Piccadilly Circus**
Mon-Sat 9-6

020 7493 8939
32-33 Burlington Arcade
London W1

tube: **Green Park/Piccadilly Circus**
Mon-Sat 9-6

020 7823 5638
149 Sloane Street
London SW1

tube: **Sloane Square**
Mon-Sat 9-6 (Wed 9-7)

020 7283 7636
6 Royal Exchange
London EC3

tube: Bank
Mon-Fri 9-6

Pied à Terre

This shoe chain owned by Nine West features its own signature collection of well-crafted, simple styles, from canvas and wicker wedges, strappy party heels, buckled mules and candy-pink ballet pumps. Prices are slightly higher than your average high street shoe store, but the selection is wide-ranging and the shoes long-lasting. *theshoestudio.com*

Moderate   *Amex/MC/V*

020 7629 1362
19 South Molton Street
London W1

tube: Bond Street
Mon-Sat 10-7
(Thurs 10-8), Sun 12-6

020 7730 3757
12 Duke of York Square
London SW3

tube: Sloane Square
Mon-Sat 9:30-6:30

The Pineal Eye

One glance in the window and you might mistake it for a gallery—you'd be half right (the staff are certainly bored and snooty enough.) This ground-floor exhibition space, where contemporary art displays change every month, is part one of The Pineal Eye. Part two is downstairs, where art magazines, Japanese books and designer clothing await. Labels are high-concept, including Dior Homme, Raf Simmons, Bernard Willhelm and Lutz. It's a cool-culture outpost in the middle of the wild west end.

Expensive   *MC/V*

020 7434 2567
49 Broadwick Street
London W1

tube: Oxford Circus
Mon-Fri 11-7, Sat 12-7

Pineapple

If you've ever watched Fame! and wished you too could live forever, you'll love this dancewear shop. Fashion undergraduates, dancers and cool Japanese students flock here for the J.Lo-esque velour sweatpants, sporty (and predominantly pink) streetwear, hooded sweatshirts, printed tees and butt-hugging black clubbing trousers. Our advice: take a good look in the mirror before venturing outside the dance studio in any of this lot. *pineapple.uk.com*

Affordable   *Amex/MC/V*

020 7836 4006
6a Langley Street
London WC2

tube: Covent Garden
Mon-Sat 10-7, Sun 11-5:30

Pink Piranha

It's a schlep to get to this corner of Camden, but the sexy, high-quality lingerie here is worth the trip. Lacy peek-a-boo bras might shock modest minnies, but on the whole, styles are tasteful, feminine and classy (and pricey). Swimwear, shoes and jewellery are also available.   *pinkpiranha.co.uk*

Expensive   *Amex/MC/V*

020 7267 1100   **tube: Chalk Farm/Camden Town**
21 Chalk Farm Road   Mon-Sat 11-7
London NW1   Sun 10:30-6:30

Please Mum   ♀

The sickening name tells you everything you need to know about the contents of this highly pretentious children's designer clothing store. If your precious son or daughter can't face the first day of pre-school without the latest Armani, this is the place to come. Featuring such designer labels as Moschino, Evisu, Roberto Cavalli and D&G, Please Mum dresses budding fashion hounds from birth to teens. The store also specializes in ballgowns for baby's first black-tie.   *please-mum.co.uk*

Expensive   *Amex/MC/V*

020 7486 1380   **tube: Knightsbridge/Hyde Park Corner**
85 Knightsbridge   Mon-Sat 9:45-6:30
London SW1   (Wed 9:45-7), Sun 10-6

Pleats Please: Issey Miyake   ♀

It makes perfect sense that a designer sometimes criticized for his unwearable, avant-garde signature collection would create a second line that is comfortable enough to sleep in (and wrinkle-free, so no one would know if you did). Miyake's selection of machine-pleated womenswear is engineered entirely of synthetic fibres and comes in his standard brilliant rainbow colours. These clothes are ideal for travelling and suited to Miyake fans who can't quite afford his main line.

Expensive   *Amex/MC/V*

020 7495 2306   **tube: Bond Street**
20 Brook Street   Mon-Sat 10-6
London W1

Plein Sud   ♀

Fans of Joseph will enjoy the equally well-tailored pieces here, although the look is harder-edged and fussier. Subtle shades of beige, pink and green offset the raw character of the clothing: a layered, leather miniskirt with an eyelet pattern and tattered hems, suede trousers with criss-crossing waist laces as well as fluid jersey dresses—everything is left a bit rough. Prices are high and the character is strong, so it's a good place to just dabble.

Expensive   *Amex/MC/V*

020 7584 8295   **tube: South Kensington**
151 Draycott Avenue   Mon-Fri 10-6:30
London SW3   Wed 10-7, Sun 1-6

Pollyanna   ♀

This little den of children's goodies is a honeypot for Fulham mums. In sizes from newborn to eight years old, the clothing is everything you'd expect, from babygrows to denim overalls to sensible shoes by Start-Rite. The store is not overrun with toys (a blessing if you're trying to navigate with a pram) but you can find a small selection of traditional playthings.

Moderate   *MC/V*

020 7731 0673   **tube: Parsons Green**
811 Fulham Road   Mon-Sat 9:30-5:30
London SW6

Pop Boutique

The moment you step into this shop you're liable to be flooded with flashbacks of schooldays and your first lunchbox. Their mantra—"Don't follow fashion, buy something already out of date"—inspires the selection of retro relics that look as fresh as the day they were made. A one-stop disco-era shop for the likes of ex-Spice Girl Geri Halliwell and the host of celebs staying next door at the Covent Garden Hotel, Pop offers tracksuits, denim jeans, corduroys, flared-collar shirts and leather jackets. Lava lamps and other kitsch housewares are also available.   *pop-boutique.com*

Affordable   *Amex/MC/V*

020 7497 5262   **tube: Covent Garden**
6 Monmouth Street   Mon-Sat 11-7, Sun 1-6
London WC2

Portobello Market

Rub shoulders with the cool crowd: Kate Moss and friends are regular visitors, and stylist Patricia Field (responsible for all our *Sex and the City* favourites) sources many outfits from this market. Friday morning is the best time to visit this stretch of Notting Hill, made famous by Hugh Grant and Julia Roberts. Saturdays are disastrous for claustrophobics, but ambitious visitors might enjoy the spectacle of a tourist stampede. On the southern end of the road you'll find a wide variety of antique shops selling everything from furniture to nautical devices to old prints. Further north, past the produce stalls, the fun begins. Once you've spotted the Westway, an overpass running across Portobello, you're heading into the fashion. Jeans, custom T-shirts, vintage shoes and leather jackets are some of the best trendy bits on hand here. While you're in the area, pop into the Portobello Arcade where some of the street's more established secondhanders hold court. Come with cash, no one takes plastic.

Affordable   *Cash/cheques only*

(no phone)   **tube: Notting Hill Gate/Ladbroke Grove**
Portobello Road   Fri 7-4, Sat 8-5
London W10   Sun 9-4 (clothing stalls)

Poste

A great one-stop shop for the man with a short attention span, Poste targets the customer who is tuned into trends in footwear. Part of the Office shoe group, this small store offers a surprisingly varied selection of international designers and styles though, as the proprietor concedes, at a price slightly above normal. A definite plus is that while he's dithering between Paul Smith and Marc Jacobs, you can nip across the road to check out the women's selection at Office.

Affordable to expensive   Amex/MC/V

020 7499 8002   **tube: Bond Street**
10 South Molton Street   Mon-Sat 10-7, Sun 12-6
London W1

Poste Mistress

As pink and fluffy as a Fifties boudoir, the interior of this store is the perfect backdrop for the quirky selection of shoes. The pleasingly unpredictable mix includes Vivienne Westwood, Dries Van Noten, Miu Miu, Moschino and Cacherel, with a few more casual acquaintances like Converse, Adidas, Camper and Birkenstock. All this, and the velvet sofas, gilded mirrors, and old Hollywood head shots (from Audrey Hepburn to Daisy and the Dukes of Hazard), set the tone for old-fashioned glamour with a bit of street cheek and some kitsch sprinkled on top.

Moderate to expensive   Amex/MC/V

020 7379 4040   **tube: Covent Garden**
61-63 Monmouth Street   Mon-Sat 10-7, Sun 12-6
London WC2

Prada

First stop for serious fashionistas: glass cases and a twinkling of skylights showcase Miuccia Prada's coveted accessories from round-toe courts to deluxe car shoes. Always one step ahead of the rest, her grown-up handbag of the season comes floral-patterned or decorated with passementerie embroidery. The clothing too has matured, and gone are the cartoon details on blouses, skirts and jackets. Instead, fabric is sculpted into the haute-couture shapes of the Fifties, and pouf sleeves and cinched waists do the talking. From athletic apparel to the little black dress, the crowd of fashion-forward guys, It-girls, young royals and Russian glitterati are never disappointed.   *prada.com*

Expensive to very expensive   Amex/MC/V

020 7647 5000   **tube: Green Park**
16-18 Old Bond Street   Mon-Sat 10-6 (Thurs 10-7)
London W1

020 7235 0008   **tube: Knightsbridge**
43-45 Sloane Street   Mon-Sat 10-6 (Wed 10-7)
London SW1

020 7626 2068   **tube: Bank**
1 The Courtyard   Mon-Fri 10-6
Royal Exchange
London EC3

Preen

The look is Victoriana set askew (à la Vivienne Westwood): puffed sleeves, layered skirts and lots of ragged edges. You might think it OTT at first glance but the handmade character and subtle colours of the collection bring it all firmly down to earth. A new accessories range continues the edgy theme. Notting Hill bohemian boldness at its best.

Expensive   *MC/V*

020 8968 1542   **tube: Ladbroke Grove**
5 Portobello Green Arcade   Thurs-Sat 10-6
London W10

Pringle

For decades this Scottish sweater brand was associated with geeks, golfers and granddads. Now, after its dramatic rejuvenation, Pringle's young, cool image is firmly in place, with Madonna, Robbie Williams and David Beckham all wearing the traditional diamond-patterned sweaters. The shops on Bond Street and Sloane Street are both light, bright and fun with heaps of the coveted cashmere separates and a few surprises thrown in too. Cute, desirable, sexy—we love it.   *pringlescotland.com*

Expensive   *Amex/MC/V*

020 7297 4580   **tube: Bond Street**
111-112 New Bond Street   Mon-Sat 10-6:30
London W1   (Thurs 10-7:30)

020 7881 3061   **tube: Sloane Square**
141-142 Sloane Street   Mon-Fri 10-6:30 (Wed 10-7)
London SW1

Proibito

Designer labels, everywhere you look—Valentino, Moschino, Versace Jeans Couture, Gianfranco Ferré, D&G, Diesel and Cavalli. This big, bright shop houses trousers, sweaters and shirts for both genders. The Bond Street location provides next season's collection, while the South Molton Street branch sells last season at a discount.

Moderate to expensive   *Amex/MC/V*

020 7493 0589   **tube: Bond Street**
94 New Bond Street   Mon-Wed 10-7
London W1   Thurs 10-8, Fri-Sat 10-7, Sun 12-6

020 7491 3244   **tube: Bond Street**
42 South Molton Street   Mon-Wed 10-7
London W1   Thurs 10-8, Fri-Sat 10-7, Sun 12-6

Public Aware

This hip clothing and accessories store off Brick Lane specialises in up-and-coming Japanese and British designers. With funky, sexy clothing ranges and shoe, jewellery and accessories collections set over two floors, Public Aware is a fashion stylist's dream.

Moderate — *Amex/MC/V*

020 7053 2185 — **tube: Liverpool Street**
Unit 7, 91 Brick Lane — Daily 11-7
London E1

Puma

Trendy sports brand Puma has sponsored Pele through World Cup Finals, Boris Becker at Wimbledon and Linford Christie on the running track. The concept store on Carnaby Street offers everyone a piece of the action, whatever their game. There's everything from track trousers and running shorts to tennis dresses and sports bras. A few more directional pieces and accessories from sunglasses to lace-up shoulder bags combine the sporty look with a fashionable modern spin. — *puma.co.uk*

Moderate to expensive — *Amex/MC/V*

020 7439 0221 — **tube: Oxford Circus/Piccadilly Circus**
52-55 Carnaby Street — Mon-Sat 10-7, Sun 12-6
London W1

☆ Push

"Sexy. Pregnant" declares the window: it's enough to make any sane girl want to go forth and multiply. There is a lengthy waiting list for their top-selling jeans by Citizens of Humanity (put your name down now), but they also stock Earl Jean's maternity range, with ingenious stretchy pockets instead of that scary expanse of kangaroo pouch elastic. We also loved the gorgeous normal-size-but-maternity-friendly clothing by Australian designer Leona Edmiston.

Expensive — *MC/V*

020 7359 2003 — **tube: Angel**
9 Theberton Street — Mon-Fri 10:30-5 (Thurs 10:30-7)
London N1 — Sat 10:30-6, Sun 12-4

Question Air

A bright boutique with a friendly staff and lots of good names such as Issey Miyake, Betsey Johnson, Joseph and Ghost. And if your man needs a wardrobe update, take him to the side-by-side his 'n' hers stores in Wimbledon Village, or to the menswear store in Covent Garden where he'll find labels such as G-star, Von Dutch, Paper Denim, Juicy Couture for men and funky Seven For all Mankind jeans. It's therapy for shopping couples. — *question-air.co.uk*

Moderate to expensive — *Amex/MC/V*

020 7221 8163 — **tube: Notting Hill Gate**
229 Westbourne Grove — Mon-Tues 10:30-6
London W11 — Wed-Sat 10:30-6:30, Sun 12-5

020 7435 9221 — **tube: Hampstead**
28 Rosslyn Hill — Mon-Wed 10:30-6, Thurs-Sat 10:30-6:30
London NW3 — Sun 12-5:30

020 8879 0366 — **tube: Wimbledon**
77/78 High Street — Mon-Sat 10-6, Sun 12-5:30
London SW19

Directory

020 8946 6288
78 High Street
London SW19

tube: Wimbledon
(opening hours as above)

020 8741 0816
129 Church Road
London SW13

station: Barnes (mainline)
Mon-Sat 10-5:30, Sun 12-5

020 8748 1772 (sale shop)
86 Church Road
London SW13

station: Barnes (mainline)
(opening hours as above)

020 8299 4252 (W)
85-87 Dulwich Village
London SE21

station: North Dulwich (mainline)
Mon-Sat 10-6, Sun 11:30-5

Quiksilver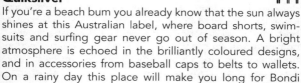

If you're a beach bum you already know that the sun always shines at this Australian label, where board shorts, swimsuits and surfing gear never go out of season. A bright atmosphere is echoed in the brilliantly coloured designs, and in accessories from baseball caps to belts to wallets. On a rainy day this place will make you long for Bondi Beach. *quiksilver-europe.com*

Affordable   *Amex/MC/V*

020 7240 5886
12 North Piazza
London WC2

tube: Covent Garden
Mon-Sat 10-7, Sun 11-5

020 7836 5371
1 & 23 Thomas Neals Centre
London WC2

tube: Covent Garden
Mon-Sat 10-7
Sun 12-6

020 7439 0436
11/12 Carnaby Street
London W1

tube: Oxford Circus
(opening hours as above)

R.M.Williams

The durable selection of khakis, oilskin jackets, thick woollens and moleskin shirts at this Australian outfitter could come in handy on a cold day. For women the pickings are slimmer, being primarily trousers and shirts. Of particular note is their signature elastic-sided leather boot, designed to provide enduring quality, structural support and a particularly rugged style. Materials like kid, nubuck and kangaroo add to the shop's rugged outback appeal. As we went to press they were planning to relocate from their old Regent Street premises; the old telephone number was 020 7629 6222, or try *rmwilliams.com.au*

Moderate to expensive   *Amex/MC/V*

R.Soles

Yee-haw! If your shoe closet has been looking a bit too city-slick lately, this is a great place to get some cowboy kicks. The store has a huge, no-holds-barred selection of cowboy boots in every conceivable style, from basic snakeskin to cow print to lime-green leather. With an assortment of matching accessories, die-hard rodeo fans can rope in the whole kit 'n' caboodle. *r-soles.com*

Expensive   *Amex/MC/V*

020 7351 5520   **tube: Sloane Square**
109a King's Road   Mon-Sat 10-7, Sun 12-6
London SW3

Rachel Riley

She won an award for her mail-order business, then opened her second London store, and now it seems there's no stopping Rachel Riley. She brings a breath of fresh air to feminine Fifties style in silk dresses with cashmere cardigans, straw hats and handbags to match. The same selection is shrunk down for the kids' collection, including Liberty print smock dresses with sunhats, sweet embroidered dungarees and Mary Janes by Start-Rite. There is a charming selection of bridesmaid and pageboy outfits, and a tailor-made service if nothing takes your fancy from the ready-to-wear selection. An enticing stop for a mother-daughter day. *rachelriley.com*

Affordable to moderate   *Amex/MC/V*

020 7935 7007   **tube: Baker Street/Bond Street**
82 Marylebone High Street   Mon-Sat 10-6
London W1

020 7259 5969   **tube: Knightsbridge**
14 Pont Street   Mon-Sat 10-6
London SW1

Racing Green

Known for practical clothes in practical cuts, Racing Green offers an extensive selection of Gap-style basics but with some big names thrown in, like Ted Baker and Pierre Cardin. Striped T-shirts, long twill skirts and cotton trousers are typical fare from this comfortable collection, which also includes tailored suits, shoes, accessories and outerwear. It all comes in durable fabrics and standard colours. Racing Green also offers a hire service for good quality suits with all the trimmings. *racinggreen.co.uk*

Moderate to expensive   *Amex/MC/V*

020 7437 4300   **tube: Oxford Circus**
195 Regent Street   Mon-Sat 10-7 (Thurs 10-8)
London W1   Sun 12-6

Ralph Lauren

From his navy sport jackets to his silk evening gowns, Ralph Lauren's signature collection is as blue-blooded as they come. Even the store on Bond Street, its walls hung with patrician portraits, is liable to evoke fantasies of a life of ease and a weekend house in the country. If you want in to this club, it'll cost you: baby-soft cable-knit cashmere sweaters, brown suede dresses, leather trousers and crisp shirts all fetch a high price. The home collection, with embroidered pillow cases, silver cocktail shakers and black and white vintage photographs is best admired at the new

Fulham Road location. If you're new to planet Lauren you may be surprised at the prices, but nosing around the stores is an education even if you don't plan to buy. The Ralph Lauren gestalt, from gentlemen's club to sportswear that almost smells of the sea and the snow, changed the way fashion presents itself. They're clothes, yes, but they're also an idea. *ukralphlauren.com*

Expensive to very expensive *Amex/MC/V*

020 7535 4600 **tube: Green Park**
1 New Bond Street Mon-Sat 10-6 (Thurs 10-7)
London W1 Sun 12-5

020 7590 7990 **tube: South Kensington**
105-109 Fulham Road Mon-Fri 10-6 (Wed 10-7)
London SW3 Sat 10-6:30, Sun 12-5

Ralph Lauren (children)

It's everything you would find at Polo Ralph Lauren, but in miniature. The Polo obsession can be met here from as early as birth and nurtured all the way to girls' size 16 and boys' size 20. You'll find swimwear, tote bags and expensive diaper bags—the perfect present for a high maintenance mummy. There's also a great selection of children's books. *ukralphlauren.com*

Expensive *Amex/MC/V*

020 7535 4888 **tube: Bond Street**
143 New Bond Street Mon-Sat 10-6 (Thurs 10-7)
London W1 Sun 12-5

Ravel

If you lack the time, interest or resources to seek out designer shoes, this store offers basic styles with no nonsense. Racks are organized by size for self-service, making it an easy, quick hit. Most of the selection reflects the latest trends, but you can also find basic black. A selection for children and juniors is also available.

Affordable *Amex/MC/V*

020 7631 4135 **tube: Oxford Circus**
184-188 Oxford Street Mon 10:30-8, Tues-Sat 10-8
London W1 Sun 11:30-6

Reiss

For more than 20 years this British retailer was devoted strictly to menswear but their womenswear collection, launched four years ago, has been a huge success, proving that these boys can do girls' stuff too. Highlights include bohemian beaded halter tops, swirl-patterned skirts and striped tops. A new lingerie line joins shoes, bags and belts to complete the picture: modern, funky but understated. *reiss.co.uk*

Moderate to expensive *Amex/MC/V*

020 7637 9112 **tube: Oxford Circus**
14-17 Market Place Mon-Sat 10-6:30 (Thurs 10-7:30)
London W1 Sun 12-6

020 7225 4910   **tube: Sloane Square**
114 King's Road   Mon-Sat 9:30-6:30 (Wed-Thurs 10-7)
London SW3   Sun 12-6

020 7493 4866   **tube: Bond Street**
78-79 New Bond Street   Mon-Sat 10-7 (Thurs 10-8)
London W1   Sun 12-6

020 7491 2208   **tube: Bond Street**
56 South Molton Street   Mon-Sat 10-7 (Thurs 10-8)
London W1   Sun 12-6

020 7240 7495   **tube: Covent Garden**
116 Long Acre   (opening hours as above)
London WC2

020 7439 4907   **tube: Oxford Circus**
172 Regent Street   (opening hours as above)
London W1

020 7431 5425   **tube: Hampstead**
52-54 Heath Street   Mon-Fri 10-6 (Thurs 10-7)
London NW3   Sun 12-6

Rellik

Set at the base of Trellick Tower, Rellik is home to three separate vintage boutiques: Identity, Laissez Faire and Affinity. Each specializes in a different era, so the selection is an eclectic mix, from reconstructed designs using antique trimmings to secondhand Vivienne Westwood—Kate Moss came here for her vintage outfit for the opening of Westwood's retrospective at the V&A. A good stop on the Notting Hill retro circuit. *relliklondon.com*

Affordable to expensive   *Amex/MC/V*

020 8962 0089   **tube: Westbourne Park**
8 Golborne Road   Tues-Sat 10-6
London W10

Replay & Sons

A must-see new children's shop on the Fulham Road, Replay & Sons is off-beat and Italian-trendy. The clothing is influenced by Peru, India, Morocco and Brazil and features cotton T-shirts with cheerful logos ("I dreamt of Hawaii and it was beautiful"), little cargo trousers, and a host of delightful denim. Colourful and playful, the styles are exactly what you want in children's clothing. The shop itself is also a joy, with huge giant bee lights hanging from the ceiling. *replay-and-sons.it*

Moderate   *Amex/MC/V*

020 7589 2870   **tube: South Kensington**
147-149 Fulham Road   Tues-Sat 10-6:30
London SW3   Sun 12-6

Ricci Burns

No other London street corner could be better suited to Ricci Burns and his brassy collection of international couture than this pricey section of Belgravia. A Vidal Sassoon protégé in the Sixties, Burns has the orange-tanned, heavily maintained look of a man who can't quite accept that his swinging days are over…who better to dress Victoria Beckham and other showy footballers' wife types? His over-the-top selection is dripping with names like Blumarine and garish gowns guaranteed to put you on the party pages of *Hello!*

Very expensive   *Amex/MC/V*

020 7823 1555   **tube: Knightsbridge**
25 Lowndes Street   Mon-Sat 10-6 (Thurs 10-7)
London SW1

Richard Anderson

The bespoke tailoring firm was formed by two ex-Huntsman men, head cutter Richard Anderson and house director Brian Lishak. Richard Anderson still cuts every suit himself, and the distinctive Anderson line is a Savile Row institution. Elegant tailored suits and shirts are the order of the day here, and a limited selection of women's business suits is also available. Clients range from pop stars to 80-year-old elder statesmen—a sure sign that they're doing everything right.   *richardandersonltd.com*

Very expensive   *Amex/MC/V*

020 7734 0001   **tube: Oxford Circus**
13 Savile Row   Mon-Fri 9-5
London W1   Saturday by appointment

Richard James

The first shop encountered on entering what everyone still calls "the Row" from the Conduit Street end, Richard James is also the street's most self-consciously fashionable store. This former Menswear Designer of the Year occupies a big-windowed, airy, subtly cool space kitted out with row upon row of vibrant shirts and distinctive long-cut, double-vented ready-to-wear suits mingling with knitwear, sportswear and trendy accessories ranging from garish socks to cuff-links. A famously rock 'n' roll bespoke service is also available—just ask Tom Cruise and Elton John. And at a Tiffany party in Spencer House, the models in formal Bruce Oldfield were well outshone by a tall male guest in a green check Richard James suit.   *richardjames.co.uk*

Expensive to very expensive   *Amex/MC/V*

020 7434 0171   **tube: Piccadilly Circus/Oxford Circus**
29 Savile Row   Mon-Fri 10-6 (Thurs 10-7), Sat 11-6
London W1

020 7626 4116   **tube: Bank**
12 The Courtyard, Royal Exchange   Mon-Fri 10-6
London EC3

Rigby & Peller

Fans of TV show *What Not To Wear* will be familiar with the sight of presenters Trinny and Susannah pushing their victim into Rigby & Peller to have her embonpoint adjusted—often with spectacular results. A family-run business specializing in made-to-measure lingerie, Rigby & Peller has held a royal warrant from the Queen since 1960. Not surprisingly, then, this is a service-oriented establishment offering bras, pants, corsets, garters, swimwear and nightwear. Labels include Prima Donna, Lise Charmel, Lejaby and Felina, and the colour spectrum is standard boudoir: blacks, whites, reds and pastels. A good place for the big-busted to get a perfect fit, but avoid lunchtimes or be prepared to wait.   *rigbyandpeller.com*

Expensive   *Amex/MC/V*

020 7491 2200   **tube: Oxford Circus**
22a Conduit Street   Mon-Sat 9:30-6 (Thurs 9:30-7)
London W1   (last fitting one hour before close)

020 7589 9293   **tube: Knightsbridge**
2 Hans Road   Mon-Sat 9:30-6 (Wed 9:30-7)
London SW3   (last fitting one hour before close)

Ritva Westenius

Understated yet original, Ritva Westenius designs fluctuate between classic and trendy, sexy and sophisticated. Using luxurious fabrics—silk organza, duchesse satin and crepe—her simple, elegant dresses come enhanced with lovely details—beading, bows, crystals and roses. Some styles do look a little bit *Footballers' Wives*, while others save the day with their Martha Stewart wholesomeness. Prices range from £1,700 to £3,500, with a full couture service available by appointment.   *ritvawestenius.com*

Expensive to very expensive   *Amex/MC/V*

020 7706 0708   **tube: Marble Arch**
28 Connaught Street   Mon-Sat 9-6 (by appointment)
London W2

River Island

Those shopping the youngster's high street, taking in Oasis and Kookaï, should add River Island to their route map. Although the store's profile is somewhat lower than its high street peers', there are some surprising treats to be had. Trendy teenagers will love the decal T-shirts, sheer shirts, caramel stiletto boots and silver bangles. Men will find khakis and jeans, leather trainers, skate shoes and casual holiday wear. The brand swiftly catches up with the latest looks and affordable prices keep hipsters happy.   *riverisland.com*

Moderate   *Amex/MC/V*

020 7491 3229   **tube: Oxford Circus**
283 Oxford Street   Mon-Sat 10-7 (Thurs 10-8)
London W1   Sun 12-6

020 7499 4018   **tube: Bond Street**
470-482 Oxford Street   Mon-Sat 10-7 (Thurs-Fri 10-8)
London W1   Sun 12-6

Robert Clergerie

The French are frustratingly good at stepping out in style. How do they do it? They've had more than a little help from Monsieur Clergerie, one of France's premier shoe designers. His moccasins and mules are perennial favourites and his summer sandals are sexy sophistication down to the last strap. Comfy insoles and soft leather linings ensure that, however fashionable, the shoes mould to your feet. There is no question that Clergerie has a magic touch. *robertclergerie.com*

Moderate to expensive   *Amex/MC/V*

020 7584 4995 (W)   **tube: South Kensington**
122 Draycott Avenue   Mon-Fri 10:30-6 (Wed 10:30-7)
London SW3   Sat 10:30-6, Sun 1-5

020 7935 3601   **tube: Bond Street**
67 Wigmore Street   Mon-Sat 10:30-6 (Thurs 10:30-7)
London W1

Robinson Valentine

Antonia Robinson and Anna Valentine have a loyal following for their chic, made-to-measure day- and eveningwear. Their background is in couture, so rest assured that quality from this designing duo is top-end: cut, subtle detailing and sumptuous fabrics are the Robinson Valentine hallmarks. Just don't expect them to gossip about their celebrity client list, which includes Camilla Parker Bowles: they are infuriatingly discreet. We weren't at all surprised that the bride was wearing a Robinson Valentine creation at the last royal wedding… *robinsonvalentine.com*

Expensive to very expensive   *MC/V*

020 7937 2900   **tube: High Street Kensington**
4 Hornton Place   Mon-Fri 10-5 (by appointment)
London W8

Rokit

Cluttered but manageable, this vintage store sells everything from Fifties shirts for men to antique hosiery for women. Trying on old prom dresses with Johnny Cash's "Desperado" floating in the background is a real treat. A hot spot for London stylists, Rokit recently launchedits own label with a range of T-shirts, sweatshirts and hoodies. *rokit.co.uk*

Moderate   *MC/V*

020 7836 6547   **tube: Covent Garden**
42 Shelton Street   Mon-Sat 10-7 (Thurs 10-8)
London WC2   Sun 11:15-6

020 7267 3046   **tube: Camden Town**
225 Camden High Street   Daily 10-7
London NW1

020 7375 3864   **tube: Liverpool Street**
101-107 Brick Lane   Mon-Fri 11-7
London E1   Sat-Sun 10-7

Roderick Charles

Less illustrious than its bespoke shirtmaker neighbours on Jermyn Street, Roderick Charles has four more stores in the City, all catering to the traditional tastes of their core 40-plus businessman customer. The ready-to-wear and made-to-measure suits, shirts and ties are of admirable quality in classic styles at affordable prices.

Moderate   *Amex/MC/V*

020 7930 4551   **tube: Piccadilly Circus/Green Park**
90 Jermyn Street   Mon-Fri 9:30-5:30 (Thurs 9:30-6)
London SW1   Sat 10-5:30

020 7929 1867   **tube: Monument**
25 Lime Street   Mon-Fri 10-5
London EC3

020 7242 4554   **tube: Chancery Lane**
79-80 Chancery Lane   Mon-Fri 10-5
London WC2

020 7248 5303   **tube: St Paul's/Mansion House**
52 Bow Lane   Mon-Fri 9-5
London EC4

020 7588 2050   **tube: Liverpool Street**
31 Blomfield Street   Mon-Fri 9-5:30
London EC2

Ronit Zilkha

A favourite with British TV presenters (is that a good thing?), the softer of Ronit Zilkha's pieces accentuate the female silhouette with tiny ruffles, shimmering sequins and strategically placed slits. But all the suits, dresses, skirts, loose trousers and eveningwear are feminine and well made. Some accessories are also available.   *ronitzilkha.com*

Moderate to expensive   *Amex/MC/V*

020 7499 3707   **tube: Bond Street**
34 Brook Street   Mon-Sat 10-7
London W1   Sun 11:30-5:30

020 7431 0253   **tube: Hampstead**
17 Hampstead High Street   Mon-Sat 9:30-6:30
London NW3   Sun 11-6

020 7730 2888   **tube: Sloane Square**
21 King's Road   Mon-Fri 9:30-6:30 (Wed 10-7)
London SW3   Sat 9:30-6:30, Sun 12-6

020 7486 6785   **tube: Bond Street/Baker Street**
107 Marylebone High Street   Mon-Sat 9:30-6:30
London W1   (Thurs 9:30-7), Sun 11-6

Ruco Line

The store is brimming with Ruco's signature lace-up leather shoes, all of which feature cartoonishly clumpy rubber soles. The women's line has a bit more flair than the men's, with pink, light blue and gold snakeskin variations, but it still comes down to one style (and not a very appealing one)

repeated to exhaustion. A range of travel bags is also available, as are metallic handbags which are just the right side of dodgy.   *rucoline.it*

Affordable to moderate   *Amex/MC/V*

020 7629 5702
64 South Molton Street
London W1

tube: Bond Street
Mon-Sat 10-6 (Thurs 10-7)

Russell & Bromley 👫

Family-owned Russell & Bromley boasts a no-nonsense environment and a large variety of shoes—some with handbags to match. The Jermyn Street branch sells only men's shoes of the classic variety from British manufacturers Church's and Barkers and American brand Sebago, famous for its loafers. Women's selection at other locations includes Stuart Weitzman, Beverly Feldman and Donna Karan. No style strays too far from the mainstream, though some people complain that prices are higher than they should be.   *russellandbromley.co.uk*

Expensive   *Amex/MC/V*

020 7629 6903
24-25 New Bond Street
London W1

tube: Bond Street
Mon-Sat 10-6:30
(Thurs 10-7:30), Sun 11-5

020 7629 4001
109-110 New Bond Street
London W1

tube: Bond Street
(opening hours as above)

020 7493 3501
494/496 Oxford Street
London W1

tube: Marble Arch
Mon-Sat 10-7
Sun 12-6

020 7409 2776
395/397 Oxford Street
London W1

tube: Bond Street
Mon-Sat 10-7, Sun 12-6

020 7589 8415
45 Brompton Road
London SW3

tube: Knightsbridge
Mon-Sat 10-6:30, Wed 10-7

020 7584 7443
77 Brompton Road
London SW3

tube: Knightsbridge
Mon-Sat 10-7, Sun 12-6

020 7584 5445
64 King's Road
London SW3

tube: Sloane Square
(opening hours as above)

020 7930 5307
95 Jermyn Street
London SW1

tube: Piccadilly Circus/Green Park
Mon-Fri 10-6, Sat 10-5

020 7938 2643
151/153 Kensington High Street
London W8

tube: High Street Kensington
Mon-Sat 10-6:30
(Thurs 10-7) Sun 11-5

Russell & Haslam 👩

You've probably already seen their designs without even knowing it. Together Gwen Russell and Janette Haslam designed the costumes for, amongst others, Michelle Pfeiffer in *Dangerous Liaisons*, Juliet Binoche in *Wuthering Heights*, Nicole Kidman in *Eyes Wide Shut* and Elizabeth Spriggs in *The Philosopher's Stone* (Harry Potter). Their couture wedding dresses are equally memorable and, not surprisingly, just as theatrical. Billowing skirts, ornate corsets and sumptuous fabrics will all ensure the Wow factor. Despite their incredible success—two Oscars for costume, two BAFTA awards and numerous other Oscar nominations—the designers remain resolutely down to earth.   russellandhaslam.com

Very expensive   *Cash or cheque only*

020 8544 1092   **(by appointment**
London SW19   at a private design studio)

Sahara

Sahara is perfect for the older woman who seeks comfortable clothing in natural earthy colours. The roomy knitwear is luxuriously soft and layered separates create a drape effect that is very forgiving. Although all the pieces are relaxed, they are by no means dull. In summer you might find a cream linen jacket enlivened with chintz-patterned pockets, and in winter the boxy jumpers and asymmetrical cardigans reflect a touch of the East. Amidst the trendy stores aimed at young shoppers this is a shining star for mature shoppers.   *saharalondon.com*

Moderate to expensive   *Amex/MC/V*

020 7351 1002   **tube: Sloane Square**
313 King's Road   Mon-Sat 10-6
London SW3   Sun 12-5

020 7487 4924   **tube: Baker Street**
58 Chiltern Street   Mon-Fri 10-6
London W1   Sat 10-5:30

Sally Parsons

A favourite haunt of smart Fulham ladies, this small French shop features an appealing array of Philippe Adec buttondowns, D Exterior separates, cardigans by Marion Foale and shoes by Dale Vincent. The classical background music is as soothing as the selection but a few stylish highlights—Gérard Darel T-shirts and cashmere sweaters by Magaschoni—turn the volume up a notch.

Expensive   *Amex/MC/V*

020 7471 4848   **tube: Parsons Green**
610 Fulham Road   Mon-Sat 10-6
London SW6

020 7584 8866   **tube: South Kensington**
15a Bute Street   Mon-Sat 10-6
London SW7

Salvatore Ferragamo

This is one of the great names of Italian style, and if you have the cash flow to shop here you can hardly go wrong. Impeccable quality, superb tailoring and every other cloth-

ing superlative you can imagine apply. The Florentine family name has long been celebrated for elegant shoes, still
revered by the most discriminating ladies. For men, the ties
in particular strike a stylish note. Ready-to-wear is available
for women only, with ribbon-trimmed jackets and softly cut
suits in linen, cotton and organza. Men will find accessories
such as shoes and briefcases. The fun-coloured children's
range fits 2-8 year-olds.   ferragamo.com

Expensive   *Amex/MC/V*

020 7629 5007   **tube: Green Park**
24 Old Bond Street   Mon-Sat 10-6
London W1

020 7838 7730   **tube: Knightsbridge**
207 Sloane Street   Mon-Sat 10-6 (Wed 10-7)
London SW1

Sassi Holford
This store offers cream dream couture bridal dresses which
will excite every bride-to-be. The shop itself could do with
refurbishment, but the smiling girls who work here infuse a
bright vibe. The dresses are simple yet decorative, with flattering lines and romantic billowing skirts. Holford is famous
for her corded lace, and her two-piece outfits where corseted bodices are teamed with slim-fitting or fuller skirts. To
compliment the collection, there are shoes from Diane
Hassall and Anello & Davide.   sassiholford.com

Expensive   *MC/V*

020 7584 1532   **tube: South Kensington**
74 Fulham Road   Mon-Sat 10-6
London SW3

Sasti
Guy Ritchie reportedly shops here, so there's reason
enough to stop by, never mind the adorable assortment
of children's clothing (think faux fur and cow prints),
booties, blankets and hats at prices that are less than a
splurge. A made-to-measure service is available for special occasions, and there's a play area to distract the little
ones while you shop. Well worth a visit, or use their good
mail order service.   sasti.co.uk

Affordable to moderate   *Amex/MC/V*

020 8960 1125   **tube: Ladbroke Grove**
Portobello Green Arcade   Mon-Sat 10-6
London W10

Savage London
Rough, tough fashion junkies craving streetwear should
make the trip to Savage. Decal T-shirts denoting different
local boroughs ("Hackney", "Peckham", "Chelsea"),
express some London pride. Clubwear is also available,
including tight leather trousers and tons of denim. In summer, this friendly shop lays on music and beer at weekends.
Go if you're cool enough.   savagelondon.com

Affordable to moderate · Amex/MC/V

020 7439 1163 · **tube: Oxford Circus**
14a Newburgh Street · Mon-Sat 10:30-7
London W1 · Sun 12-5

Scabal

Despite the ring-to-enter system, this London boutique of a Brussels-based international menswear chain has a more modern feel than many of its neighbours. The slick but slightly anodyne air to the shop's interior is reflected a little too well in the range of well-made but somewhat unremarkable made-to-measure and ready-to-wear suits. Uncut fabrics are also available, as well as a high-quality range of accessories. *scabal.com*

Expensive · Amex/MC/V

020 7734 8963 · **tube: Piccadilly Circus/Oxford Circus**
12 Savile Row · Mon-Fri 9-6, Sat 10-4
London W1

Scorah Pattullo

Brainchild of shoe fetishists Johnny Pattullo and Frances Scorah comes this great store offering a diverse range of shoes from Stella McCartney to Red or Dead to Gucci. The flash of Julien Macdonald, the danger of Narciso Rodriguez, the panache of Christian Louboutin—it's all brought together in this special spot. What's more, Scorah and Pattullo launched their own collection last year which includes platforms, round toes, ballerinas and sandals. *scorahpattullo.com*

Moderate to expensive · Amex/MC/V

020 7226 9342 · **tube: Angel**
137 Upper Street · Mon-Fri 10:30-6:30
London N1 · Sun 1-5

Seconda Mano

Obsessive Virgos should probably steer clear: this is another overcrowded, musty-smelling vintage store which will throw compulsive hand-washers into fits. The rest of us should take a deep breath and have fun. We found Earl jeans for £18 (pipe cleaner-size, admittedly), grey flannel trousers by Pringle for £35 and an unworn Maria Grachvogel silk polka-dot dress for £135, as well as a smorgasbord of reasonably-priced shoes and bags.

Moderate · MC/V

020 7359 5284 · **tube: Angel**
111 Upper Street · Mon-Tues 10-5, Wed-Sat 10-5
London N1 · (Thurs 10-7), Sun 11-5

Sefton

One of a handful of the neighbourhood's truly reputable boutiques, Sefton stocks a mix of backbone designers—Temperley, Gharani Strok and Joseph—as well as lesser-known labels like Madeleine Press or Eley Kishimoto. Everything has a quirky touch here, from T-shirts to suits with bright diagonal stitching and pleats in strange places. There's also Diptyque perfume, Anya Hindmarch change purses and shoes by Marc Jacobs. The menswear shop across the road has a similarly stellar line-up, with Costume National, Paul & Joe, Hussein Chalayan and ex-Prada designer Neil Barrett amongst others. If you've made the trip to Islington, Sefton is a must.

Expensive   *MC/V*

020 7226 9822 (W)   **tube: Highbury & Islington**
271 Upper Street   Mon-Sat 10-6:30 (Thurs-Fri 10-7)
London N1   Sun 12-6

020 7226 9822 (M)   **tube: Highbury & Islington**
196 Upper Street   (opening hours as above)
London N1

☆ Selfridges

A firm favourite—the best just keeps getting better. Selfridges is the coolest department store in London, owned by the Weston family who also own Fortnum & Mason, with a mind-boggling mix of traditional designers, new talents and mainstream fashion to satisfy the most voracious of London's label hounds. New brands include Antik Batik, Basso & Brooke, Marc Jacob accessories and See by Chloé. Even the children's department is chock-full of designer names: Evisu, Burberry and D&G. For those shoppers long on style but short on time, the personal shopping service comes to the rescue. Add accessories, cosmetics, books, toys, homewares and the famous food hall, and you can see why Selfridges comes up trumps time and time again. There's a great selection of restaurants and bars on every floor: whether you fancy a Moroccan tagine or a Brazilian caipirinha, you'll find it here. Don't miss the store's dramatic themed makeover in summer—past themes have included Bollywood, Brazil and Vegas Supernova.   *selfridges.com*

Affordable to very expensive   *Amex/MC/V*

0870 837 7377   **tube: Bond Street**
400 Oxford Street   Mon-Fri 10-8 (Thurs 10-9)
London W1   Sat 9:30-8, Sun 12-6

☆ Selina Blow

One of Britain's most eccentric designers, Selina Blow is best known for her coats, from smock to smoking. Simple, classic, but never boring, they are beautifully cut and come in rich fabrics—Harris tweed, silk brocade, velvet, wool—and bold colours—toffee brown, mustard yellow or orange. This confident use of colour extends to the new shop on Ellis Street: the exterior is raspberry pink, the interior a vibrant cobalt blue. Blow's fans include Joan Collins, Anjelica Houston and Ulrika Jonsson, but her prices are incredibly good (£350-£600) when you consider the superb quality of the pieces. There are also coats and ties for men, and a delightful mini collection for children.   *selinablow.com*

Moderate to expensive   *Amex/MC/V*

020 7730 2077
1 Ellis Street
London SW1

tube: Sloane Square
Mon-Fri 10-6, Sat 11-6

☆ **Semmalina** ♀

Semmalina is a children's fairytale come true. There is a fantasy drawbridge that kids love and the clothing ranges from fairy costumes and tutus to labels such as Bubsie and Freoli. Sizes run up to age eight, but the new "Whizz" collection downstairs features pretty jewellery, Indian kaftans and handbags that will suit girls-at-heart of all generations and is ideal for a mother-daughter shopping spree. Party bags and vintage toys add further appeal, as does the service. Sweet down to the last detail, Semmalina will wrap your goodies in layers of tissue paper with lollipops, sequins and hairpins hidden within. Perfect for games of pass the parcel.

Moderate   *Amex/MC/V*

020 7730 9333
225 Ebury Street
London SW1

tube: Sloane Square
Mon-Sat 9:30-5:30

Seraphine ♀♂

This store is a haven for stylish new mums and offers refreshingly chic maternity wear, cute baby basics and sophisticated nursery furniture. Fresh fabrics and soft colours ensure that the clothing is far from stuffy. For everyday there are low-waist bootleg jeans and combat trousers; for a smarter look the pinstripe suits, blouses and linen trousers are elegantly comfortable, and for evenings and parties there are plenty of bias-cut dresses. The combination of practicality and prettiness is ideal and will ensure that this baby is here to stay.   *seraphine.com*

Moderate   *MC/V*

020 7937 3156
28 Kensington Church Street
London W8

tube: High Street Kensington
Mon-Sat 10:30-6
Sun 12-5

Shanghai Tang ♂♀♂

David Tang's Chinese-inspired fashion and clothes emporium is as much a hit in England as in Shanghai and Hong Kong. The luxurious silk pyjamas, velvet Chinese jackets and quilted silk slippers are a splurge. But there are some well-priced prezzies, including teddy bears decked out in colourful eastern garb and a dim sum watch with dumplings denoting the hours (presented in its own bamboo basket).   *shanghaitang.com*

Expensive   *Amex/MC/V*

020 7235 8778
6a/b Sloane Street
London SW1

tube: Knightsbridge
Mon-Sat 10-7, Sun 12-6

Sharon Cunningham ♀

Having worked with such top designers as Catherine Walker and Ben de Lisi, Sharon Cunningham opened her own bridal shop in fashionable Marylebone in 1999. Her designs are simple, elegant, modern and well suited to an hourglass figure. Off the peg you'll find bias-cut gowns and column dresses enhanced with delicate embroidery or beaded with fresh water pearls or Swarovski crystals. Prices start at £1,500. If you prefer to wear something unique expect to pay above £3,000 for bespoke designs. *sharoncunningham.com*

Very expensive   *Amex/MC/V*

020 7724 7002   **tube: Marble Arch**
23 New Quebec Street   Mon-Sat 10-6 (by appointment)
London W1

Shellys

A big, buzzing footwear chain, Shellys won't win any design accolades but there's tons of variety on hand for the fashion-conscious high street buyer, all at good prices. With a staggering range, from high-heeled boots to standard loafers to sporty sneakers, there's a shoe here for everyone. The selection is easy to browse, organized by style and displayed on different levels.   *shellys.co.uk*

Affordable   *Amex/MC/V*

020 7478 1730   **tube: Oxford Circus**
266-270 Regent Street   Mon-Sat 10-7
London W1   (Thurs 10-8), Sun 12-6

020 7437 5842   **tube: Oxford Circus**
159 Oxford Street   (opening hours as above)
London W1

020 7240 3726   **tube: Covent Garden**
14-18 Neal Street   (opening hours as above)
London WC2

020 7581 5537   **tube: Sloane Square**
124b King's Road   Mon-Sat 10-7
London SW3   Sun 12-6

020 7938 1082   **tube: High Street Kensington**
40 Kensington High Street   Mon-Sat 9:30-6:30
London W8   (Thurs 10-7:30), Sun 12-6

Shi Cashmere

In the luxurious heart of Belgravia, this shop offers pulse-stoppingly expensive cashmere in designs that are truly avant-garde. Julia Roberts, Naomi Campbell and Minnie Driver are all fans of the innovative styles which range from backless polo-necks to lacy funnel jumpers to floaty tunic dresses, plus a stunning selection of evening dresses. Some styles, and some of the acid colours, are too bold for those who prefer to err on the edge of caution, but those with cash to splash and a confident personal style will be happy here.   *shicashmere.com*

Expensive   *Amex/MC/V*

020 7235 3829   **tube: Knightsbridge**
30 Lowndes Street   Mon-Sat 9:30-6 (Wed 9:30-7)
London SW1

Shipton & Heneage

Specialising in men's dress shoes, Shipton & Heneage has a huge choice of the highest quality designs crafted in supple leather. From brogues, oxfords and loafers to town boots, sailing shoes and slippers, the emphasis here is on smart, conservative footwear. Most pairs cost under £200, which is excellent value when you consider the craftsmanship. The handmade slippers take three to six weeks to make, in velvet, tartan or silk, and with any motif you might fancy. There are also some colourful cotton socks, leather accessories and a small range for women.   shipton.com

Expensive   *Amex/MC/V*

020 7738 8484   **tube: Sloane Square, then 137 bus**
117 Queenstown Road   Mon-Fri 9-6
London SW8   Sat 10-4

Shirin Guild

You have to ring a doorbell to gain entry to Shirin Guild's shop, but once inside the staff are friendly and the collection easy to view. Inspired by the crisp simplicity of the traditional clothing in her native Iran, Guild's loose-layered designs are all about comfort and understated style. You'll find wide-leg trousers with wraparound belts, over-sized round-neck tops with square kimono sleeves and her ubiquitous box sweaters. Guild uses luxurious fabrics such as cashmere, tweed and flannel and her clothes come in subtle colours—brown, blue, grey, black and white. A small homeware selection rounds out the look with pebble-shaped soaps and light white china.

Expensive   *Amex/MC/V*

020 7351 2766   **tube: South Kensington**
241 Fulham Road   Mon-Sat 10-6
London SW3

Shizue

Waiting to be buzzed into a shop can make one feel like Julia Roberts in *Pretty Woman*: "It's very expensive. You couldn't afford it. Please leave." At Shizue, it is very expensive, you might not be able to afford it, but you'll still receive a warm welcome. Once you get past the door, you'll enter an Aladdin's cave of blue and pink snakeskin slingback shoes with diamanté, black and beige leather ankle boots, beige leather luggage—all handmade in Italy. The orange and blue decor is cheerful with girly boudoir chandeliers. Kylie, Victoria Beckham and Liz Hurley are all members of Shizue's jet-set fan club.   shizue.co.uk

Expensive to very expensive   *Amex/M/V*

020 7491 3322   **tube: Bond Street**
93 Mount Street   Mon-Fri 10-6
London W1   (Sat by appointment)

Shoon

A lifestyle store for outdoorsy types: beware, it's the sort of place you go to buy your dad some golf shoes and end up leaving with loads of stuff for yourself. There is nothing fancy about the range of Helly Hansen, Whitestuff, Timberland or Gant. It's practical, good-quality clothing and footwear with useful bits and bobs in-between. African tribal music beats in the background and before you know it you've got a full basket—PF Flyers plimsolls, a useful sailing fleece, a mini torch and 50 ways to kill a slug. It's not as dull as it looks.   shoon.com

Affordable to moderate   MC/V

020 7487 3001   **tube: Bond Street/Baker Street**
94 Marylebone High Street   Mon-Sat 10-6:30
London W1   Sun 11-5

Sign of the Times

If you want to get rid of some old designer clothes, hotfoot it here. For 25 years, Sign of the Times has offered high-end secondhand clothing and accessories. Designer names include (deep breath) Prada, Gucci, Chanel, Dolce & Gabbana, Yohji Yamamoto and Marc Jacobs, some still with the tags on. Upstairs you'll find Jimmy Choos and Manolos just begging to be broken in.

Moderate   MC/V

020 7589 4774   **tube: South Kensington**
17 Elystan Street   Mon-Fri 10-6
London SW3   (Wed 10-7:30), Sat 10-5:30

Sisley

This is Benetton's big sister—a little more sophisticated and streamlined than her colourful sibling. It's also a label best known for fine knitwear but the London location carries every variation of men's and women's clothing, from coats to dyed denim to bikinis. We're betting it's best for ladies-in-training.   sisley.com

Affordable   Amex/MC/V

020 7376 2437   **tube: High Street Kensington**
129-131 Kensington High Street   Mon-Sat 10-7
London W8   (Thurs 10-8), Sun 12-6

Sixty 6

The mature women will love the modern but classic day- and eveningwear in this treasure-chest of a shop. Materials are gorgeous—cashmere, silk, suede and leather all feature strongly—and the colour spectrum is bold.

Moderate   Amex/MC/V

020 7224 6066   **tube: Bond Street**
66 Marylebone High Street   Mon-Fri 10:30-6:30
London W1   Sat 10-6, Sun 1-5

Size?

If you're looking for the latest fashionable sneaker, look no further. All the top names are here—Adidas, Puma, Lacoste, Converse, Nike and Vans—in the season's most popular colours and styles. It's a treat not to have to trek up to heaving Oxford Street any more for sneakers, but be aware that this selection is more for posing than for sport.

Moderate   *Amex/MC/V*

020 7823 8182   **tube: Sloane Square**
104 King's Road   Daily 10-6 (Sun 11-6)
London SW3

020 7240 1736   **tube: Covent Garden**
17-19 Neal Street   Mon-Fri 9:30-7:30 (Thurs 9:30-8)
London WC2   Sat-Sun 12-6

020 7287 4016   **tube: Oxford Circus**
31 Carnaby Street   Mon-Sat 10-7:30 (Thurs 10-8)
London W1   Sun 12-6

020 7792 8494   **tube: Ladbroke Grove**
200 Portobello Road   Mon-Sat 9:30-6:30, Sun 11-5
London W11

Skin Machine

Famous among leather-loving celebrities, Skin Machine provides high-style hide off-the-peg or made-to-measure. For sexy sorts, there are tight red leather trousers, black tube dresses and diamanté-studded halters with matching minis. If this sounds a bit too raunchy, you'll also find classic suede jackets and warm winter coats lined with wool. A solid selection of hats and goggles will please the biker buffs.

Expensive   *Amex/MC/V*

020 7937 3297   **tube: High Street Kensington**
25 Kensington Church Street   Mon-Fri 10-6:30
London W8   (Thurs, Sat 10-7), Sun 12-5

So aei kei

When Djurdja Watson, a jewellery designer raised in what was Yugoslavia, set up shop, the result was an ultra-hip new store in Portobello's up-and-coming Golborne Road. Watson's decadent range of jewellery (she was head designer at Erickson Beamon for 10 years) offers the perfect accompaniments in the form of jade and coral necklaces, dangly earrings and chunky bangles all colours of the rainbow.   *aeikei.com*

Moderate to expensive   *Amex/MC/V*

020 8960 8442   **tube: Ladbroke Grove/Notting Hill Gate**
357 Portobello Road   Tues-Sat 11-6
London W10

Soboye Soong

Stylist Samson Soboye and womenswear designer E-Sinn Soong combined their talents to open this chic boutique in Shoreditch. Soong's silk chiffon panelled skirts are elegant and her tulip silk satin tie-front dresses exude sexiness—her fan club includes Matthew Williamson, Julien Macdonald and Joanna Lumley. The store also offers a selection of contemporary soft furnishings such as cushions and throws, accessories by Ally Cappellino as well as hand-blown glass by Columbia Glassworks. A great store with super-friendly staff. *soboyesoong.com*

Expensive   *MC/V*

020 7729 3521   **tube: Liverpool Street/Old Street**
13 Calvert Avenue   Thurs 12-7, Fri-Sun 11-5
London E2

Sole Trader

With a relaxed atmosphere and stagey lighting effects, Sole Trader is yet another Neal Street home of trendy shoes. The store carries a wide range of styles, from trainers to leather lace-ups to high-heeled boots. Shoes hark from such designers as DKNY, Paul Smith and Boss, and sneakers from Adidas and Converse to Puma and Vans. *sole-trader.co.uk*

Affordable   *Amex/MC/V*

020 7836 6777   **tube: Covent Garden**
72 Neal Street   Mon-Sat 10:30-7 (Thurs 10:30-7:45)
London WC2   Sun 12-6

020 7361 1560   **tube: High Street Kensington**
96a Kensington High Street   Mon-Sat 10-7
London W8   (Thurs 10-8), Sun 12-6

Sonia Rykiel

She is a Grande Dame of chic Parisian fashion and her famous designs in knitwear have earned Sonia Rykiel the title Queen of Sweaters. Her soft fitted designs, often black or in primary colours, come enhanced with fun, eye-catching details—rainbow stripes, bright spots, sequins and rhinestones. While Rykiel is always in tune with fashion's ever-changing whims, her aesthetic remains reassuringly wearable. Her daughter Nathalie is the company's creative director and has successfully made her presence felt in young, flirtier styles such as metal-studded handbags, sexy white linen suits and floppy felt hats. *soniarykiel.com*

Expensive   *Amex/MC/V*

020 7493 5255   **tube: Bond Street**
27-29 Brook Street   Mon-Sat 10-6:30 (Thurs 10-7)
London W1

☆ Souvenir

Owners Anna Namiki and Anthony Manell capture the spirit of the Left Bank in Sixties Paris when fashion saw the collision of couture-house glamour and bohemian cool. Designers like Sara Berman, Paul & Joe, Les Prairies de Paris and Anna Sui create an inspired mix of new talents and luxury labels. The slightly out-of-the-way locations further enhance the magic of these tiny treasure-houses.

Moderate to expensive   *Amex/MC/V*

020 7287 9877   **tube: Piccadilly Circus/Oxford Circus**
47 Lexington Street   Mon-Sat 11-7, (Thurs 11-7:30)
London W1   Sun 12-6

020 7287 8708
53 Brewer Street
London W1

tube: Oxford Circus
(opening times as above)

Sox Kamen

This bright boutique by World's End on the King's Road offers a lovely selection of Asian-inspired dresses, trousers and tops made from silk specially chosen for its versatility and beauty. The designs are sophisticated but loose and comfortable. With a touch of eastern mystery, the range is colourful and unique.   *sox-kamen.com*

Moderate   *Amex/MC/V*

020 7795 1830
394 King's Road
London SW10

tube: Sloane Square
Mon-Fri 10-5:30, Sat 10:30-5:30

☆ Space.NK

What's a beauty shop doing in a fashion guide, you ask? Well, we love this place so much, we couldn't leave it out (don't say we don't look after you). Almost every woman has a horror story about buying cosmetics—domineering sales staff criticizing your skin, makeovers that leave you looking like a drag queen. Not so at Space.NK, where the staff are more like sympathetic girlfriends than lip-linered lynch-women. All this, plus a new men's store in Broadwick Street, over 2,500 products on the website, the best of the hard-to-get brands including Eve Lom, Laura Mercier, Dr Sebagh and Kiehl's and their own delicious label. Other highlights include Acqua di Parma perfume, Freeze 24-7—a natural alternative to botox—and the very best selection of self-tanners.   *spacenk.com*

Moderate   *Amex/MC/V*

020 7727 8063
127-131 Westbourne Grove
London W2

tube: Notting Hill Gate
Mon-Sat 10-7
(Wed-Thurs 10-8), Sun 12-6

020 7486 8791
83a Marylebone High Street
London W1

tube: Baker Street/Bond Street
Mon-Fri 10-6:30
(Thurs 10-7), Sat 10-6, Sun 12-5

020 7355 1727
45-47 Brook Street
London W1

tube: Bond Street
Mon-Sat 10-6:30 (Thurs 10-7)

020 8740 2085
8-10 Broadwick Street
London W1

tube: Oxford Circus
Daily 10-6

020 7379 7030
4 Thomas Neals Centre
37 Earlham Street
London WC2

tube: Covent Garden
Mon-Sat 10-7
(Thurs 10-7:30), Sun 12-5

020 7256 2303
137 Bishopsgate
London EC2

tube: Liverpool Street
Mon-Wed 8:30-6:30
Thurs-Fri 8:30-7

020 7589 8250
307 Brompton Road
London SW3

tube: South Kensington
Mon-Sat 10-6, Sun 12-5

020 7351 7209
307 King's Road
London SW3

tube: Sloane Square
(opening hours as above)

020 7586 0607
73 St John's Wood High Street
London NW8

tube: St John's Wood
Mon-Sat 10-6
Sun 12-6

020 7730 9841
27 Duke of York Square
London SW3

tube: Sloane Square
Mon-Tues, Sat 10-6:30
Wed-Fri 10-7, Sun 11-6

020 7376 2870
3 Kensington Church Street
London W8

tube: High Street Kensington
Mon-Sat 10-6:30
Thurs 10-7, Sun 12-6

020 7726 2060
145-147 Cheapside
London EC2

tube: St Paul's
Mon-Fri 8:30-6

Spaghetti

Walls decorated with big bowls of pasta make a rather strange setting for couture. Chalk it up to homesickness for Italian designer Nadia La Valle whose dresses, tops, trousers and wedding gowns are covered in hand embroidery and elaborate beading. Styles befit the more mature woman, and prices the more mature bank account. If the decor makes you crave carbonara, San Lorenzo is just across the street.

Expensive   *Amex/MC/V*

020 7584 0631
32 Beauchamp Place
London SW3

tube: Knightsbridge
Mon-Fri 9:30-6, Sat 10-6

Spencer Hart

These bespoke and off-the-peg suits and shirts are designed with a touch of old-time movie-star magic. Elegant single-breasted jackets with sharp tapered labels sit next to 11 variations on the classic white shirt. We love the travel coat, which has discreetly tailored pockets for passport, cigars, phone, tickets and palm pilot. Also check out the station-to-station capsule collection, which comes thoughtfully pre-packed in a Bill Amberg leather holdall— ideal if you're jetting off for an illicit Brief Encounter (or even if you're not.)   *spencerhart.com*

Expensive to very expensive   *Amex/MC/V*

020 7434 0000
36 Savile Row
London W1

tube: Oxford Circus
Mon-Sat 10:30-6:30

Spice

If you are looking for a cute summer sandal, look no further. Spice is a light, modern boutique which makes you feel as if you have the time and the means to try on every shoe in the store. The collection of shoes by leading designers including Paul Smith, Camper and Audley is neatly interspersed with Coccinelle handbags—the overriding theme is chic and elegant. *spiceshu.co.uk*

Expensive *Amex/MC/V*

020 7722 2478 **tube: Chalk Farm**
162 Regent's Park Road Mon 10:30-6:30, Tues-Fri 10-6:30
London NW1 Sat 10-6, Sun 12:30-5:30

020 7704 0043 **tube: Angel/Higbury & Islington**
309 Upper Street (opening hours as above)
London N1

☆ Start

Stop by Start if you have a chance. Situated in the cools of Shoreditch, where hip fashion is plentiful, these savvy boutiques are a must. Owned by a former rock 'n' roll guitarist, the shops are quirky, spacious and full of character. The clothing is equally funky with Helmut Lang, Miu Miu, Adidas Vintage and Philosophy by Alberta Ferretti intermingled with an impressive collection of jeans by Seven For All Mankind, Citizens For Humanity and the limited-edition Levi Vintage. The accessories are particularly gorgeous: a glass cabinet full of vintage sunglasses, and sparkling necklaces by Spanish jewellery designer Susan Suell, a favourite of Madonna's. *start-london.com*

Moderate to expensive *Amex/MC/V*

020 7739 3636 **tube: Old Street**
42 & 59 Rivington Street Mon-Fri 10-6:30
London EC2 Sat 11-6, Sun 1-5

☆ Steinberg & Tolkien

Vintage is big news and anyone with a passion for the past will think they've died and gone to heaven, or perhaps the 1920s, at this treasure-house of recovered relics. From the 1840s to the 1980s you'll find top quality, top label pieces. The packed racks are organized by style (tea dresses, piano shawls, fur wraps), or designer (Pucci, Chanel, Yves Saint Laurent). There is also a mouth-watering selection of accessories including crocodile handbags, collectable costume jewellery, stunning powder compacts and period shoes.

Expensive *Amex/MC/V*

020 7376 3660 **tube: Sloane Square**
193 King's Road Tues-Sat 11-6:30, Sun 12-6
London SW3

Stella McCartney

In 1995 Stella McCartney, daughter of Beatle Paul, graduated from St Martin's London with a collection that revealed a rare designing talent and was almost immediately snapped up by Browns, Joseph and Neiman Marcus. During her stint as creative director of the house of Chloé in Paris, she established a reputation for combining sharp tailoring with sexy femininity. Her Bruton Street shop has a surprisingly friendly, homey atmosphere—no model wannabes giving you dirty looks here. Expect to find strong geometric patterns, a sexy sportswear sensibility and plenty of experimenting with construction, as well as striking high-heeled shoes (but strictly no animal materials), lingerie, her perfume and body line as well as trainers she has designed for Adidas. *stellamccartney.com*

Expensive   *Amex/MC/V*

020 7518 3100   **tube: Green Park/Bond Street**
30 Bruton Street   Mon-Sat 10-6 (Thurs 10-7)
London W1

Stephane Kélian

If you have a weakness for shoes you'll want to see what Stephane Kélian has been up to. Not one to chase the fashion pack, he sticks to the classics, so styles remain fairly constant from one season to the next but are never dull. From flowered mules to comfy flats, Kélian takes what works best in footwear and makes it one step better.

Expensive   *Amex/MC/V*

020 7235 9459   **tube: Knightsbridge**
48 Sloane Street   Mon-Sat 10-6 (Wed 10-7)
London SW1

020 7629 8920   **tube: Green Park**
13 Grafton Street   Mon-Sat 10-6 (Thurs 10-7)
London W1

Stewart Parvin

Stewart Parvin has built up an impressive international clientele and includes the Queen amongst his loyal customers. His talent is crafted couture in simple colours and traditional styles. The bridal boutique on Motcomb Street, decorated with ivory walls, leather sofas and sparkling mirrors, houses a signature collection of romantic contemporary styles infused with a touch of Fifties glamour. A couture service is also on offer, along with going away outfits and plenty of pretty accessories. Prices start from £1,600 and rise to around £6,500. *stewartparvin.com*

Very expensive   *Amex/MC/V*

020 7235 1125   **tube: Hyde Park Corner**
14 Motcomb Street   Mon-Sat 10-6 (Sat by appointment)
London SW1

Still...

The emphasis at this vintage store is on dresses from the Fifties and Sixties but you can also find other retro relics, from roller-skates to pre-Calvin Klein underwire bras. On a recent visit we found beautifully embroidered kimonos, flower-print tops and pretty pastels. In an area rife with vintage, the selection here is obviously from the attic, but also appropriately "now".

Affordable to moderate   *MC/V*

020 7243 2932
61d Lancaster Road
London W11

tube: Ladbroke Grove
Mon-Sat 11-6, Sun 12-4

Stone

The rails of neon-bright separates and ingenious glass floor panels containing flip-flops and bikinis instantly scream Ibiza. You may not have heard of any of the designers sold here, but don't let this put you off—owner Andrea Gillard has a policy of seeking out promising new names, like Munthe plus Simonsen whose beaded dresses are a favourite of Cindy Crawford's. Even if you don't buy anything, go to admire "the dalek", an extraordinary silver sculpture wriggling between the ground and first floors.

Moderate   *Amex/MC/V*

020 7226 9504
48 Upper Street
London N1

tube: Angel
Mon-Sat 10-7, Sun 11-6:30

Story

This magical store is hidden away on a little side street in Spitalfields and sells a mixture of homewares, organic cosmetics and clothing from lesser-known designers such as Ray Harris. With lampshades made from shells from the Philippines next to vintage floral-print dresses and elegant, one-off jewellery pieces, the content of the store depends entirely on the whim of its owners.

Moderate   *Amex/MC/V*

020 7377 0313
4 Wilkes Street
London E1

tube: Liverpool Street
Daily 1-7

Stussy

Once just a California T-shirt brand, Stüssy was among the first to mass-market skateboard style back in the Eighties. Today the clothing collection is more diversified, incorporating skate and preppy influences (cargo pants, baseball shirts, camouflage caps and wide-leg jeans) but the name still suggests cool urban gear.   *stussystore.co.uk*

Affordable   *Amex/MC/V*

020 7836 9418
19 Earlham Street
London WC2

tube: Covent Garden
Mon-Sat 11-7
Sun 1-5:30

Sub Couture

There's nothing substandard about this popular Notting Hill shop, where the atmosphere is casual and the designer selection hip...Nolita, Tashia, Poleci and Essentiel. But here big names do not mean big attitude. The staff are friendly and promote a villagey feel—if you find a skirt but no top to match, they'll call round the other neighbourhood shops for you; if you fall in love with something which doesn't quite fit, they'll tailor it for you. The effect is completed with sunglasses, bags and shoes to suit every woman in the hunt for a refined look.

Moderate to expensive   MC/V

020 7229 5434   **tube: Notting Hill Gate**
204 Kensington Park Road   Mon-Sat 10:30-6:30
London W11   Sun 12-5

Sukie's

The daring designs of owner H.Salimen, who commissions his own interpretations of catwalk styles, have proved so popular that Sukie's has now opened a second store just a few doors down. For men there are Camper-style trainers, handmade ostrich lace-ups and rubber-soled boots with upturned toes. Women will find pointy mules, colourful slingbacks and comfy loafers with striking character. It's all a bit hit-and-miss, and definitely not for the faint-footed.

Expensive   Amex/MC/V

020 7352 3431   **tube: Sloane Square**
285 & 289 King's Road   Mon-Sat 10-7, Sun 1-6
London SW3

Super Lovers

Part of a Japanese chain, this shop with its bright turquoise exterior is difficult to miss. Inside you'll find kitsch streetwear with club roots, including an extensive collection of colourful logo'd merchandise featuring wide-eyed cartoon characters. Tie-dyed T-shirts declaring "Love is the Message" and tank tops stating "non-violence" will appeal to club kids with a Seventies sensibility.   *superlovers.co.jp*

Affordable to moderate   Amex/MC/V

020 7240 5248   **tube: Covent Garden**
64 Neal Street   Mon-Sat 10:30-6:30
London WC2   (Thurs 10:30-7:30), Sun 12-6

Swaine Adeney Brigg/Herbert Johnson

A long-established leather goods specialist holding several royal warrants, Swaine sells sumptuous traditional luggage and accessories such as gloves, umbrellas and riding whips. Luxury items include champagne bottle holders complete with beautiful fluted glasses, perfect for opera-interval picnics at Glyndebourne. The adjoining hatter, Herbert Johnson, supplies a large range of casual and formal hats to complete the look, from bowlers to cosy fur trappers.

Expensive   Amex/MC/V

020 7409 7277 (Swaine Adeney Brigg)   **tube: Green Park**
020 7408 1174 (Herbert Johnson)   **Mon-Sat 10-6**
54 St James's Street
London SW1

Swear

The bright orange exterior sets the tone for the collection within, where yellow and white checked deck shoes, ruched tan high heels and chunky rubber-soled shoes from the skateboarder collection give the shop a cartoonish feel. Come here to stand out from the crowd. *swear-net.net*

Affordable to moderate   *Amex/MC/V*

020 7734 1690   **tube: Oxford Circus**
22 Carnaby Street   Mon-Sat 11-7, Sun 1-6
London W1

020 7485 7182   **tube: Camden Town**
Unit 6, Stables Market   Mon-Fri 11-6
Chalk Farm Road   Sat-Sun 10:30-6:30
London NW1

Sweatshop

Think function not fashion at this small sports shop that carries a selection of top action brands—USA Pro, Nike and Adidas. Choose from a large assortment of logo'd T-shirts, cosy hooded sweatshirts, running shoes and sleek tank tops. There are also Speedo swimsuits—better for doing laps than turning heads—and baggy cream T-shirts with matching leggings for yogis. Backpacks, goggles, sunglasses and a huge variety of socks round out the sporty selection. Not as trendy as Sweaty Betty, but it does the job. *sweatshop.co.uk*

Moderate   *Amex/MC/V*

020 7351 4421   **tube: Gloucester Road**
188 Fulham Road   Mon-Fri 10-8
London SW10   Sat-Sun 10-6

020 7497 0820   **tube: Covent Garden**
9a Endell Street   Mon, Thurs 11-8, Tues-Wed 8-8
London WC2   Fri 11-6:30, Sat 10-6, Sun 10-4

Sweaty Betty

Oh, the eternal female dilemma: gym or shopping? Shopping or gym? Ease your guilt at one of London's first fashion sports boutiques, where the final score is a tie between being comfortable and looking cute. For those who actually make it to the gym, there are Adidas stretch tops with matching trousers, USA Pro biking shorts and shock-absorbing bras by Berlei, while gym-at-home types could reach for the stretching mats, skipping ropes and yoga travel kits. If you'd rather just look the part, you'll find Nike trainers, Puma bags, Quiksilver cropped trousers, diamanté halternecks and a wide assortment of bikinis and swimwear for posing by the pool. *sweatybetty.com*

Moderate   *MC/V*

020 7937 5523   **tube: High Street Kensington**
5 Kensington Church Street   Mon-Sat 10:30-7
London W8   Sun 12-5

020 7751 0228   **tube: Parsons Green**
833 Fulham Road   Mon-Fri 10-6:30
London SW6   Sat 10-6, Sun 12-5

020 7287 5128   **tube: Piccadilly Circus**
21 Beak Street   Mon-Sat 11-7
London W1   Sun 12-5

020 7794 2914
35 Heath Street
London NW3

tube: Hampstead
Mon-Sat 10-6
Sun 12-5

020 7513 0666
Cabot Place East
London E14

tube: Canary Wharf
Mon-Fri 9-7, Sat 10-6
Sun 12-6

Sybil Stanislaus

You could walk straight past, but this is a diamond find much beloved by A-list celebs and society ladies. Sybil Stanislaus specializes in sophisticated, sexy looks for women who are body-confident but discreet. We're talking Beyoncé, not Jordan. The Asian-inspired clothing includes everything from beautiful kaftans and kimonos to pretty tea dresses and cocktail dresses. Think plunging necklines and luxurious slashed fabrics, including Italian chiffons and satin silks. Everything in the shop is designed by Sybil and is a one-off. Prices are just as exclusive.

Very expensive

Amex/MC/V

020 7245 4424
11 Grosvenor Place
London SW1

tube: Hyde Park Corner
(by appointment)

T&G Clothing

T&G Clothing started back in 1989 in Cowes on the Isle of Wight, the home of yachting. Still going strong, the casual collection of nautical wear embodies a wholesome image of fresh air, sea and sunshine. In England, of course, it may be raining, but this is just the sort of practical, comfortable clothing you want to keep you warm. For men there are cotton shirts, waterproof jackets and khaki trousers; mother-earth women will revel in the lilac fleeces, moleskin skirts and simple cotton T-shirts.

tandg.co.uk

Moderate

Amex/MC/V

020 7731 5215
580 Fulham Road
London SW6

tube: Fulham Broadway
Mon-Sat 10-6, Sun 11-4

T.M.Lewin

Although it's one of London's longest established shirtmakers (since 1898), T.M.Lewin is also one of those leading the charge to attract a younger, more trend-conscious customer. This is achieved mainly through opening up the shops with brighter, cleaner interiors and introducing younger, friendly staff without compromising quality—and it works. No fewer than 10 branches in the City show just how much businessmen and women like their Lewin shirts. Casualwear, accessories and ready-to-wear suits (from £500) are also available.

tmlewin.co.uk

Moderate

Amex/MC/V

020 7930 4291 (M)
106/108 Jermyn Street
London SW1

tube: Piccadilly Circus/Green Park
Mon-Sat 9:30-6
(Wed 10-6, Thurs 10-7), Sun 11-5

020 7487 5941 (M)
St Christopher's Place
London W1

tube: Bond Street
(opening hours as above)

020 7283 1277 (M)
34-36 Lime Street
London EC2

tube: Bank
Mon-Fri 9:30-6
(Wed 10-6)

020 7920 0787 (M)
32-33 Blomfield Street
London EC2

tube: Liverpool Street
(opening hours as above)

020 7256 6584 (M)
67 Moorgate
London EC2

tube: Moorgate
(opening hours as above)

020 7242 3180 (M)
27a Chancery Lane
London WC2

tube: Chancery Lane
(opening hours as above)

020 7242 1409 (W)
9a Chichester Rents
London WC2

tube: Chancery Lane
(opening hours as above)

020 7329 5337 (M)
59 Ludgate Hill
London EC4

tube: St Paul's
(opening hours as above)

020 7329 2258 (W)
49 Bow Lane
London EC4

tube: Bank
(opening hours as above)

020 7283 4644 (W, casual)
9-9a Cullum St
London EC3

tube: Bank
(opening hours as above)

020 7606 2995 (M, casual)
85 Cheapside
London EC3

tube: Bank
(opening hours as above)

020 7519 6292
18 Canada Place Mall
London E14

tube: Canary Wharf
Mon-Fri 8:30-7
Sat 10-6, Sun 12-5

Tabio

This Japanese sock shop will open your mind to the creative potential of the humble wardrobe staple. There's every conceivable style (long or short, stripy or spotty, cotton or wool, fishnet or crocheted) minus the cartoon characters and geometric patterns that seem to haunt most sock shops. If you treasure absolute freedom of movement, some even come with separated toes. Quality fabrics and reasonable price range make this a reliable choice for the well-heeled. *tabio.co.uk*

Affordable   *Amex/MC/V*

020 7591 1960
94 King's Road
London SW3

tube: Sloane Square
Mon-Sat 10-7, Sun 12-6

020 7836 3713 (W)
66 Neal Street
London WC2

tube: Covent Garden
Mon-Sat 10-7, Sun 12-6

Talbots

This American import will never turn heads, so if you dress to get noticed, move on. But Talbots has its niche for its wide selection of classic business and casualwear, particularly among conservative, mature dressers. Sensible suits, trousers, dresses and skirts are mixed with T-shirts and soft knitwear. Petite sizes, accessories and shoes are also available. *talbots.com*

Affordable to expensive   *Amex/MC/V*

020 7494 9272   **tube: Piccadilly Circus**
115 Regent Street   Mon-Sat 10-7
London W1   (Thurs 10-8), Sun 12-6

Tanner Krolle

Formed in 1856, this small handbag and luggage shop offers stylish, colourful cases for the fashionably high-minded. Durability is guaranteed and, with proper care, fabrics are liable to last a lifetime—this is the stuff that fashion heirlooms are made of. From alligator to plaid, from small and structured to giant weekender bag, from look-at-me showy to quietly classic, the variety of colours and styles makes choosing tough. An exciting new range of bags and and shoes comes in delicious browns, pinks and damsons—our favourite is the money bag based on an old London style. *tannerkrolle.com*

Expensive   *Amex/MC/V*

020 7287 5121   **tube: Green Park**
3 Burlington Gardens   Mon-Sat 10:6:30
London W1

020 7823 1688   **tube: Knightsbridge**
5 Sloane Street   Mon-Sat 10-7
London SW1   Sun 12-6

020 7623 2123   **tube: Bank**
7 Royal Exchange   Mon-Fri 10-7
London EC3

Tartine et Chocolat

Stepping into this shop is like stepping back in time, with linen pinafores of a quality not seen since our grandmothers were girls. It's a great stop for elegant christening presents: from pastel smock dresses to tiny twill trousers, this is childrenswear at its most adorably refined. Mothers-to-be can prep with the small selection of baby blankets, booties and bibs. Sizes run from newborn to age 10.

Moderate   *Amex/MC/V*

020 7629 7233   **tube: Bond Street**
66 South Molton Street   Mon-Sat 10-6
London W1

Tashia

A den of fashionable goodies in otherwise conservative Walton Street, Tashia offers young designer styles with a contemporary spin. Biya, Gharani Strok and Roland Mouret are just some of the exciting names you'll want to grab. From hip handbags to swirling skirts, the vibe is girly, modern and super-sweet. Try and persuade owner Sara Chiaramonte to give you tea or coffee in the garden at the back.   *tashia.com*

Expensive   *Amex/MC/V*

020 7589 0082   **tube: South Kensington**
178 Walton Street   Mon-Sat 10-6
London SW3

Ted Baker

For those who are fashion-conscious but don't feel compelled to prove it, Ted Baker is more sophisticated than the high street shops but not quite dashing designer. The clothing is modern and grounded, with his especially popular linen and cotton shirts, wool suits and a women's collection that includes comfortable denim, trendy silk tops and decal T-shirts. A full range of accessories is also available, and there's a limited but stylish selection of homewares to spruce up any interior. All in all, more exciting than the prosaic name might suggest.   *tedbaker.co.uk*

Moderate to expensive   *Amex/MC/V*

020 7836 7808   **tube: Covent Garden**
9-10 Floral Street   Mon-Sat 10-7 (Thurs 10-8)
London WC2   Sun 12-6

020 7497 8862   **tube: Covent Garden**
1-4 Langley Court   Mon-Fri 10-7 (Thurs 10-8)
London WC2   Sat 10-7, Sun 12-6

020 7493 6251   **tube: Oxford Circus**
245 Regent Street   (opening hours as above)
London W1

020 7881 0850   **tube: Sloane Square**
19 Duke of York Square   Mon-Tues 10-6:30, Wed-Sat 10-7
London SW3   Sun 12-6

020 7519 6588   **tube: Canary Wharf**
Unit 5, Canada Place   Mon-Fri 9-7
London E14   Sat 10-6, Sun 12-6

Temperley

Every woman should own a Temperley dress. Feminine and stylishly sexy, they are championed by well-dressed celebrities and fashion editors alike who put their orders in as soon as the collection is previewed. Unfortunately there is no store yet, but ladies who lunch come to the large boudoir showroom with their friends and make it a social event. Catwalk designs come in a range of colours and many of her dresses are ordered in cream for weddings.   *temperleylondon.com*

Expensive   *Amex/MC/V*

020 7229 7957   **tube: Notting Hill Gate**
6-10 Colville Mews, Lonsdale Road   (by appointment)
London W11

Directory

Texier

Head here for Christmas presents for awkward relatives. Texier sells leather goods as we like 'em—of impeccable quality and classic design. The business has been family-owned since 1951 and the folks have spent half a century perfecting their craft. The result is a collection of briefcases, travel bags, handbags and wallets that the French have been known to go mad for.

Moderate   *Amex/MC/V*

020 7935 0215   **tube: Bond Street/Baker Street**
6 New Cavendish Street   Tues-Sat 9:30-5:30
London W1

Thailandia

From Bombay to Bali, this is an unexpected Aladdin's Cave in otherwise mundane Munster Road. Old Etonian Jeremy Reiss travels to India and throughout southeast Asia to seek out the beautiful and the unique for this surprising store. Ethnic clothing doesn't get much better: there are shirts, dresses and much else in every exotic shape, delicious colour and desirable material. You'll also find Indian crystals, Buddhas of every sort, some of the finest silver in London and stunning jewellery in turquoise, coral and moonstone. If, despite the calming atmosphere of the shop, you're feeling stressed out, try an hour in the flotation tank downstairs; it's particularly popular with tennis players during Wimbledon.

Moderate   *Amex/MC/V*

020 7610 2003   **tube: Parsons Green**
222 Munster Road   Mon-Sat 11-6
London SW6

The Lazy Ones

This tiny boutique is tucked away on a side street off Brick Lane and was opened in April 2004 by Catalan brother and sister team Diego and Natalia Colom. You'll find a mix of vintage pieces from the Sixties and Seventies, shirts by new London designers and items from their own label, Des Moines.

Moderate   *Amex/MC/V*

07812 957 276   **tube: Liverpool Street**
102 Sclater Street   Tues-Sun 11:30-7
London E1

Their Nibs

If Gap Kids doesn't quite do it for you, head to this new shop for children up to 12 years old. Kate Moss and singer Sharleen Spiteri have shopped for their children from the selection of vintage, velvet dresses, flower-printed kaftans, fairy dresses, denims and combats. It's a bit of a one-stop shop, with a hairdresser, play area and a range of accessories and toys also on offer.   *theirnibs.com*

Moderate to expensive   *Amex/MC/V*

020 7221 4263
214 Kensington Park Road
London W11

tube: Westbourne Park
Mon-Fri 9:30-6
Sat 10-6, Sun 12-5

Thomas Pink

This popular brand is named after an 18th-century tailor whose legendary coats first inspired the phase "in the pink". The casual and formal mix of shirts you'll find here certainly lives up to old-fashioned standards. It may be one of the most forward-looking of the traditional shirtmakers on Jermyn Street, with a modern open-plan store and unstuffy staff, but the quality and tailoring of a Pink shirt are renowned and have not been compromised. The stiff, semi-cutaway collars look better worn with a tie, while the classic linen line is casual enough to be worn on holiday. Pink is the company that has been largely responsible for attracting younger customers, men and women, to the joys of English shirtmaking and that has also been expanding in the City. Good mail-order service. *thomaspink.co.uk*

Moderate to expensive *Amex/MC/V*

020 7930 6364
85 Jermyn Street
London SW1

tube: Piccadilly Circus/Green Park
Mon-Fri 10-6 (Thurs 10-7)
Sat 10-6:30, Sun 12-5

020 7245 0202
74 Sloane Street
London SW1

tube: Knightsbridge/Sloane Square
Mon-Fri 10-6 (Wed 10-7)
Sat 10-6:30, Sun 12-5

020 7499 4580
18 Davies Street
London W1

tube: Bond Street
Mon-Fri 10-6:30 (Thurs 9:30-7)
Sat 10-6:30

020 7430 2667
82 Chancery Lane
London WC2

tube: Chancery Lane
Mon-Fri 9:30-6

020 7374 2800
16 Blomfield Street
London EC2

tube: Liverpool Street/Moorgate
Mon-Fri 9:30-6

020 7623 4300
24 Cullum Street
London EC3

tube: Bank
Mon-Fri 9:30-6

020 7489 7916
60 Cannon Street
London EC4

tube: Cannon Street
Mon-Fri 9-6

020 7513 0303
Cabot Place East
London E14

tube: Canary Wharf
Mon-Fri 8:30-7 (Thurs 8:30-8)
Sat 10-6, Sun 12-6

Tim Little

Worn leather club chairs, an antique rug and blues playing in the background—not exactly what you'd expect in a shoe store. But the Fifties bachelor vibe is a perfect complement to Tim Little's traditional men's footwear—all made from superior French calfskin and each named after a song of the era. There's the "Whisky and Women" loafer, the "Stormy

Monday" ankle boot and their bestseller, the "Red House" lace-up, as well as a made-to-measure service. Women will find a similar selection in smaller sizes. The sleek, classic aesthetic is Terence Conran for the feet. No surprise then that the home guru himself created his own shoe for the collection, a slip-on loafer made from kangaroo.   timlittle.com

Expensive   *Amex/MC/V*

020 7736 1999   **tube: Fulham Broadway**
560 King's Road   Mon-Sat 10-6, Sun 11-5
London SW6

Timberland

The clothing here is tough enough for a mountain trek, a river crossing or even a stroll through Piccadilly Circus. Once an American outpost for durable waterproof boots, Timberland has grown into a major source of outdoor wear divided into three lines, Trek Travel, Rugged Casual and The Classic Line. There are state-of-the-art entron jackets, fleeces, sturdy bags and dense wool socks, as well as simple thick sweaters, oxford shirts and soft chinos. The hiking boots top the lot, guaranteed to withstand the rigours of nature.   timberland.com

Moderate   *Amex/MC/V*

020 7495 2133   **tube: Bond Street**
72 New Bond Street   Mon-Sat 10-6
London W1   (Thurs 10-7), Sun 12-6

020 7240 4484   **tube: Covent Garden**
125 Long Acre   Mon-Sat 10-7 (Thurs 10-8)
London WC2   Sun 12-6

020 7588 8544   **tube: Liverpool Street**
Unit 6, Bishopsgate Arcade   Mon-Fri 9-6 (Thurs 9-7)
London EC2

Timothy Everest

A visit to Timothy Everest's store, set in an elegant and inconspicuous Georgian house in the heart of Spitalfields, is a memorable experience. Besides the stylish shirts, ultra-cool ties and bespoke tailored suits displayed throughout, Everest also sells gems such as a slimline Mackintosh in midnight blue. Such is the popularity of their shirts, they have recently opened a shirt shop around the corner in Artillery Lane. The top floor of the house has been converted into an exhibition room where a detailed step-by step introduction to the art of bespoke tailoring is displayed. Booking an appointment is highly recommended.

Very expensive   *Amex/MC/V*

020 7377 5220   **tube: Liverpool Street**
32 Elder Street   Mon-Fri 9-6, Sat 10-4
London E1

020 7377 8755   **tube: Liverpool Street**
52 Artillery Lane   Mon-Fri 9-6, Sat 10-4
London E1

Tod's

The hand-stitched leather driving shoes, with distinctive pebble soles, are a stylish staple in any shoe collection and have gained international status as a chic but comfortable essential. Nowadays they are just as likely to be seen in St Tropez as in the car, although they are still the perfect style for travelling. Along with dressier designs, including the Ferrari Red range, designer Diego Della Valle has also turned his hand to handbags which are equally luscious, in the softest leather and boxy shapes. Just be warned that low heels bear high prices. *tods.com*

Expensive   *Amex/MC/V*

020 7235 1321   **tube: Knightsbridge**
35-36 Sloane Street   Mon-Fri 10-6
London SW1   Sat 10:30-6

020 7493 2237   **tube: Green Park**
2-5 Old Bond Street   Mon-Sat 10-7
London W1   (Thurs 10-8)

020 7283 6611   **tube: Bank**
15 The Courtyard   Mon-Fri 10-6
Royal Exchange
London EC3

Tomasz Starzewski

Traditionally a society dresser and a firm favourite of the late Diana, Princess of Wales, Tomasz Starzewski (pronounced star-jeff-ski) designs elegant eveningwear for a high-profile clientele. His suits are sharply tailored and conservative, his dresses are glamorous and ladylike, and his wedding dresses are ruffled sensations. The tucked-away studio is almost as inaccessible as a royal residence. Be sure to book an appointment because popping-in is severely frowned upon. *starzewski.com*

Very expensive   *Amex/MC/V*

020 7244 6138   **tube: Gloucester Road**
14 Stanhope Mews West   Mon-Fri 10-6 (by appointment)
London SW7

Tommy Hilfiger

Good clean American fun, Tommy Hilfiger features boldly coloured casual wear with Ivy League style. There's a young, fresh spirit to the collection, from chinos and shirts for the guys to fitted dresses and jeans for the dolls, evoking outdoor living as well as urban cool. American prep doesn't get better. *tommy.com*

Expensive   *Amex/MC/V*

020 7235 2500   **tube: Knightsbridge**
6 Sloane Street   Mon-Sat 10-6
London SW1   (Wed 10-7), Sun 12-6

Top Gun

The name may be a little dated but it pays homage to Tom Cruise's big-screen rebel who helped bring back the bomber jacket, found in all its macho glory at this made-to-measure leather shop. It may not be the danger zone but you'll still find a racy range of styles, from turquoise snake-skin to black suede. Long or short, shiny or weathered, zip-up or button-down—you want it, they got it.

Moderate *Amex/MC/V*

020 7376 0823 **tube: High Street Kensington**
23 Kensington High Street Mon-Sat 10-7 (Thurs 10-8)
London W8 Sun 12:30-6:30

☆ Top Shop

If like us, you sometimes find the whole Top Shop experience just too much—then book their new personal shopping service. It's free and there is no obligation to buy. Alternatively, just call Top Shop To Go. Brief a Top Shop sales consultant by phone, and within hours packages filled with goodies will be delivered to your doorstep. This store continues to earn accolades for the trendiest and most affordable designs to hit the high street. Don't be put off by the banging music and hordes of skinny teens in the changing-rooms (shop during school hours to avoid the latter). Fashion stylists, mums-to-be and celebs from Beyoncé to Gwyneth Paltrow pay homage in the three giant floors, which feature sleek and cheap designer copies and basic mix-and-match separates for women and men. The bottom floor features one-off designer and vintage pieces, while upstairs you'll find a massive selection of accessories, extending beyond the basic belts and bags to include cosmetics, Kangol visors, body jewellery and every other conceivable club-kid treat as well as Top Man—check out the fab slogan T-shirts. With rock-bottom prices and dead-on designs, you'd be crazy not to join in the fun. *topshop.co.uk*

Affordable *Amex/MC/V*

020 7636 7700 **tube: Oxford Circus**
214 Oxford Street Mon-Sat 9-8 (Thurs 9-9)
London W1 Sun 12-6

020 7938 1242 **tube: High Street Kensington**
42-44 Kensington High Street Mon-Sat 10-7
London W8 (Thurs 10-8), Sun 12-6

020 7839 4144 **tube: Charing Cross**
32 The Strand Mon-Fri 10:30-7 (Thurs 10:30-8)
London WC2 Sat 10:30-7, Sun 12-6

020 7512 1996 **tube: Canary Wharf**
Unit 3, Canada Square Mon-Fri 8:30-7
London E14 Sat 9-6, Sun 12-6

Tops & Bottoms

Girls blessed with God-given figures might find something suitable in this store where the theme seems to be the tighter, the better. There are skin-hugging bodysuits, suede trousers with barely enough room to breathe and tiny tees by Anti-flirt that will do the strutting for you.

Moderate   *MC/V*
020 7349 8822   **tube: South Kensington**
3 Cale Street   Mon-Fri 10-6, Sat 11-6
London SW3

Travelling Light

The Riviera, the Costa Smeralda, Malaga—all are just a few hours away but beachwear is often difficult to come by in London. Not so at Travelling Light, where the slogan is "hot weather clothing all year round" and the speciality is travel, safari, cruise and beachwear. The clothes are bright and the fabrics light and comfortable. The styles may be a bit dowdy, but if you're going on safari you won't be glamming up anyway. Accessories are also available, and we've heard great things about their mail order service.   *travellinglight.com*

Moderate   *MC/V*
020 7629 7000   **tube: Green Park**
35 Dover Street   Mon-Fri 10-5:30, Sat 10-5
London W1

Trésor

If your wallet is a bit sad, cheer yourself up at this cramped secondhand store in Chelsea Green. Packed with dresses by the likes of Christian Dior and Emanuel Ungaro, as well as a fabulous collection of chic coats, handbags and designer shoes, a spree here will leave your friends green with envy, especially if you disclose how little you paid for your new-found gems. Remember: money can't buy you style.

Moderate   *Cheque or cash only*
020 7349 8829   **tube: South Kensington/Sloane Square**
13 Cale Street   Mon 2:30-6, Tues-Sat 11-6
London SW3   (closed 1:15-2:15 daily)

Tricker's

Shoemakers by royal appointment to the Prince of Wales, Tricker's has been going strong since 1829 and is one of the giants of traditional English shoe crafting. In addition to brogues, oxfords and derbys, the family-run store is renowned for its unique monogrammed velvet slippers, which are lined in leather and can be customised with many motifs, from dragons to family crests. Popular with American customers, some of these slippers are known to walk the sunny streets of LA and Miami. The small intimate interior of the shop and the old-fashioned service are still distinctly British.   *trickers.com*

Very expensive   *Amex/MC/V*
020 7930 6395   **tube: Piccadilly Circus/Green Park**
67 Jermyn Street   Mon-Fri 9:30-6, Sat 9:30-5:30
London SW1

Trotters

A bright and bubbly children's store, Trotters offers colourful clothing for up to 10-year-olds with mini pieces by

Diesel, Oilily and Petit Bateau. Lively patterns bring the looks to life and the basic separates are perfect playwear. The super-friendly staff do expert shoe fittings while your darling one sits aboard the Trotter's Express Train, and there's also a great hairdresser who will tidy-up babies' and children's hair with lightning speed. *trotters.co.uk*

Moderate   *Amex/MC/V*

020 7259 9620   **tube: Sloane Square**
34 King's Road   Mon-Sat 9-7
London SW3   Sun 10-6:30

020 7937 9373   **tube: High Street Kensington**
127 Kensington High Street   Mon-Sat 9-7
London W8   Sun 10:30-6:30

Trudy Hanson

Whether you want a slim, sexy gown reminiscent of a glamorous evening dress, or a full princess-line skirt teamed with a strapless bodice, Hanson's creations range from the sleek to the opulent. Her salon, situated on trendy All Saints Road, is airy and friendly with over 40 display dresses to draw inspiration from. Handmade veils and tiaras are designed to match the dresses and a tiny blue bow is sewn inside each made-to-measure gown as a token of good luck. They will dye bags and shoes to match creations in the shop, and it's also a great place for bridesmaids' dresses. *trudyhanson.co.uk*

Expensive   *MC/V*

020 7792 1300   **tube: Westbourne Park**
25 All Saints Road   Mon-Sat 10-5:30 (Thurs 10-7:30)
London W11   (by appointment)

☆ Turnbull & Asser

Al Pacino, Michael Caine, Prince Charles and Governor Schwarzenegger have all been seduced into shopping at Turnbull & Asser. The country house interior, complete with grandfather clocks and heavy panelling, and historic atmosphere (the company was founded in 1885) draw the customers in, but it is the immaculate, sharply-tailored shirts that keep them coming back. Cut from over 400 fabrics, with prices starting at £130, the bespoke and off-the-peg shirts are some of the best money can buy. With mother of pearl buttons, specially woven Sea Island cotton and broad three-button cuffs, the quality is so good that fathers have been known to pass T&A shirts on to their sons 10 years after they were first purchased. There is also a stunning selection of ties, cufflinks, socks, handkerchiefs and sumptuous colourful dressing-gowns. No wonder this is one of Jermyn Street's best known shops. *turnbullandasser.co.uk*

Very expensive   *Amex/MC/V*

020 7808 3000   **tube: Piccadilly Circus/Green Park**
71-72 Jermyn Street   Mon-Fri 9-6, Sat 9:30-6
London SW1

Uniqlo

Like its compatriot Muji, this Japanese chain offers utilitarian basics at low prices. Although fabrics can be cheap, and styles a bit boring, the plain cotton T-shirts, warm fleeces and simple trousers will blend perfectly with more expensive pieces in your wardrobe. For essential modern separates, from black pullovers to white vest tops, this is a number one stop-off. *uniqlo.com*

Affordable *Amex/MC/V*

020 7734 5369 **tube: Oxford Circus**
The Plaza, 120 Oxford Street Mon-Sat 10-7
London W1 Sun 12-6

020 7434 9688 **tube: Piccadilly Circus**
84-86 Regent Street Mon-Sat 10-7 (Thurs 10-8)
London W1 Sun 12-6

United Colors of Benetton

Shoppers of a certain generation will remember when the green and blue Benetton rugby shirts were ubiquitous. At times this Italian company makes more headlines for its controversial ad campaigns than for its designs, but Benetton continues to be a reliable source of well-made knitwear in a brilliant spectrum of solid colours. Sweaters, dresses, trousers and skirts are the staples of the women's selection; men can choose from suits and casualwear. For the colour-shy there is even the odd bit of black, white and brown. Avoid the slightly tacky trendy stuff and stick to affordable basics. *benetton.com*

Affordable *Amex/MC/V*

020 7647 4200 **tube: Oxford Circus**
255-259 Regent Street Mon-Wed 10-7:30
London W1 Thurs-Sat 10-8, Sun 11:30-6

020 7591 0925 **tube: Knightsbridge**
23 Brompton Road Mon-Sat 10-7
London SW3 Sun 12-6

Urban Outfitters

The English cousin of the American chain, this store is a huge industrial-style warehouse for retro/modern culture. You may go in looking for just one thing, but you're liable to leave with credit card damage. The basement houses a men's garage-meets-grunge clothing collection with a secondhand effect. Thumping music will draw you to the DJ booth where you can purchase the latest sounds. Upstairs, the women's section offers a variety of styles, from too-cool-to-care T-shirts to Sixties striped sweaters to basic button-downs. Accessories include funky bag lines by Ollie & Nic and Religion, trailer-trash plastic slip-on shoes and a wall of gadgets that will keep teens occupied for hours. Huge Chinese lanterns, velvet pillows and suede ottoman cubes will perk up any drab pad. The overall effect is mismatched and proud of it. *urbanoutfitters.com*

Affordable to moderate *Amex/MC/V*

020 7761 1001
36-38 Kensington High Street
London W8

tube: High Street Kensington
Mon-Sat 10-7
(Thurs 10-8), Sun 12-6

020 7907 0800
200 Oxford Street
London W1

tube: Oxford Circus
(opening hours as above)

020 7759 6390
42-56 Earlham Street
London WC2

tube: Covent Garden
(opening hours as above)

Valentino

Dazzling dresses are Valentino's forte and his elegant, demure couture is legendary. Women can select from sophisticated ready-to-wear including knitwear, separates, trousers and suits. Men who prefer dressing down can bypass the business section for a collection of casual but equally well-crafted clothes. Known around the world for razor-sharp suits and glamorous evening gowns, the Valentino label is the mark of chic opulence.   *valentino.it*

Very expensive   *Amex/MC/V*

020 7235 5855
174 Sloane Street
London SW1

tube: Knightsbridge
Mon-Fri 10-6, Sat 10:30-6

Vans

This skateboarders' haven has a courtyard at the back which is a great place to relax and give yourself a shopping break. As well as the trademark sporty sneakers, mens' and womens' sportswear is also available.   *vans.com*

Affordable   *Amex/MC/V*

020 7287 9235
47 Carnaby Street
London W1

tube: Oxford Circus
Mon-Fri 10-7 (Thurs 10-8)
Sun 12-6

Venise Collection

On a road where some shops have been standing for years, this is the new kid on the block, but its sexy shoes have already established an ardent following amongst Chelsea style seekers. The French footwear designs are sometimes quirky, sometimes classic, but always wearable. Find towering boots, jewelled slingbacks and court shoes with demoniacally pointed toes—all at good prices.

Moderate   *Amex/MC/V*

020 7351 7707
163 King's Road
London SW3

tube: Sloane Square
Mon-Sat 10-7, Sun 12-6

020 7499 1267
37 Brook Street
London W1

tube: Bond Street
Mon-Sat 10:30-7 (Thurs 10:30-8)
Sun 12-6

020 7836 3116
41 Monmouth Street
London WC2

tube: Leicester Square
(opening hours as above)

Ventilo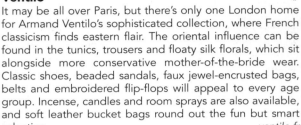

It may be all over Paris, but there's only one London home for Armand Ventilo's sophisticated collection, where French classicism finds eastern flair. The oriental influence can be found in the tunics, trousers and floaty silk florals, which sit alongside more conservative mother-of-the-bride wear. Classic shoes, beaded sandals, faux jewel-encrusted bags, belts and embroidered flip-flops will appeal to every age group. Incense, candles and room sprays are also available, and soft leather bucket bags round out the fun but smart selection. *ventilo.fr*

Moderate Amex/MC/V

020 7491 3666 **tube: Bond Street**
70 New Bond Street Mon-Fri 10:30-6 (Thurs 10-7)
London W1 Sat 10-6:30

Versace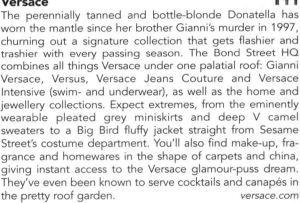

The perennially tanned and bottle-blonde Donatella has worn the mantle since her brother Gianni's murder in 1997, churning out a signature collection that gets flashier and trashier with every passing season. The Bond Street HQ combines all things Versace under one palatial roof: Gianni Versace, Versus, Versace Jeans Couture and Versace Intensive (swim- and underwear), as well as the home and jewellery collections. Expect extremes, from the eminently wearable pleated grey miniskirts and deep V camel sweaters to a Big Bird fluffy jacket straight from Sesame Street's costume department. You'll also find make-up, fragrance and homewares in the shape of carpets and china, giving instant access to the Versace glamour-puss dream. They've even been known to serve cocktails and canapés in the pretty roof garden. *versace.com*

Expensive to very expensive Amex/MC/V

020 7355 2700 **tube: Bond Street/Oxford Circus**
113-115 New Bond Street Mon-Sat 10-6 (Thurs 10-7)
London W1

020 7259 5700 **tube: Knightsbridge**
183-184 Sloane Street Mon-Sat 10-6
London SW1

Vertice Uomo

An approachable boutique featuring designer menswear without the hype. Labels include Alessandrini, Neil Barrett, Costume National, Antonio Mallas, Xavier Delcour, and DSquared2. Check out the pimp-chic lizard and diamanté boots and customised T-shirts decorated with buttons. Styles are wearable and prices within reason. Worth a glance if you're walking by.

Affordable Amex/MC/V

020 7408 2031 **tube: Bond Street**
16 South Molton Street Mon-Sat 10-6:15
London W1 (Thurs 10-7)

Vilebrequin ♂

A real favourite of *Vogue* editor Alexandra Schulman and inspired by its roots in sunny St Tropez, this airy store stocks hundreds of men's swimming trunks in fun colourful prints. From plain blue to Hawaiian flowers to red chillies to dancing elephants, the choice is endless. You'll also find a small selection of linen shirts, shorts, beach towels and soft leather sandals. Perfect for lazy summer days by the swimming-pool. *vilebrequin.com*

Moderate *Amex/MC/V*

020 7589 8445 **tube: South Kensington**
56 Fulham Road Mon-Sat 10-6 (Wed 10-7)
London SW3

020 7499 6558 **tube: Green Park/Piccadilly Circus**
1-2 Burlington Arcade Mon-Sat 10-6
London W1

Ville St Cassien ♀

Seriously sexy shoes from the likes of Sergio Rossi, Dolce & Gabbana and Baldini make this a favourite haunt for ladies who lunch. Delicate heels are crafted in vintage-style floral fabrics, perfect for summer tea parties, and Robert Clergerie ankle boots are effortlessly chic teemed with bootleg trousers. The new King's Road shop is a gleaming white space with chunky silver shelves displaying the shoes like artworks. If you are tired from all the footwork of shopping, have a seat in one of the lime-green retro-style chairs.

Expensive *Amex/MC/V*

020 7351 5155 **tube: Sloane Square**
251 King's Road Mon-Sat 10-6:30
London SW3 Sun 12-6

Virginia ♀

John Galliano might drop by to discuss the finer points of corsetry, such is the esoteric character of Virginia (a former actress) and her vintage shop which features women's clothing from the 1880s to the 1930s. It's all displayed in an over-the-top boudoir where literally everything is pink—imagine a grandmother's crowded dressing-room, her frilly knickers resting on a day-bed that's draped with an embroidered piano shawl. There's no rhyme or reason to the selection, it's whatever Virginia likes...evening gowns, lingerie, hats, bags and decorative objets. One thing she definitely doesn't like: customers who gripe about her prices, which generally start around £200—petty cash for Virginia's A-list clientele which includes Nicole Kidman and Naomi Campbell.

Expensive *Amex/MC/V*

020 7727 9908 **tube: Holland Park**
98 Portland Road Mon-Fri 11-6, Sat by appointment
London W11

Vivienne Westwood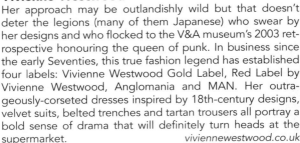

Her approach may be outlandishly wild but that doesn't deter the legions (many of them Japanese) who swear by her designs and who flocked to the V&A museum's 2003 retrospective honouring the queen of punk. In business since the early Seventies, this true fashion legend has established four labels: Vivienne Westwood Gold Label, Red Label by Vivienne Westwood, Anglomania and MAN. Her outrageously-corseted dresses inspired by 18th-century designs, velvet suits, belted trenches and tartan trousers all portray a bold sense of drama that will definitely turn heads at the supermarket.   *viviennewestwood.co.uk*

Expensive   *Amex/MC/V*

020 7439 1109   **tube: Oxford Circus**
44 Conduit Street   Mon-Sat 10-6 (Thurs 10-7)
London W1

020 7629 3757   **tube: Bond Street**
6 Davies Street   (opening hours as above)
London W1

020 7352 6551   **tube: Sloane Square**
430 King's Road   Mon-Sat 10-6
London SW10

Viyella

The shop still hasn't had its long-overdue facelift and nor have the designs. Elastic waistband trousers, basic blouses and long, roomy skirts take no apparent notice of the latest fashion trends. The mixed separates and suits at Viyella feature basic fabrics like cotton and linen and mostly solid shades of beige, brown and navy. We were bored stiff here, but there's bound to be someone looking for such safe, practical casualwear. Unexciting bags, shoes and belts continue the snooze-worthy theme.

Moderate   *Amex/MC/V*

020 7734 7524   **tube: Oxford Circus**
179-183 Regent Street   Mon-Fri 10-6:30 (Thurs 10-8)
London W1   Sat 10-6, Sun 12-5

Voyage

The ups and downs of the Voyage voyage are fashion legend. First it was well in with fashion luvvies, then it was well and truly out. The boho-chic clothing in lush fabrics was popular, but a discriminating entrance policy and unfriendly staff were distinctly off-putting. Now there is no door policy at their Mayfair store (the Covent Garden diffusion shop is no longer) and service is much less intimdating—but shopping here is still an experience. Recent highlights include rhinestone-studded, acid-coloured prints, sequined sandals and enough glitter to put any drag queen to shame. At best the Voyage look is slightly outlandish and, despite the shop's more welcoming vibe, the styles on offer are not for the faint-hearted.

Expensive to very expensive   *Amex/MC/V*

020 7287 9989   **tube: Oxford Circus**
50 Conduit Street   Mon-Sat 9:30-6 (Thurs 9:30-7)
London W1

Wall

Launched in 1997 by Herman and Judith Balcazar and influenced largely by Peruvian and oriental designs, the womenswear here reflects an earthy, organic style sense in such materials as Pima cotton, alpaca wool and Irish linen. Colours are inspired by the great outdoors, with sea-green shirts, sky-blue tunic dresses and sandy-beige cropped trousers. Cuts are large and forgiving, and probably best for a mature shopper with a boho bent. They are also a mail order company, if you're too tired to make it over to Notting Hill. Order a catalogue or shop online.   *wall-london.com*

Moderate to expensive   *Amex/MC/V*

020 7243 4623   **tube: Notting Hill Gate**
1 Denbigh Road   Mon-Fri 10:30-6:30, Sat 10-6
London W11   (for mail order, 0870 350 7373)

Wallis

If making the style pages has never been at the top of your to-do list, you might find this a good source for benign basics. It's certainly a place to visit for the seasonal changing of the guard, when a glance through your wardrobe reveals nothing reliable to wear. Elegant blouses, bright tops, perennial trousers and sexy evening bits achieve the look of the moment without risking much, but the classic cuts and commendable petite selection really make it worth stopping by.   *wallis-fashion.co.uk*

Affordable to moderate   *Amex/MC/V*

020 7437 0076   **tube: Oxford Circus**
217 Oxford Street   Mon-Fri 10-8 (Thurs 10-9)
London W1   Sat 107, Sun 12-6

020 7408 0639   **tube: Marble Arch/Bond Street**
532-536 Oxford Street   (opening hours as above)
London W1

Wardrobe

Susie Faux offers women a uniquely individualized shopping experience. Meeting with customers one-on-one, she helps working women build their core business wardrobe—a great service for the shopping illiterate and those who don't have time to learn the tricks. The emphasis is on Italian designers such as Sergio Rossi, TSE, Piazza Sempione and many others, with expert guidance through the sea of suedes, tweeds, florals, stripes and leather. Beyond business, there are dresses and eveningwear as well. If you want to overhaul more than your closet, there's also a beautician on hand.   *wardrobe.co.uk*

Moderate to expensive   *Amex/MC/V*

020 7494 1131
42 Conduit Street
London W1

tube: **Oxford Circus**
Mon-Sat 10-6 (Fri 8-6)
(or by appointment)

Warehouse 👤

Tapping into the under-25 market and feeding its rabid appetite for trend, Warehouse brings the latest runway looks to the masses. Girls love the jeans, tight tanks, party wear, black trousers and cheap silver jewellery, as well as the more casual line of sporty shirts and denim. Designs are primarily flashy and bright (but not of exceptional quality) and the latest trends are well represented. If Kookaï and Oasis are your guilty pleasures, this will also please. *warehousefashion.com*

Affordable   *Amex/MC/V*

020 7437 7101
19-21 Argyll Street
London W1

tube: **Oxford Circus**
Mon-Sat 10-7
(Thurs 10-8), Sun 12-6

020 7436 4179
The Plaza, 120 Oxford Street
London W1

tube: **Oxford Circus**
(opening hours as above)

020 7240 8242
24 Long Acre
London WC2

tube: **Covent Garden**
Mon-Fri 10-7:30 (Thurs 10-8)
Sat 10-7, Sun 12-6

020 7584 0069
96 King's Road
London SW3

tube: **Sloane Square**
Mon-Sat 10-6:30
(Wed 10-7), Sun 12-6

020 7221 2699
Whiteley's, Queensway
London W2

tube: **Queensway/Bayswater**
Mon-Sat 10-8
Sun 12-6

020 7938 3550
2 Barkers Arcade
Kensington High Street
London W8

tube: **High Street Kensington**
Mon-Wed 10-7, Thurs 10-8
Fri-Sat 10-7, Sun 12-6

020 7794 8559
8 Hampstead High Street
London NW3

tube: **Hampstead**
Daily 10-6 (Sun 12-6)

020 7606 5558
99a Cheapside
London EC2

tube: **Bank**
Mon-Fri 8:30-6:30

020 7256 8976
26 Blomfield Street
London EC2

tube: **Liverpool Street**
Mon-Fri 8:30-6:30

020 7519 1662
14 Canada Square
London E14

tube: **Canary Wharf**
Mon-Fri 9-7
Sat 10:30-6:30, Sun 11-5

The Wedding Shop 👤

Reminiscent of *My Fair Lady* and Audrey Hepburn, a stripey wallpapered stairway leads to the only Carolina Herrera and Vera Wang collections in London: from vintage lace designs to the contemporary bandeau styles of today. Add girlfriends and champagne and you have the perfect wedding-dress shopping experience. You can also view Elie Saab's collection (he dressed Halle Berry for the Oscars) or consult the in-house couture designer. Dresses start at £2,000 and they do a fab wedding list too.   *theweddingshoponline.com*

Expensive   *Amex/MC/V*
020 7838 0171   **tube: South Kensington**
171 Fulham Road   (by appointment)
London SW3

Welsh & Jefferies

The military prints on the wall, the front-of-shop cutting table and the plush, carpeted atmosphere in this small, welcoming establishment single out Welsh & Jefferies as an archetypal Savile Row gentleman's tailors. The firm has been in business for over 100 years (with a royal warrant to make military wear for the Prince of Wales), offering a completely bespoke service to an equally typical range of stockbrokers, big businessmen and landowners.   *welshandjefferies.co.uk*

Very expensive   *Amex/MC/V*
020 7734 3062   **tube: Piccadilly Circus/Oxford Circus**
20 Savile Row   Mon-Fri 9-5
London W1

West Village

Named after one of Manhattan's most celebrated neighbourhoods, West Village hocks an eclectic selection of international designers. Style fanatics will swoon for the selection, featuring names like Antik Batik and Nanaki and the signature label, The West Village, alongside Ugg boots and Havaianas flip-flops. If you're looking for a girly gift, pick up one of the popular West Village white Ts pre-packed in its own cute box. Candles, beaded bracelets and flowery hairclips are also on hand. It's all very cool.

Expensive   *Amex/MC/V*
020 7243 6912   **tube: Notting Hill Gate**
35 Kensington Park Road   Mon-Sat 10-6, Sun 12-5
London W11

☆ Whistles

More boutique than mainstream, this well-loved chain offers the most imaginative and directional pieces on the high street. The collection is fashionable and feminine, characterised by handcrafted details such as beadwork and embroidery. Whistles consistently offers clothing refreshingly different from the norm, whether it be a beautifully tailored pin-striped suit with shocking pink lining or a sheer summer dress with little cap sleeves; a lot of the tops work brilliantly as maternity wear too.   Besides the store's own label you'll find bias-cut skirts, candy coloured T-shirts and covetable denim from an eclectic selection of designers, including Cacherel, Antik Batik and Alberta Ferretti.   *whistles.com*

Expensive   *Amex/MC/V*

020 7823 9134
303 Brompton Road
London SW3

tube: South Kensington
Mon-Sat 10-6:30
(Wed 10-7), Sun 12-5

020 7487 4484
12 St Christopher's Place
London W1

tube: Bond Street
Mon-Sat 10-6
(Thurs 10-7), Sun 12-5

020 7730 2006
31 King's Road
London SW3

tube: Sloane Square
Mon-Fri 10-7
Sat 10-6:30, Sun 12-6

020 7379 7401
20 The Market
London WC2

tube: Covent Garden
Mon-Wed 10:30-6:30, Thurs 10:30-7:30
Fri-Sat 10:30-7, Sun 12-6

020 7935 7013
1 Thayer Street
London W1

tube: Bond Street
Mon-Sat 10-6
(Thurs 10-7), Sun 12-5

020 7431 2395
2-4 Hampstead High Street
London NW3

tube: Hampstead
Mon-Sat 10-6
(Thurs 10-7), Sun 12-6

020 7586 8282
51 St John's Wood High Street
London NW8

tube: St John's Wood
Mon-Sat 10-6, Sun 12-5

020 7226 7551
135 Upper Street
London N1

tube: Highbury & Islington/Angel
Mon-Sat 10:30-6:30 (Thurs 10:30-7:30)
Sun 12-6

020 7792 2488
218 Westbourne Grove
London W2

tube: Bayswater/Notting Hill Gate
Mon-Sat 10-6:30 (Thurs 10-7)
Sun 12-6

020 7491 0597
32 South Molton Street
London W1

tube: Bond Street
Mon-Sat 10-6 (Thurs 10-7)
Sun 12-6

020 7519 6132
Unit 33, Jubilee Place
London E14

tube: Canary Wharf
Mon-Sat 9-6 (Thurs 9-8)
Sun 12-6

020 8739 0112
28 High Street
London SW19

tube: Wimbledon
Mon-Sat 10-6
Sun 11-5

White Stuff　👨👩

Chilled-out, outdoor clothing for surfing, snowboarding dudes (and wannabes.) It all started when two Englishmen set off to sell T-shirts in the French Alps. Fifteen stores later, the selection is still inspired by the alpine tourist seasons—skiwear in the winter and beachwear when the sun shines. Capri trousers and tank tops, snowboarding jackets and slick goggles all get their turn on the floor.　*whitestuff.com*

Affordable　　　　　　　　　　　　　　　　　　　　*MC/V*

020 7371 0174
845 Fulham Road
London SW6

tube: Parsons Green
Mon-Sat 10-6:30
Sun 11-5

020 7228 7129
49 Northcote Road
London SW11

station: Clapham Junction (mainline)
Mon-Sat 9:30-5:30
Sun 11-5:30

020 7354 8204   **tube: Angel**
12-14 Essex Road   Mon-Sat 10-6 (Thurs 10-7)
London N1   Sun 11-5

020 7313 9544   **tube: Bayswater/Notting Hill Gate**
66 Westbourne Grove   Daily 10-6 (Sun 12-5)
London W2

William Hunt   👤

William Hunt, even more so than Richard James, plays the Savile Row upstart with aplomb. The utterly, instantly flamboyant appearance of his brilliantly bohemian shop (which boasts a piano and a red carpet overlaid with a cow-print rug) is perfect for the larger-than-life clothes with which he has made his name over the past few years. Bespoke and ready-to-wear suits boast signature flared cuffs and theatrical linings while a superb range of high-collared, full-colour, fitted shirts fights for attention with casual (but no less colourful) trousers and half-sleeve shirts. *williamhunt-savilerow.com*

Expensive   *Amex/MC/V*

020 7439 1921   **tube: Piccadilly Circus/Oxford Circus**
41 Savile Row   Mon-Sat 10-6
London W1

Wolford   👤

Where there are stockings there will be runs, right? Not so for Wolford, whose high-tech stretch hosiery is said to withstand the rigours of repeated wear. Classic tights sit next to naughty fishnets, support hose and knee-highs, sheer or opaque—Wolford has a leg up on every stocking trend. Best of all, they've eliminated waistbands from their designs, thereby banishing the embarrassing belly-bulge effect. Samples are hung throughout the store so customers can pull and stretch to their heart's content, and the staff are knowledgeable and helpful. You'll never have another clear nail polish emergency. *wolfordboutiquelondon.co.uk*

Affordable   *Amex/MC/V*

020 7499 2549   **tube: Bond Street**
3 South Molton Street   Mon-Sat 10-6 (Thurs 10-7)
London W1

Woodhouse   👤

Not the most inspiring shop, but Woodhouse is a great stop-off for fashion clueless males happy to rely on designer names. Conventional labels—Armani, Boss and Burberry—offer quality basics including structured suits, smart shirts, jeans and khakis. Everything is as you would expect it to be; fashion-forward style-setters should look elsewhere.

Expensive   *Amex/MC/V*

020 7823 3014   **tube: Sloane Square**
97 King's Road   Mon-Sat 10-6:30
London SW3   (Wed 10-7), Sun 12-6

020 7240 2008   **tube: Covent Garden**
138 Long Acre   Mon-Sat 10-7 (Thurs 10-8)
London WC2   Sun 11-5

020 7486 1099   **tube: Bond Street**
28-32 St Christopher's Place   Mon-Sat 10-6:30
London W1   (Thurs 10-7), Sun 11-5

The World According To *(formerly known as Shop)*

Neon pink lighting leads the way to this basement Soho store where you'll find a cutting-edge combination of girly fashion and sexy kitsch. The list of labels is enough to make a shopoholic reach for her Amex: Eley Kishimoto, Vivienne Westwood, Adidas vintage, Sonia Rykiel, Cacharel... To top it all, plenty of sparkly accessories.

Moderate to very expensive   *Amex/MC/V*

020 7437 1259   **tube: Piccadilly Circus**
4 Brewer Street   Mon-Fri 11-6:30, Sat 11-6:30
London W1

Yohji Yamamoto

His name is synonymous with cutting-edge, androgynous Japanese fashion. Yamamoto's modern, architectural designs come from a mostly black, white and beige palette. Men can choose from suits while women browse among tailored trousers, shirts, jackets and wrap skirts in intricate Persian carpet prints. The pieces in this ready-to-wear collection are structural works of art. Naturally, creative genius comes at a price.

Very expensive   *Amex/MC/V*

020 7491 4129   **tube: Oxford Circus**
14-15 Conduit Street   Mon-Sat 10-6 (Thurs 10-7)
London W1

YD.UK

The name stands for "You Decide" as in "Wear what you like and don't be hung up on labels and fashion fads". Step into the mauve-walled, stone-floored store and you almost forget you're in self-conscious, self-important Hampstead: we could happily while away a morning here, browsing through the eclectic, colour-fuelled range of established names and lesser-known labels. YD's fans include rock bad boy Liam Gallagher and Naked Chef Jamie Oliver, who've clearly learnt a thing or two from this bunch of non-conformists.   *yduk.com*

Expensive   *Amex/MC/V*

020 7431 9242   **tube: Hampstead**
82 Heath Street   Daily 10-6:30 (Sun 11-6:30)
London NW3

Young England

Balloon-sleeved pinafores, linen smock dresses and mini cotton checked shirts: traditional children's clothing is the speciality here, with sizes ranging from newborn to 10. In addition to classic cotton frocks with bows at the back, there are little sleeveless pink dresses, and, for boys, plaid shorts and sailor suits. The Baby Graziella label is on hand, as well as colourful booties, embroidered bed sheets, tiny straw handbags and a small selection of toys. All this, plus a made-to-measure service (for bridesmaid dresses and mini cutaways), makes Young England one of the best kids' shops in London. *youngengland.com*

Expensive   *Amex/MC/V*

020 7259 9003   **tube: Victoria/Sloane Square**
47 Elizabeth Street   Mon-Fri 10-5:30, Sat 10-3
London SW1

Yves Saint Laurent: Rive Gauche

Tom Ford put the sex back into Yves Saint Laurent and Stefano Pilati who bravely stepped into his shoes has now designed two collections for Yves Saint Laurent's glamorous heroine. Hollywood loved his debut of frou-frou red-carpet dresses, but his second collection was more worthy of fashion column inches and embraced the new mood for structured shapes; stiff suits and high necklines are softened with pussy-bows. Watch out for the Bow bag, the next must-have item sure to be seen on the shoulders of Cameron Diaz and suchlike. Menswear is stylish with sleek suiting, soft cashmere and luxurious accessories. *ysl.com*

Expensive to very expensive   *Amex/MC/V*

020 7493 1800   **tube: Bond Street**
33 Old Bond Street   Mon-Sat 10-6 (Thurs 10-7)
London W1

020 7235 6706   **tube: Knightsbridge**
171-172 Sloane Street   Mon-Sat 10-6 (Wed 10-7)
London SW1

☆ Zara

We haven't had her for long, but how did we do without her? Women of every age love this Spanish chain for its low prices and high style sense. With a selection that ranges from sporty to girlishly hip to downright classic, they recreate every major seasonal look, often before anyone else. Jeans and baby tees are mingled with leather skirts and sleek business suits. There's so much good stuff, you can't try it on fast enough. Accessories and the new range of homewear (available at the Brompton Road store) are the icing on the cake. Keep coming back—the selection changes constantly. *zara.com*

Affordable   *Amex/MC/V*

020 7590 6900   **tube: Knightsbridge**
78-91 Brompton Road   Mon-Sat 10-7
London SW3   Sun 12-6

020 7534 9500   **tube: Piccadilly Circus**
118 Regent Street   Mon-Sat 10-8
London W1   Sun 12-6

020 7318 2700	**tube: Oxford Circus**
242-248 Oxford Street	(opening hours as above)
London W1	
020 7368 4680	**tube: High Street Kensington**
48-52 Kensington High Street	(opening hours as above)
London W8	
020 7518 1550	**tube: Bond Street**
333 Oxford Street	(opening hours as above)
London W1	
020 7438 9900	**tube: Covent Garden**
52-56 Long Acre	(opening hours as above)
London WC2	

Zee & Co

We're sure we saw a couple of boy band members in here—or perhaps we were confused by the try-hard-trendy clothing. It's all very gorgeous (as are the smiley staff) and label-tastic – Fake London, Maharishi, Armani, D&G, Stone Island, Hugo Boss – but we prefer our men a bit more dressed down, please. The womenswear branch way out east in Bow (020 8980 2122) carries a similarly high-profile range of designers. *zeeandco.co.uk*

Expensive *MC/V*

020 7354 5855	**tube: Angel**
36 Upper Street	Mon-Sat 10-6:30
London N1	Sun 12-5:30

Zibba

Located near the edge of Hyde Park, this girly den of shoes and clothing requires a bit of a detour. Once inside, however, you'll find a sophisticated but restrained shoe selection ranging from solid black pumps to cute kitten heels with tiny bows. The clothing is a bit edgier, featuring funky shawls and chunky knits.

Moderate *Amex/MC/V*

020 7235 3344	**tube: Knightsbridge/Hyde Park Corner**
61 Knightsbridge	Mon-Sat 10-6:30
London SW1	(Wed 10-7), Sun 11-5

MAIL ORDER/INTERNET

Boden

For its detractors, Johnny Boden's mail-order empire represents everything that is worst about middle England: bland, overpriced, anti-fashion comfort clothing worn by mumsy frumps and rugger bores. For its fans, the arrival of the new Boden catalogue is an excuse to open a bottle of wine and hammer the credit card. Love it or hate it (we love it), Boden has taken Britain by storm. Designs are fun, colourful and good quality and there's something for everybody—from pretty ruffled T-shirts for women, soft linen shirts for men and basic cotton trousers from Mini Boden for kids. Sizing is almost always spot-on, the clothes are modelled by real people, and if you decide you don't like what you've ordered simply return it and get the refund. Shopping from the comfort of your armchair has never been easier.   *boden.co.uk*

Moderate to expensive   *Amex/MC/V*

0845 677 5000   **Mon-Sat 8-8**
Boden
Meridian West
Meridian Business Park
Leicester LE 19 1PX

Harry Duley

She did not set out to be a maternity designer but Harry Duley's clothes are the perfect pregnancy wear. They're soft, comfortable and flattering; most important of all, they're made of a brilliant stretch fabric that will expand over your tummy and then bounce back after the baby is born. Styles are simple and lovely enough to be worn whether you're pregnant or not. Signature items include a ruche-sided top with three-quarter-length sleeves, a below-the-knee skirt and a simple frill dress. There are hand-knitted tank tops, cardigans and jumpers for babies in contrasting colours and a sweetly simple children's clothing collection. Every Harry Duley piece comes decorated with a small embroidered spider, so arachnophobics beware.   *harryduley.co.uk*

Moderate   *MC/V*

0870 975 2142   **Mon-Fri 10-6**
Unit 2, 77 Fortess Road
London NW5

☆ Lucky Me

In an ideal world, every new baby would have a white-haired, apple-cheeked granny with the spare time and skill to knit pram blankets, tiny cardigans and warm woolly sweaters. Fortunately for those of us in the real world, we've found Lucky Me: a mail-order company specialising in hand-knitted children's clothes (aged 0-4) as well as smocked dresses and chic sheepskin gilets to match Mummy's Joseph number. Every piece is handmade in Scotland, from Australian lambswool. Such loving attention to detail doesn't come cheap, but just think of all the knitting hours and dropped stitches Granny will be spared. For autumn 2005, they are introducing matinee jackets, cashmere hat and mitten sets, all beautifully packaged and ready to be sent to the luckiest children in the UK.   *luckyme-uk.com*

Moderate   *Amex/MC/V*

020 7738 8555   **station: Battersea Park (mainline)**
3 Cupar Road   (by appointment only)
London SW11

Mitty James

This is the candyfloss clothing that your kids, nieces and nephews will be wearing in those mantelpiece holiday photos. Stripy and plain towelling hoodies, retro bathing costumes and bikinis in cotton ginghams and florals will make your little ones the cutest on the beach. For surf-babe teenagers and Sloaney mummies, pink and turquoise hotpants, skirts and jogging bottoms are perfect for the British summer. The new website is quite small but we are looking forward to seeing what they come up with next. *mittyjames.com*

Affordable   *MC/V*

08456 120240   **Mon-Fri 9-5:30**
New Rock
Chilcompton
Bath BA3 4JE

Peruvian Connection

Peru is renowned for two luxurious fabrics, hand-harvested pima cotton, velvety soft and smooth, and silky precious alpaca. This mail-order company offers the best of both. The team of UK-based designers produces detailed sketches, inspired by everything from Andean textiles to Turkoman carpets. Skilled Andean knitters in South America, who employ a range of knit and crochet techniques, then translate these sketches into reality. The resulting garments are soft, bold and full of character. Strong geometric patterns and warm rustic shades may be a bit too dowdy for the younger generation, but who can resist the warm, weightless long-haired alpaca blankets. *peruvianconnection.com*

Moderate   *Amex/MC/V*

0800 550000   **Mon-Fri 8-7, Sat 9-5**
3 Thames Court
Goring on Thames
Berkshire RG8 9AQ

Plumo

Plumo has been going strong for a few years now and its colourful catalogue still offers an eclectic range of inspiring goodies sourced from all over the world. There are massage slippers, sequin-embroidered floral bags from France, Moroccan lanterns, delicate paper lamps from Japan and heart-shaped embroidered cushions. The Chinese bead bracelets are wonderful gifts and the pretty Edwardian umbrella is perfect for sun or rain. Clothing highlights include a jersey wrap dress, a lace cardigan, embroidered drawstring trousers and ribboned ballet shoes. You'll be tempted by something if you're in the spending mood. *plumo.com*

Moderate to expensive   *MC/V*

0870 241 3590   **(24-hour ordering service)**
Leroy House, Unit 30
436 Essex Road
London N1

Tati

From gingham hooded jackets and traditional romper suits for babies, to smart shorts and cricket sweaters for boys, to floral kaftans and pin-tuck blouses for women, this line of women's and children's clothing and accessories is the epitome of understated English good taste. Prices are reasonable and every order is meticulously wrapped and beautifully presented in a fabric bag.   *tati.co.uk*

Moderate   MC/V

01794 323 633
The Coach House at the Old Rectory
Sherfield English
Hants SO51 6FL

Toast

Simple, subtle and yet always interesting, the clothing offered by mail-order company Toast is apparently favoured by Nigella Lawson and Kate Winslet. Styles are a combination of vintage, eastern and classic and come in lovely soft colors such as sage blue, dusty plum and ivory. For women there are Fifties print skirts and swimsuits, canvas fatigues, towelling kimonos and linen jackets. The overall look is understated and informal and is continued in a great selection of shoes and accessories.   *toastbypost.co.uk*

Moderate to expensive   MC/V
0870 240 5200   **Mon-Fri 9-8, Sat 10-6**
Unit D, Lakeside
Llansamlet
Swansea SA7 9FF

Tulip & Nettle (formerly Dromedary)

Don't be put off by the slightly home-made look of the brochure; low-key cosiness is exactly what appeals abut this Northumberland-based mail-order company. The clothing is mostly for children (although some popular designs are now available for adults) and the range starts at 12 months and goes up to 12 years. There is a strong emphasis on stripes, ginghams, florals and denims and the overall look is old-fashioned country garden. The selection includes baby bloomers, sailor suits, Hero shirts, Yum Yum sundresses and toggle fleeces. If only everything was this sweet.

Moderate   MC/V
0143 467 3961   **Mon-Fri 9-5:30**
Healey Hall
Riding Mill
Northumberland NE44 6BH

The White Company

It's a simple concept: a mail-order company that specializes in a stylish collection for the home—cotton bed linen, throws, bedspreads, towels, bathrobes and china—all predominantly in white. So successful has the idea proved that The White Company now has three shops in London and has incorporated a small casual selection of clothing also in white, but with a few pieces in baby pink, sky blue, beige and black thrown in. The jerseywear is soft and comfortable with simple T-shirts, cami tops and bottoms, all great for lounging around at home in. The cotton nightwear—pyjamas, nightdresses and gowns—is fresh and crisp, and the activewear is reminiscent of Gap but without the logos, while babies' pyjamas, dressing gowns and quilts make the most perfect presents.   *thewhiteco.com*

Moderate to expensive   *Amex/MC/V*

020 7823 5322   **tube: Sloane Square**
8 Symons Street   Mon-Sat 9:30-6:30
London SW3   Sun 11-5

020 7935 7879   **tube: Bond Street**
12 Marylebone High Street   Mon-Sat 9-7, Sun 11-5
London W1   Sun 11-5

020 7881 0783 (children)   **tube: Sloane Square**
261 Pavilion Road   Mon-Sat 9:30-6:30
London SW1   Sun 11-5
Returns: Unit 30
Perivale Park
Horsenden Lane South
Greenford, Middlesex UB6 7RJ

Stores by Neighborhood

London Area Map

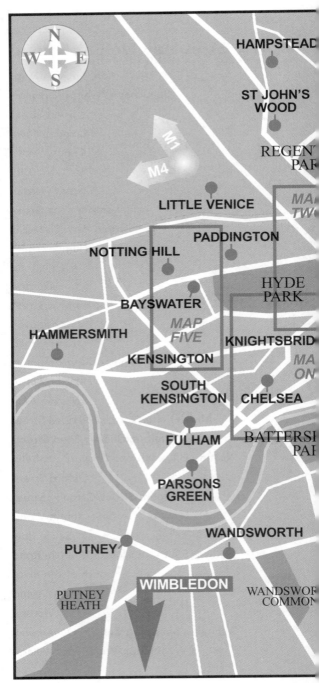

London Area Map

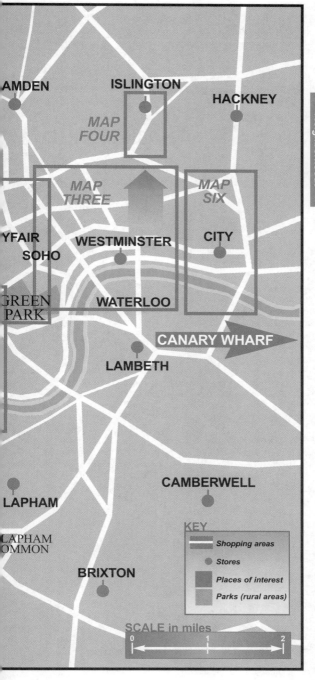

CAMDEN

ISLINGTON

HACKNEY

MAP FOUR

MAP THREE

MAP SIX

MYFAIR
SOHO

WESTMINSTER

CITY

GREEN PARK

WATERLOO

CANARY WHARF

LAMBETH

CAMBERWELL

CLAPHAM

CLAPHAM COMMON

BRIXTON

KEY

Shopping areas

Stores

Places of interest

Parks (rural areas)

SCALE in miles

0   1   2

Beauchamp Place / King's Road / South Ken

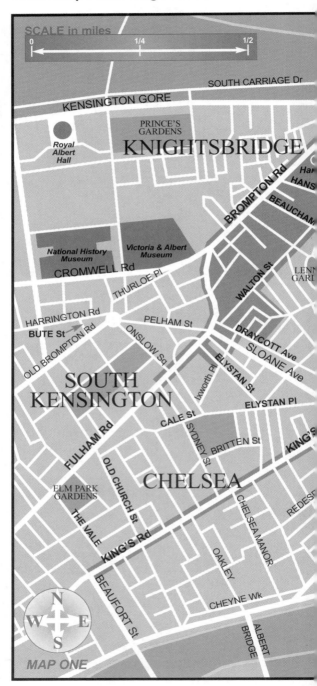

SCALE in miles
0   1/4   1/2

SOUTH CARRIAGE Dr

KENSINGTON GORE

PRINCE'S GARDENS

KNIGHTSBRIDGE

Royal Albert Hall

BROMPTON Rd

Har

HANS

BEAUCHAM

National History Museum

Victoria & Albert Museum

CROMWELL Rd

THURLOE PL

WALTON St

LENN GARI

HARRINGTON Rd

BUTE St

PELHAM St

ONSLOW Sq

DRAYCOTT Ave

SLOANE Ave

OLD BROMPTON Rd

lxworth Pl

ELYSTAN St

SOUTH KENSINGTON

ELYSTAN Pl

CALE St

SYDNEY St

BRITTEN St

KING'S

FULHAM Rd

OLD CHURCH St

CHELSEA

CHELSEA MANOR

REDESF

ELM PARK GARDENS

THE VALE

KING'S Rd

OAKLEY

BEAUFORT St

CHEYNE Wk

N
W E
S

MAP ONE

ALBERT BRIDGE

230

Knightsbridge / Belgravia

Mayfair / Oxford Street / Marylebone

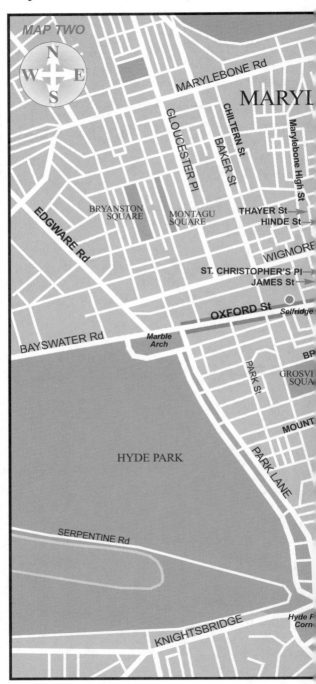

MAP TWO

N
W E
S

MARYLEBONE Rd

MARYL

GLOUCESTER Pl

CHILTERN St

BAKER St

Marylebone High St

EDGWARE Rd

BRYANSTON SQUARE

MONTAGU SQUARE

THAYER St →
HINDE St →

WIGMORE

ST. CHRISTOPHER'S Pl
JAMES St →

OXFORD St

Selfridge

BAYSWATER Rd

Marble Arch

BR

PARK St

GROSVE
SQUA

MOUNT

HYDE PARK

PARK LANE

SERPENTINE Rd

KNIGHTSBRIDGE

Hyde P
Corn

Bond Street / Regent Street / Jermyn Street

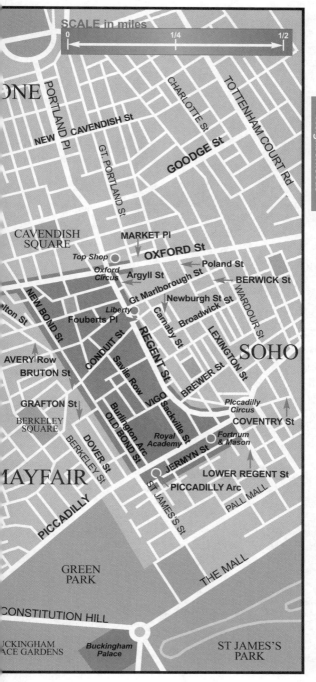

233

Covent Garden / Soho

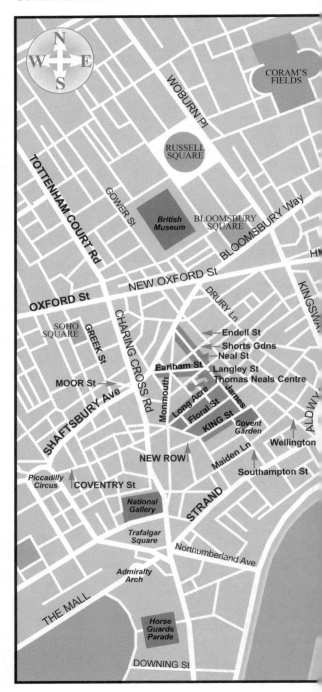

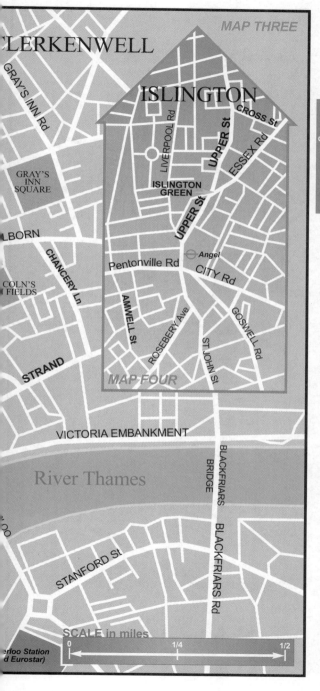

MAP THREE

CLERKENWELL

ISLINGTON

GRAY'S INN Rd

CROSS St

LIVERPOOL Rd

UPPER St

ESSEX Rd

GRAY'S INN SQUARE

ISLINGTON GREEN

UPPER St

LBORN

CHANCERY Ln

Pentonville Rd

Angel

CITY Rd

COLN'S FIELDS

AMWELL St

GOSWELL Rd

ROSEBERY Ave

ST JOHN St

STRAND

MAP FOUR

VICTORIA EMBANKMENT

River Thames

BLACKFRIARS BRIDGE

BLACKFRIARS Rd

STANFORD St

BLACKFRIARS Rd

SCALE in miles

0   1/4   1/2

erloo Station
d Eurostar)

Neighborhoods

Notting Hill / Kensington

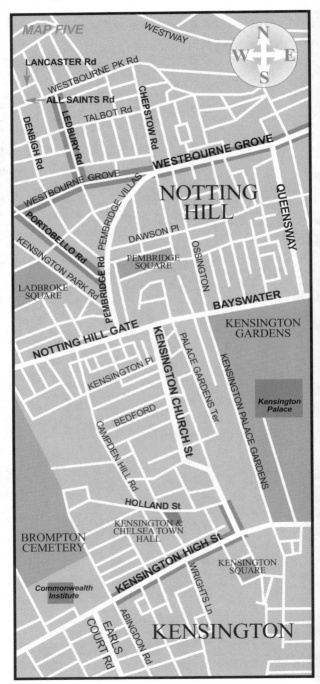

City

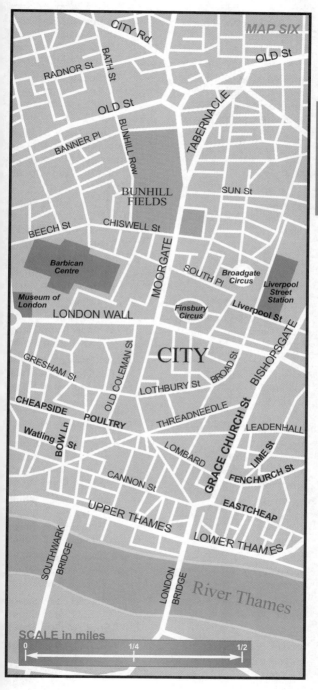

237

Beauchamp/Walton/Draycott (SW3)

See map pages 230–231

Abu Jani Sandeep Khosla	55 Beauchamp Place
Bertie Golightly	48 Beauchamp Place
Betsey Johnson	106 Draycott Avenue
Blossom	164 Walton Street
Bruce Oldfield	27 Beauchamp Place
Caroline Charles	56-57 Beauchamp Place
Caroline Holmes	176 Walton Street
Cashmere London	180 Walton Street
Caz	177 Draycott Avenue
Eliot Zed	117-119 Walton Street
Gigi	124 Draycott Avenue
Guys & Dolls	172 Walton Street
Isabell Kristensen	33 Beauchamp Place
Janet Reger	2 Beauchamp Place
Jean Paul Gaultier Boutique	171-175 Draycott Avenue
Katch	91 Walton Street
Kruszynska	35 Beauchamp Place
Laurence Tavernier	77 Walton Street
Liola	69 Walton Street
M-A-G	20 Beauchamp Place
Marie-Chantal	148 Walton Street
Monogrammed Linen Shop	168 Walton Street
Paddy Campbell	17 Beauchamp Place
Patrizia Wigan Designs	19 Walton Street
Plein Sud	151 Draycott Avenue
Robert Clergerie	122 Draycott Avenue
Spaghetti	32 Beauchamp Place
Tashia	178 Walton Street

Bond Street (W1)

See map pages 232–233

Aftershock	12 South Molton Street
Alexander McQueen	4 Old Bond Street
Anne Fontaine	30 New Bond Street
Armani Collezioni	43 New Bond Street
Avi Rossini	46 New Bond Street
Bally	116 New Bond Street
Bally	30 Old Bond Street
Berluti	43 Conduit Street
Bernini	95-96 New Bond Street
Bertie	36 South Molton Street
Bonpoint	38 Old Bond Street
Bottega Veneta	15 Old Bond Street
Brioni	32 Bruton Street
Browns	23-27 South Molton Street
Browns Focus	38-39 South Molton Street
Browns Labels For Less	50 South Molton Street
B-Store	6 Conduit Street

Burberry	21-23 New Bond Street
Butler & Wilson	20 South Molton Street
Calvin Klein	65 New Bond Street
Calvin Klein	65 South Molton Street
Camper	8-11 Royal Arcade, Old Bond Street
Canali	122 New Bond Street
Catimini	52a South Molton Street
Cecil Gee	92 New Bond Street
Celine	160 New Bond Street
Chanel	26 Old Bond Street
Church's	133 New Bond Street
Clio	75 New Bond Street
Comme des Garçons	17-18 Dover Street
Connolly	41 Conduit Street
Crombie	105 New Bond Street
D&G	53-55 New Bond Street
DKNY	27 Old Bond Street
Daks	10 Old Bond Street
Dolce & Gabbana	6-8 Old Bond Street
Donna Karan	19-21 New Bond Street
Dover Street Market	17-18 Dover Street
Dune	18 South Molton Street
Edward Green	12-13 Burlington Arcade
Eliot Zed	4 Avery Row
Emanuel Ungaro	150-151 New Bond Street
Emporio Armani	112a New Bond Street
Episode	69 New Bond Street
Ermenegildo Zegna	37-38 New Bond Street
Etro	14 Old Bond Street
Fenwick	63 New Bond Street
Formes	33 Brook Street
F.Pinet	47-48 New Bond Street
Fratelli Rossetti	177 New Bond Street
French For Less	8 South Molton Street
Furla	31 New Bond Street
Gina	9 Old Bond Street
G.J.Cleverley	13 The Royal Arcade
Gordon Scott	29 New Bond Street
Hermès	155 New Bond Street
Hobbs	47-49 South Molton Street
Holland & Holland	31-33 Bruton Street
Issey Miyake	52 Conduit Street
Jigsaw (& Jigsaw Junior)	126-127 New Bond Street
Jigsaw (accessories)	49 South Molton Street
Jimmy Choo	27 New Bond Street
John Richmond	54 Conduit Street
John Smedley	24 Brook Street
Jones the Bootmaker	15 South Molton Street
Joseph	23 Old Bond Street

Joseph	28 Brook Street
Karen Millen	46 & 57 South Molton Street
Kate Kuba	26 Brook Street
Krizia	24-25 Conduit Street
Kurt Geiger	65 South Molton Street
Lanvin	108 New Bond Street
L.K.Bennett	25 & 31 Brook Street
Loewe	130 New Bond Street
Louis Féraud	68 New Bond Street
Louis Vuitton	17-18 New Bond Street
Marina Rinaldi	39 Old Bond Street
Matthew Williamson	28 Bruton Street
MaxMara	19-21 Old Bond Street
Mayfair Rat	37 South Molton Street
Miu Miu	123 New Bond Street
Moschino	28-29 Conduit Street
Mulberry	41-42 New Bond Street
Nicole Farhi	158 New Bond Street
Nine West	9 South Molton Street
Nitya	118 New Bond Street
Office	55 South Molton Street
Petit Bateau	62 South Molton Street
Pied à Terre	19 South Molton Street
Pleats Please: Issey Miyake	20 Brook Street
Poste	10 South Molton Street
Prada	16-18 Old Bond Street
Pringle	111-112 New Bond Street
Proibito	94 New Bond Street
Proibito	42 South Molton Street
Ralph Lauren	1 New Bond Street
Ralph Lauren (children)	143 New Bond Street
Reiss	78-79 New Bond Street
Reiss	56 South Molton Street
Rigby & Peller	22a Conduit Street
Ronit Zilkha	34 Brook Street
Ruco Line	64 South Molton Street
Russell & Bromley	24-25 & 109-110 New Bond Street
Salvatore Ferragamo	24 Old Bond Street
Sonia Rykiel	27-29 Brook Street
Space.NK	45-47 Brook Street
Stella McCartney	30 Bruton Street
Tartine et Chocolat	66 South Molton Street
Timberland	72 New Bond Street
Ventilo	70 New Bond Street
Versace	113-115 New Bond Street
Venise Collection	37 Brook Street
Vertice Uomo	16 South Molton Street
Vivienne Westwood	44 Conduit Street
Voyage	50 Conduit Street
Wardrobe	42 Conduit Street

Whistles	32 South Molton Street
Wolford	3 South Molton Street
Yohji Yamamoto	14-15 Conduit Street
Yves Saint Laurent: Rive Gauche	137 New Bond Street

Camden Town (NW1)

Anna	126 Regent's Park Road
Buffalo Boots	190 Camden High Street
Camden Market	Camden High Street
Cyberdog	Stables Market, Chalk Farm Road
Episode	26 Chalk Farm Road
Gap	6-12 Parkway
Graham & Green	164 Regent's Park Road
Marks & Spencer	143 Camden High Street
Offspring	221 Camden High Street
Pamela Shiffer	75 Regent's Park Road
Pink Piranha	21 Chalk Farm Road
Rokit	225 Camden High Street
Spice	162 Regent's Park Road
Swear	Stables Market, Chalk Farm Road

Canary Wharf (E14)

Cecil Gee	Unit 27, Canada Square
Church's	Cabot Place East
Dorothy Perkins	24 Canada Place
Fiorelli	45 Bank Street
French Connection	18 Jubilee Place
Gap	16-17 Canada Square
Gap Kids	Cabot Place East
Hobbs	4 Canada Place Mall
Jones the Bootmaker	Cabot Place East
L.K.Bennett	31 Jubilee Place
Mark Stephen Marengo	West India Quay
Monsoon	21-22 Canada Square
Next	11-12 Canada Place
Oasis	19 Canada Square
Phase Eight	Cabot Place East
Space.NK	Cabot Place East
Ted Baker	Unit 5, Canada Place
Thomas Pink	Cabot Place East
T.M.Lewin	18 Canada Place Mall
Top Shop	Unit 3, Canada Square
Warehouse	14 Canada Square
Whistles	Unit 33, Jubilee Place

City/Liverpool Street/Brick Lane *See map page 237*

Absolute Vintage	15 Hanbury Street, E1
Accessorize	84 Cheapside, EC2
Agent Provocateur	5 Royal Exchange, EC3
Austin Reed	1-2 Poultry, EC2

Austin Reed	13-23 Fenchurch Street, EC3
Austin Reed	1-14 Liverpool Street, EC2
Bodas	29 Lime Street, EC3
Cecil Gee	153 Fenchurch Street, EC3
Charles Tyrwhitt	43 Bow Lane, EC4
Church's	28 Royal Exchange, EC3
Church's	90 Cheapside, EC2
Church's	89 Chancery Lane, WC2
Crockett & Jones	25 Royal Exchange, EC3
Ede & Ravenscroft	93 Chancery Lane, WC2
Ede & Ravenscroft	2 Gracechurch Street, EC3
Emmett Shirts	4 Eldon Street, EC2
Episode	Bishopsgate Arcade, 137 Bishopsgate, EC2
Ethos	Bishopsgate Arcade, 137 Bishopsgate, EC2
Frockbrokers	115 Commercial Street, E1
Gap	4 Poultry, EC2
Gucci	9 Royal Exchange, EC3
Hackett	19 Eastcheap, EC3
Hermès	2-3 Royal Exchange, EC3
Hobbs	64-72 Leadenhall Market, EC3
Hobbs	Bishopsgate Arcade, 137 Bishopsgate, EC2
Hope + Glory	Broadgate Link, EC2
Jesiré	Bishopsgate Arcade, 137 Bishopsgate, EC2
Jigsaw	31 Leadenhall Market, EC3
Jigsaw	44 Bow Lane, EC2
Jones the Bootmaker	15 Cullum Street, EC3
Jones the Bootmaker	70-71 Watling Street, EC4
Jones the Bootmaker	320 High Holborn, WC1
Jones the Bootmaker	119 Cannon Street, EC4
Karen Millen	Bishopsgate Arcade, 137 Bishopsgate, EC2
Karen Millen	1-2 Royal Exchange Buildings, EC3
Knickerbox	69 Fleet Street, EC4
The Lazy Ones	102 Sclater Street, E1
L.K. Bennett	1-2 Royal Exchange Buildings, EC3
Louis Vuitton	5-6 Royal Exchange, EC3
Lulu Guinness	23 Royal Exchange, EC3
Mark Stephen Marengo	32 Artillery Lane, E1
Marks & Spencer	70 Finsbury Pavement, EC2
Monsoon	87 Gracechurch Street, EC3
Moss Bros	35 Blomfield Street, EC2
Moss Bros	83 Cheapside, EC2
Moss Bros	81 Gracechurch Street, EC3
Oasis	85-86 Old Broad Street, EC2
Oasis	4 Queen Victoria Street, EC4
Old Spitalfields Market	Brushfield Street, EC1
Oliver Sweeney	135 Middlesex Street, E1
Paul Smith	7 The Courtyard, Royal Exchange, EC3
Pickett	6 Royal Exchange, EC3
Public Aware	91 Brick Lane, E1
Prada	1 The Courtyard, Royal Exchange, EC3

Richard James	12 The Courtyard, Royal Exchange, EC3
Roderick Charles	31 Blomfield Street, EC2
Roderick Charles	25 Lime Street, EC3
Roderick Charles	52 Bow Lane, EC4
Roderick Charles	79-80 Chancery Lane, WC2
Rokit	101-107 Brick Lane, E1
Soboye Soong	13 Calvert Avenue, E2
Space.NK	Bishopsgate Arcade, 137 Bishopsgate, EC2
Space.NK	145-147 Cheapside, EC2
Start	42 & 59 Rivington Street, EC2
Story	4 Wilkes Street, E1
T.M.Lewin	34-36 Lime Street, EC2
T.M.Lewin	32-33 Blomfield Street, EC2
T.M.Lewin	67 Moorgate, EC2
T.M.Lewin	85 Cheapside, EC2
T.M.Lewin	9-9a Cullum Street, EC3
T.M.Lewin	59 Ludgate Hill, EC4
T.M.Lewin	49 Bow Lane, EC4
T.M.Lewin	27a Chancery Lane, WC2
T.M.Lewin	9a Chichester Rents, WC2
Tanner Krolle	7 Royal Exchange, EC3
Thomas Pink	16 Blomfield Street, EC2
Thomas Pink	24 Cullum Street, EC3
Thomas Pink	60 Cannon Street, EC4
Thomas Pink	82 Chancery Lane, WC2
Timberland	Unit 6, Bishopsgate Arcade, EC2
Timothy Everest	32 Elder Street, E1
Timothy Everest Shirts	52 Artillery Lane, E1
Tod's	15 The Courtyard, Royal Exchange, EC3
Warehouse	26 Blomfield Street, EC2
Warehouse	99a Cheapside, EC2

Covent Garden (WC2)   *See map pages 234–235*

Accessorize	25 The Market, 35 Neal Street & 5-6 James Street
Adolfo Dominguez	15 Endell Street
agnès b.	35-36 Floral Street
Aldo	3-7 Neal Street
All Saints	5 Earlham Street
American Classics	20 Endell Street
Angels	119 Shaftesbury Avenue
Aquaint	38 Monmouth Street
Arrogant Cat	42 Shorts Gardens
Base	55 Monmouth Street
Bertie	25 Long Acre
Birkenstock	70 Neal Street
Blackout II	51 Endell Street
Blunauta	69-76 Long Acre
Boxfresh	13 Shorts Gardens
Buffalo Boots	65-67 Neal Street

Burro	44 Monmouth Street
Camper	39 Floral Street
Carhartt	56 Neal Street
Carhartt	15-17 Earlham Street
Cath Kidston	28-32 Shelton Street
Diesel	43 Earlham Street
Dockers	Unit 8, North Piazza
Duffer of St George	29 & 34 Shorts Gardens
East	16 The Piazza
Egoshego	76 Neal Street
Ellis Brigham	30-32 Southampton Street
Fat Face	13 Thomas Neals Centre
Field & Trek	42 Maiden Lane
Foot Locker	30-32 Neal Street
Formes	28 Henrietta Street
Fred Perry	14 The Piazza
Fred Perry	6-7 Thomas Neals Centre
French Connection	11 James Street
French Connection	99-103 Long Acre
Gamba	3 Garrick Street
Gap	2-3 James Street
Gap	30-31 Long Acre
Gap Kids	121-123 Long Acre
H&M	27-29 Long Acre
Hackett	31-32 King Street
Hackett	38 Floral Street
High Jinks	25 Thomas Neals Centre
Hobbs	17 The Market
Hobbs	124 Long Acre
Hope + Glory	30 Nottingham House, Shorts Gardens
Hugo Boss	47 Long Acre
Jesire	28 James Street
Jigsaw	21 Long Acre
Jones	13-15 Floral Street
Jones the Bootmaker	16 New Row
Jones the Bootmaker	7-8 Langley Court
Joseph 1	5 Floral Street
Jungle	7 Earlham Street
Karen Millen	22-23 James Street
Koh Samui	65-67 Monmouth Street
Kookaï	39 Long Acre
Levi's	117a Long Acre
L.K.Bennett	130 Long Acre
The Loft	35 Monmouth Street
Maharishi	19a Floral Street
Maharishi (Dpmhi)	2-3 Great Pulteney Street
Mango/MNG	8-12 Neal Street
Mexx	112-115 Long Acre
Miss Sixty	39 Neal Street

Monsoon	23 The Piazza
Monsoon	5-6 James Street
Moss Bros	27 King Street
Muji	135 Long Acre
The Natural Shoe Store	21 & 37 Neal Street
Next	15-17 Long Acre
Nigel Hall	18 Floral Street
Nine West	1 James Street
Oasis	13 James Street
Office	57 Neal Street
Office	60 St Martin's Lane
Offspring	60 Neal Street
O'Neill	9-15 Neal Street
Paul & Joe	33 Floral Street
Paul Smith	40-44 Floral Street
Paul Smith	9-11 Langley Court
Pegaso	33 Neal Street
Pineapple	6a Langley Street
Pop Boutique	6 Monmouth Street
Poste Mistress	61-63 Monmouth Street
Quiksilver	12 North Piazza
Quiksilver	1 & 23 Thomas Neals Centre
Reiss	116 Long Acre
Rokit	42 Shelton Street
Shellys	14-18 Neal Street
Size?	17-19 Neal Street
Sole Trader	72 Neal Street
Space.NK	4 Thomas Neals Centre
Stussy	19 Earlham Street
Super Lovers	64 Neal Street
Sweatshop	9a Endell Street
Tabio	66 Neal Street
Ted Baker	1-4 Langley Court
Ted Baker	9-10 Floral Street
Timberland	125 Long Acre
Urban Outfitters	42-56 Earlham Street
Warehouse	24 Long Acre
Whistles	20 The Market
William Hunt	68 Neal Street
Woodhouse	138 Long Acre
Zara	52-56 Long Acre

Neighborhoods

Fulham/Parsons Green (SW6)

Angela Stone	257 New King's Road
Anna	590 King's Road
Blooming Marvellous	725 Fulham Road
Cath Kidson	668 Fulham Road
Crew Clothing Co	203 New King's Road
Dressage	299 New King's Road

Fat Face	827 Fulham Road
Harriet Gubbins	813b Fulham Road
Jenesis	52 New King's Road
Kit Clothing/Twentieth Century Frox	614 Fulham Road
Laura Tom	Redloh House, 2 Michael Road
Mimmo	602 Fulham Road
Pantalon Chameleon	28 & 187 New King's Road
Phillipa Lepley	494 Fulham Road
Pollyanna	811 Fulham Road
Sally Parsons	610 Fulham Road
Sweaty Betty	833 Fulham Road
T&G Clothing	580 Fulham Road
Thailandia	222 Munster Road
Tim Little	560 King's Road

Green Park/Piccadilly (W1)   *See map pages 232–233*

Accessorize	1 Piccadilly Circus
Aware	25a Old Compton Street
Bally	30 Old Bond Street
Berk	6 & 46-49 Burlington Arcade
Brioni	32 Bruton Street
Budd	3 Piccadilly Arcade
Camper	8-11 Royal Arcade, 28 Old Bond Street
Chanel	26 Old Bond Street
Church's	58-59 Burlington Arcade
Claire's Accessories	13 Coventry Street
Crockett & Jones	20-21 Burlington Arcade
DKNY	27 Old Bond Street
Daks	10 Old Bond Street
Dolce & Gabbana	6-8 Old Bond Street
Dormeuil	35 Sackville Street
Dover Street Market	17 Dover Street
Ede & Ravenscroft	8 Burlington Gardens
Edward Green	12-13 Burlington Arcade
Elégance	14a Grafton Street
Etro	14 Old Bond Street
Fallan & Harvey	7 Sackville Street
Favourbrook	19-21 Piccadilly Arcade
Fortnum & Mason	181 Piccadilly
Franchetti Bond	7 Burlington Arcade
Frontier	9 Brewer Street
G.J.Cleverley & Co	13 The Royal Arcade
	28 Old Bond Street
Gap	1-7 Shaftesbury Avenue
Georgina Goodman	12-14 Shepherd Street
Gina	9 Old Bond Street
Gucci	34 Old Bond Street
House of Cashmere (Barbour)	8-9 Burlington Arcade
Jil Sander	7 Burlington Gardens

Joseph	23 Old Bond Street
Kanves	19-20 Brewer Street
Kokon to Zai	57 Greek Street
Lacoste	233 Regent Street
Lillywhites	24-36 Lower Regent Street
Louis Vuitton	17-18 New Bond Street
Marina Rinaldi	39 Old Bond Street
Neil Cunningham	28 Sackville Street
N.Peal	37 & 71-72 Burlington Arcade
Offspring	49 Old Compton Street
Orvis	36a Dover Street
Ozwald Boateng	9 Vigo Street
Paule Ka	13a Grafton Street
Pickett	32-33 & 41 Burlington Arcade
Prada	16-18 Old Bond Street
Ralph Lauren	1 New Bond Street
Souvenir	53 Brewer Street
Stephane Kélian	13 Grafton Street
Tanner Krolle	3 Burlington Gardens
Tod's	2-5 Old Bond Street
Travelling Light	35 Dover Street
Vilebrequin	1-2 Burlington Arcade
The World According To	4 Brewer Street

Hampstead (NW3)

agnès b.	58-62 Heath Street
Cochinechine	74 Heath Street
Exclusivo	24 Hampstead High Street
Formes	66 Rosslyn Hill
French Connection	29 Hampstead High Street
Frontier	18 Hampstead High Street
Hampstead Bazaar	31 Heath Street
Hobbs	9 & 15 Hampstead High Street
Jigsaw (& Jigsaw Junior)	58 & 83 Heath Street
Karen Millen	4 Hampstead High Street
L.K.Bennett	23 Hampstead High Street
Linea	8 Heath Street
Look Who's Walking	78 Heath Street
Mirage	76 Hampstead High Street
Monsoon	1 Hampstead High Street
Nicole Farhi	27 Hampstead High Street
Oasis	58-62 Heath Street
Question Air	28 Rosslyn Hill
Reiss	52-54 Heath Street
Ronit Zilkha	17 Hampstead High Street
Sweaty Betty	35 Heath Street
Warehouse	8 Hampstead High Street
Whistles	2-4 Hampstead High Street
YD.UK	82 Heath Street

Neighborhoods

Islington (N1)   *See map page 235*

Broadway	152 Upper Street
Brora	186 Upper Street
Clusaz	56 Cross Street
Diverse	286 & 294 Upper Street
Diverse Kids	46 Cross Street
Emma Hope	33 Amwell Street, EC1
Microzine	66-67 Colebrooke Row
Monsoon	Shopping Centre, 10 Parkfield Street
Noa Noa	146 Upper Street
Oasis	10 Upper Street
Phase Eight	211-212 Upper Street
Push	9 Theberton Street
Scorah Pattullo	137 Upper Street
Seconda Mano	111 Upper Street
Sefton	196 & 271 Upper Street
Spice	309 Upper Street
Stone	48 Upper Street
Whistles	135 Upper Street
White Stuff	12-14 Essex Road
Zee & Co	36 Upper Street

Jermyn Street (SW1)   *See map pages 232–233*

Bates Gentleman's Hatter	21a Jermyn Street
Charles Tyrwhitt	92 Jermyn Street
Church's	108-110 Jermyn Street
Coles the Shirtmakers	101 Jermyn Street
Crockett & Jones	69 Jermyn Street
Crombie	99 Jermyn Street
Daks	101 Jermyn Street
Dunhill	48 Jermyn Street
Emma Willis	66 Jermyn Street
Fabri	75 Jermyn Street
Favourbrook	55 Jermyn Street
Favourbrook	18 Piccadilly Arcade
Fortnum & Mason	181 Piccadilly
Foster & Son	83 Jermyn Street
Hackett	87 Jermyn Street
Harvie & Hudson	77 & 97 Jermyn Street
Hawes & Curtis	23 Jermyn Street
Henry Maxwell	83 Jermyn Street
Herbert Johnson	54 St James's Street
Herbie Frogg	18-19 & 21 Jermyn Street
Hilditch & Key	37 & 73 Jermyn Street
John Bray	78-79 Jermyn Street
John Lobb	88 Jermyn Street
John Lobb	9 St James's Street
Jones the Bootmaker	112 Jermyn Street
Links of London	94 Jermyn Street

Lock & Co	6 St James's Street
Manucci	108 Jermyn Street
New & Lingwood	53 Jermyn Street
Roderick Charles	90 Jermyn Street
Russell & Bromley	95 Jermyn Street
Swaine Adeney Brigg	54 St James's Street
T.M.Lewin	106-108 Jermyn Street
Thomas Pink	85 Jermyn Street
Tricker's	67 Jermyn Street
Turnbull & Asser	71-72 Jermyn Street

See map page 236

Kensington (W8)

Accessorize	123a Kensington High Street
Aldo	14 Kensington High Street
Annello and Davide	15 St Alban's Grove
Atticus	14 Kensington Church Street
Barkers of Kensington	63 Kensington High Street
Bonpoint	17 Victoria Grove
Cecil Gee	172 Kensington High Street
Claire's Accessories	169 Kensington High Street
Clarks	98 Kensington High Street
Designer Bargains	29 Kensington Church Street
Diesel	38a Kensington High Street
Dune	66 Kensington High Street
East	143 Kensington High Street
Ellis Brigham	178 Kensington High Street
Fenn Wright Manson	Barkers Arcade Kensington High Street
French Connection	168-170 Kensington High Street
Gap & Gap Kids	99-101 Kensington High Street
H&M	103-111 Kensington High Street
Hats Etc	36b Kensington Church Street
Hobbs	63 Kensington High Street
Jauko	34c Kensington Church Street
Jigsaw	65 Kensington High Street
Jones the Bootmaker	26 Kensington Church Street
Karen Millen	4 Barkers Arcade, Kensington High Street
Kew	123c Kensington High Street
Knickerbox	Kensington Arcade, Kensington High Street
Kookaï	123d Kensington High Street
Kurt Geiger	133 Kensington High Street
L.K.Bennett	1 Kensington Church Street
Levi's	171 Kensington High Street
Marks & Spencer	113 Kensington High Street
Miss Sixty	42 Kensington High Street
Monsoon	5 Barkers Arcade, Kensington High Street
Muji	157 Kensington High Street
Musa	31 Holland Street
Next	54-56 Kensington High Street

Neighborhoods

Nine West	155 Kensington High Street
Oasis	128a Kensington Church Street
Pegaso	275 Kensington High Street
Robinson Valentine	4 Hornton Place
Russell & Bromley	151-153 Kensington High Street
Seraphine	28 Kensington Church Street
Shellys	40 Kensington High Street
Sisley	129-131 Kensington High Street
Skin Machine	25 Kensington Church Street
Sole Trader	96a Kensington High Street
Space.NK	3 Kensington Church Street
Sweaty Betty	5 Kensington Church Street
Top Gun	23 Kensington High Street
Top Shop	42-44 Kensington High Street
Trotters	127 Kensington High Street
Urban Outfitters	36-38 Kensington High Street
Warehouse	2 Barkers Arcade, Kensington High Street
Zara	48-52 Kensington High Street

King's Road (SW1, 3 & 10) *See map pages 230–231*

9 London	8 Hollywood Road, SW10
Accessorize	102 King's Road, SW3
Ad Hoc	153 King's Road, SW3
Anne Fontaine	14 Sloane Street, SW1
Aftershock	194 King's Road, SW3
agnès b	31-32 Duke of York Square, SW3
à la mode	10 Symons Street, SW3
All Saints	3 Duke of York Square, SW3
Allegra Hicks	28 Cadogan Place, SW1
American Classics	398-400 King's Road, SW10
Antique Boutique	155 King's Road, SW3
Arrogant Cat	311 King's Road, SW3
Audley	72 Duke of York Square, SW3
Austique	330 King's Road, SW3
Bally	92 King's Road, SW3
Basia Zarzycka	52 Sloane Square, SW1
Blue Velvet	174 King's Road, SW3
Brora	344 King's Road, SW3
Calvin Klein	68 King's Road, SW3
Cath Kidston	12 Cale Street, SW3
Cathryn Grosvenor	3 Elystan Street, SW3
Catimini	33c King's Road, SW3
Chloé	152-152 Sloane Street, SW1
cm Store	121 King's Road, SW3
Coccinelle	13 Duke of York Square, SW3
Coco Ribbon	133 Sloane Street, SW1
Collette Dinnigan	26 Cale Street, SW3
Couverture	310 King's Road, SW3
Cozmo Jenks	London SW3

Crew Clothing Co	Unit 6, B Block
	Duke of York Square, SW3
Daisy & Tom	181-183 King's Road, SW3
Diesel	72 King's Road, SW3
Dollargrand	124a King's Road, SW3
Due Passi	192 King's Road, SW3
Dune	33b King's Road, SW3
East	105 King's Road, SW3
Eda Lingerie	132 King's Road, SW3
Emma Hope	53 Sloane Square, SW1
Emmett Shirts	380 King's Road, SW3
Escapade	141 King's Road, SW3
Eskandar	134 Lots Road
Fat Face	126 King's Road, SW3
Fenn Wright Manson	19 King's Road, SW3
Fifi Wilson	1 Godfrey Street, SW3
Franchetti Bond	12 Symons Street, SW3
French Connection	140-144 King's Road, SW3
French Sole	6 Ellis Street, SW1
Furla	17 King's Road, SW3
Gap (& Gap Kids)	122 King's Road, SW3
General Trading Company	2 Symons Street, SW3
Georgina von Etzdorf	4 Ellis Street, SW1
Gieves & Hawkes	33 Sloane Square, SW1
Ginka	137 Fulham Road, SW3
Gloss	159 King's Road, SW3
Graham & Green	340 King's Road, SW3
Hackett	136-138 Sloane Street, SW1
Harley-Davidson	125 King's Road, SW3
Harvest	136 King's Road, SW3
Hawes & Curtis	39 King's Road, SW3
Heidi Klein	257 Pavilion Road, SW1
Hilditch & Key	131 Sloane Street, SW1
Hobbs	88 King's Road, SW3
Hogan	10 Sloane Street, SW1
Iana	186 King's Road, SW3
iBlues	23 King's Road, SW3
Jaeger	145 King's Road, SW3
James Lakeland	113 King's Road, SW3
Jane Shilton	164 King's Road, SW3
Jigsaw & Jigsaw Junior	6 Duke of York Square, SW3
Jimmy Choo	32 Sloane Street, SW1
Jones the Bootmaker	57-59 King's Road, SW3
Joseph	53 King's Road, SW3
Joseph	76, Duke of York Square, SW3
Kate Kuba	22-23 Duke of York Square, SW3
Karen Millen	33e King's Road, SW3
Kenneth Cole	33 King's Road, SW3
Kew	124 King's Road, SW3

King's Road Sporting Club	38-42 King's Road, SW3
Knickerbox	28 Sloane Square, SW1
Kookaï	27a Sloane Square, SW3
L.K.Bennett	83, 97, 219 & 239 King's Road, SW3
L.K.Bennett	20 Duke of York Square, SW3
La Scala	39 Elystan Street, SW3
Links of London	16 Sloane Square, SW1
Lulu Guinness	3 Ellis Street, SW1
Mandy	139 King's Road, SW3
Manolo Blahnik	49 Old Church Street, SW3
Margaretta	309 King's Road, SW3
Maria Grachvogel	162 Sloane Street, SW1
Marks & Spencer	85 King's Road, SW3
MiMi	309 King's Road, SW3
Mirage	73 Duke of York Square, SW3
Monsoon	37 King's Road, SW3
Muji	118 King's Road, SW3
Naf Naf	13-15 King's Road, SW3
The Natural Shoe Store	325 King's Road, SW3
Nine West	90 King's Road, SW3
Oasis	76-78 King's Road, SW3
Office	58 King's Road, SW3
Oliver Sweeney	29 King's Road, SW3
One Night Stand	8 Chelsea Manor Studios Flood Street, SW3
Pantalon Chameleon	50 Duke of York Square, SW3
Patrick Cox	129 Sloane Street, SW1
Paul & Joe	134 Sloane Street, SW1
Paul Ka	161 Sloane Street, SW1
Peter Jones	Sloane Square, SW1
Petit Bateau	106-108 King's Road, SW3
Phase Eight	97 Lower Sloane Street, SW1
Phase Eight	34 Duke of York Square, SW3
Phlip	191 King's Road, SW3
Pickett	149 Sloane Street, SW1
Pied à Terre	2 Duke of York Square, SW3
Pringle	141-142 Sloane Street, SW1
R.Soles	109a King's Road, SW3
Reiss	114 King's Road, SW3
Ronit Zilkha	21 King's Road, SW3
Russell & Bromley	64 King's Road, SW3
Sahara	313 King's Road, SW3
Selina Blow	1 Ellis Street, SW1
Shellys	124b King's Road, SW3
Sign of the Times	17 Elystan Street, SW3
Size?	104 King's Road, SW3
Sox Kamen	394 King's Road, SW10
Space.NK	307 King's Road, SW3
Space.NK	27 Duke of York Square, SW3
Steinberg & Tolkien	193 King's Road, SW3

Sukie's	285/289 King's Road, SW3
Tabio	94 King's Road, SW3
Ted Baker	19 Duke of York Square, SW3
Thomas Pink	74 Sloane Street, SW1
Tops & Bottoms	3 Cale Street, SW3
Trésor	13 Cale Street, SW3
Trotters	34 King's Road, SW3
Venise Collection	163 King's Road, SW3
Ville St Cassien	251 King's Road, SW3
Vivienne Westwood	430 King's Road, SW10
Warehouse	96 King's Road, SW3
Whistles	31 King's Road, SW3
Woodhouse	97 King's Road, SW3

Neighborhoods

Knightsbridge/Belgravia (SW1 & 3)

See map pages 230–231

Abu Jani Sandeep Khosla	55 Beauchamp Place, SW3
Accessorize	53 Brompton Road, SW3
Agent Provocateur	16 Pont Street, SW1
Alberta Ferretti	205-206 Sloane Street, SW1
Anya Hindmarch	15-17 Pont Street, SW1
Belinda Robertson	4 West Halkin Street, SW1
Ben de Lisi	40 Elizabeth Street, SW1
Bonpoint	35b Sloane Street, SW1
Bottega Veneta	33 Sloane Street, SW1
Boyd	42 Elizabeth Street, SW1
Browns	6c Sloane Street, SW1
Burberry	2 Brompton Road, SW1
Camper	35 Brompton Road, SW3
Chanel	167-170 Sloane Street, SW1
Chanel	278-280 Brompton Road, SW3
Christian Dior	31 Sloane Street, SW1
Christian Louboutin	23 Motcomb Street, SW1
Church's	143 Brompton Road, SW3
Club	9 West Halkin Street, SW1
Coco Ribbon	133 Sloane Street, SW1
Connolly	32 Grosvenor Crescent Mews, SW1
Dolce & Gabbana	175 Sloane Street, SW1
Egg	36 & 69 Kinnerton Street, SW1
Elspeth Gibson	7 Pont Street, SW1
Emma Somerset	69 Knightsbridge, SW1
Emporio Armani	191 Brompton Road, SW3
Escada	194-195 Sloane Street, SW1
Feathers	42 Hans Crescent, SW1
Favourbrook	11 Pont Street, SW1
Fogal	3a Sloane Street, SW1
Formes	313 Brompton Road, SW3
Fratelli Rossetti	196 Sloane Street, SW1
French Connection	44 Brompton Road, SW3
Gant USA	47-49 Brompton Road, SW3

Gianfranco Ferré	29 Sloane Street, SW1
Gina	189 Sloane Street, SW1
Giorgio Armani	37 Sloane Street, SW1
Gucci	17 Sloane Street, SW1
H&M	17-21 Brompton Road, SW3
Harrods	87-135 Brompton Road, SW1
Harvey Nichols	109-125 Knightsbridge, SW1
Harvie & Hudson	55 Knightsbridge, SW1
Herbie Frogg	13 Lowndes Street, SW1
Hermès	179 Sloane Street, SW1
High & Mighty	81-83 Knightsbridge, SW1
Hobbs	37 Brompton Road, SW3
Jacques Azagury	50 Knightsbridge, SW1
Jaeger	16-18 Brompton Road, SW1
Jane Norman	59 Brompton Road, SW3
Jigsaw	31 Brompton Road, SW3
Jitrois	6f Sloane Street, SW1
Jones the Bootmaker	187 Brompton Road, SW3
Joseph	16 Sloane Street, SW1
Joseph Azagury	73 Knightsbridge, SW1
Karen Millen	33 Brompton Road, SW3
Kenneth Cole	3 Sloane Street, SW1
Kookaï	5-7 Brompton Road, SW3
La Perla	163 Sloane Street, SW1
Lacoste	20 Brompton Road, SW1
The Library	268 Brompton Road, SW3
Liza Bruce	9 Pont Street, SW1
Loro Piana	47 Sloane Street, SW1
Louis Vuitton	190-192 Sloane Street, SW1
Louise Kennedy	11 West Halkin Street, SW1
Marni	16 Sloane Street, SW1
Mexx	75 Brompton Road, SW3
Mirage	193-195 Brompton Road, SW3
Monsoon	48 Brompton Road, SW3
Mulberry	171-175 Brompton Road, SW3
Nicole Farhi	193 Sloane Street, SW1
Office	61 Brompton Road, SW3
Oilily	9 Sloane Street, SW1
Patricia Roberts	60 Kinnerton Street, SW1
Paul & Joe	309 Brompton Road, SW3
Philip Treacy	69 Elizabeth Street, SW1
Please Mum	85 Knightsbridge, SW1
Prada	43-45 Sloane Street, SW1
Rachel Riley	14 Pont Street, SW1
Ricci Burns	25 Lowndes Street, SW1
Rigby & Peller	2 Hans Road, SW3
Russell & Bromley	45 & 77 Brompton Road, SW3
Salvatore Ferragamo	207 Sloane Street, SW1
Semmalina	225 Ebury Street, SW1

Shanghai Tang	6a/b Sloane Street, SW1
Shi Cashmere	30 Lowndes Street, SW1
Stephane Kélian	48 Sloane Street, SW1
Stewart Parvin	14 Motcomb Street, SW1
Sybil Stanislaus	1 Grosvenor Place, SW1
Tanner Krolle	5 Sloane Street, SW1
Thomas Pink	74 & 161 Sloane Street, SW1
Tod's	35-36 Sloane Street, SW1
Tommy Hilfiger	6 Sloane Street, SW1
United Colors of Benetton	23 Brompton Road, SW3
Valentino	174 Sloane Street, SW1
Versace	183-184 Sloane Street, SW1
Young England	47 Elizabeth Street, SW1
Yves Saint Laurent: Rive Gauche	33 Sloane Street, SW1
Zara	78-91 Brompton Road, SW3
Zibba	61 Knightsbridge, SW1

Little Venice (W9)

Joujou & Lucy	32 Clifton Road

Marble Arch (W1)
See map pages 232–233

Bally	472 Oxford Street
Clarks	476 Oxford Street
Faith	488 Oxford Street
H&M	481 Oxford Street
High & Mighty	145-147 Edgware Road, W2
Jimmy Choo (couture)	18 Connaught Street, W2
Marks & Spencer	458 Oxford Street
Monsoon	498-500 Oxford Street
Morgan	391-393 Oxford Street
Next	508-520 Oxford Street
Ritva Westenius	28 Connaught Street, W2
Russell & Bromley	494-496 Oxford Street
Sharon Cunningham	23 New Quebec Street
Wallis	217 Oxford Street

Marylebone/North of Oxford Street (W1)
See map pages 232–233

agnès b.	40-41 Marylebone High Street
Bang Bang	21 Goodge Street
Brora	81 Marylebone High Street
Cath Kidston	51 Marylebone High Street
Due Passi	27 James Street
Fenn Wright Manson	95 Marylebone High Street
Gary Anderson	12-15 Chiltern Street
Ghost	14 Hinde Street
Hampstead Bazaar	45 Charlotte Street
Jesus Lopez	69 Marylebone High Street
Johanna Hehir	10-12 Chiltern Street
Ken Smith Designs	6 Charlotte Place

Neighborhoods

Long Tall Sally	21-25 Chiltern Street
Madeleine Press	90 Marylebone High Street
Margaret Howell	34 Wigmore Street
Monsoon	96 Marylebone High Street
Parallel	22 Marylebone High Street
Parallel Intimo	85 Marylebone High Street
Philip Somerville	38 Chiltern Street
Rachel Riley	82 Marylebone High Street
Robert Clergerie	67 Wigmore Street
Ronit Zilkha	107 Marylebone High Street
Sahara	58 Chiltern Street
Shoon	94 Marylebone High Street
Sixty	6 Marylebone High Street
Space.NK	83a Marylebone High Street
Texier	6 New Cavendish Street
Whistles	1 Thayer Street

Mayfair *(excluding Bond Street)* **(W1)**

See map pages 232–233

Brioni	32 Bruton Street
Comme des Garçons	59 Brook Street
Douglas Hayward	95 Mount Street
Elégance	14a Grafton Street
Eliot Zed	4 Avery Row
Formes	33 Brook Street
Golden Glow	31 Avery Row
Holland & Holland	31 & 33 Bruton Street
James Purdey & Sons	57-58 South Audley Street
John Smedley	24 Brook Street
Joseph	28 Brook Street
Kate Kuba	26 Brook Street
Links of London	32 Brook Street
L.K.Bennett	25 & 31 Brook Street
Matthew Williamson	28 Bruton Street
Orvis	36a Dover Street
Paule Ka	13a Grafton Street
Pleats Please: Issey Miyake	20 Brook Street
Ronit Zilkha	34 Brook Street
Shizue	93 Mount Street
Sonia Rykiel	27-29 Brook Street
Space.NK	45-47 Brook Street
Stella McCartney	30 Bruton Street
Stephane Kélian	13 Grafton Street
Thomas Pink	18 Davies Street
Travelling Light	35 Dover Street
Venise Collection	37 Brook Street
Vivienne Westwood	6 Davies Street

Notting Hill/Ladbroke Grove/Portobello (W2, 10 & 11)

See map page 236

The 1920s-1970s Crazy Clothes Connection
134 Lancaster Road, W11
Accessorize   237 Portobello Road, W11
Agent Provocateur   305 Westbourne Grove, W11
agnès b.   233-235 Westbourne Grove, W11
Aimé   32 Ledbury Road, W11

Ann Wiberg   170 Westbourne Grove, W11
Ananya   196 Kensington Park Road, W11
Anya Hindmarch   63 Ledbury Road, W11
Armand Basi   189 Westbourne Grove, W11

Ballantyne Cashmere   303 Westbourne Grove, W11
Beatrice von Tresckow   9 Portobello Road, W11
Bill Amberg   21-22 Chepstow Corner, W2
Bodas   38b Ledbury Road, W11

Bonpoint   197 Westbourne Grove, W11
Brora   66-68 Ledbury Road, W11
Bumpsville   33 Kensington Park Road, W11
Camper   214 Westbourne Grove, W11

Cath Kidston   8 Clarendon Cross, W11
Catherine Buckley   302 Westbourne Grove, W11
Coco Ribbon   21 Kensington Park Road, W11
The Cross   141 Portland Road, W11

Diane von Furstenberg   83 Ledbury Road, W11
The Dispensary   200 Kensington Park Road, W11
Dolly Diamond   51 Pembridge Road, W11
Duchamp   75 Ledbury Road, W11

Earl Jean   40 Ledbury Road, W11
Egoshego   158 Portobello Road, W11
Ember   206 Portobello Road, W11
Emma Hope   207 Westbourne Grove, W11

Euforia   61b Lancaster Road, W11
Euforia   281 Portobello Road, W10
Feathers   176 Westbourne Grove, W11
French Connection   191 Westbourne Grove, W11

Gap   132-136 Notting Hill Gate, W11
Ghost   36 Ledbury Road, W11
The Gladys   253 Portobello Road, W11
Graham & Green   4 & 10 Elgin Crescent, W11
Heidi Klein   174 Westbourne Grove, W11

The Hive   3 Lonsdale Road, W11
J&M Davidson   42 Ledbury Road, W11
J.W.Beeton   48-50 Ledbury Road, W11
The Jacksons   5 All Saints Road, W11

Jigsaw (& Jigsaw Junior) 190-192 Westbourne Grove, W11
Joseph   236 Westbourne Grove, W11
Katch   185 Westbourne Grove, W11
L.K.Bennett   220 Westbourne Grove, W11

Neighborhoods

The L Boutique	28 Chepstow Corner, W2
Laundry Industry	186 Westbourne Grove, W11
Marilyn Moore	7 Elgin Crescent, W11
Matches	60-64 & 85 Ledbury Road, W11
Myla	77 Lonsdale Road, W11
The Natural Shoe Store	181 Westbourne Grove, W11
Nicole Farhi	202 Westbourne Grove, W11
Office	206 Portobello Road, W11
OG2	367 Portobello Road, W10
Olivia Morris	355 Portobello Road, W10
One of a Kind	253 & 259 Portobello Road, W11
Pamela Shiffer	25 Kensington Park Road, W11
Paul & Joe	39-41 Ledbury Road, W11
Paul Smith	122 Kensington Park Road, W11
Pepe Jeans	172 Westbourne Grove, W11
Pepe Jeans	309 Portobello Road, W10
Petit Bateau	73 Ledbury Road, W11
Phase Eight	164 Notting Hill Gate, W11
Portobello Market	Portobello Road, W11
Preen	281 Portobello Road, W10
Question Air	229 Westbourne Grove, W11
Rellik	8 Golborne Road, W10
Sasti	281 Portobello Road, W11
Size?	200 Portobello Road, W11
So aei kei	357 Portobello Road, W10
Space.NK	127-131 Westbourne Grove, W2
Still…	61d Lancaster Road, W11
Sub Couture	204 Kensington Park Road, W11
Temperley	6-10 Colville Mews, Lonsdale Road, W11
Titri	1 Denbigh Road, W11
Trudy Hanson	25 All Saints Road, W11
Virginia	98 Portland Road, W11
West Village	35 Kensington Park Road, W11
Whistles	218 Westbourne Grove, W2
White Stuff	66 Westbourne Grove, W2

Oxford Street (W1)

See map pages 232–233

Accessorize	The Plaza, 120 Oxford Street
Aldo	309 Oxford Street
Ann Harvey	266 Oxford Street
Cecil Gee	170 & 287 Oxford Street
The Changing Room	10a Gees Court
Claire's Accessories	108 Oxford Street
Claire's Accessories	18-20 Oxford Street
Claire's Accessories	West One Shopping Centre 379 Oxford Street
Dorothy Perkins	118-132 New Oxford Street, WC1
Clarks	15, 260 & 476 Oxford Street
Debenhams	334-348 Oxford Street
Dorothy Perkins	189 & 379 Oxford Street

Dune	The Plaza, 120 Oxford Street
Esprit	283 Oxford Street
Faith	192-194 & 488 Oxford Street
Foot Locker	363-367 Oxford Street
Foot Locker	309 Oxford Street
French Connection	396 Oxford Street
Gap	223-235, 315 & 376-384 Oxford Street
Gap Kids	223-235, 315 & 376-384 Oxford Street
H&M	174-176 & 360-366 Oxford Street
Hampstead Bazaar	1 Gees Court
High & Mighty	The Plaza, 120 Oxford Street
House of Fraser	318 Oxford Street
Jeans West	5 Harewood Place
Jeans West	The Plaza, 120 Oxford Street
Jigsaw	St Christopher's Place
John Lewis	278-306 Oxford Street
Kamara	3 Gees Court
Kookaï	257-259 Oxford Street
La Senza	162 Oxford Street
Mango/MNG	233 Oxford Street
Marks & Spencer	173 Oxford Street
Mash	73 Oxford Street
Miss Selfridge	214 Oxford Street
Miss Sixty	31-32 Great Marlborough Street
Monsoon	264 Oxford Street
Morgan	270 & 391-393 Oxford Street
Moss Bros	299 Oxford Street
Muji	187 Oxford Street
Muji	6 Tottenham Court Road
Mulberry	11-12 Gees Court
New Look	175-179 Oxford Street
Next	201-205 & 325-329 Oxford Street
Niketown London	236 Oxford Street
Oasis	The Plaza, 120 Oxford Street
Paddy Campbell	8 Gees Court
Ravel	184-188 Oxford Street
Reiss	14-17 Market Place
River Island	470-482 & 283 Oxford Street
Russell & Bromley	395-397 Oxford Street
Selfridges	400 Oxford Street
Shellys	159 Oxford Street
T.M.Lewin	St Christopher's Place
Top Shop	214 Oxford Street
Urban Outfitters	200 Oxford Street
Wallis	532-536 Oxford Street
Warehouse	The Plaza, 120 Oxford Street
Whistles	12 St Christopher's Place
Woodhouse	28-32 St Christopher's Place
Zara	242-248 & 333 Oxford Street

Neighborhoods

259

Regent Street/Carnaby Street (W1)

See map pages 232–233

Accessorize	35-36 Great Marlborough Street
Adolfo Dominguez	129 Regent Street
Agent Provocateur	6 Broadwick Street
All Saints	6 Foubert's Place
Aquascutum	100 Regent Street
Austin Reed	103-113 Regent Street
Barker Shoes	215 Regent Street
Base London	30 Carnaby Street
Beau Monde	20 Kingly Street
Burberry	165 Regent Street
Camper	57 Foubert's Place
Carhartt	13 Newburgh Street
Church's	201 Regent Street
Clarks	101 & 203 Regent Street
Design Works	42-44 Broadwick Street
Diesel	24 Carnaby Street
The Dispensary	8-9 Newburgh Street
Esprit	178-182 Regent Street
French Connection	249 Regent Street
French Connection	10 Argyll Street
Gap Kids	208 Regent Street
Gymboree	198 Regent Street
H&M	261-271 Regent Street
Hackett	143-147 Regent Street
Henri Lloyd	48 Carnaby Street
High Jinks	13-14 Carnaby Street
Hobbs	217-219 Regent Street
Hugo Boss	184-186 Regent Street
Jaeger	200-206 Regent Street
Jigsaw	9 Argyll Street
Jones the Bootmaker	15 Foubert's Place
Karen Millen	262-264 Regent Street
Knickerbox	281a Regent Street
Levi's	174-176 & 269 Regent Street
Liberty	210-220 Regent Street
Liz Claiborne	211-213 Regent Street
Mango/MNG	106-112 Regent Street
Mark Stephen Marengo	9 Quadrant Arcade Regent Street
Massimo Dutti	156 Regent Street
Moss Bros	88 Regent Street
Muji	41 Carnaby Street
Next	160 Regent Street
Oasis	292 Regent Street
Oasis	12-14 Argyll Street
Office	35 Carnaby Street
O'Neill	5-7 Carnaby Street
Pepe Jeans	42 Carnaby Street

The Pineal Eye	49 Broadwick Street
Puma	52-55 Carnaby Street
Quiksilver	11-12 Carnaby Street
Racing Green	195 Regent Street
Reiss	172 Regent Street
Savage London	14a Newburgh Street
Shellys	266-270 Regent Street
Size?	31 Carnaby Street
Souvenir	47 Lexington Street
Swear	22 Carnaby Street
Talbots	115 Regent Street
Ted Baker	5-7 Foubert's Place
Uniqlo	84-86 Regent Street
United Colors of Benetton	255-259 Regent Street
Vans	47 Carnaby Street
Viyella	179-183 Regent Street
Warehouse	19-21 Argyll Street
Zara	118 Regent Street

St John's Wood (NW8)

Gap Kids	47-49 St John's Wood High Street
Joseph	21 St John's Wood High Street
Space.NK	73 St John's Wood High Street
Whistles	51 St John's Wood High Street

Savile Row (W1)   *See map pages 232–233*

40 Savile Row	40 Savile Row
Anderson & Sheppard	32 Old Burlington Street
Anthony J. Hewitt/Airey & Wheeler	9 Savile Row
Davies & Son	38 Savile Row
Dege & Skinner	10 Savile Row
Gary Anderson	34-35 Savile Row
Gieves & Hawkes	1 Savile Row
Hardy Amies	14 Savile Row
Henry Poole & Co	15 Savile Row
Huntsman	11 Savile Row
James Levett	13 Savile Row
Kilgour French Stanbury	8 Savile Row
Maurice Sedwell	19 Savile Row
Paraboot	37 Savile Row
Richard Anderson	13 Savile Row
Richard James	29 Savile Row
Scabal	12 Savile Row
Spencer Hart	36 Savile Row
Welsh & Jefferies	20 Savile Row
William Hunt	41 Savile Row

South Kensington/Fulham Road (SW3, 7 & 10)
See map pages 230–231

agnès b.	111 Fulham Road, SW3
Amanda Wakely	80 Fulham Road, SW3

Neighborhoods

Anne Fontaine	151 Fulham Road, SW3
Beatrice von Tresckow	273 Fulham Road, SW10
Bertie Wooster	284 Fulham Road, SW10
Betty Jackson	311 Brompton Road, SW3
Butler & Wilson	189 Fulham Road, SW3
Caramel Baby & Child	291 Brompton Road, SW3
Catherine Walker	46 Fulham Road, SW3
The Chelsea Collections	90 Fulham Road, SW3
Claudia Sebire	136 Fulham Road, SW10
Courtezan	84 Fulham Road, SW3
East	192 Fulham Road, SW10
Gap (& Gap Kids)	145-149 Brompton Road, SW3
Ginka	137 Fulham Road, SW3
Great Expectations	78 Fulham Road, SW3
Iselin	72 Fulham Road, SW3
Issey Miyake	270 Brompton Road, SW3
Jigsaw	91-97 Fulham Road, SW3
Jigsaw Junior	97 Fulham Road, SW3
Joseph	77 & 299 Fulham Road, SW3
Joseph	74 Sloane Avenue, SW3
Joseph	315 Brompton Road, SW3
Kenzo	70 Sloane Avenue, SW3
Le Silla1	33 Fulham Road, SW3
The Library	268 Brompton Road, SW3
Massimo Dutti	71 Brompton Road, SW3
Nicole Farhi	115 Fulham Road, SW3
Night Owls	78 Fulham Road, SW3
Paul Smith	84-86 Sloane Avenue, SW3
Phase Eight	345 Fulham Road, SW10
Ralph Lauren	105-109 Fulham Road, SW3
Replay & Sons	147-149 Fulham Road, SW3
Sally Parsons	15a Bute Street, SW7
Sassi Holford	74 Fulham Road, SW3
Shirin Guild	241 Fulham Road, SW3
Space.NK	307 Brompton Road, SW3
Sweatshop	188 Fulham Road, SW10
Thomas Starzewski	14 Stanhope Mews West, SW7
Vilebrequin	56 Fulham Road, SW3
The Wedding Shop	171 Fulham Road, SW10
Whistles	303 Brompton Road, SW3

South of the River (SW11, 13, 15, & SE21)

Fifi Wilson	51 Abbeville Road, SW4 (Clapham)
Jigsaw	114 Putney High Street, SW15 (Putney)
Lilli Diva	32 Lavender Hill, SW11 (Battersea/Clapham)
Monsoon	25 Putney Exchange Shopping Centre, SW15 (Putney)
Question Air	86 & 129 Church Road, SW13 (Barnes)

Question Air	85-87 Dulwich Village, SE21
	(Dulwich Village)
White Stuff	49 Northcote Road, SW11
	(Battersea/Clapham)

The Strand (WC2)

Jigsaw	449 The Strand
Moss Bros	92-93 The Strand
Top Shop	32 The Strand

Victoria (SW1)

Christiana Couture	53 Moreton Street
Cornucopia	12 Upper Tachbrook Street
Dorothy Perkins	Victoria Station
La Senza	8 Kingsgate Parade, Victoria Street
New Look	Upper Concourse, Victoria Station

Whiteley's Shopping Centre, Queensway (W2)

Accessorize
Dune
H&M
Karen Millen
Kew
Marks & Spencer
Muji
Nine West
Oasis
Warehouse

Wimbledon/Wimbledon Village (SW19)

Brora	17 High Street
Cath Kidston	3 High Street
Fat Face	18 The Broadway
Jaeger	27 High Street
Joseph	64 High Street
Matches (4!)	34, 38, 39 & 56b High Street
Monsoon	Centre Court Shopping Centre
New Look	Centre Court Shopping Centre
Phase Eight	31 High Street
Russell & Haslam	(private design studio)
Question Air	77 & 78 High Street
Whistles	28 High Street

Neighborhoods

Stores by Category

Women's

Men's

Children's

Tweens

Women's Accessories

Accessorize
Basia Zarzycka
Claire's Accessories
Coccinelle
Dollargrand
Fenwick
Franchetti Bond
Georgina von Etzdorf
Ginka
Golden Glow
Harrods
Harvey Nichols

Jane Shilton
The Jacksons
Liberty
Massimo Dutti
Margaretta
Mulberry
Net-a-porter
Ninivah Khomo
Selfridges
So aei kei
Tabio
Top Shop

Women's Activewear

Crew Clothing Co
Ellis Brigham
Fat Face
Field & Trek
Foot Locker
Fred Perry
Gamba
Harley-Davidson
Heidi Klein
Henri Lloyd
Holland & Holland
Jungle
King's Road Sporting Club
Lacoste
Lillywhites

Liza Bruce
Loro Piana
O'Neill
Orvis
Puma
Quiksilver
R.M.Williams
Shoon
Sweatshop
Sweaty Betty
T&G Clothing
Timberland
Travelling Light
White Stuff

Women's Bridal

Amanda Wakely
Angela Stone
Anello and Davide
Basia Zarzycka
Beau Monde
Bruce Oldfield
Caroline Holmes
Catherine Buckley
Catherine Walker
Christiana Couture
Eda Lingerie
Harriet Gubbins

Isabell Kristensen
Johanna Hehir
Kruszynska
Neil Cunningham
Phillipa Lepley
Ritva Westenius
Russell & Haslam
Sassi Holford
Sharon Cunningham
Stewart Parvin
Trudy Hanson
The Wedding Shop

Women's Cashmere/Knitwear

Ballantyne Cashmere
Belinda Robertson
Ben de Lisi

Berk
Brioni
Brora

Women's Cashmere/Knitwear *(continued)*

Cashmere London
Cathryn Grosvenor
Caz
Gigi
House of Cashmere
John Smedley
Krizia
Liola

Loro Piana
Louise Kennedy
M-A-G
Marilyn Moore
N.Peal
Oilily
Patricia Roberts
Shi Cashmere

Women's Casual

Blunauta
Broadway
Duffer of St George
Episode
Eskandar
Esprit
Fenn Wright Manson
French for Less
Gap
Ginka
The Gladys
Hampstead Bazaar
J.W.Beeton
James Lakeland
Kew
Kit Clothing/
 Twentieth Century Frox
Laundry Industry
Laura Tom

Levi's
Massimo Dutti
Mirage
Muji
Pamela Shiffer
Pantalon Chameleon
Pepe Jeans
Phase Eight
Phlip
Sahara
Sally Parsons
Shoon
Sisley
Ted Baker
Tops & Bottoms
Uniqlo
United Colors of Benetton
Wall
White Stuff

Women's Classic

40 Savile Row
Adolfo Dominguez
Aquascutum
Armand Basi
Beau Monde
Betty Jackson
Brioni
Burberry
Catherine Walker
Caroline Charles
Cerruti 1881
Claudia Sebire
Daks
Elégance
Emanuel Ungaro
Emma Somerset
Feathers

Fenwick
Gigi
Hobbs
J&M Davidson
Jaeger
Jean Paul Gaultier Boutique
Louise Kennedy
Maria Grachvogel
Mirage
Mulberry
Paddy Campbell
Pantalon Chameleon
Paule Ka
Sahara
Sixty 6
Spaghetti
Talbots

Women's Contemporary

Armani Collezioni	Justin Kara
à la mode	Kamara
Aimé	Kanves
Allegra Hicks	Katch
Ann Wiberg	Kenneth Cole
Anna	Kew
Aquaint	Koh Samui
Arrogant Cat	Kokon to Zai
Arté	Lilli Diva
Austique	L.K.Bennett
Ben de Lisi	Machiko Jinto
Betsey Johnson	Matches
Browns Focus	Marilyn Moore
Butler & Wilson	MiMi
The Changing Room	Mirage
Clusaz	Musa
Coco Ribbon	Noa Noa
Cochinechine	The Pineal Eye
The Cross	Preen
Designer Club	Proibito
Diane von Furstenberg	Question Air
Diverse	Rachel Riley
Dover Street Market	Sefton
Egg	Shirin Guild
Euforia	Soboye Soong
Fifi Wilson	Story
General Trading Company	Sub Couture
Gloss	Tashia
Graham & Green	Tokïo
Heidi Klein	Ventilo
The Hive	Voyage
The Jacksons	Wardrobe
Jesiré	West Village
Jones	The World According To

Women's Department Store*
& High Street Chains

Austin Reed	*John Lewis
*Debenhams	Karen Millen
Dorothy Perkins	Kookaï
East	*Liberty
*Fenwick	*Lillywhites
*Fortnum & Mason	Mango/MNG
French Connection	Marks & Spencer
Gap (& Gap Kids)	Miss Sixty
H&M	Monsoon
*Harrods	Morgan
*Harvey Nichols	Muji
Hobbs	New Look
House of Fraser	Next
Jigsaw (& Jigsaw Junior)	Oasis

Women's Department Store*
& High Street Chains *(continued)*

*Peter Jones
Phase Eight
Reiss
Russell & Bromley
*Selfridges
Space.NK

Top Shop
United Colors of Benetton
Wallis
Whistles
Zara

Women's Designer

agnès b.
Alberta Ferretti
Alexander McQueen
Amanda Wakely
Anne Fontaine
Betsey Johnson
Brioni
Bruce Oldfield
Calvin Klein
Celine
Chanel
Chloé
Christian Dior
Collette Dinnigan
Comme des Garçons
Diane von Furstenberg
Dolce & Gabbana
Donna Karan
Earl Jean
Elspeth Gibson
Emanuel Ungaro
Emporio Armani
Escada
Eskandar
Etro
Frockbrokers
Georgina von Etzdorf
Ghost
Gianfranco Ferré
Giorgio Armani
Gucci
Isabell Kristensen
Issey Miyake
Jacques Azagury
Jean Paul Gaultier Boutique
Jil Sander
John Richmond
Joseph
Kenneth Cole
Kenzo
Krizia
The L Boutique

Linea
Liz Claiborne
Liza Bruce
Louis Féraud
Louis Vuitton
Louise Kennedy
Madeleine Press
Maharishi
Mararishi (Dpmhi)
Maria Grachvogel
Marilyn Moore
Marni
Matthew Williamson
MaxMara
Miu Miu
Moschino
Net-a-porter
Nicole Farhi
OG2
Paul & Joe
Pleats Please: Issey Miyake
Plein Sud
Prada
Pringle
Ralph Lauren
Robinson Valentine
Ronit Zilkha
Selina Blow
Shirin Guild
Sonia Rykiel
Stella McCartney
Temperley
Thomas Starzewski
Tommy Hilfiger
Tracey Boyd
Valentino
Versace
Vivienne Westwood
Voyage
Yohji Yamamoto
Yves Saint Laurent

Categories

Women's Ethnic (& Asian)

Abu Jani Sandeep Khosla
Ananya
East
Graham & Green
Jauko
Monsoon
Nitya

Noa Noa
Shanghai Tang
Sox Kamen
Sybil Stanislaus
Thailandia
Titri
Wall

Women's Formalwear, Eveningwear & Special Occasions

Aftershock
Amanda Wakely
Angela Stone
Angels
Ann Wiberg
Beatrice von Tresckow
Betsey Johnson
Brioni
Bruce Oldfield
Cashmere London
Catherine Walker
The Chelsea Collections
Courtezan
Emanuel Ungaro
Emma Willis
Escada
Escapade

Favourbrook
Gianfranco Ferré
Isabell Kristensen
Iselin
Joanna Hehir
Kit Clothing/
  Twentieth Century Frox
The L Boutique
Maria Grachvogel
One Night Stand
Ricci Burns
Robina
Robinson Valentine
Sixty 6
Temperley
Valentino
Wardrobe

Women's Handbags

Aldo
Anya Hindmarch
Bally
Bill Amberg
Coccinelle
Dollargrand
Fenwick
Fiorelli
Franchetti Bond
Furla
Georgina Goodman
Gigi
Gucci

Hermès
Karen Millen
Kate Kuba
Louis Vuitton
Lulu Guinness
Mimi
Miu Miu
Mulberry
Pantalon Chameleon
Pickett
Prada
Russell & Bromley
Tanner Krolle

Women's Hats

The Chelsea Collections
Cozmo Jenks
Fenwick
Harvey Nichols
Hats Etc

Liberty
Philip Somerville
Philip Treacy
Selfridges

Women's Leathergoods

Bill Amberg
Connolly
Furla
Harley-Davidson
Hermès
Mayfair Rat

Mulberry
Osprey
Pickett
Skin Machine
Texier
Top Gun

Women's Lingerie & Nightwear

Agent Provocateur
Bodas
Couverture
Eda Lingerie
Fogal (hosiery specialist)
Janet Reger
Knickerbox
La Perla
La Senza

Laurence Tavernier
Marks & Spencer
Monogrammed Linen Shop
Myla
Night Owls
Parallel Intimo
Pink Piranha
Rigby & Peller
Wolford (hosiery specialist)

Maternity

9 London
Blooming Marvellous
Blossom
Bumpsville
Formes

Great Expectations
Long Tall Sally
Push
Seraphine

Women's Petite Sizes

Dorothy Perkins
Jaeger
Liz Claiborne
Miss Sixty
Next

Talbots
Top Shop
Viyella
Wallis

Women's Plus Sizes (& tall women)

Ann Harvey
Base
Dorothy Perkins
Gordon Scott (for shoes)

Ken Smith Designs
Long Tall Sally
Marina Rinaldi

Categories

Women's Secondhand, Leftovers & Exchange

Bang Bang
Bertie Golightly
Browns Labels for Less
Blackout II
Cornucopia
Designer Bargains
Dressage

La Scala
The Loft
One of a Kind
Proibito
Sign of the Times
Trésor

Women's Shirts

Anne Fontaine
Charles Tyrwhitt
Emma Willis
Louise Kennedy

Thomas Pink
T.M.Lewin
Turnbull & Asser

Women's Shoes

Aldo
Anello & Davide
Atticus
Audley
Bally
Bertie
Bertie Golightly
Birkenstock
Blue Velvet
Buffalo Boots
Camper
Christian Louboutin
Church's
Clarks
Clio
Dollargrand
Due Passi
Dune
Egoshego
Eliot Zed
Emma Hope
Ethos
F.Pinet
Faith
Farrutx
Fiorelli
Foot Locker
Franchetti Bond
Fratelli Rossetti
French Sole
Frontier
Georgina Goodman
Gigi
Gina

Golden Glow
Hobbs
Hogan
Jane Shilton
Jesus Lopez
Jimmy Choo
Jimmy Choo Couture
John Lobb
Jones the Bootmaker
Joseph Azagury
Karen Millen
Katch
Kate Kuba
Kenneth Cole
Koh Samui
Kurt Geiger
L.K.Bennett
Le Silla
Manolo Blahnik
Miu Miu
The Natural Shoe Store
Niketown
Nine West
Offspring
Olivia Morris
OG2
Pantalon Chameleon
Paraboot
Parallel
Patrick Cox
Pied à Terre
Poste Mistress
Puma
R.Soles

Women's Shoes (continued)

Ravel
Robert Clergerie
Ruco Line
Russell & Bromley
Salvatore Ferragamo
scorah pattullo
Shellys
Shizue
Size?
Sole Trader

Spice
Stephane Kélian
Sukie's
Swear
Tod's
Vans
Venise Collection
Ville St Cassien
Zibba

Women's Trend & Streetwear

American Classics
Arrogant Cat
Black & Brown
Boxfresh
B-Store
Carhartt
cm Store
Cyberdog
D&G
Diesel
The Dispensary
Dockers
Earl Jean
Fat Face
French Connection
Frockbrokers
High Jinks
Hope + Glory
Jane Norman
Jeans West
Jenesis
Jitrois
Kookaï
Laden Showroom
Mandy
Mango/MNG
Mash

Miss Selfridge
Miss Sixty
Morgan
New Look
Oasis
O'Neill
Pepe Jeans
Phlip
Pineapple
Pop Boutique
Public Aware
Quiksilver
River Island
Savage London
Start
Stone
Stussy
The Lazy Ones
Tops & Bottoms
Urban Nation
Urban Outfitters
V.I.P.
The Vestry
Warehouse
Whistles
YD.UK
Zara

Women's Vintage/Retro

The 1920s-1970s Crazy
 Clothes Connection
Absolute Vintage
Bang Bang
Blackout II
Butler & Wilson
Camden Market

Cath Kidston
Cenci
Cornucopia
Courtezan
Dolly Diamond
Dressage
Ember

Categories

Women's Vintage/Retro *(continued)*

Episode
Exclusivo
Laden Showroom
The Lazy Ones
Musa
Old Spitalfields Market
One of a Kind
Pop Boutique
Portobello Market

Rachel Riley
Rellik
Rokit
Seconda Mano
Souvenir
Steinberg & Tolkien
Still…
Virginia

Men's Accessories

Aware
Budd
Dege & Skinner
Duchamp
Duffer of St. George
Dunhill
Gieves & Hawkes

Massimo Dutti
New & Lingwood
Richard James
Tabio
Turnbull & Asser
Vilebrequin

Men's Activewear

Berluti
Ellis Brigham
Fat Face
Field & Trek
Foot Locker
Fred Perry
Harley-Davidson
Henri Lloyd
Holland & Holland
House of Cashmere
James Purdey & Sons
Jungle
King's Road Sporting Club

Lacoste
O'Neill
Orvis
Puma
Quiksilver
R.M.Williams
Shoon
T&G Clothing
Timberland
Travelling Light
Vilebrequin
White Stuff

Men's Cashmere/Knitwear

Ballantyne Cashmere
Berk
Brioni
Brora

Connolly
John Smedley
Loro Piana
N.Peal

Men's Casual

Armand Basi
Base London
Crew Clothing Co
Dockers
Duchamp
Duffer of St. George
Dunhill
Ermenegildo Zegna
Fabri
Fat Face
Gant USA
Hackett

John Bray
Lacoste
Massimo Dutti
O'Neill
Quiksilver
Racing Green
Shoon
Tommy Hilfiger
Urban Outfitters
Versace
White Stuff
William Hunt

Men's Classic

40 Savile Row
Adolfo Dominguez
Anthony J. Hewitt/Airey
 & Wheeler
Aquascutum
Avi Rossini
Bernini
Brioni
Browns
Budd
Canali
Cerruti 1881
Crombie
Daks
Davies & Son
Dege & Skinner
Dunhill
Ermenegildo Zegna
Gieves & Hawkes

Hackett
Henry Poole & Co
Herbie Frogg
Huntsman
James Levett
James Purdey & Sons
John Bray
Kilgour French Stanbury
Lanvin
Levi's
Mark Stephen Marengo
Maurice Sedwell
Mulberry
Pegaso
Richard Anderson
Roderick Charles
Spencer Hart
Welsh & Jefferies

Men's Contemporary

Armani Collezioni
Browns Focus
Design Works
Dover Street Market
Duchamp
Egg
Hackett
Kanves
Kilgour French Stanbury
The Library
Manucci
Maurice Sedwell
Nigel Hall
OG2

Pegaso
The Pineal Eye
Question Air
Richard James
Scabal
Sefton
Sox Kamen
Ted Baker
Urban Outfitters
Vertice Uomo
William Hunt
Woodhouse
Yohji Yamamoto

Categories

Men's Department Store*
& High Street Chains

Austin Reed
Cecil Gee
*Debenhams
Dickins & Jones
French Connection
Gap
H&M
*Harrods
*Harvey Nichols
House of Fraser
Jigsaw

*John Lewis
*Liberty
*Lillywhites
Marks & Spencer
Next
Office
*Peter Jones
Reiss
*Selfridges
Top Shop
United Colors of Benetton

Men's Designer

Brioni
Burberry
Calvin Klein
Comme des Garçons
Dolce & Gabbana
Donna Karan
Earl Jean
Emporio Armani
Etro
Ghost
Giorgio Armani
Gucci
Hermès
Hugo Boss
Issey Miyake
Jil Sander
Joseph
Kenneth Cole
Kenzo

Krizia
Linea
Louis Vuitton
Maharishi
Maharishi (Dpmhi)
Moschino
Nicole Farhi
Ozwald Boateng
Paul & Joe
Paul Smith
Prada
Pringle
Ralph Lauren
Selina Blow
Valentino
Versace
Yves Saint Laurent
Zee & Co

Men's Formalwear & Special Occasions

Brioni
Favourbrook
Gary Anderson

Hawes & Curtis
Moss Bros

Men's Hats

Bates Gentleman's Hatter
Douglas Hayward
Ede & Ravenscroft
Harvey Nichols

Herbert Johnson
Lock & Co
Skin Machine

Men's Leathergoods

Bill Amberg
Connolly
Duchamp
Dunhill
Leather Rat Classics

Mulberry
Proudfoot
Skin Machine
Texier
Top Gun

Men's Plus Sizes

Gordon Scott (for shoes)
High & Mighty

Men's Secondhand, Leftovers & Exchange

Bertie Wooster
Blackout II
Browns Labels for Less

The Loft
Proibito

Men's Shirts

Brioni
Charles Tyrwhitt
Coles the Shirtmakers
Dege & Skinner
Duchamp
Dunhill
Emma Willis
Emmett Shirts
Ermenegildo Zegna
Gieves & Hawkes
Hackett
Harvie & Hudson
Hawes & Curtis

Henry Poole & Co
Hilditch & Key
Huntsman
John Bray
New & Lingwood
Richard James
Roderick Charles
T.M.Lewin
Thomas Pink
Timothy Everest
Turnbull & Asser
William Hunt

Men's Shoes

Aldo
Audley
Bally
Barker Shoes
Berlut
Birkenstock
Buffalo Bootskids
Camper
Church's
Clarks
Crockett & Jones
Design Works
Edward Green

Egoshego
Eliot Zed
Ethos
F.Pinet
Foot Locker
Foster & Son
Fratelli Rossetti
Frontier
G.J.Cleverley
Georgina Goodman
Gordon Scott
Hogan
John Lobb

Categories

Men's Shoes (continued)

Jones the Bootmaker
Kurt Geiger
Microzine
The Natural Shoe Store
New & Lingwood
Niketown London
Offspring
Oliver Sweeney
Paraboot
Patrick Cox
Pegaso
Poste
Puma
R.Soles
Ravel
Robert Clergerie
Robot
Ruco Line
Russell & Bromley
Salvatore Ferragamo
Scorah Pattullo
Shellys
Shipton & Heneage
Shoon
Size?
Sole Trader
Sukie's
Swear
Tim Little
Tod's
Tricker's
Vans
Venise

Men's Trend & Streetwear

American Classics
Antique Boutique
Boxfresh
B-Store
Burro
Carharrt
Cyberdog
D&G
Diesel
The Dispensary
Earl Jean
High Jinks
Hope + Glory
J.W.Beeton
Jones
The Lazy Ones
Microzine
Pepe Jeans
Phlip
Pop Boutique
Public Aware
River Island
Savage London
Start
Stussy
YD.UK
Zee & Co

Men's Vintage/Retro

The 1920s-1970s Crazy
  Clothes Connection
Ember
Episode
Exclusivo
Microzine
Pop Boutique
Rokit
Seconda Mano
The Lazy Ones

Children's (* for Children's Shoes)

Anna
Blooming Marvellous
Bonpoint
Brora
*Bumpsville
Burberry
*Caramel Baby & Child
*Catimini
Couverture
Crew Clothing
The Cross
D&G
*Daisy & Tom
Debenhams
*The Dispensary
*Diverse Kids
Field & Trek
*Foot Locker
*Gamba
Gant USA
*Gap Kids & Baby Gap
Gucci
*Guys & Dolls
Gymboree
H&M
*Harvey Nichols
Hermès
House of Fraser
Iana
*Jigsaw Junior
*John Lewis
*Joujou & Lucy
La Scala
Lillywhites
*Look Who's Walking

Maharishi
Marks & Spencer
Marie-Chantal
Mimmo
Monogrammed Linen Shop
Monsoon
*Next
*Niketown London
*Oilily
Patricia Roberts
Patrizia Wigan Designs
*Paul Smith
Petit Bateau
Please Mum
*Pollyanna
*Prada
*Rachel Riley
Ralph Lauren
*Ravel
Replay & Sons
R.Soles
*Ruco Line
Sasti
Selina Blow
Semmalina
Shellys
Shanghai Tang
*Tartine et Chocolat
Their Nibs
*Timberland
*Tod's
*Trotters
*United Colors of Benetton
Young England

Categories

Tweens (* for Tweens' Shoes)

Accessorize
*Atticus
*Bertie
*Blue Velvet
Boxfresh
Buffalo Boots
Camden Market
Camper
Carhartt
Claire's Accessories
cm Store
Diesel
Dorothy Perkins
*Dune
Esprit
*Faith
Fat Face
*Foot Locker
French Connection
Gap
H&M
Jauko
Jeans West
Knickerbox
Kookaï
Levi's
Mandy
Mango
Marks & Spencer

Miss Selfridge
Miss Sixty
Morgan
New Look
Next
Niketown
*Nine West
Oasis
*Office
Old Spitalfields Market
Pepe jeans
Phlip
Portobello Market
Quiksilver
River Island
*Shellys
*Shoon
Sisley
*Size?
Stussy
Sweaty Betty
Ted Baker
Top Gun
Top Shop/Top Man
Uniqlo
United Colors of Benetton
Urban Outfitters
*Vans
Zara

In-store Restaurants

All are recommended, but a star (☆) indicates that they are our particular favourites.

Art Bar Café (at Liberty)   020 7734 1234
210-220 Regent Street, W1
(also Arthur's on the lower ground floor)

The Caffé (at Emporio Armani)   020 7581 0854
191 Brompton Road, SW3

The Café at French Connection   020 7229 8325
191 Westbourne Grove, W11

☆ **Carluccio's (at Fenwick)**   020 7629 9161
63 New Bond Street, W1

DKNY Bar (at DKNY)   020 7399 1978
27 Old Bond Street, W1

Fifth Floor Café (at Harvey Nichols)   020 7823 1839
109-125 Knightsbridge, SW1

Fifth Floor Restaurant (at Harvey Nichols)   020 7235 5250
109-125 Knightsbridge, SW1

The Fountain (at Fortnum & Mason)   020 7734 8040
181 Piccadilly, W1
(also The Patio, and the St. James Restaurant)

The Georgian (at Harrods)   020 7730 1234
87-135 Brompton Road, SW1
(also more than 20 other restaurants,
on every floor except the 5th)

Iguacu (at Selfridges)   020 7318 3937
42 Duke Street, W1

Joe's Café (at Gigi)   020 7225 2217
126 Draycott Avenue, SW3

Joe's Café (at Joseph)   020 7235 9869
16 Sloane Street, SW1

☆ **Joe's Restaurant (at Fenwick)**   020 7495 5402
63 New Bond Street, W1

☆ **Nicole's (at Nicole Farhi)**   020 7499 8408
158 New Bond Street, W1

☆ **202 Restaurant at (Nicole Farhi)**   020 7727 2722
202 Westbourne Grove, W11

YO! Sushi (at Selfridges)   020 7318 3944
Oxford Street, W1 (also other restaurants on every floor)

Restaurants

Shop 'til you drop…ideally into a comfortable chair at any of the following restaurants. Our list has been chosen specially for lunching during your shopping spree.

N1 (Islington)

Brasserie La Trouvaille   020 7704 8323
353 Upper Street
quintessential French brasserie

Frederick's   020 7359 2888
Camden Passage
modern European

NW1 (Primrose Hill)

☆ **Lemonia**   020 7586 7454
89 Regent's Park Road
the most popular Greek restaurant in London

Lucca   020 7485 6864
63 Parkway
hugely friendly family-run Italian

Odette's   020 7586 5486
130 Regent's Park Road
modern British

NW3 (Hampstead)

Black & Blue   020 7443 7744
205-207 Haverstock Hill
mid-market steakhouse

ZeNW3   020 7794 7863
83-84 Hampstead High Street
Chinese

NW8 (St. John's Wood)

L'Aventure   020 7624 6232
3 Blenheim Terrace
French; outside terrace on fine days

La Casalinga   020 7722 5959
64 St. John's Wood High Street
Italian; outside tables on fine days

Rosmarino   020 7328 5014
1 Blenheim Terrace
Italian; outside terrace on fine days

SW1 (Knightsbridge/Belgravia)

Boxwood Café   020 7235 1010
The Berkeley Hotel
Wilton Place
*European cuisine but with something
of a New York atmosphere*

☆ **Drones**   020 7235 9555
1 Pont Street
French/Mediterranean; celebrity favourite

☆ **Olivo**   **020 7730 2505**
21 Eccleston Street
Italian, very social

☆ **Oriel**   **020 7730 4275**
50-51 Sloane Square
brasserie for café society, very popular rendezvous

Signor Sassi   **020 7584 2277**
14 Knightsbridge Green
up-market Italian

☆ **Zafferano**   **020 7235 5800**
15 Lowndes Street
Italian, very high reputation

SW1 (St. James's)

The Avenue   **020 7321 2111**
7 St. James's Street
modern European; airy, spacious, stylish

☆ **Le Caprice**   **020 7629 2239**
Arlington Street
modern British; A-list clientele

Quaglino's   **020 7930 6767**
16 Bury Street
modern European

☆ **Wheeler's of St James's**   **020 7930 2460**
12a Duke of York Street
*fish, at the original Wheeler's as revived
by Marco Pierre White*

SW3 (Chelsea, South Ken, Fulham Road)

☆ **The Admiral Codrington**   **020 7581 0005**
17 Mossop Street
modern British, superb wines; heartland of the beau monde

Area   **020 7589 7613**
162 Brompton Road
Italian

Bacio   **020 7351 9997**
386 King's Road
*a nostalgic throwback to the vibrant Italian trattorias
of the Seventies*

☆ **Bibendum Oyster Bar**   **020 7589 1480**
81 Fulham Road
*famous for seafood; worth visiting for the Michelin
building alone*

Bluebird   **020 7559 1000**
350 King's Road
northern European

☆ **Brasserie St Quentin**　　　　　　**020 7589 8005**
243 Brompton Road
French; with a superb wine list chosen by
Patrick Sandeman of high-rep vintners Lea & Sandeman

Carpaccio　　　　　　　　　　**020 7352 3433**
4 Sydney Street
Italian

☆ **Eight over Eight**　　　　　　　**020 7349 9934**
392 King's Road
pan-Asian sister to E&O in Notting Hill

El Gaucho　　　　　　　　　　**020 7376 8514**
125 Sydney Street
Argentinian, i.e. serious red meat

Floriana　　　　　　　　　　　**020 7838 1500**
15 Beauchamp Place
Italian; celebrity favourite

Itsu　　　　　　　　　　　　**020 7590 2400**
118 Draycott Avenue
Japanese

☆ **La Brasserie**　　　　　　　　**020 7584 1668**
272 Brompton Road
traditional brasserie; favourite with the beau monde

Le Colombier　　　　　　　　**020 7351 1155**
145 Dovehouse Street
classic French

Manicomio　　　　　　　　　**020 7730 3366**
85 Duke of York Square
traditional Italian

Patisserie Valerie　　　　　　**020 7730 7094**
81 Duke of York Square
very popular French café (check out Gelateria Valerie
for London's best ices just around the corner)

Picasso　　　　　　　　　　**020 7352 4921**
127 King's Road
traditional coffee bar, evergreen favourite;
no one can remember a time before Picasso

Racine　　　　　　　　　　　**020 7584 4477**
239 Brompton Road
classic French

☆ **San Lorenzo**　　　　　　　　**020 7584 1074**
22 Beauchamp Place
Italian; A-list celebrity favourite

Scalini　　　　　　　　　　**020 7225 2301**
1-3 Walton Street
Italian classics

☆ **Tartine**　　　　　　　　　　**020 7589 4981**
114 Draycott Avenue
special daily dishes, but tartines always

SW6 (Fulham)

Blue Elephant   020 7385 6595
3 Fulham Broadway
Thai, and a wonderful rainforest decor

Jim Thompson's   020 7731 0999
617 King's Road
Oriental

Mao Tai   020 7731 2520
58 New King's Road
Chinese

The Salisbury Tavern   020 7381 4005
21 Sherbrooke Road
*modern British, excellent wines; you need a taxi to find it,
but the food and wine are worth it*

SW7 (Knightsbridge)

Café Lazeez   020 7581 9993
93-95 Old Brompton Road
Indian, brasserie-style

☆ **Zuma**   020 7584 1010
5 Raphael Street
Japanese

SW10 (further out the Fulham and King's roads)

Aubergine   020 7352 3449
11 Park Walk
French

Carluccio's   020 7376 5960
236 Fulham Road
traditional Italian

La Famiglia   020 7351 0761
7 Langton Street
Italian

Randall & Aubin   020 7823 3515
329-331 Fulham Road
Continental

Tampopa   020 7370 5355
140 Fulham Road
fashionable noodle bar

Vama   020 7351 4118
438 King's Road
north Indian

Vingt Quatre   020 7376 7224
325 Fulham Road
contemporary English for the smart young set, open 24/7

W1 (Mayfair & Marylebone)

Alloro　　　　　　　　　　**020 7495 4768**
19-20 Dover Street
Italian

Cecconi's　　　　　　　　　**020 7434 1500**
5a Burlington Gardens
Italian, excellent bar

☆ **Cipriani**　　　　　　　　　**020 7399 0500**
25 Davies Street
the name says it all; shoulder-to-shoulder celebrities

☆ **Hush**　　　　　　　　　　**020 7659 1500**
8 Lancashire Court, New Bond Street
brasserie downstairs, French restaurant upstairs,
tables out in the courtyard on fine days

Itsu　　　　　　　　　　　**020 7491 9799**
1 Hanover Square
sushi and Japanese-inspired food—
a favourite with the Vogue girls

Mosaico　　　　　　　　　　**020 7409 1011**
13 Albemarle Street
northern Italian

☆ **Noble Rot**　　　　　　　　**020 7629 8877**
3 Mill Street
modern European; superb bar/club downstairs

Nobu　　　　　　　　　　　**020 7447 4747**
The Metropolitan, 19 Old Park Lane
Japanese, about as up-market as you can go

The Providores　　　　　　　**020 7935 6175**
109 Marylebone High Street
fusion, one of the better pub conversions

Sketch　　　　　　　　　　**0870 777 4488**
9 Conduit Street
have lunch in the Library, not in the Gallery (which is the
UK's most expensive restaurant)

☆ **Sotheby's Café**　　　　　　　**020 7293 5077**
34-35 New Bond Street
international, very social (free art viewing)

☆ **The Wolseley**　　　　　　　**020 7499 6996**
160 Piccadilly
immensely popular from breakfast onwards,
in a spectacular former banking hall

W8 (Kensington)

The Ark　　　　　　　　　　**020 7229 4024**
122 Palace Gardens Terrace
Italian

☆ **Clarke's**　　　　　　　　　**020 7221 9225**
124 Kensington Church Street
modern British/Mediterranean, with excellent American
wines (and a wonderful shop attached)

Ken Lo's Memories of China   **020 7603 6951**
353 Kensington High Street
Chinese

Kensington Place   **020 7727 3184**
201-209 Kensington Church Street
modern European, very fashionable

The Terrace   **020 7937 3224**
33c Holland Street
modern British/Mediterranean

W9 (Little Venice)

Café Rouge   **7286 2266**
30 Clifton Road
French brasserie style, open right through from breakfast

Raoul's Café   **020 7289 7313**
13 Clifton Road
international, sidewalk tables on fine days

W2/10/11 (Notting Hill, Westbourne Grove)

Cow Dining Rooms ("the Cow")   **020 7221 0021**
89 Westbourne Park Road
casual gastropub below, more formal upstairs

☆ **E&O**   **020 7229 5454**
14 Blenheim Crescent
pan-Asian and very, very fashionable

☆ **Electric Brasserie**   **020 7908 9696**
191 Portobello Road
modern British, and the Notting Hill rendezvous

Four Seasons   **020 7229 4320**
84 Queensway
Chinese, where the Chinese themselves eat

Mediterraneo   **020 7792 3131**
37 Kensington Park Road
Italian, popular Euro haunt

☆ **Notting Hill Brasserie**   **020 7229 4481**
92 Kensington Park Road
good enough for Joan Collins's pre-wedding party

Osteria Basilico   **020 7727 9372**
29 Kensington Park Road
Italian favourite with the Euro crowd

☆ **Ottolenghi**   **020 7727 1121**
63 Ledbury Road
friendly, chic Italian

Rotisserie Jules   **020 7221 3331**
133 Notting Hill Gate
spit-roast chicken and lamb

☆ **Tom's Café**   **020 7221 8818**
226 Westbourne Grove
popular café/deli

Restaurants

Zucca   020 7727 0060
188 Westbourne Grove
modern Italian

WC2 (Covent Garden)

☆ **Bertorelli's**   020 7836 3969
44 Floral Street
modern Italian

Café des Amis du Vin   020 7379 3444
11 Hanover Place
Mediterranean

Café Pacifico   020 7379 7728
5 Langley Street
Mexican; Margarita heaven

Christopher's   020 7240 4222
18 Wellington Street
modern American and very stylish

☆ **Joe Allen**   020 7836 0651
13 Exeter Street
europeanised American, perennially popular

J.Sheekey   020 7240 2565
28-32 St. Martin's Court
fish, part of the Ivy/Caprice group

Manzi's   020 7734 0224
1-2 Leicester Street
fish

☆ **Mon Plaisir**   020 7836 7243
21 Monmouth Street
*family-owned classic French, and the oldest
French restaurant in London*

Neal Street Restaurant   020 7836 8368
26 Neal Street
Italian

City

Caravaggio   020 7626 6206
107 Leadenhall Street, EC3
Italian

Le Coq d'Argent   020 7395 5002
1 Poultry, EC2
French

Perc%nto   020 7778 0010
26 Ludgate Hill, EC4
Italian

Prism   020 7256 3888
147 Leadenhall Street, EC3
modern British

Sweetings   020 7248 3062
39 Queen Victoria Street, EC4
fish & seafood, famous old City favourite

Tatsuso   020 7638 5863
32 Broadgate Circle, EC2
*fearfully expensive Japanese: teppan yaki on the ground
floor or remove your shoes and head downstairs
for sushi and sashimi*

Health & Beauty

Barbers

Hair Salons

Hair Removal

Beauty Treatments

Manicures

Day Spas

Fitness Studios

Massage Therapists

Yoga, Pilates, Alexander technique

Tanning

Make-up Artists

Barbers

Cuts
39 Frith Street
London W1

020 7734 2171
tube: Piccadilly Circus
Mon-Fri 11-7, Sat 10-6, Sun 12-5

Flittner
86 Moorgate
London EC2

020 7606 4750
tube: Moorgate
Mon-Fri 8-6 (Thurs 8-6:30)

Fourth Floor
4 Northington Street
London WC1

020 7405 6011
tube: Chancery Lane
Mon 9-4, Tues-Fri 9-7, Sat 9-6

Fish
30 D'Arblay Street
London W1

020 7494 2398
tube: Oxford Circus/
Tottenham Court Road
Mon-Fri 10-7 (Thurs 10-8), Sat 10-5

Gentleman's Tonic
31a Bruton Place
London W1

020 7297 4343
tube: Bond Street
Mon 10-7, Tues, Weds 10-8, Thurs 10-9
Fri 9-7, Sat 10-6, Sun 11-5

George F. Trumper
9 Curzon Street
London W1

020 7499 1850
tube: Green Park
Mon-Fri 9-5:30, Sat 9-1

George F. Trumper
20 Jermyn Street
London SW1

020 7734 6553
tube: Piccadilly Circus
Mon-Fri 9-5:30, Sat 9-5

The Refinery
60 Brook Street
London W1

020 7409 2001
tube: Bond Street
Mon-Tues 10-7, Wed-Fri 10-9
Sat 9-6, Sun 11-5

Sadlers Wells Barbers Shop
110 Rosebery Avenue
London EC1

020 7833 0556
tube: Angel
Mon-Sat 8-6

Truefitt & Hill
71 St. James's Street
London SW1

020 7493 2961
tube: Green Park
Mon-Fri 8:30-5, Sat 8:30-4

Urban Rites
151 Sydney Street
London SW3

020 7352 6888
tube: Sloane Square/
South Kensington
Mon-Fri 10-7 (Thurs 11-8), Sat 10-6, Sun 11-5

Hair Salons

Charles Worthington
7 Percy Street
London W1

020 7631 1370
tube: Tottenham Court Road
Mon-Thurs 8-8, Fri 10:15-7
Sat 9:15-6, Sun 10-5

Charles Worthington
34 Great Queen Street
London WC2

020 7831 5303
tube: Covent Garden/Holborn
Mon-Thurs 8-9, Fri 10-7, Sat 9-6
Sun 10-5

Charles Worthington
The Dorchester
Park Lane
London W1

020 7317 6321
tube: Hyde Park Corner/Marble Arch
Mon-Thurs 9:30-8, Fri 10-7
Sat 9:30-6, Sun 10-5

Daniel Galvin
58-60 George Street
London W1

020 7486 9661
tube: Bond Street/Baker Street
Mon-Sat 9-6

Daniel Hersheson
45 Conduit Street
London W1

020 7434 1747
tube: Oxford Circus
Mon-Sat 8:45-6 (Thurs-Fri 9-8)

Errol Douglas
18 Motcomb Street
London SW1

020 7235 0110
tube: Knightsbridge
Mon 9-6, Tues-Sat 9-7

Groom
49 Beauchamp Place
London SW3

020 7581 1248
tube: Knightsbridge
Tues, Fri 10-6, Wed 11-7
Thurs 12-8, Sat 9-6, Sun 11-6

Harringtons
14 Great Marlborough Street
London W1

020 7292 2890
tube: Oxford Circus
Mon-Fri 10:30-7:30
(Thurs 11:30-8:30), Sat 9:30-6:30

Hari's Salon
305 Brompton Road
London SW3

020 7581 5211
tube: South Kensington
Mon-Fri 9:30-6:30, Sat 9-6:30

Jo Hansford
19 Mount Street
London W1

020 7495 7774
tube: Bond Street
Tues-Sat 9-6

John Frieda
75 New Cavendish Street
London W1

020 7636 1401
tube: Oxford Circus
Mon-Sat 9-5

John Frieda @ Claridge's
54-55 Brook Street
London W1

020 7499 3617
tube: Bond Street
Mon-Sat 9-5

John Frieda
4 Aldford Street
London W1

020 7491 0840
tube: Bond Street
Mon-Sat 9-5

Martyn Maxey
18 Grosvenor Street
London W1

020 7629 6161
tube: Bond Street/Green Park
Mon-Sat 9-6

Michaeljohn
25 Albemarle Street
London W1

020 7629 6969
tube: Green Park
Mon-Sat 8-6

Neville
5 Pont Street
London SW1

020 7235 3654
tube: Sloane Square/Knightsbridge
Mon-Sat 9-6

Nicky Clarke
130 Mount Street
London W1

020 7491 4700
tube: Bond Street/Green Park
Tues-Sat 9-5:30

Nyumba, Michael Charalambous
The House of Hair and Beauty
6-7 Mount Street
London W1

020 7408 1489
tube: Marble Arch
Tues-Sat 9-6 (Thurs 9-8)

Paul Edmonds
166 Brompton Road
London SW3

020 7589 5958
tube: Knightsbridge
Mon 9-6, Tues-Sat 9-7

Real
6-8 Cale Street
London SW3

020 7589 0877
tube: South Kensington/Sloane Square
Mon-Sat 9-6:30

Trevor Sorbie
27 Floral Street
London WC2

020 7379 6901
tube: Covent Garden
Mon, Tues, Sat 9-6, Wed 9-7
Thurs-Fri 9-7:45

Hair Removal

Feré Parangi (hot wax)
at Neville Hair & Beauty
5 Pont Street
London SW1

020 7235 3654
tube: Sloane Square/
Knightsbridge
Mon-Sat 8-5 (closed Wed)

Kamini Vaghela (threading)
6-7 Mount Street
London W1

020 7408 1489
tube: Bond Street/Green Park
Wed 10:30-6, Thurs 2-7, Fri 10:30-6

Martine Henry (electrolysis & laser)
at The Beauty Clinic
122 Knightsbridge
London SW1

020 7823 7882
tube: Knightsbridge
Wed-Sat 10-6

Beauty Treatments

Bharti Vyas Therapy & Beauty Centre
24 Chiltern Street
London W1

020 7935 5312
tube: Baker Street
Mon-Sat 9:30-6 (Wed, Fri 9:30-7)

Chantecaille Beauty Room
3rd Floor, Fenwick
63 New Bond Street
London W1

020 7629 9161
tube: Bond Street
Mon-Sat 10-6:30 (Thurs 10-8)

Eve Lom Clinic
2 Spanish Place
London W1

020 7935 9988
tube: Bond Street
Mon-Sat 9-5

Greenhouse
142 Wigmore Street
London W1

020 7486 6800
tube: Bond Street
Mon-Fri 10-6:30, Sat 10-4

Guinot
17 Albemarle Street
London W1

020 7491 9971
tube: Green Park
Mon-Fri 9:30-6:30 (Wed-Thurs 9:30-8)
Sat 9:30-5:30

Kirsty McLeod
106 Draycott Avenue
London SW3

020 7225 3939
tube: Sloane Square
Tues 11-8, Wed-Thurs 11-6, Fri-Sat 10-6

Pout
32 Shelton Street
London WC2

020 7379 0379
tube: Covent Garden
Mon-Sat 10-7 (Thurs 10-8)
Sun 12-6

Pure Alchemy
3 Violet Hill
London NW8

020 7624 1022
tube: St John's Wood
Mon-Fri 10-6, Sat 9:30-6

Sophie Thorpe (semi-permanent make-up)   **020 7589 5899**
106 Draycott Avenue
London SW3

tube: South Kensington
(by appointment only)

Urban Retreat
5th Floor, Harrods
87-135 Brompton Road
London SW1

020 7730 1234
tube: Knightsbridge
Mon-Sat 10-7

Vaishaly Patel
51 Paddington Street
London W1

020 7224 6088
(by appointment)

Manicures

The Country Club
101 Moore Park Road
London SW6

020 7731 4346
tube: Fulham Broadway
Tues, Sat 10-6, Wed-Fri 10-8

Nails Inc
41 South Molton Street
London W1
Sat 10-7, Sun 12-6

020 7499 8333
tube: Bond Street
Mon-Weds 9-7, Thurs-Fri 9-8

Nails Inc
46 Bishopsgate
London EC1

020 7382 9353
tube: Liverpool Street
Mon-Fri 8-7

Nails Inc @ Fenwick
63 New Bond Street
London W1

020 7491 1155
tube: Bond Street
Mon-Sat 10-6:30 (Thurs 10-8)

Nails Inc @ House of Fraser
318 Oxford Street
London W1

020 7529 4798
tube: Oxford Circus
Mon-Fri 10-8 (Thurs 10-9), Sun 12-6

Nails Inc
1 Canada Square
London E14

020 7519 1669
tube: Canary Wharf
Mon-Fri 9-7, Sat 10-6, Sun 11-5

Rene Rainbird
at Daniel Hersheson
45 Conduit Street
London W1

020 7434 1747
tube: Oxford Circus
Mon-Sat 9-6 (except Wed)

New York Nail Company
38 Marylebone High Street
London W1

020 7224 5898
tube: Baker Street
Mon, Sat 10-7, Tues-Fri 10-8, Sun 11-6

New York Nail Company
7 Kensington Church Street
London W8

020 7376 9376
tube: High Street
Kensington
Mon, Sat 10-7, Tues-Fri 10-8, Sun 10:30-6

New York Nail Company
118 Westbourne Grove
London W2

020 7229 4321
tube: Notting Hill Gate
(opening hours as above)

New York Nail Company
21 Kensington High Street
London W8

020 7938 3456
tube: High Street Kensington
(opening hours as above)

New York Nail Company
17 South Molton Street
London W1

020 7409 3332
tube: Bond Street
(opening hours as above)

Day Spas

Agua
The Sanderson
50 Berners Street
London W1

020 7300 1414
tube: Oxford Circus/
Tottenham Court Road
Daily 9-10

The Aveda Urban Retreat
174 High Holborn
London WC1

020 7759 7355
tube: Covent Garden/Holborn
Mon-Fri 9:30-7, Sat 9-6:30

Balance
250 King's Road
London SW3

020 7565 0333
tube: Sloane Square
Mon, Sat 9-6, Tues, Fri 9-7
Wed-Thurs 9-8, Sun 10-4

Bliss London
60 Sloane Avenue
London SW3

020 7584 3888
tube: South Kensington/Sloane Square
Mon-Fri 9:30-8, Sat 9:30-6:30

Calmia Inner Beauty Day Spa
52-54 Marylebone High Street
London W1

020 7224 3585
tube: Baker Street
Mon-Sat 9-9, Sun 10-7

The Dorchester Spa
The Dorchester
Park Lane
London W1

020 7495 7335
tube: Hyde Park Corner/Marble Arch
Daily 7-9:30

Elemis Day Spa
2-3 Lancashire Court
London W1

020 7499 4995
tube: Bond Street
Mon-Thurs 9-9, Fri-Sat 10-8, Sun 10-6

Elizabeth Arden Red Door
Hair & Beauty Spa
29 Davies Street
London W1

020 7629 4488
tube: Bond Street
Mon 10-7, Tues 9-7, Wed-Fri 9-8
Sat 9-7, Sun 11-5

The Hale Clinic
7 Park Crescent
London W1

020 7631 0156
tube: Regents Park/
Great Portland Street
Mon-Fri 8:30-8:30, Sat 9-5

Olympus Suite Spa @ Claridge's
54-55 Brook Street
London W1

020 7409 6565
tube: Bond Street
Mon-Fri 6:30-9, Sat-Sun 8-8

Spa Illuminata
63 South Audley Street
London W1

020 7499 7777
tube: Bond Street
Mon-Fri 10-9, Sat 10-6

The Parlour   **020 7729 6969**
3 Ravey Street   tube: Old Street/Liverpool Street
London EC2   Mon-Thurs 11:30-8, Fri 10:30-7, Sat 10-5

The Sanctuary   **08700 630300**
12 Floral Street   tube: Covent Garden
London WC2   Mon-Fri 9:30-6, Sat-Sun 10-8
                                Wed-Fri Evening Spa (5-10)

The Spa @ Mandarin Oriental   **020 7838 9888**
Mandarin Oriental Hyde Park   tube: Knightsbridge
66 Knightsborough   Daily 7-10
London SW1

The Spa @ Chancery Court   **020 7829 7058**
Renaissance Hotel   tube: Holborn
252 High Holborn   Mon-Fri 8-9, Sat-Sun 10-7
London WC1

Spa NK   **020 7727 8002**
127-131 Westbourne Grove   tube: Notting Hill Gate
London W2   Mon, Fri, Sat 10-7, Tues-Thurs 9-9, Sun 10-5

Spa Studio   **020 7259 5599**
The Lanesborough   tube: Hyde Park Corner
Hyde Park Corner   Mon-Fri 8-10, Sat-Sun 10-8
London SW1

The Temple   **020 7229 2828**
22 Powis Terrace   tube: Ladbroke Grove
London W11   Mon-Fri 6:30-9:30, Sat 8-5, Sun 11-5

Unlisted London   **0870 225 5007**
Luxury up-to-the-minute treatments in your home, office or
hotel room. Whether it's girly nights in for the Kate Moss
crowd, massages for stressed-out city girls or revitalising
treatments for tourists, New Yorker Deborah-Jean Faraces's
team come to you and make you feel a million dollars. From
hair treatments to manicures to four-hand massages, rest
assured they'll be the newest and best on the market.
33 Davies Street   tube: Bond Street
London W1   Daily 9-9

Fitness Studios

The Berkeley Spa & Club   **020 7201 1699**
The Berkeley   tube: Knightsbridge/Hyde Park Corner
Wilton Place   Mon-Fri 6:30-10, Sat-Sun 8-8
London SW1

The Circle Health Club   **020 7722 1234**
41 Mackennal Street   tube: St. John's Wood
London NW8   Mon-Thurs 7-10, Fri 7-8, Sat-Sun 9-7

Lotte Berk   **020 7385 2477**
465 Fulham Road   tube: Fulham Broadway
London SW6   (call for class timetable)

The Peak Health Club   **020 7858 7008**
Carlton Tower   tube: Knightsbridge
Cadogan Place   Mon-Fri 6:30-10
London SW1   Sat-Sun 7:30-9

Health & Beauty

The Third Space　　　　　　　　**020 7439 6333**
13 Sherwood Street　　　　tube: Piccadilly Circus
London W1　　　Mon-Fri 6:30-11, Sat-Sun 8:30-8:30

Massage Therapists

Amanda Birch　　　　　　　　**020 7629 6969**
Michaeljohn Ragdale Clinic　　　tube: Green Park
25 Albemarle Street　　　　Tues-Sat 9:30-5:30
London W1　　　　　　　　　　(except Wed)

Clarins @ Fenwick　　　　　　**020 7493 1901**
60 New Bond Street　　tube: Bond Street/Oxford Circus
London W1　　　　　　Mon-Sat 10-5 (Thurs 10-8)

Kannika Parker　　　　　　　**020 7409 6565**
Olympus Suite Spa @ Claridge's　　tube: Bond Street
54-55 Brook Street　　　　　　(by appointment)
London W1

Micheline Arcier Aromatherapy　　**020 7235 3545**
7 William Street　　　　　　tube: Knightsbridge
London SW1　　　Mon-Sat 9-6 (Tues, Thurs 10-7)

Nari Sadhuram　　　　　　　**020 7328 5452**
(call to arrange home visit)

This Works　　　　　　　　**020 7584 1887**
18 Cale Street　　　　　　tube: Sloane Square
London SW3　　　　　　　　Mon-Sat 10-6

Yoga, Pilates, Alexander technique

Danceworks　　　　　　　　**020 7629 6183**
16 Balderton Street　　tube: Marble Arch/Bond Street
London W1　　　　Mon-Fri 8:30-10, Sat-Sun 9-6:30

The Life Centre　　　　　　**020 7221 4602**
15 Edge Street　　　　　tube: Notting Hill Gate
London W8　　　Mon-Fri 7:30-9:30, Sat-Sun 9-7:30

Lynne Pinette　　　　　　　**020 7580 4400**
Portland Hospital (pregnancy & post-natal yoga)
234 Great Portland Street　　tube: Oxford Circus
London W1　　Mon 12:45-2, Thurs 4:45-6 (by appointment)

Triyoga Centre　　　　　　　**020 7483 3344**
6 Erskine Road　　　　　　tube: Chalk Farm
London NW3　　　　Mon-Fri 6-10, Sat-Sun 8-8

Noel Kingsley (Alexander technique)　**020 7491 3505**
19 Cavendish Square　　　tube: Oxford Circus
London W1　　　　　　　(by appointment)

Pilates off the Square　　　　**020 7935 8505**
4 Mandeville Place　　　　tube: Bond Street
London W1　　　　　　Mon-Fri 8-7, Sat 9-3

Stephanie Wright (Kum Nye)　　**020 7881 5800**
Eden Medical Centre　　　tube: Sloane Square
63a King's Road　　　　　　Mon-Fri 11-7
London SW3

Tanning

Fantasy Tan **0795 777 1503**
Susie Lung tube: Bond Street
Basement Studio, 50 Manchester Street
London W1 (by appointment)

Golden Glow (one-minute mist-on tans) **020 7495 7677**
31 Avery Row tube: Bond Street
London W1 Mon-Sat 10-6

St Tropez (spray tan) @ Debenhams **020 7495 7445**
334-338 Oxford Street tube: Bond St/Oxford Circus
London W1

St Tropez (original tan) @ House of Fraser **020 7529 4700**
318 Oxford Street tube: Bond Street/Oxford Circus
London W1 Tues-Sat 11-6 (Thurs-Fri 11-7)
(The St Tropez general number is 0115 983 6363)

Make-up Artists

Chanel Colour Studio **020 7823 1735**
Harvey Nichols tube: Knightsbridge
London SW1 Mon-Fri 10-8, Sat 10-7, Sun 12-6

Jackie Hamilton-Smith **020 7434 3202**
(by appointment)

Repairs & Services

Dry Cleaners

Mending, Alterations & Custom Tailoring

Shoe Repair

Trimmings

Personal Shoppers

Dry Cleaners

Blossom & Brown Sycamore **020 7727 2635**
73a Clarendon Road tube: Holland Park
London W11 Mon-Fri 8:30-5:30 (Thurs 8:30-4:30)
Sat 8:30-3 (closed for lunch 1-2)

Buckingham Dry Cleaners **020 7499 1253**
83 Duke Street tube: Bond Street
London W1 Mon-Fri 8-6, Sat 9:30-12:30

Cashmere Clinic **020 7584 9806**
Flat 5, 53 Redcliffe Gardens tube: South Kensington/
London SW10 Earls Court
(by appointment)

Celebrity Cleaners **020 7437 5324**
(wedding dress specialists) tube: Oxford Circus
9 Greens Court Mon-Fri 8:30-6:30
London W1

Chalfont Dryers & Cleaners **020 7935 7316**
222 Baker Street tube: Baker Street
London NW1 Mon-Fri 8:30-5:30, Sat 9-1

Concorde of Knightsbridge **020 7584 0784**
3 Motcomb Street tube: Knightsbridge
London SW1 Mon-Fri 8-6, Sat 9-5

Elias **020 7589 5851**
85 Walton Street tube: South Kensington
London SW3 Mon-Fri 8:30-5:30, Sat 9-5

Elias **020 7584 1246**
16-17 Glendower Place tube: South Kensington
London SW7 Mon-Sat 7:30-6:30, Sat 9-5

Elias **020 7722 2212**
68 St. John's Wood High Street tube: St. John's Wood
London NW8 Mon-Sat 8-6, Sun 11-4

Jeeves of Belgravia **020 7235 1101**
8-10 Pont Street tube: Knightsbridge/Sloane Square
London SW1 Mon-Fri 8:30-7, Sat 8:30-6

Jeeves of Belgravia **020 7589 9229**
123 Fulham Road tube: South Kensington
London SW3 Mon-Fri 8:30-7, Sat 8:30-6

Jeeves of Belgravia **020 7262 0200**
59 Connaught Street tube: Marble Arch
London W2 Mon-Fri 8:30-6, Sat 8-5:30

Jeeves of Belgravia **020 7603 0484**
271 Kensington High Street tube: High Street Kensington
London W8 Mon-Fri 8:30-5:30, Sat 8:30-5

Jeeves of Belgravia **020 7491 8885**
54 South Audley Street tube: Bond Street
London W1 Mon-Fri 8-7, Sat 8-5

Jeeves of Belgravia **020 7794 4100**
11 Heath Street tube: Hampstead
London NW3 Mon-Fri 8:30-5:30, Sat 8:30-5, Sun 11-3

Jeeves of Belgravia
94 High Street
London SW19

020 8946 0665
tube: Wimbledon
Mon-Fri 8:30-5:30, Sat 8:30-5

Jeeves of Belgravia
131 Fleet Street
London EC4

020 7353 3532
tube: Blackfriars
Mon-Fri 8-6

Jeeves of Belgravia
43-45 Leadenhall Market
London EC3

020 7623 3266
tube: Bank/Monument
Mon-Fri 8:30-6

Mr Buttercup
49 Pimlico Road
London SW1

020 7730 2912
tube: Sloane Square
Mon-Fri 8-6, Sat 9-4:30

Perkins Dry Cleaners
28 Thayer Street
London W1

020 7935 3072
tube: Bond Street
Mon-Fri 8:15-7 (Thurs 8:15-6), Sat 8:15-3

Peters & Falla
281 New King's Road
London SW6

020 7731 3255
tube: Parsons Green
Mon-Fri 8:30-6:15, Sat 9:30-2

Peters & Falla
179 New King's Road
London SW6

020 7731 5114
tube: Parsons Green
Mon-Fri 8:30-6, Sat 9:30-2

Seven Dials
37 Monmouth Street
London WC2

020 7240 9274
tube: Covent Garden
Mon-Fri 8-6, Sat 9-2

Valentino Dry Cleaners
(suede & leather specialists)
125 Shaftesbury Avenue
London WC2

020 7240 5879
tube: Tottenham Court Road
Mon-Fri 8:30-6, Sat 9-1

Clothes Storage

Linda Agran Clothes Storage
www.lindaagran.co.uk

020 8893 4411
by appointment

Mending, Alterations & Custom Tailoring

The Alterations Station
29 The Pavement
London SW4

020 7627 0167
tube: Clapham Common
Mon-Fri 8-6:30, Sat 10-2

Bob Tailoring
58 Maddox Street
London W1

020 7495 4099
tube: Bond Street/Oxford Circus
Mon-Fri 10-6, Sat 10-3

British Invisible Mending Service
32 Thayer Street
London W1

020 7935 2487
tube: Bond Street
Mon-Fri 8:30-5:30, Sat 10-1

First Tailored Alterations
(leather, suede & sheepskin specialists)
85 Lower Sloane Street
London SW1

020 7730 1400
tube: Sloane Square
Mon-Sat 9-6

General Leather Company　　　**020 7935 1041**
56 Chiltern Street　　　　　　tube: Baker Street
London W1　　　　　　　　Mon-Fri 10-6, Sat 10-5

George the Tailor　　　　　　**020 7437 6876**
83-84 Berwick Street　tube: Oxford Circus/Piccadilly Circus
London W1　　　　　　Mon-Fri 6-5, Sat 6-2, Sun 6-12

KS Tailoring Service　　　　　**020 7437 9345**
13 Savile Row　　　tube: Piccadilly Circus/Oxford Circus
London W1　　　　　　　Mon-Fri 9:30-5:30, Sat 10-2

Mike Mandalia Tailors　　　　**020 7629 4021**
22 South Molton Street　　　　tube: Bond Street
London W1　　　　　　　Mon-Fri 10-6, Sat 11-5:30

Stitchcraft　　　　　　　　**020 7629 7919**
7 South Molton Street　　　　tube: Bond Street
London W1　　　　　　　Mon-Fri 9-5, Sat 10-4

Shoe Repair

The Complete Cobbler　　　　**020 7636 9040**
26 Tottenham Street　　　　tube: Goodge Street
London W1　　　　　　　Mon-Fri 8-7, Sat 11-5

Fifth Avenue Shoe Repairs　　**020 7636 6705**
41 Goodge Street　　　　　tube: Goodge Street
London W1　　　　　　Mon-Fri 8-6:30, Sat 10-6

The Heel Bar　　　　　　　**020 7580 6024**
35 Tottenham Street　　　　tube: Goodge Street
London W1　　　　　　Mon-Fri 9-6, Sat 9:30-1

Special Footwear & Orthotics　**020 7486 4664**
12 New Cavendish Street　　　tube: Bond Street
London W1　　　　　　　Mon-Fri 9-6, Sat 10-2

Trimmings

Allans of Duke Street (fabrics)　**020 7629 3781**
75 Duke Street　　　　　　　tube: Bond Street
London W1　　Mon-Fri 9:30-6, Thurs 10-7, Sat 10-5:30

The Button Queen　　　　　**020 7935 1505**
19 Marylebone Lane　　　　　tube: Bond Street
London W1　　Mon-Wed 10-5, Thurs-Fri 10-6, Sat 10-4

Ells & Farrier (beads)　　　　**020 7629 9964**
(mail order catalogue 01494 778818)
20 Beak Street　　tube: Oxford Circus/Piccadilly Circus
London W1　　　　　　　Mon-Fri 9-5:15, Sat 10-5

Joel & Son (fabrics)　　　　　**020 7724 6895**
75-83 Church Street　　　　tube: Edgware Road
London NW8　　　　　　　　　Mon-Sat 9-5

John Lewis　　　　　　　　**020 7629 7711**
278 Oxford Street　　tube: Oxford Circus/Bond Street
London W1　　Mon-Sat 9:30-7 (Thurs 10-8), Sun 12-6

Liberty
210-220 Regent Street
London W1

020 7734 1234
tube: Oxford Circus
Mon-Sat 10-7, Thurs 10-8, Sun 12-6

MacCulloch & Wallis
25 Dering Street
London W1

020 7629 0311
tube: Oxford Circus/Bond Street
Mon-Fri 10-6 (Thurs 10-7), Sat 10:30-5

Soho Silks
22 D'Arblay Street
London W1

020 7434 3305
tube: Oxford Circus/
Tottenham Court Road
Mon-Sat 9:30-6

V V Rouleaux (ribbons)
54 Sloane Square
London SW1

020 7730 3125
tube: Sloane Square
Mon-Sat 9:30-6 (Weds 9:30-6:30)

V V Rouleaux (ribbons)
6 Marylebone High Street
London W1

020 7224 5179
tube: Bond Street
Mon-Sat 9:30-6

Personal Shoppers

Being Seen

07870 564 937
beingseen.co.uk

Personal shopping and styling for any age, sex, taste, budget and, of course, style. Nicola Robinson offers discounts at designer stores, boutiques and jewellers, access to sample and preview sales, and access to Italian designer outlets.

Jane Thompson   **020 7229 0287**

Jane specialising in dressing women of a certain age (over 50s) who have fallen into a style rut. She'll get you thinking young again and can create a whole new wardrobe to suit any budget. She is as confident spotting high street trends as she is in the designer shops, and believes that you can mix and match if you wish. For a home consultation (London only) she charges £60.

Judi Bitel

020 7291 4540
1 Harley Street   judibitel@hotmail.com
London W1

The full wardrobe overhaul. Judi will rummage through your closets, persuade you to throw away some of the contents, then take you shopping to fill the gaps. She is also happy to take on single commissions, for example a wedding dress or an interview suit.

Lucy Pridden

07889 005 042
16 Stratford Road   lucypridden@lpps.co.uk
London W8

Lucy has worked for top labels—Cartier, Yves Saint Laurent, Tomasz Starzewski and—has solved style problems for everyone from rock stars to royalty. She'll introduce you to the city's best kept shopping secrets, guide you through department store sales, or come up with the best gift ideas, all wrapped and delivered.

Repairs & Services

Mary Young
The Shopping Service
PO Box 31329
London SW11

020 7350 1877
vipshoppinglondon.com

Will take clients out on a tailor-made shopping spree with special appointments at each store.

Y Shop (Camilla Yonge)

07711 277 969
y-shop.co.uk

After a consultation with Camilla in the privacy of your own home, you are whisked off to find that perfect outfit (or, if your wardrobe needs serious updating, outfits). Camilla has access to preview, sample and new season sales as well as entrance to trade previews during London Fashion Week (September and February), so you are sure to find just what you are after.

Fashion Speak

Avant-garde: forward-thinking or advanced. When referring to art or costume, sometimes implies erotic or startling. Derived from the French for "advance guard".

Bridge collection: a collection that is priced between designer and mass market.

Couture: French word used throughout fashion industry to describe the original styles, the ultimate in fine sewing and tailoring, made of expensive fabrics, by designers. The designs are shown in collections twice a year—spring/summer and fall/winter.

Custom-made/tailor-made, also called bespoke: garments made by tailor or couture house for an individual customer following couturier's original design. Done by either fitting a model form adjusted to the customer's measurements or by several personal fittings.

Diffusion line: a designer's second and less expensive collection.

Ensemble: an entire costume, including accessories, worn at one time. Two or more items of clothing designed and coordinated to be worn together.

Fashion trend: direction in which styles, colors and fabrics are moving. Trends may be influenced by political events, films, personalities, dramas, social and sporting events or indeed any human activity.

Faux: false or counterfeit, imitation: used in connection with gems, pearls and leathers. Faux fur (fake fur) is commonplace today, as is what is sometimes known as "pleather" (plastic leather). Artificial gems, especially pearls, are often made from a fine kind of glass known as "paste", and are accordingly sometimes called "paste" for short.

Haberdashery: a store that sells men's apparel and furnishings.

Knock-off: trade term for the copying of an item of apparel, e.g. a dress or a coat, in a lower price line. Similar to piracy.

Made-to-measure: clothing (dress, suit, shirt etc) made according to individual's measurement. No fittings required.

One-off: a unique, one-of-a-kind item that will not be found in any other store or produced again in the future, e.g. a customized denim skirt or a rare vintage cocktail dress. Can also refer to made-to-measure and couture garments designed for a particular person and/or event, such as a dress for the Oscars.

Prêt-à-porter: French term which literally means ready-to-wear, i.e. to take (or wear) straight out of the shop.

Ready-to-wear (rtw): apparel that is mass-produced in standard sizes. Records of the ready-to-wear industry tabulated in the U.S. Census of 1860 included hoop skirts, cloaks, and mantillas; from 1890 shirtwaists and wrappers were added; and, after 1930, dresses.

5 very good reasons why you should become a *Where to Wear* online subscriber

1. Access the guide online from wherever you are.

2. Take the guide on a laptop or CD ROM.

3. Find a particular designer, type of clothing or boutique easily by just typing in what you want and seeing the result.

4. Results printed out to show information and location, member concessions, special offers and promotions from stores.

5. Exclusive seasonal offers available to *Where to Wear* members only from selected stores.

Visit our new exclusive members website at
www.wheretowear.com/member.htm

How to order *Where to Wear*

Where to Wear publishes guides to the following cities: *London, New York, Paris, Los Angeles, San Francisco, Italy* (which includes Florence, Milan and Rome), *Australia* (which includes Sydney, Melbourne, Adelaide), *Las Vegas* and *Florida*. Each edition retails at £9.99 or $14.95.

There is also a gift box set, *Shopping Guides to the World's Fashion Capitals*, available for £29.99 or $49.99 which includes the *London, New York, Paris* and *Italy (Milan, Florence, and Rome)* guides (four books for the price of three).

If you live in the UK or Europe, you can order your copies of *Where to Wear* by contacting our London office at:

10 Cinnamon Row
Plantation Wharf
London SW11 3TW
TEL: 020 7801 1381
EMAIL: uk@wheretowear.com

If you live in the USA, you can order your copies of *Where to Wear* by contacting our New York office at:

666 Fifth Avenue
PMB 377
New York, NY 10103
TEL: 212-969-0138
TOLL-FREE: 1-877-714-SHOP (7467)
EMAIL: usa@wheretowear.com

Or simply log on to our website: www.wheretowear.com
Where to Wear delivers worldwide.

Where to Wear
to
LONDON

PLACE YOUR
CORPORATE LOGO
HERE

FASHION SHOPPING FROM A-Z

CUSTOMIZE TO MEET YOUR OBJECTIVES

Where to Wear, the only recognized brand name in fashion shopping guides, is an effective marketing tool for your business. *Where to Wear* can customize any of its city guides to reflect your company's brand identity. Our corporate clients have used *Where to Wear* in a variety of different ways: subscription renewals, hotel in-room gift, magazine cover mount, event or holiday gift, or a much needed thank-you to key clients.

Where to Wear has its own in-house design team who will work with you to co-brand our guides:

- Stamp your corporate logo onto the *Where to Wear* front cover
- Create co-branded covers with additional pages detailing your important information
- Offer mini guides with specially selected stores to your demographic profile
- Design leather pocket-size agenda books for men and women
- Cover full-size editions of *Where to Wear* in beautiful leather or suede in a variety of colors
- Create a box set, including different cities, with a co-branded cover

Notes

Notes

Notes